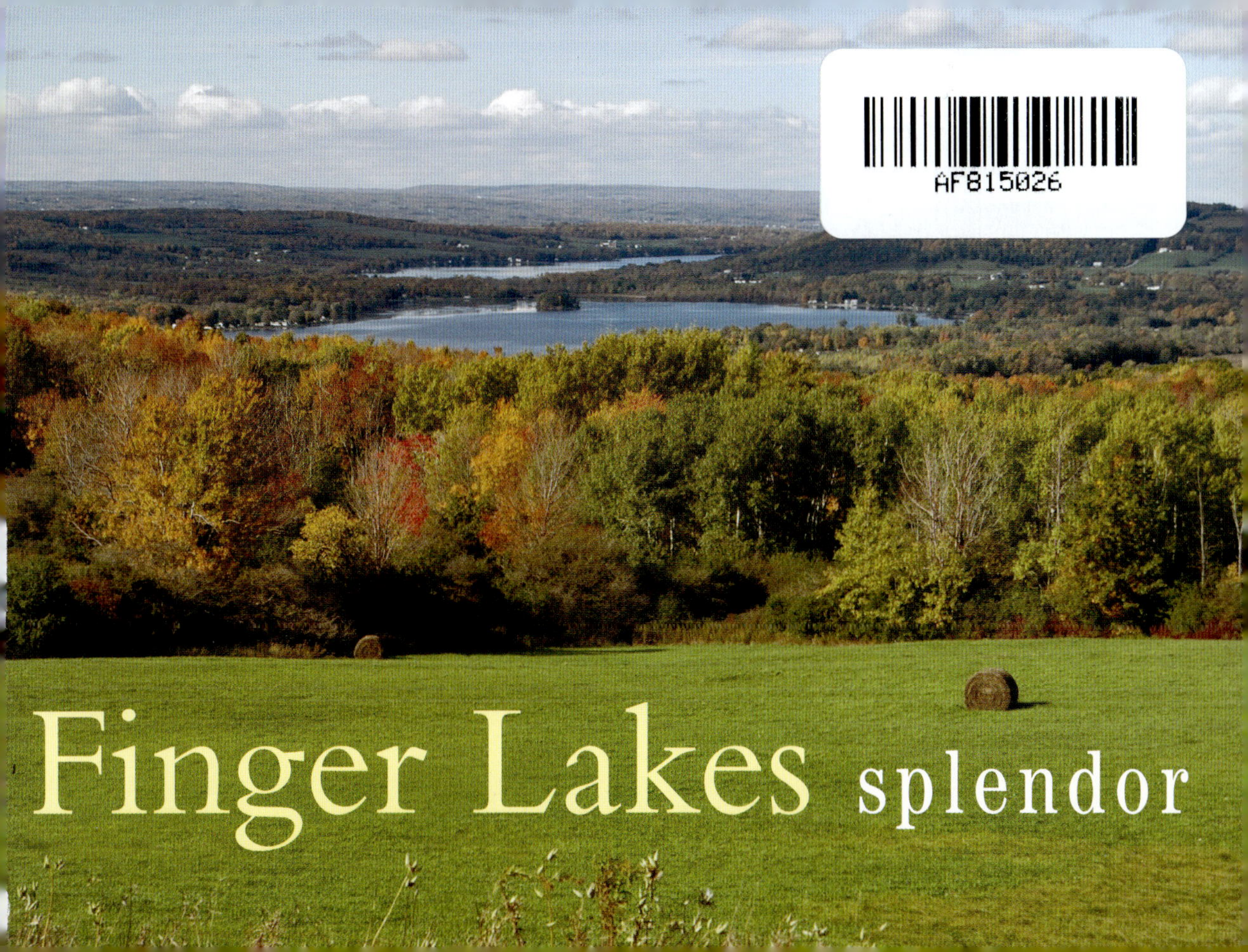

Finger Lakes splendor

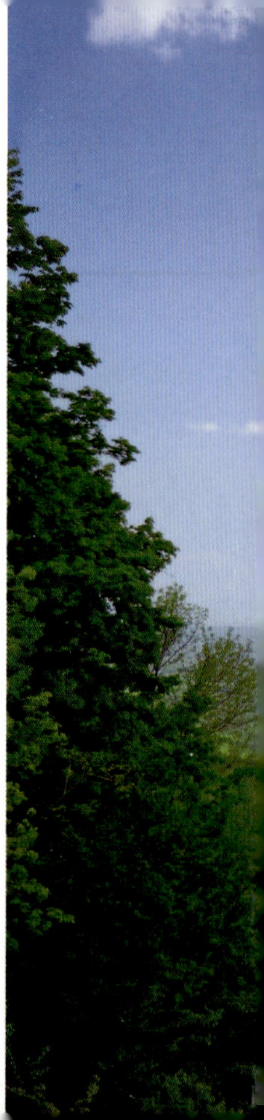

right Spring view of Honeoye Lake from Harriet Hollister State Park.
previous Waneta and Lamoka Lakes.

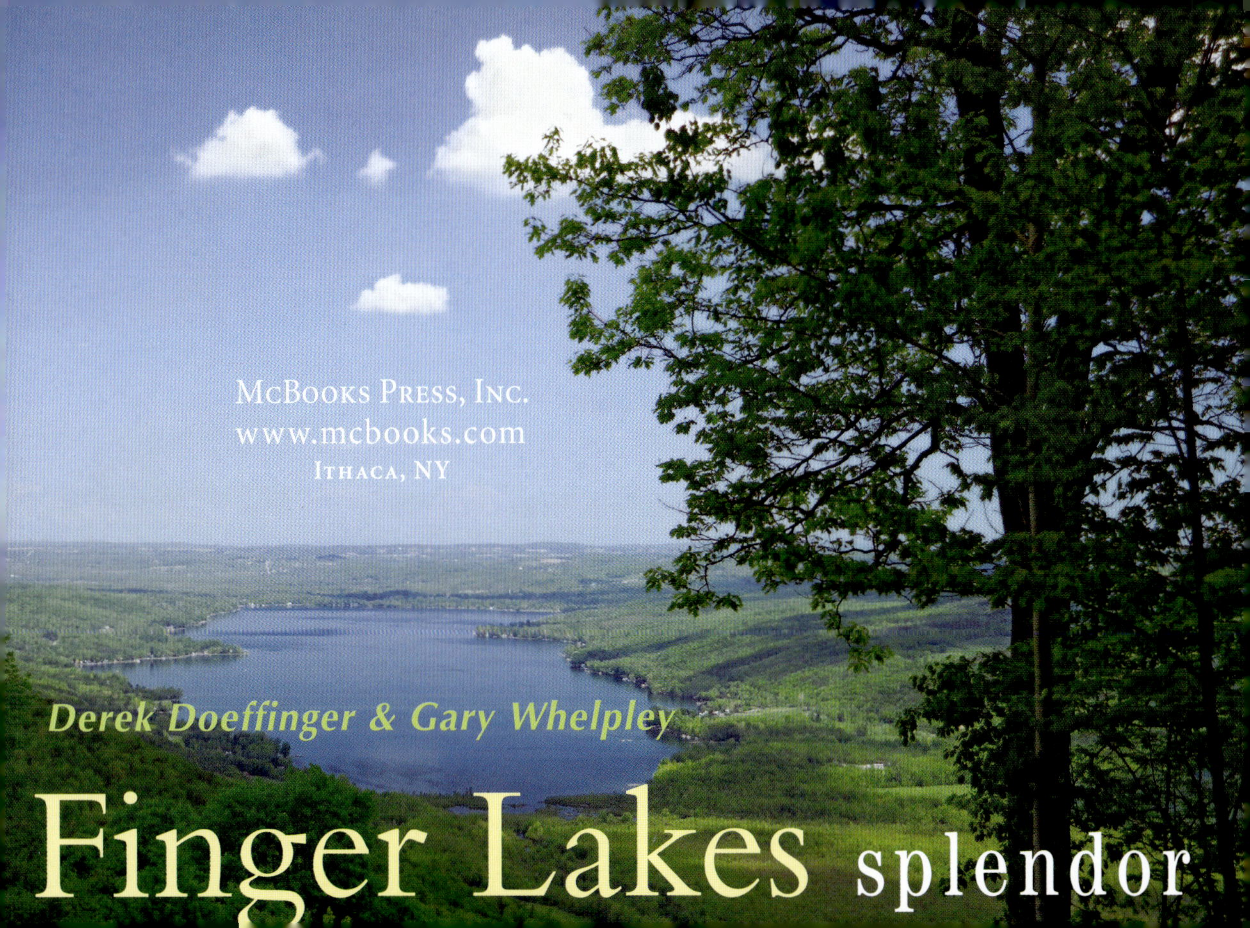

Finger Lakes splendor

Derek Doeffinger & Gary Whelpley

McBooks Press, Inc.
www.mcbooks.com
Ithaca, NY

Published by McBooks Press 2007

Concept, book design and digital imaging by Panda Musgrove.

Library of Congress Cataloging-in-Publication Data

Doeffinger, Derek.

Finger Lakes splendor / by Derek Doeffinger and Gary Whelpley.

p. cm.

ISBN 978-1-59013-145-9 (hardcover : alk. paper)

1. Finger Lakes (N.Y.)–Pictorial works. 2. Finger Lakes Region (N.Y.)--Pictorial works. I. Whelpley, Gary, 1945- II. Title.

F127.F4D64 2007

974.7'80440222--dc22

2007012851

Distributed to the trade by Independent Publishers Group

814 North Franklin Street Chicago, IL 60610, (800) 888-4741, www.ipgbook.com

Visit the McBooks Press website at www.mcbooks.com.

Printed in China

9 8 7 6 5 4 3

right The Finger Lakes region boasts eleven lakes and loads of summer fun.

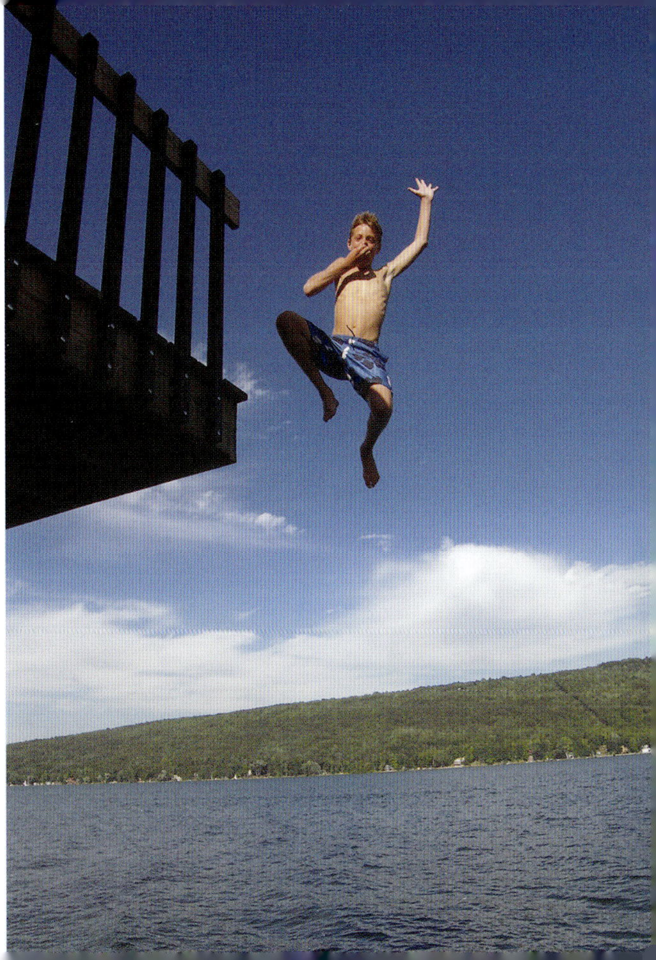

Introduction

Rolling hills, snaking gorges, deep lakes, sun-drenched vineyards, sweeping views and endless vistas: what first brings us to the Finger Lakes is not always what calls us back a second or third or tenth time. Compelled by the beauty and variety of the region, many of us return and run rapids at Keuka Outlet, hike or bike some of the eight hundred miles that make up the Finger Lakes Trail, collect autographs from NASCAR drivers at Watkins Glen, ride the mail boat around Skaneateles Lake, or sail across Seneca Lake on the two-masted schooner *Malabar X*. We stomp grapes; listen to bluegrass; or venture up to Ganondagon to explore an Iroquois longhouse, listen to a creation myth, or learn traditional Native American dances.

Others return for different reasons: a relaxing day of winery hopscotch with frequent sippings of white wine, red wine, ice wine, Merlot, Cabernet Franc, Cabernet Sauvignon, Pinot Noir–then an evening of hot jazz or cool sailing.

Whatever the season, the Finger Lakes are always ready for us: fresh powder on Bristol Mountain, crackling logs and cordial innkeepers, music festivals, farmers' markets, stately homes; amber maple syrup in March and scarlet and gold leaves in October; salmon (very hungry salmon) and record-breaking trout in April; blue skies and purple pies in September.

Amazingly, we drive to our pies and vineyards on routes established thousands of years ago. Those first paths were made by some of the earliest inhabitants of the Finger Lakes: ice age mastodons and woolly mammoths seeking salt licks. And the paths they created were used by the first human inhabitants and then by the pioneer road builders–and today, by us.

The origin of the salt licks is tied into the origin of the region. It goes back millions of years–long before the lakes were born–to a vast inland sea spreading as far as Ohio. As the waters evaporated, thick veins of salt were left behind. Currently, extensive salt mines run under both Cayuga and Seneca Lakes. Tunnels created by Cargill Inc. burrow 2,400 feet under Cayuga Lake, forming the deepest salt mine in North America.

When the inland sea departed, it left behind a series of gently flowing rivers–forerunners of the lakes. During the last few million years, several ice ages resulted in glaciers invading the region. They plowed into the river beds and gouged them ever deeper. The last glacier, a mile thick and of such a fantastic weight that it compressed the earth's crust to a depth of nearly a quarter-mile, retreated only 10,000 years ago.

It left behind the landscape we see now: over one hundred waterfalls scattered among eleven Finger Lakes. From east to west the Indian-named lakes spread out about one hundred miles: Otisco (waters died away), Skaneateles (long lake), Owasco (crossing place), Cayuga (boat landing), Seneca (place of the stone), Keuka (canoe landing), Canandaigua (chosen place), Honeoye (finger lying), Canadice (long lake), Hemlock (the only one named by Europeans), and Conesus (always beautiful). The longest, Cayuga, stretches forty miles. The deepest, Seneca, extends down six hundred feet. The shortest, Canadice, is just three miles long. The shallowest, Honeoye, is a mere thirty feet deep.

First to call the Finger Lakes home were the Native Americans. Led by Hiawatha (the real man, not the mythical hero of Longfellow's poem), six tribes joined to form a powerful confederacy–the Iroquois. Soon European settlers brought their own social customs and interests. Joseph Smith, who lived in Palmyra, founded the Mormon faith. Elizabeth Cady Stanton and Susan B. Anthony joined together in Seneca Falls to fight for women's equality and the right to vote. Glenn Curtiss, of Hammondsport, invented one of the earliest airplanes–the JN-4 "Jenny"–and just missed the fame of the Wright brothers. George Eastman turned the complex and costly process of early photography into inexpensive Brownie cameras that transformed the way we see and remember the world.

Two less-famous people may have left the most enduring legacy of the region. With their generous donations of land, both William Pryor Letchworth and Robert Treman preserved some of the most outstanding natural beauty in the Finger Lakes.

Whether visitor or resident, those who traipse through the Finger Lakes seem to find the experience uplifting and inspiring. Visitor Frank Capra saw the human possibilities and revealed them in the Seneca Falls–based movie *It's a Wonderful Life*. Similarly, Frank L. Baum, resident of Chittenango, took us on a yellow-brick road adventure of the human spirit in *The Wonderful Wizard of Oz*. He may well have been speaking of the Finger Lakes when he has Dorothy tell us, "It wasn't a dream. It was a place."

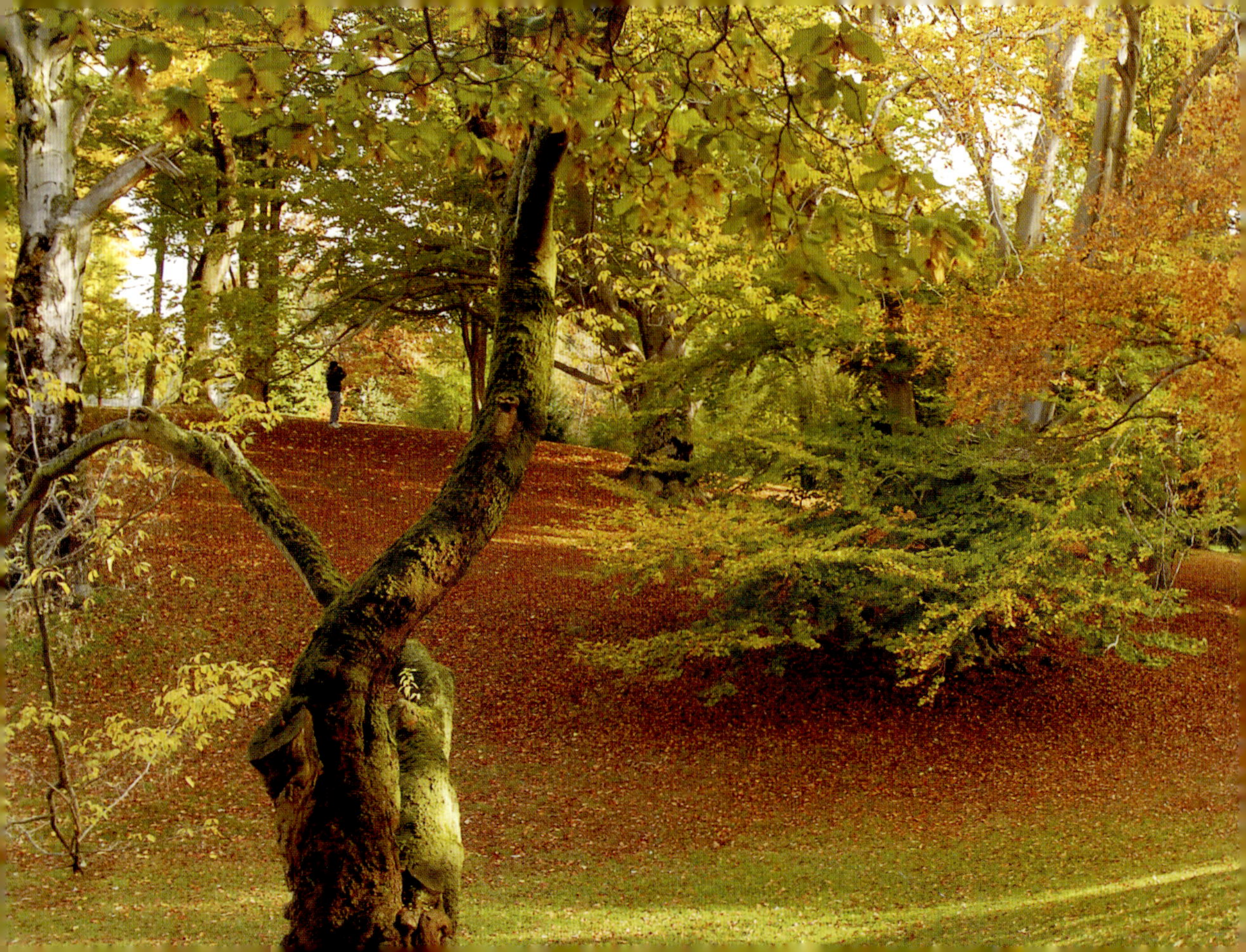

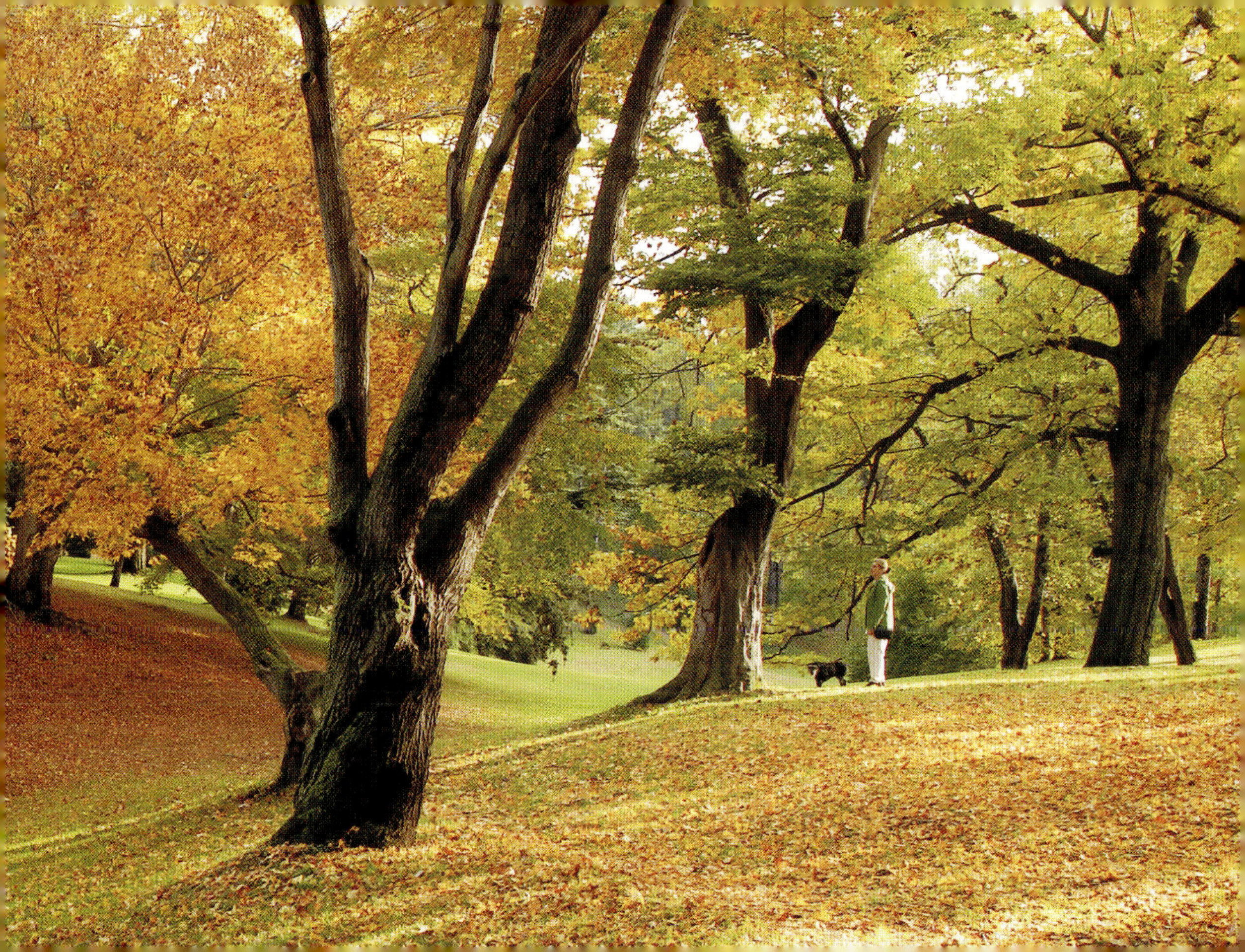

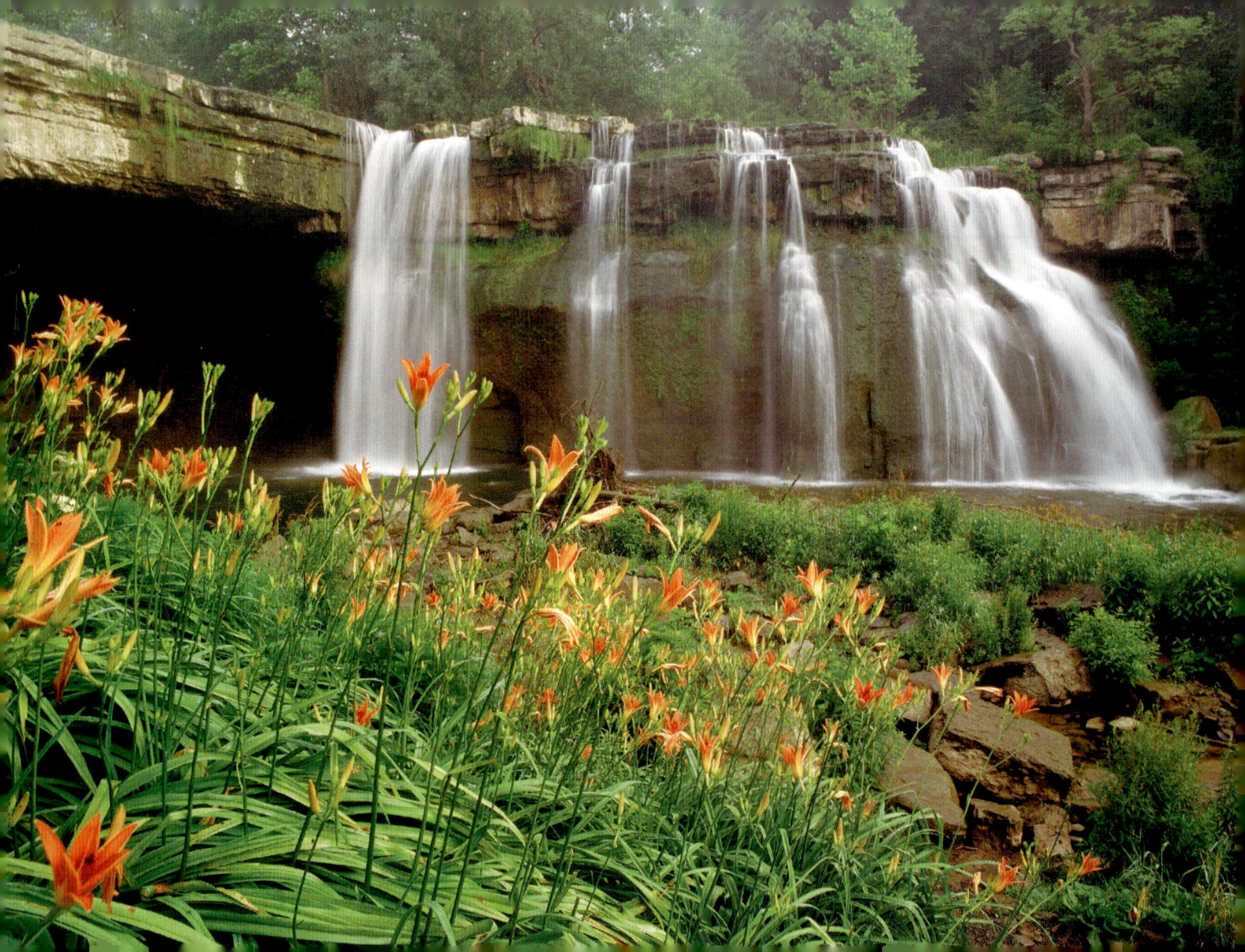

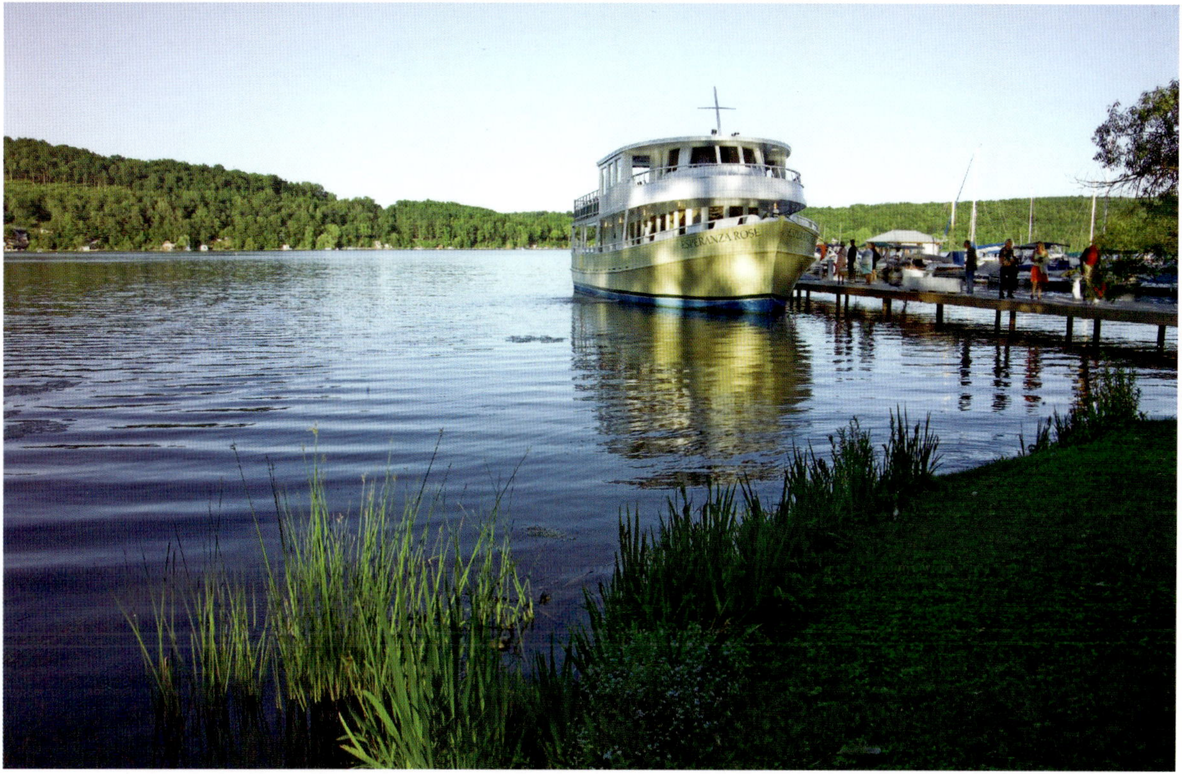

above The 65-foot *Esperanza Rose* docks in Branchport on Keuka Lake. left Ludlowville Falls was part of the 600-acre Revolutionary War grant given to army enlistee Thomas Ludlow. previous Highland Park in Rochester, a 155-acre arboretum designed by Frederick Law Olmsted.

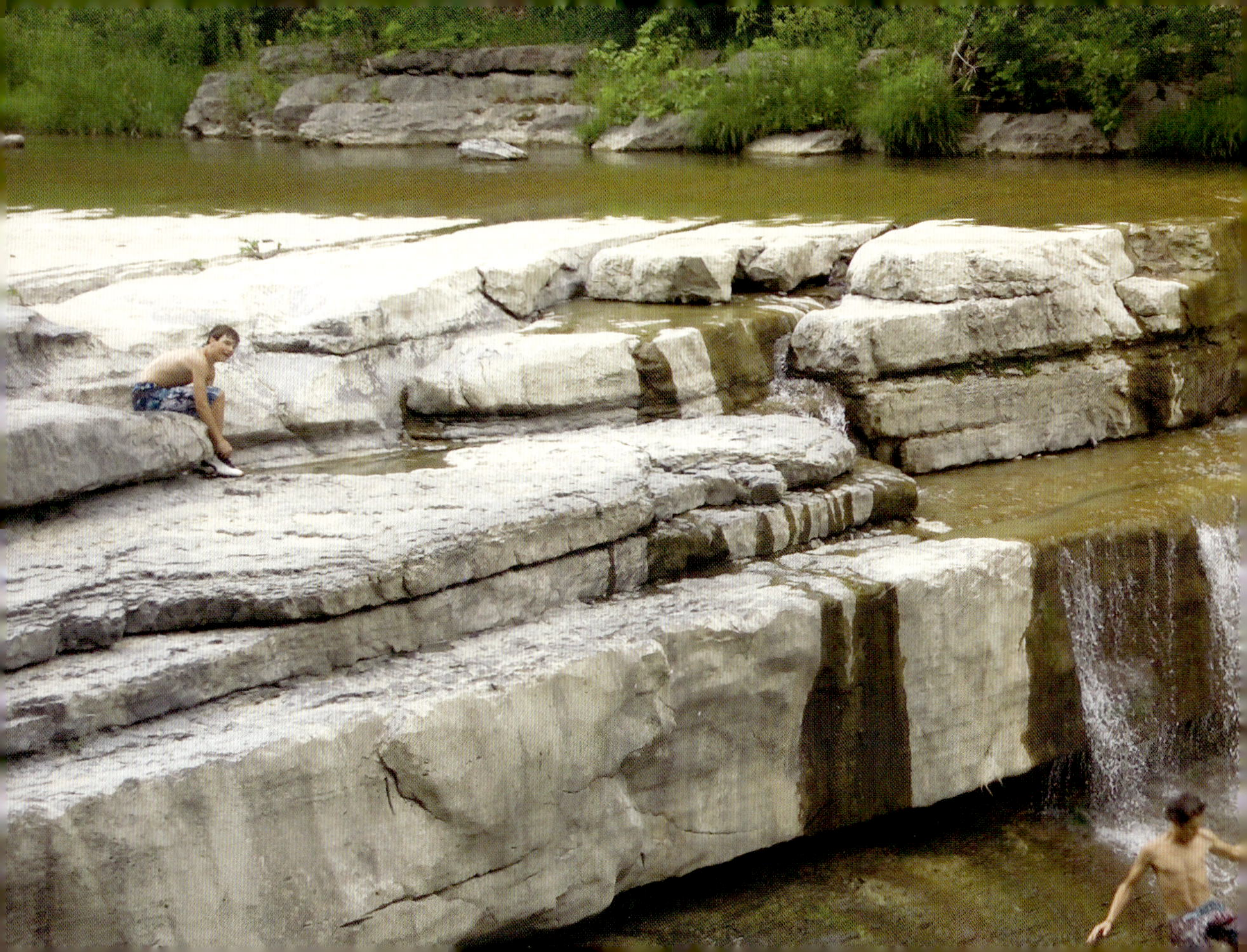

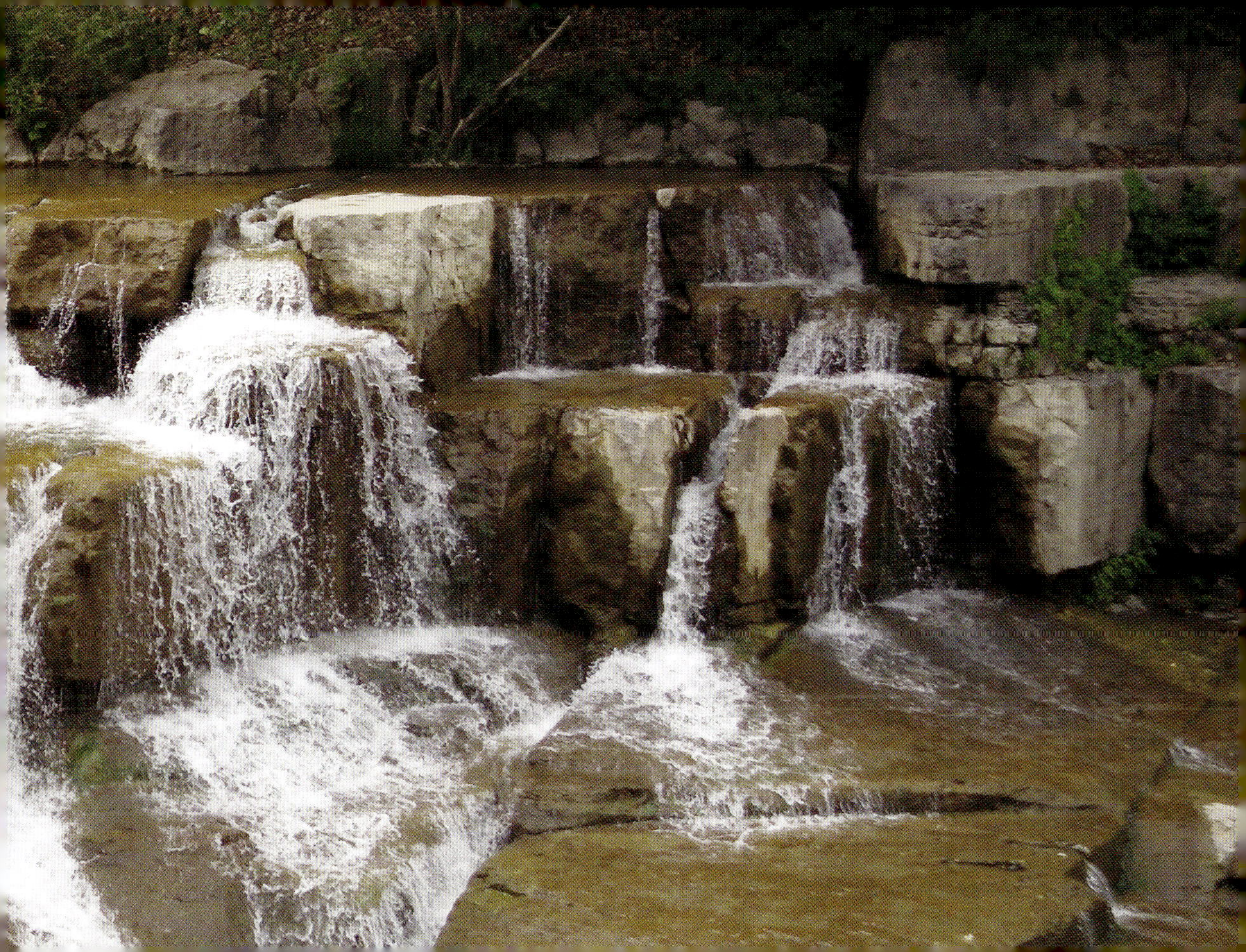

right Hikers on the gorge trail at Watkins Glen State Park. previous The gorge at Taughannock Falls State Park in Trumansburg is over a mile long. next A fisherman calls it a day at Canadice Lake.

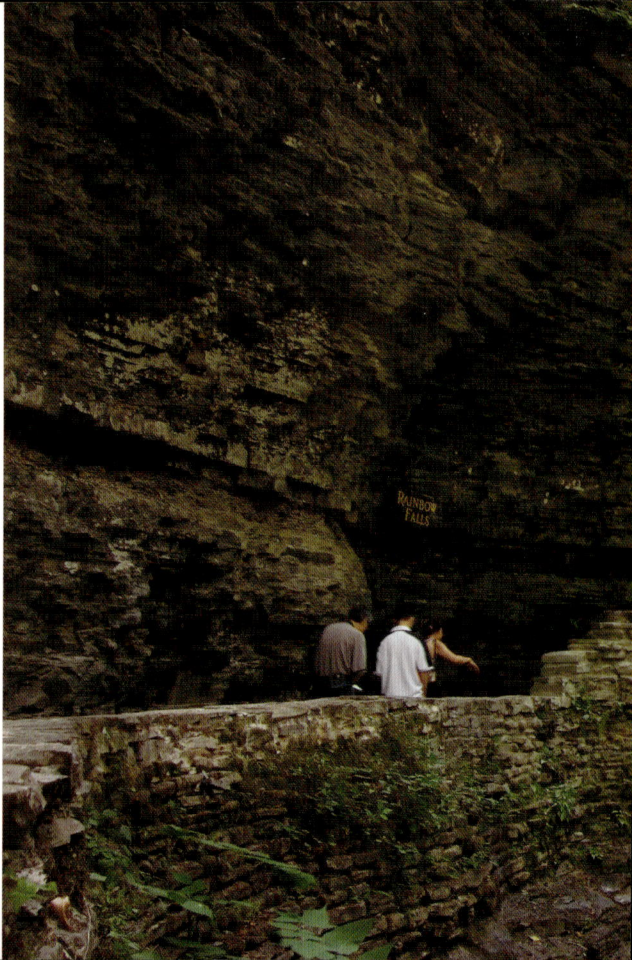

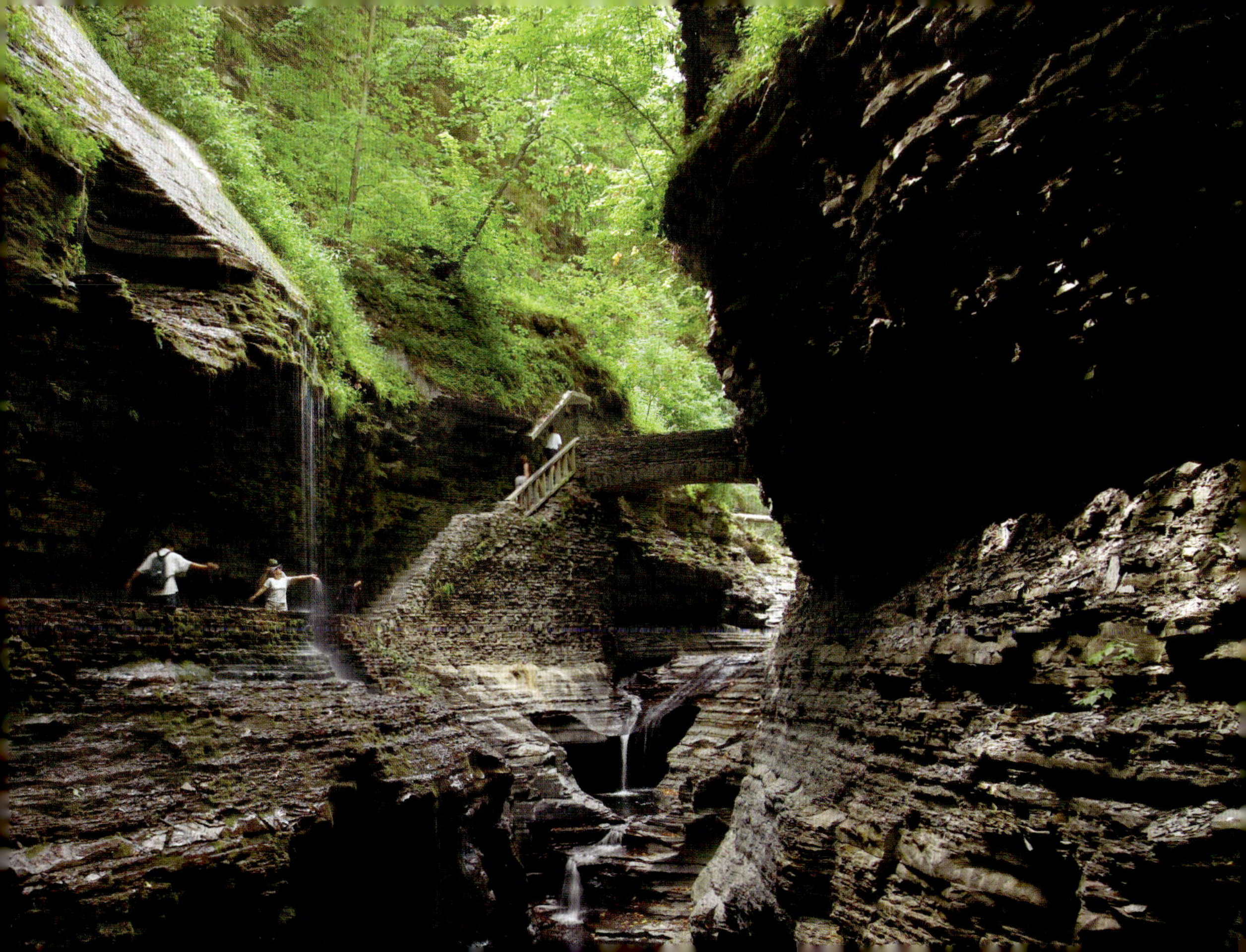

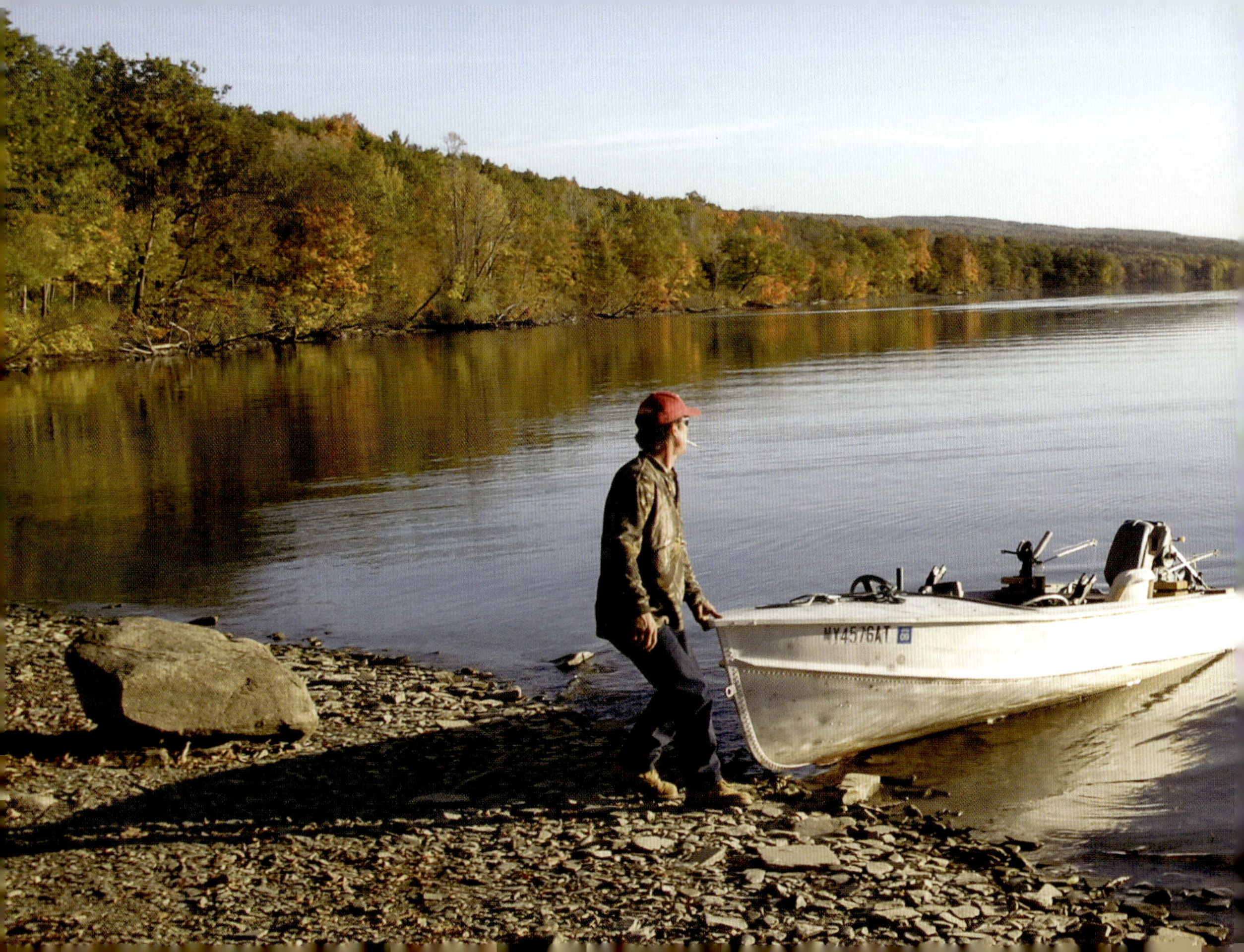
NY4576AT

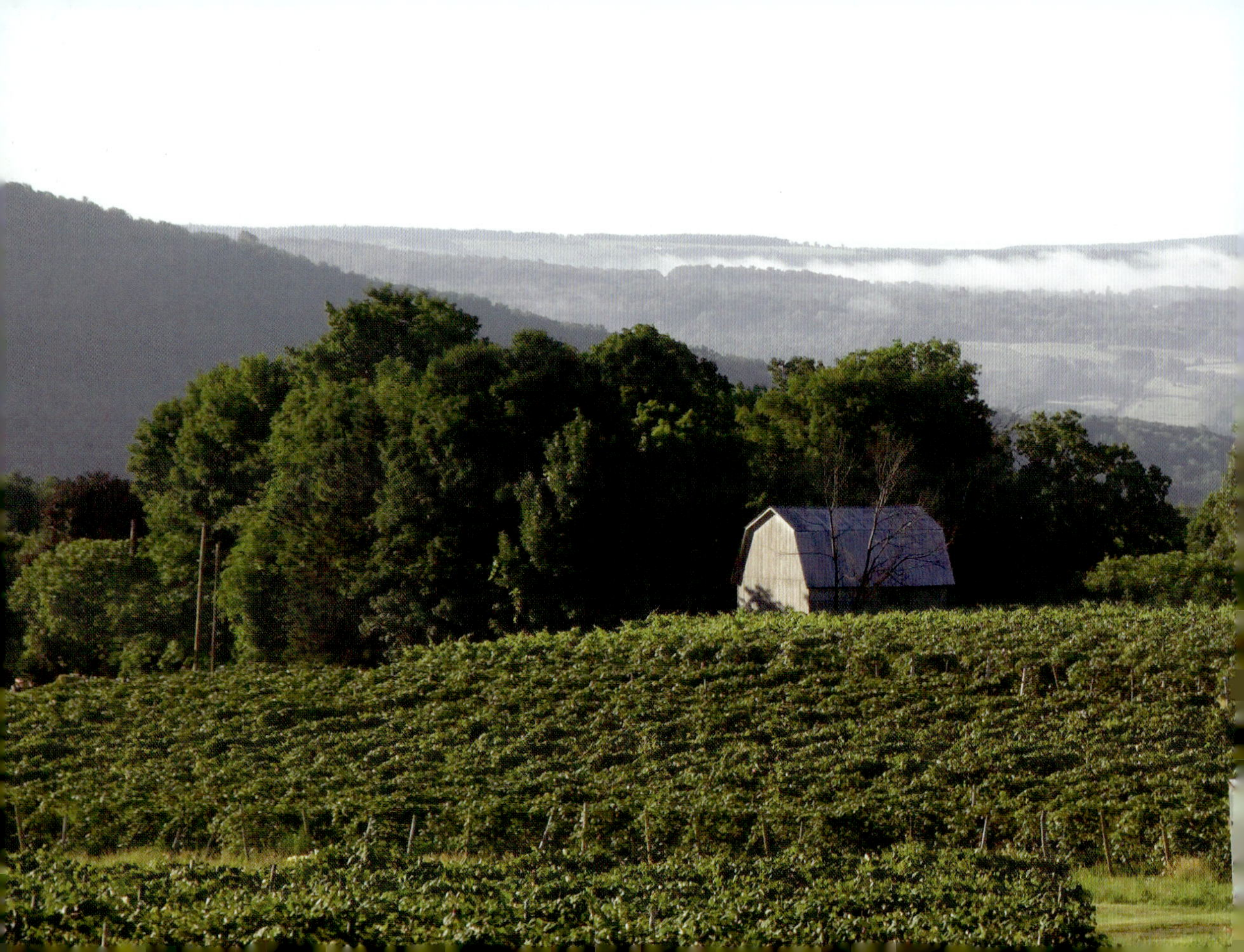

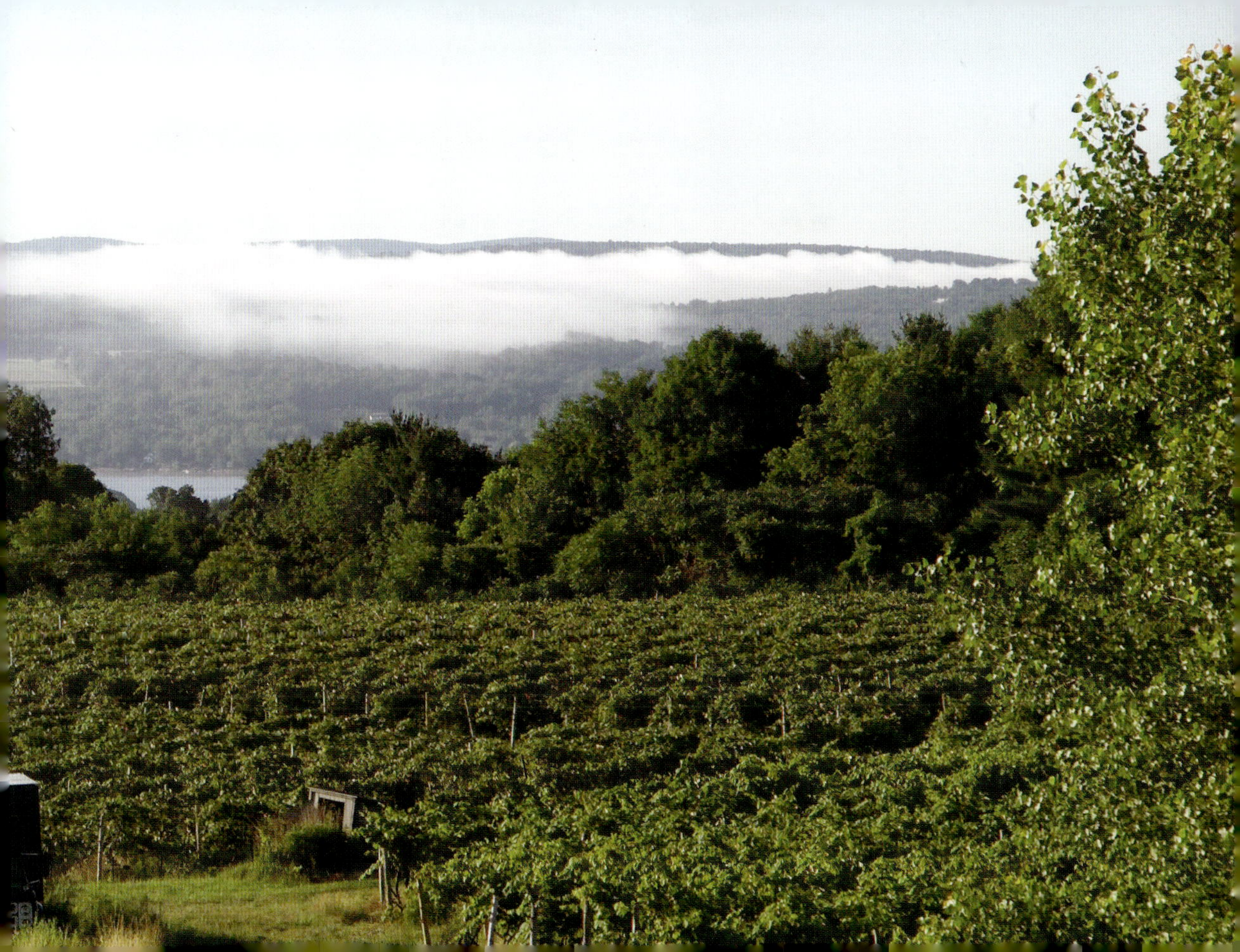

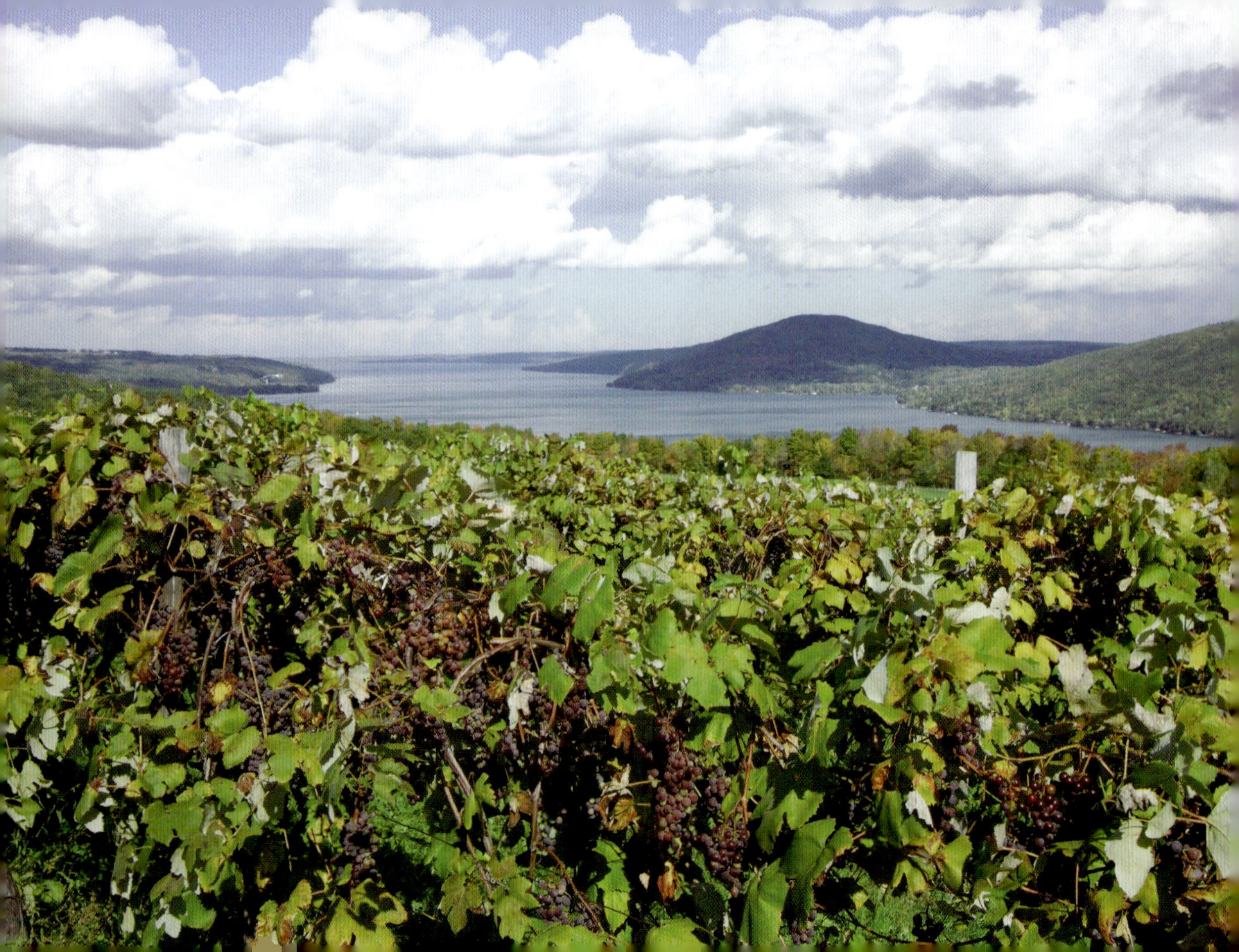

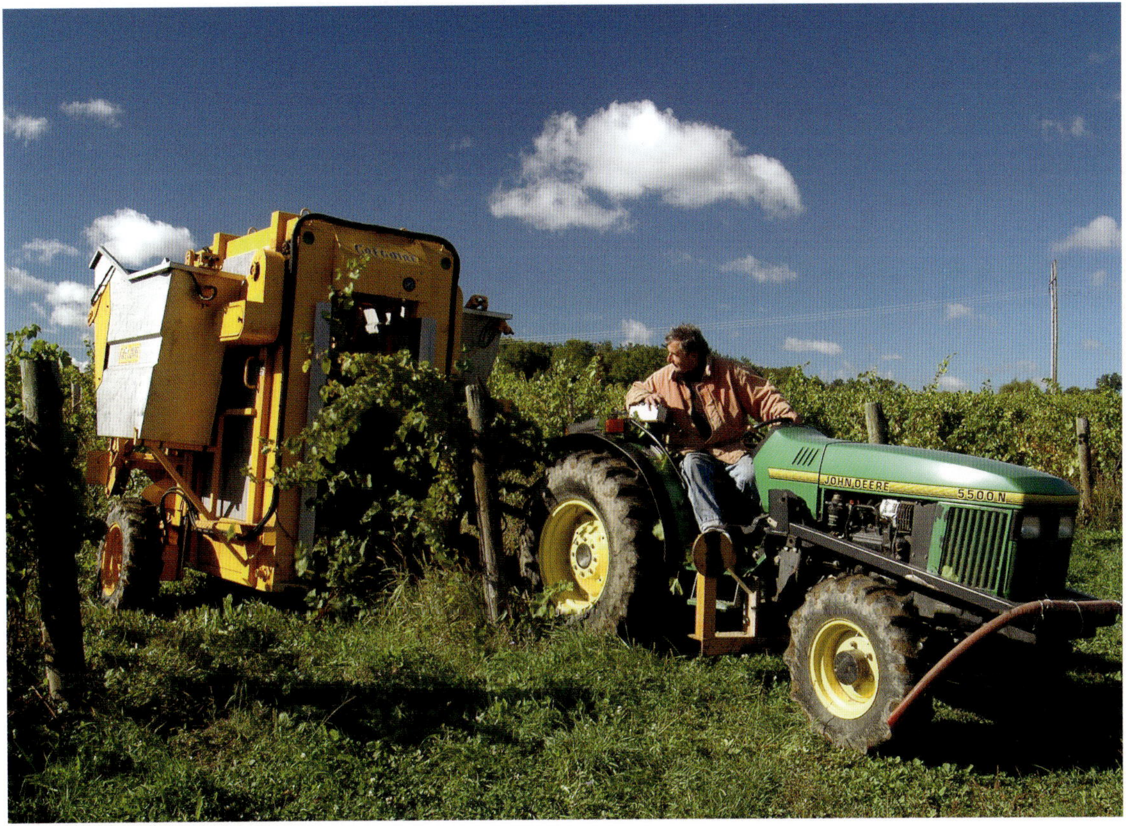

above, left, and previous The narrow, deep Finger Lakes create microclimates perfect for growing vinifera grapes that produce award-winning wines. next Balloons sail over the nearly 600-foot-deep gorge at Letchworth State Park.

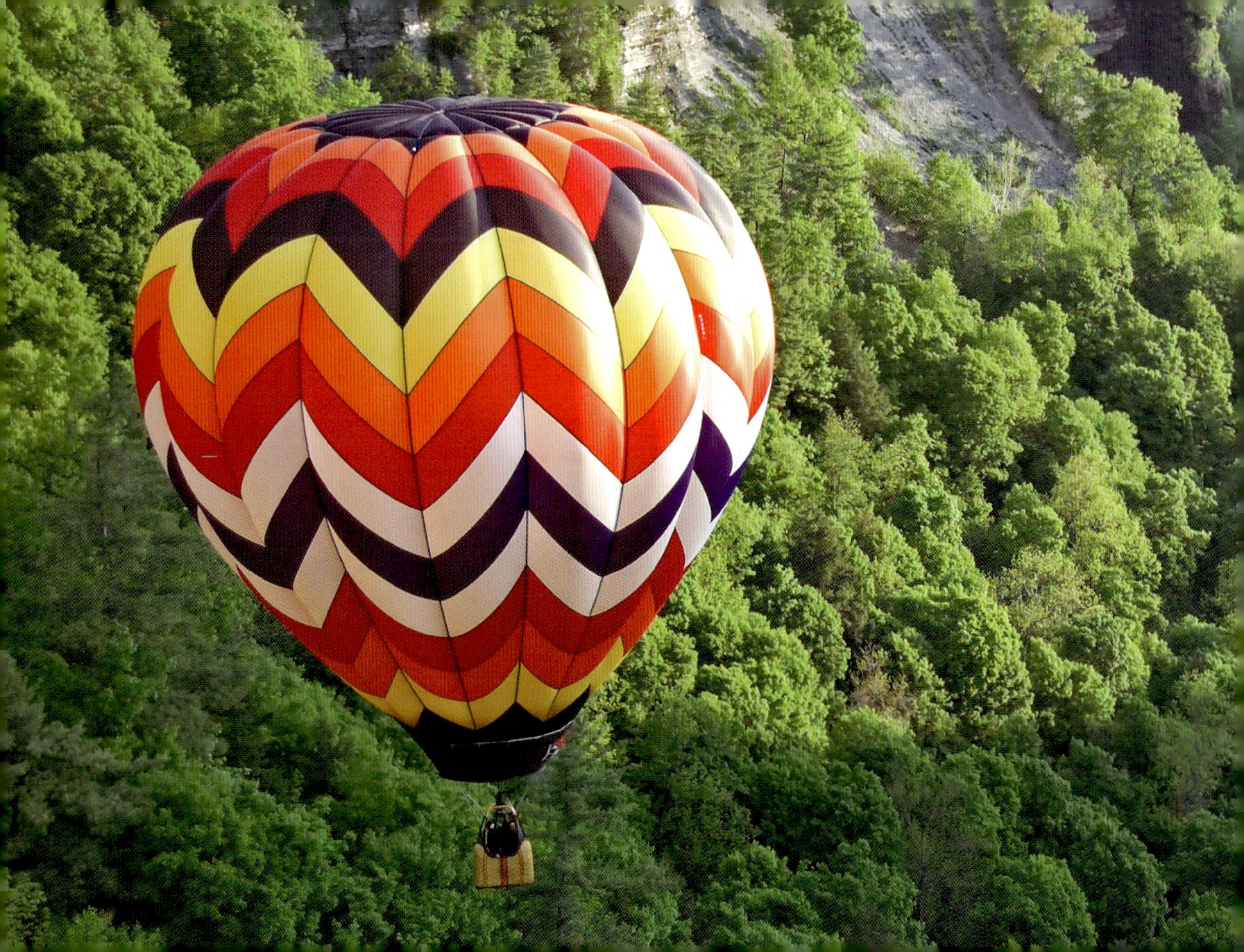

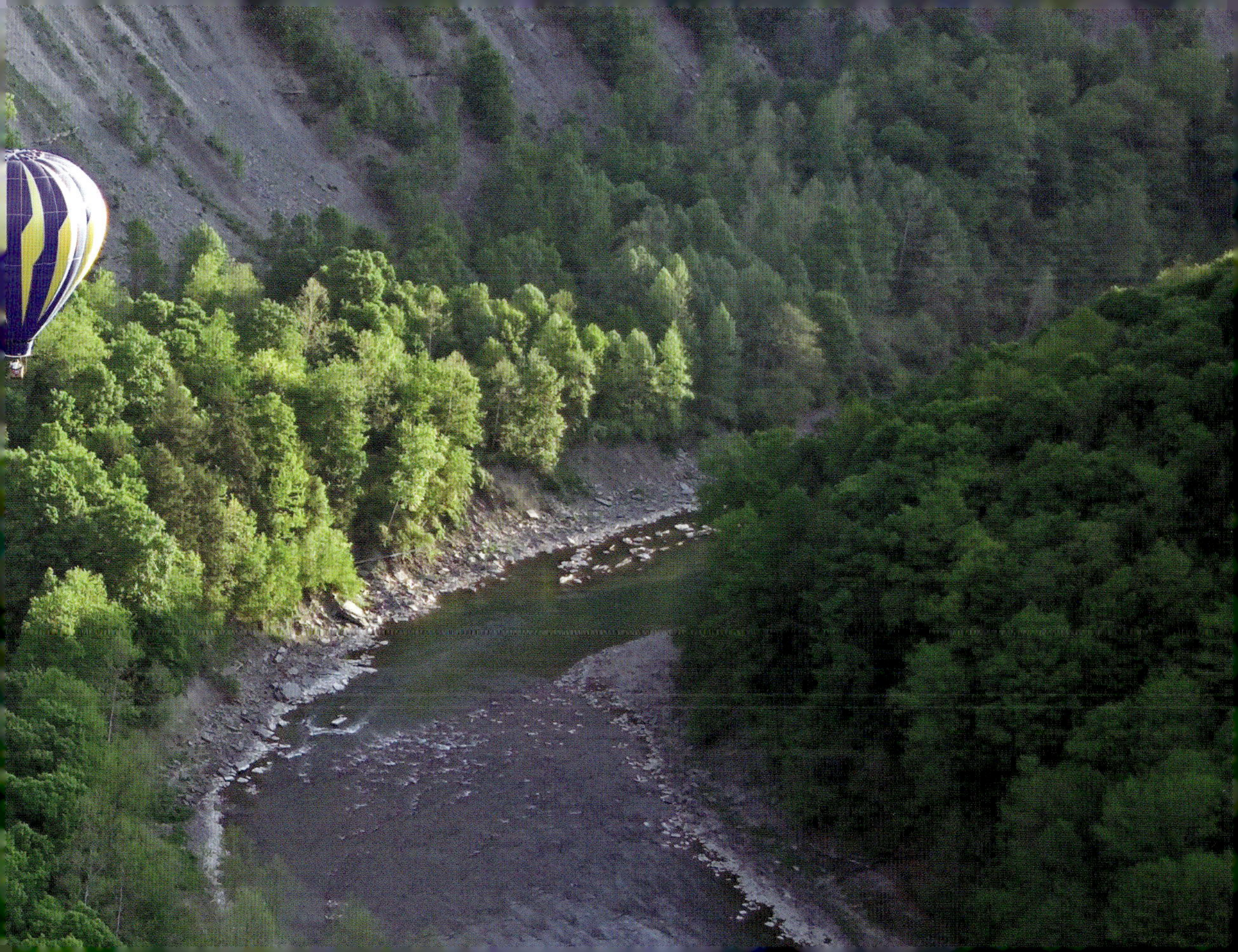

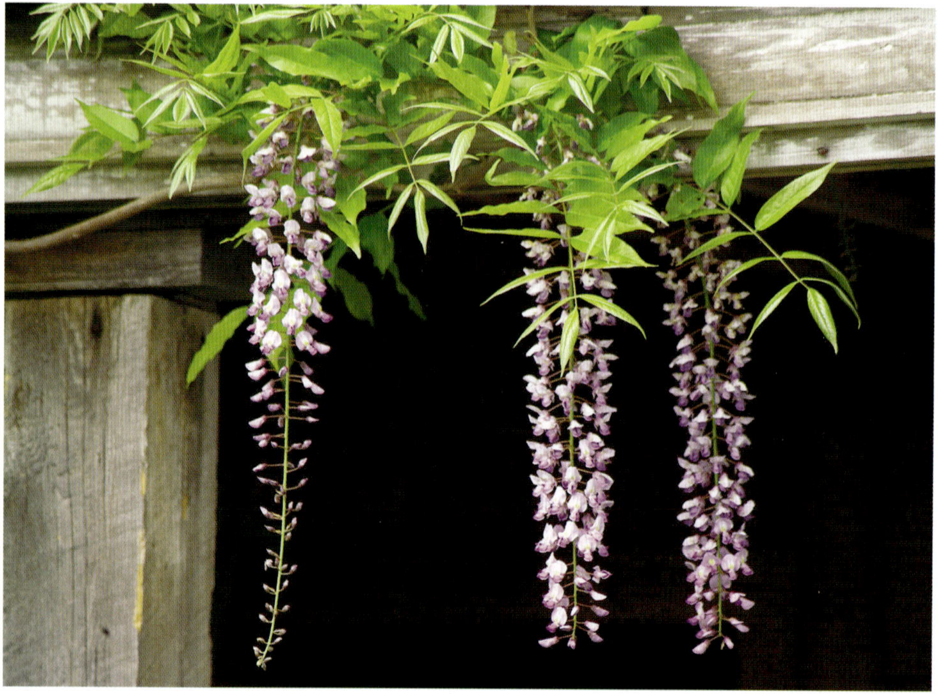

above Wisteria brightens a lintel. right Colorful row houses on Main Street, Geneva.
next The annual Ithaca Festival parade celebrates the start of summer.

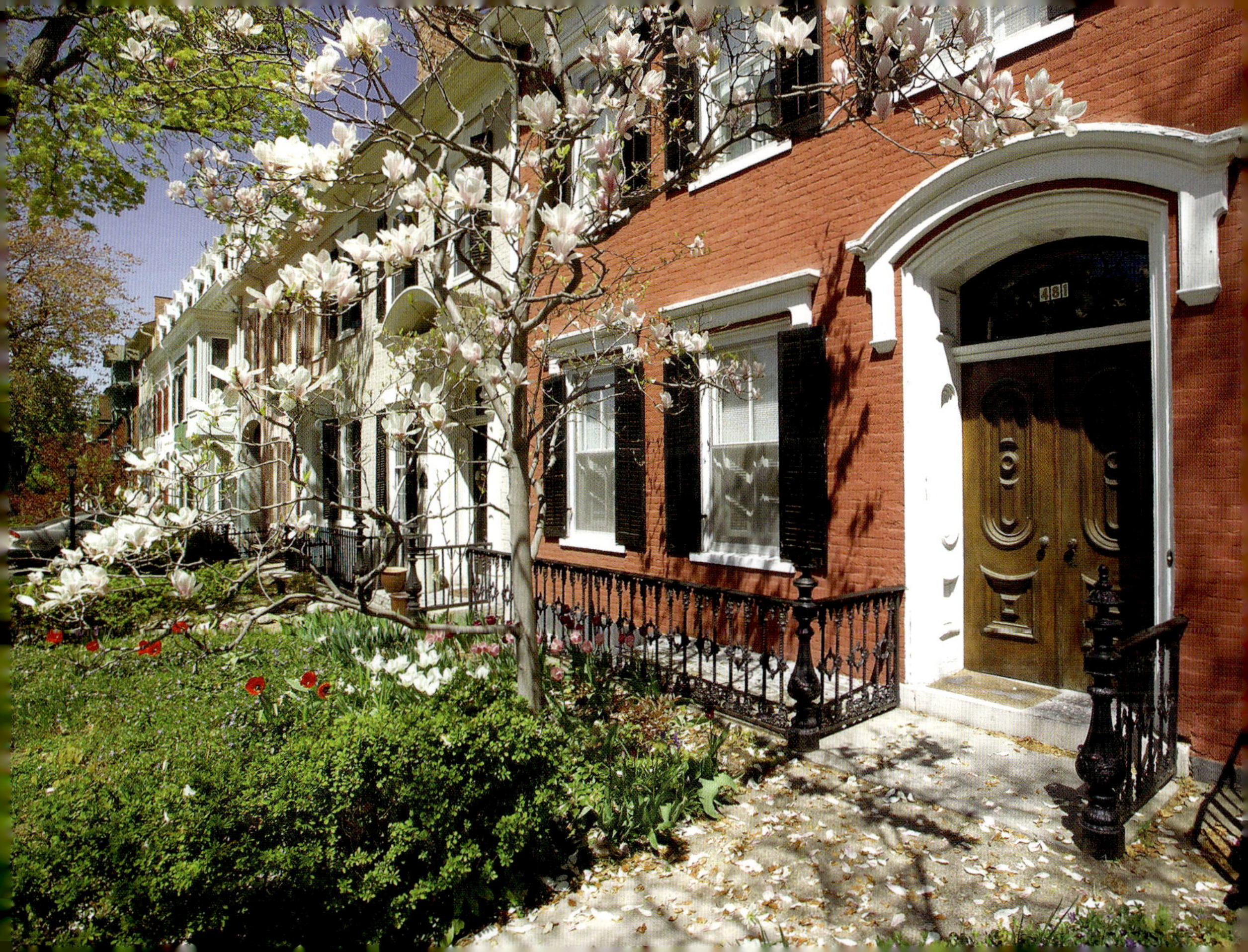
481

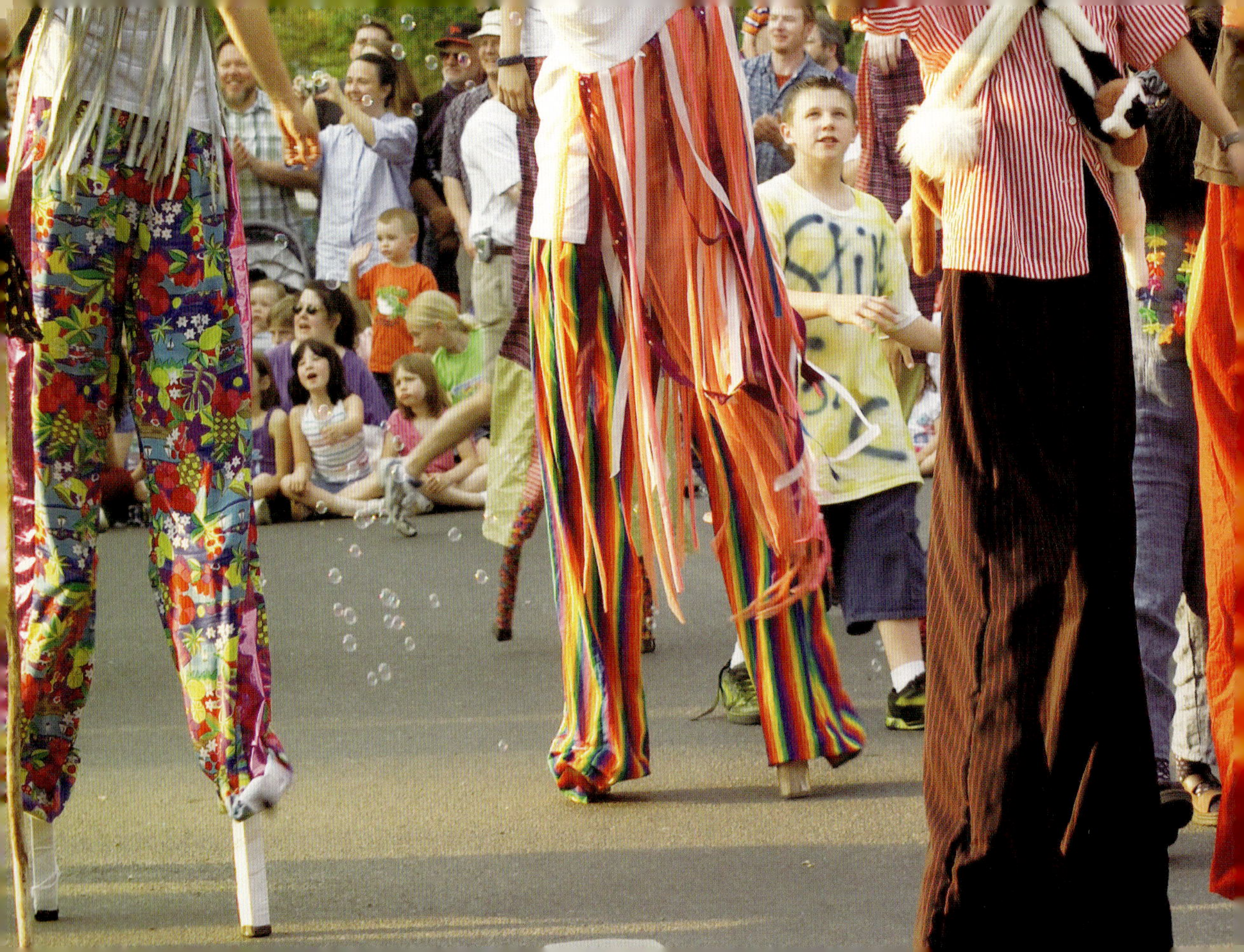

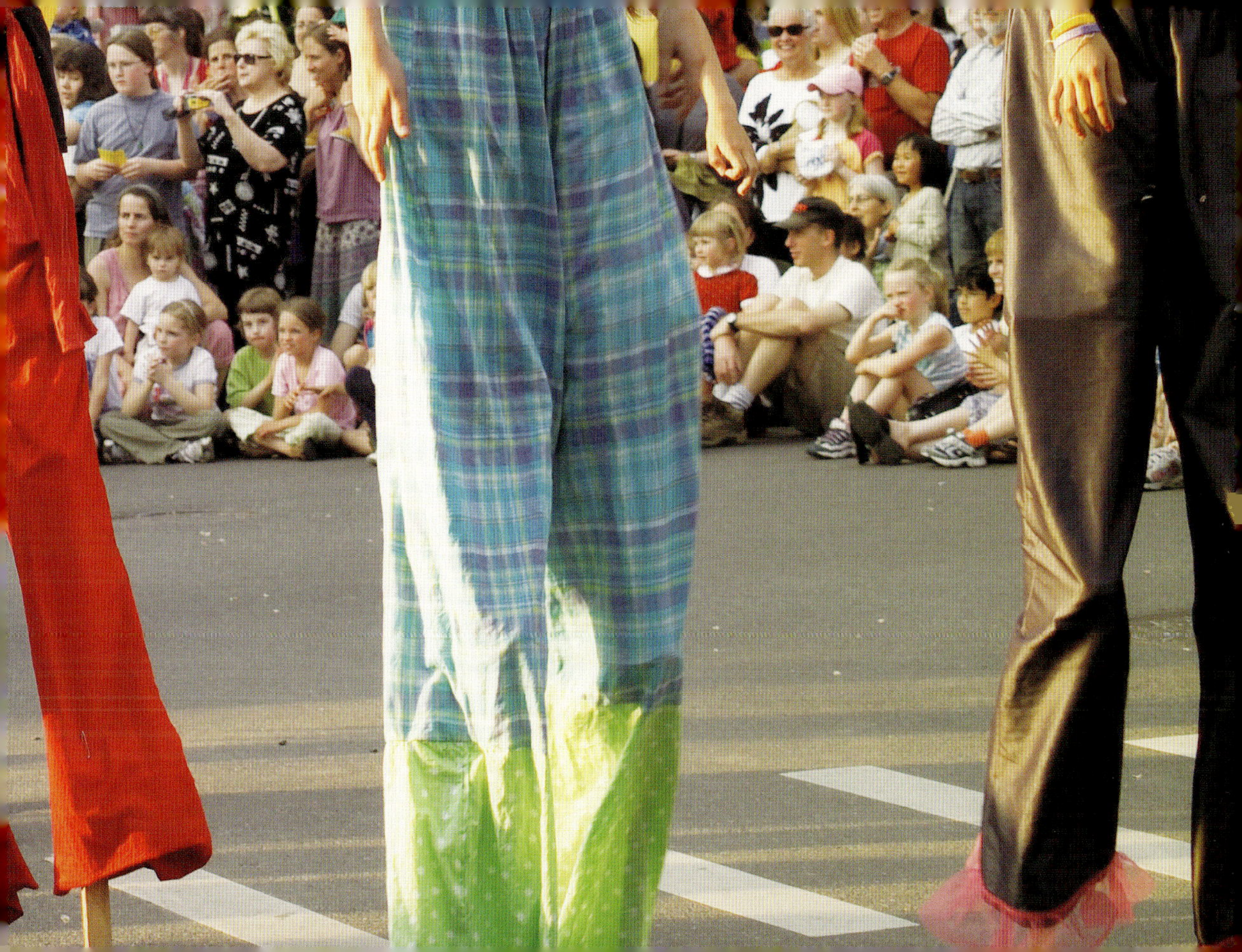

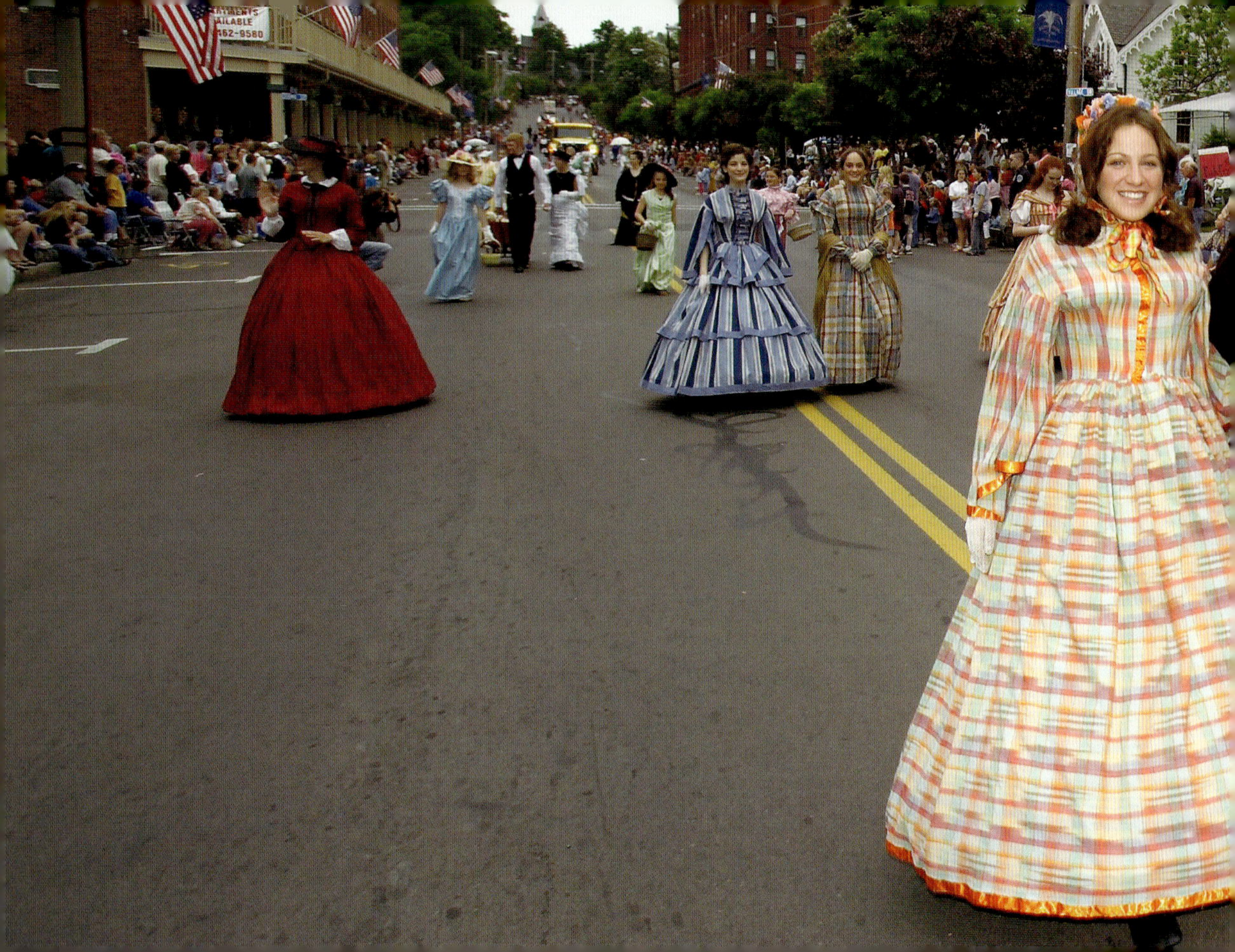

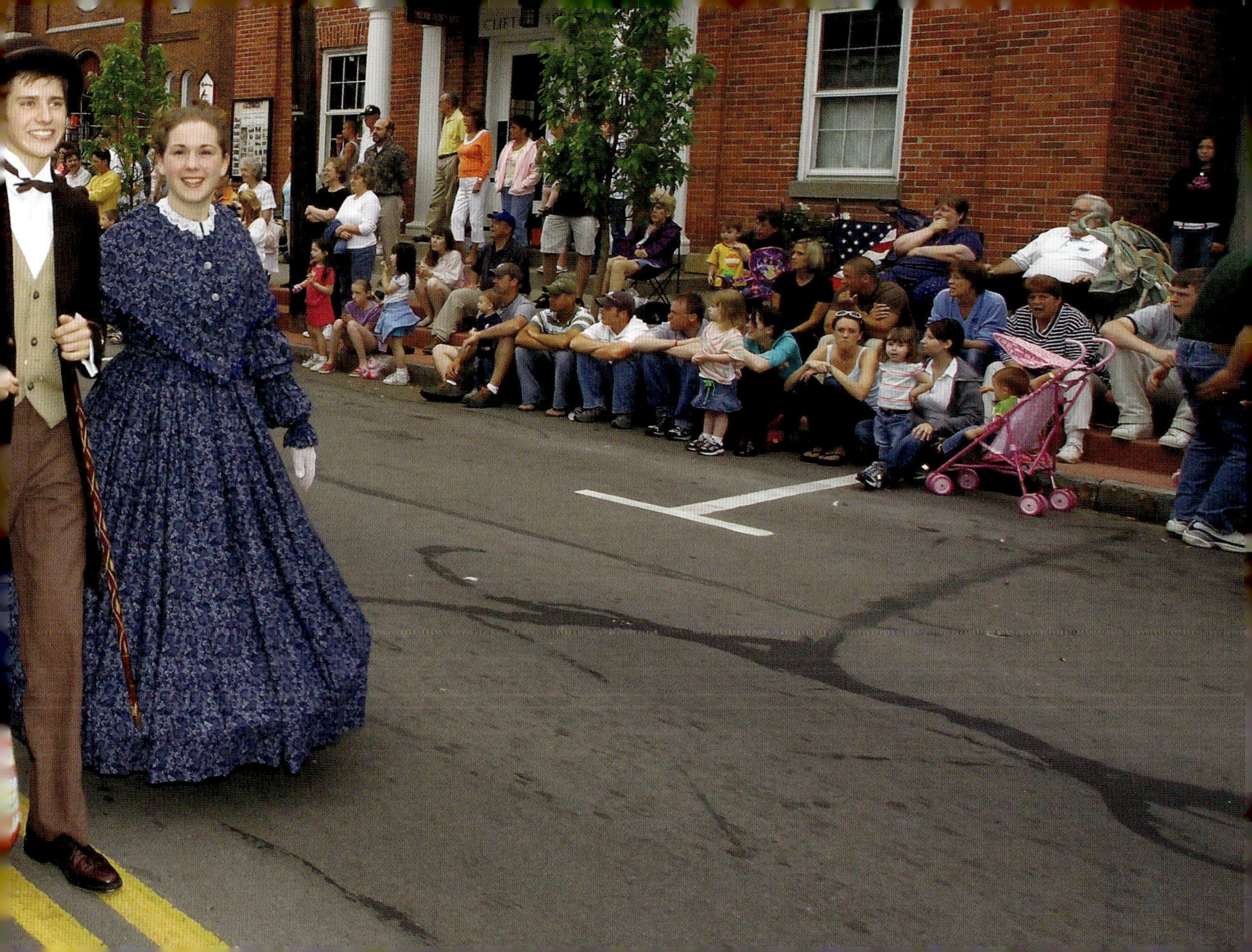

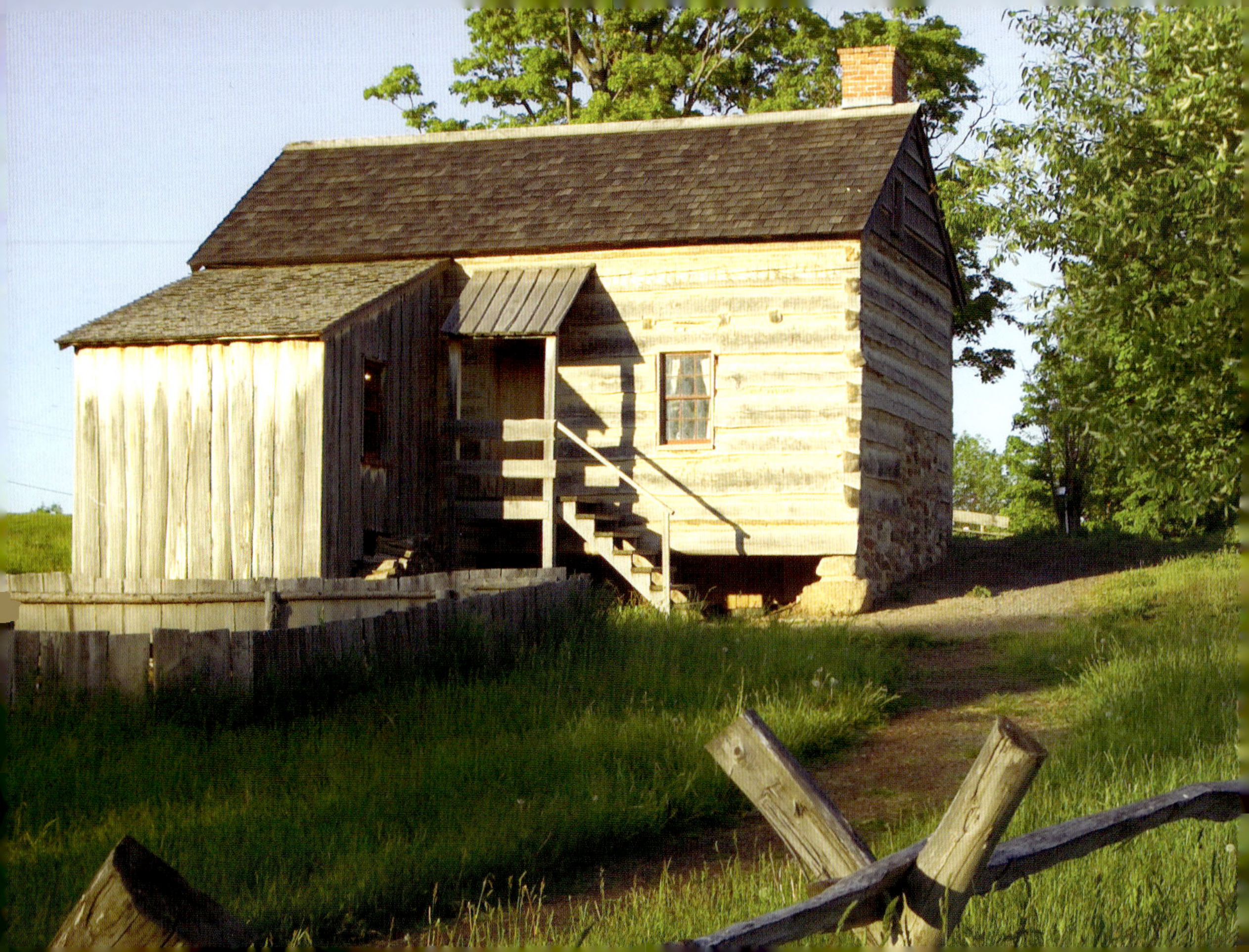

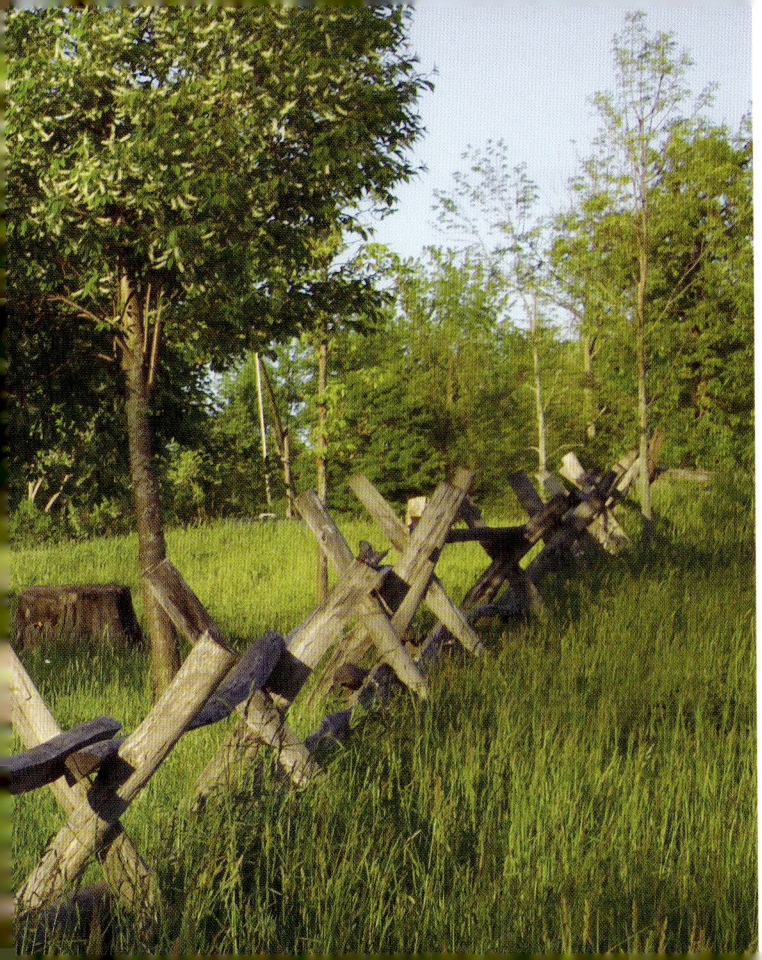

left The reconstructed homestead in Palmyra of Joseph Smith, founder of the Mormon faith. previous The parade at the Sulfur Springs Festival in Clifton Springs. next An Amish farmer plows his fields near Prattsburg.

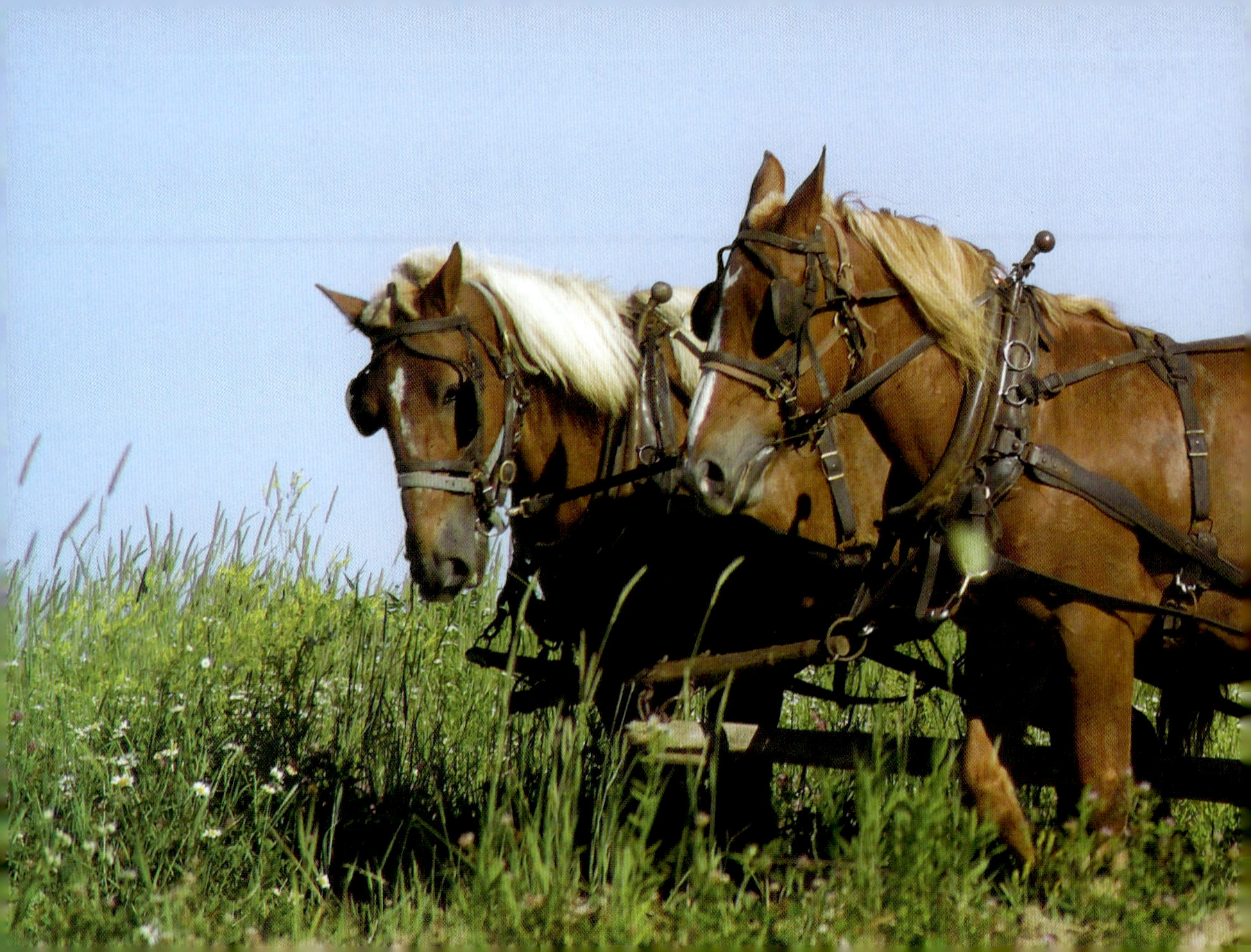

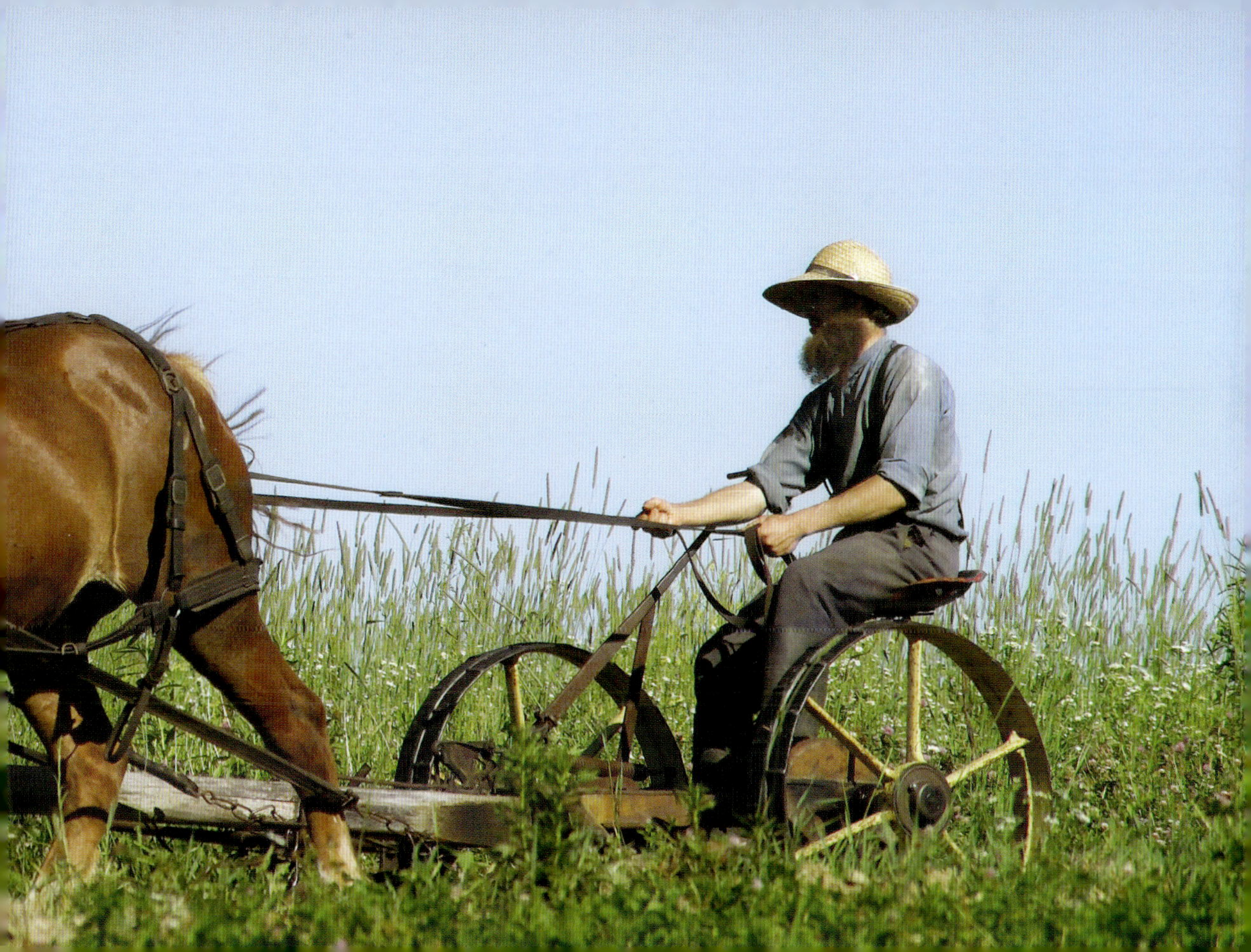

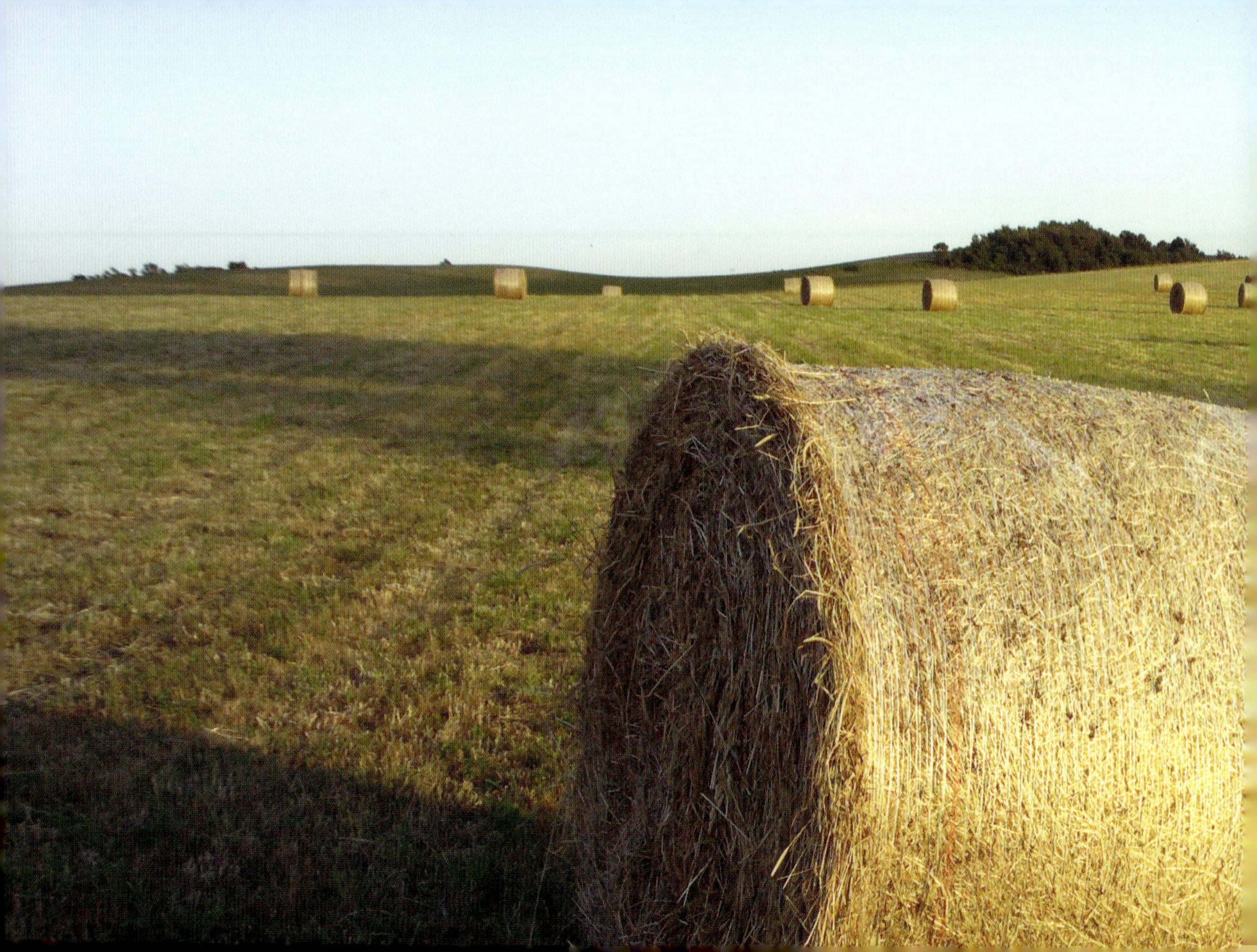

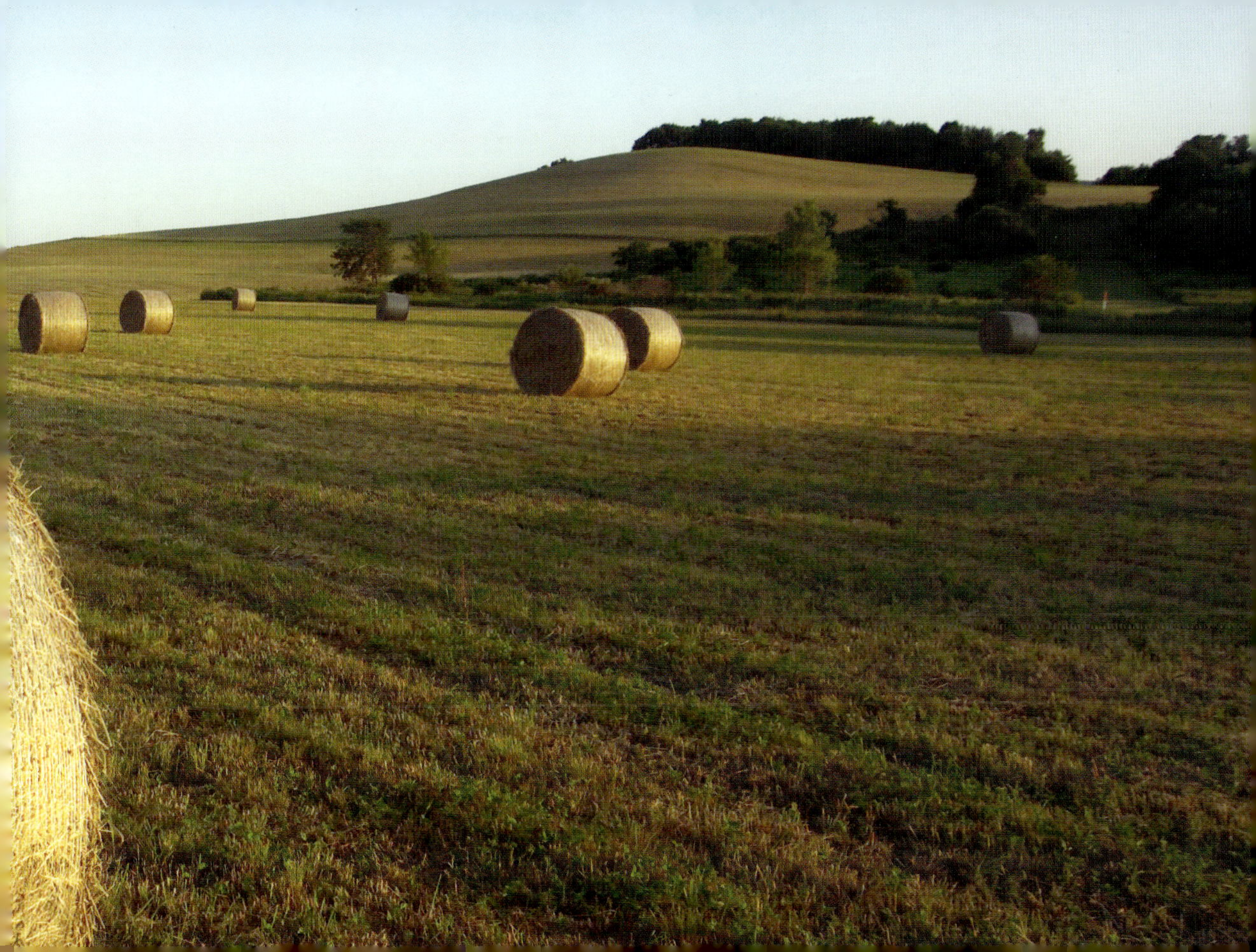

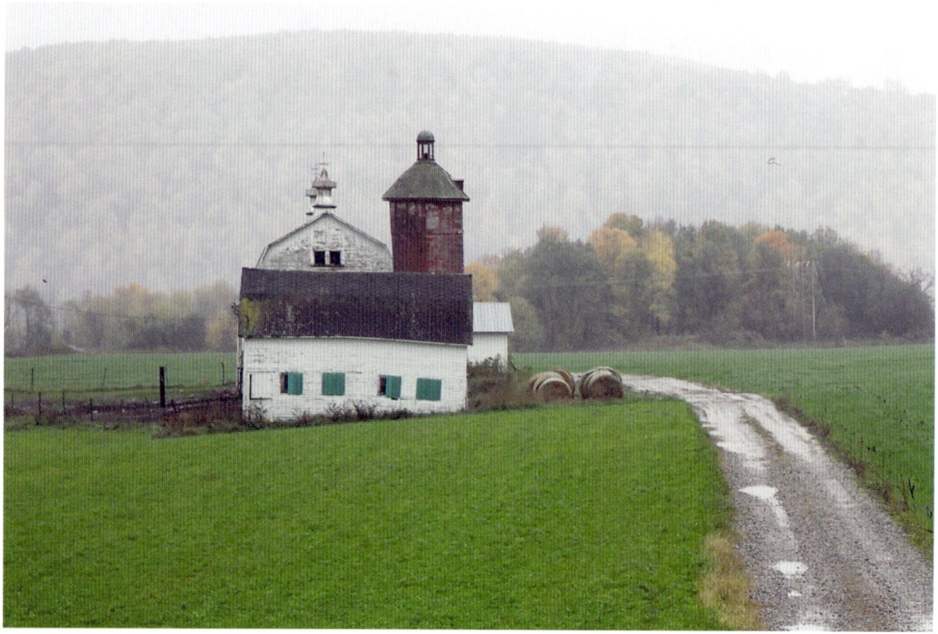

above, right and previous Independent farmers still work the land between the lakes. next Glacier-created drumlins south of Naples.

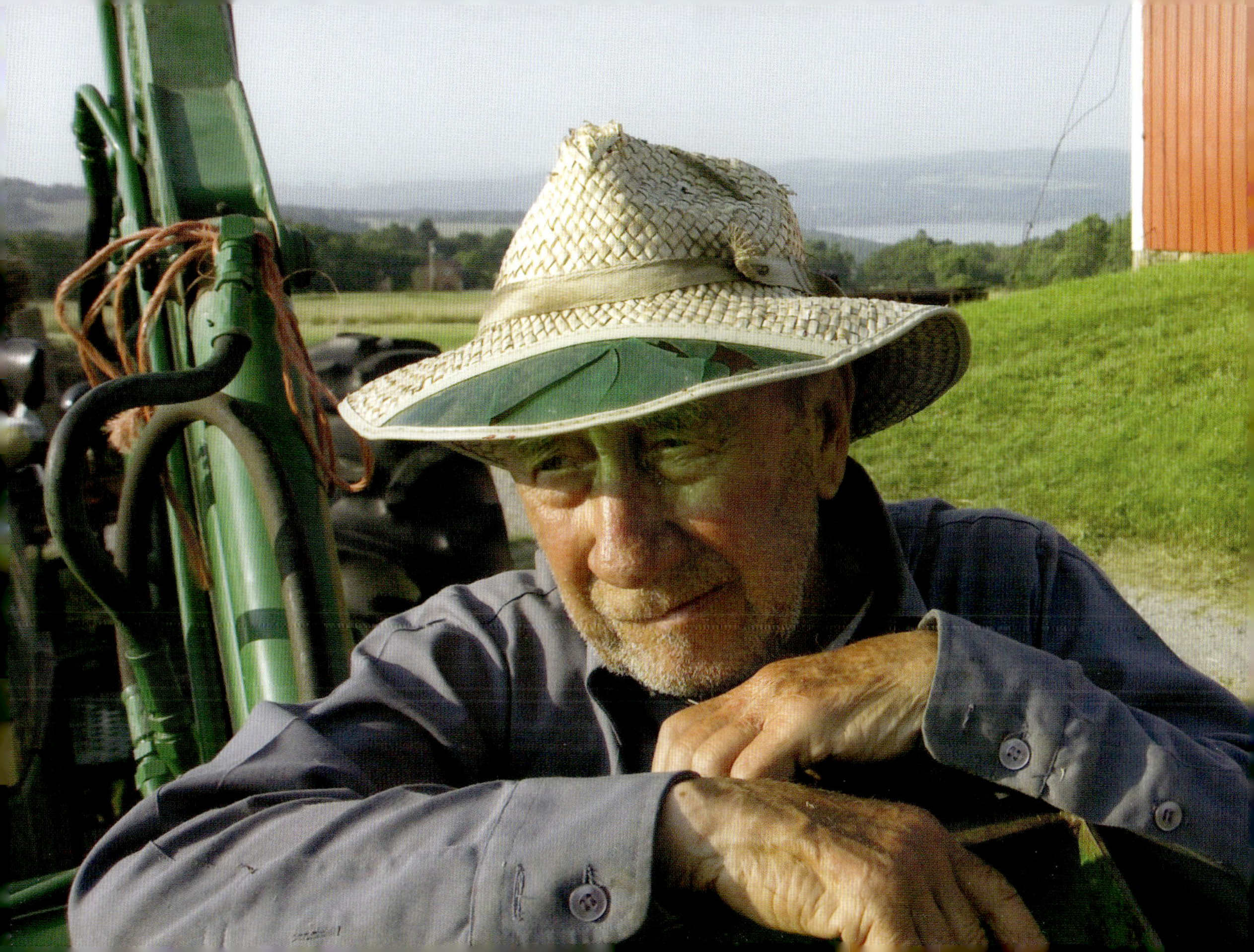

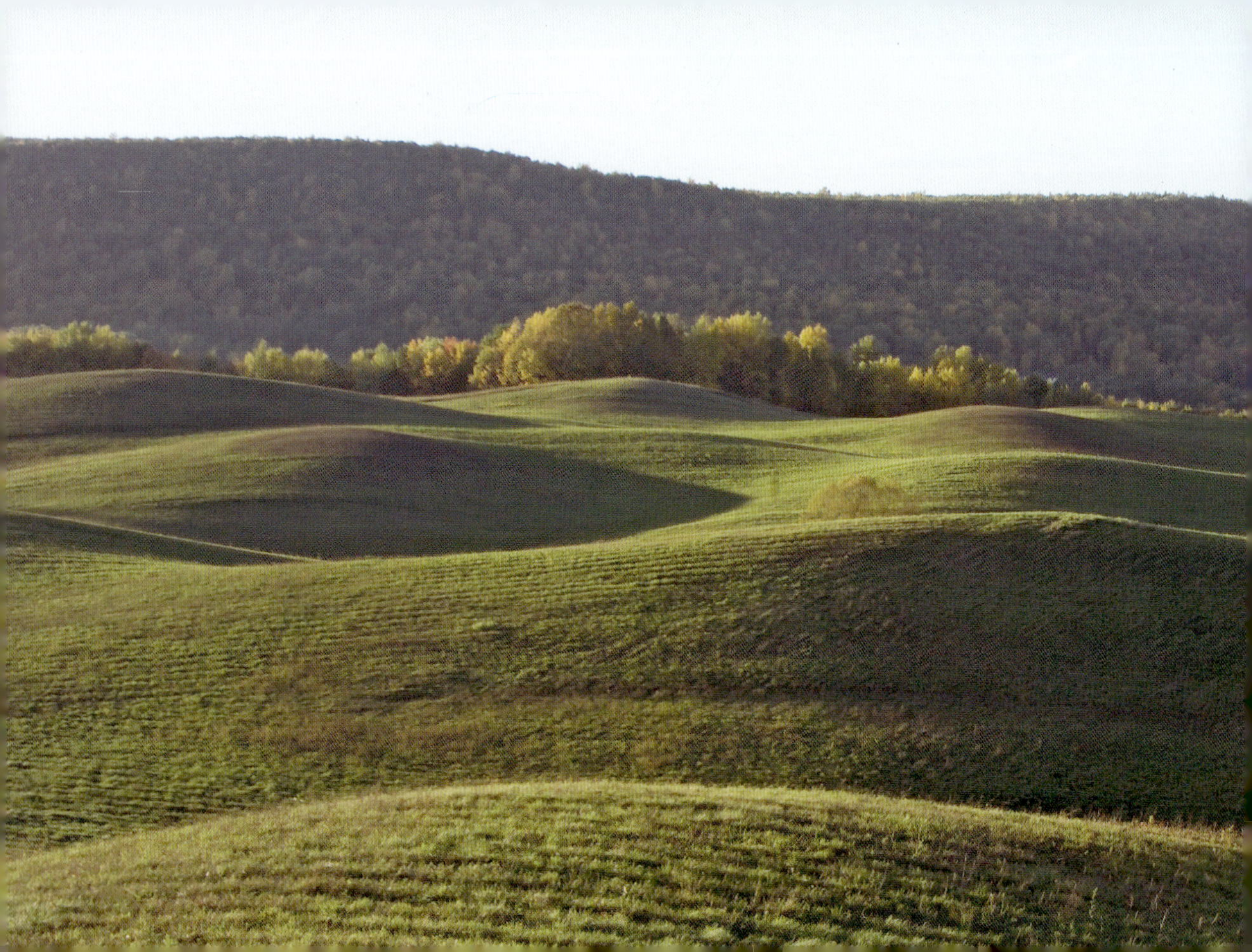

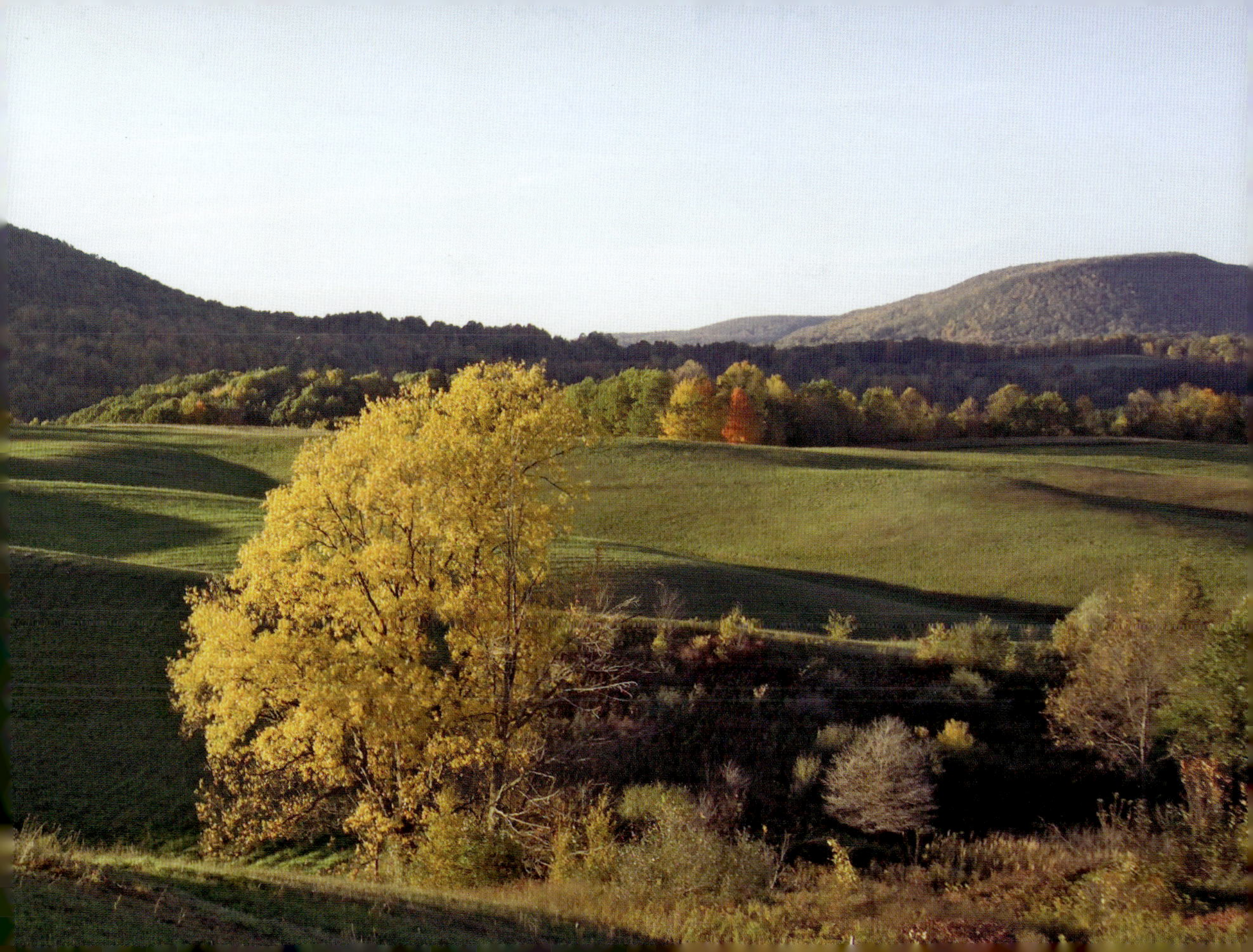

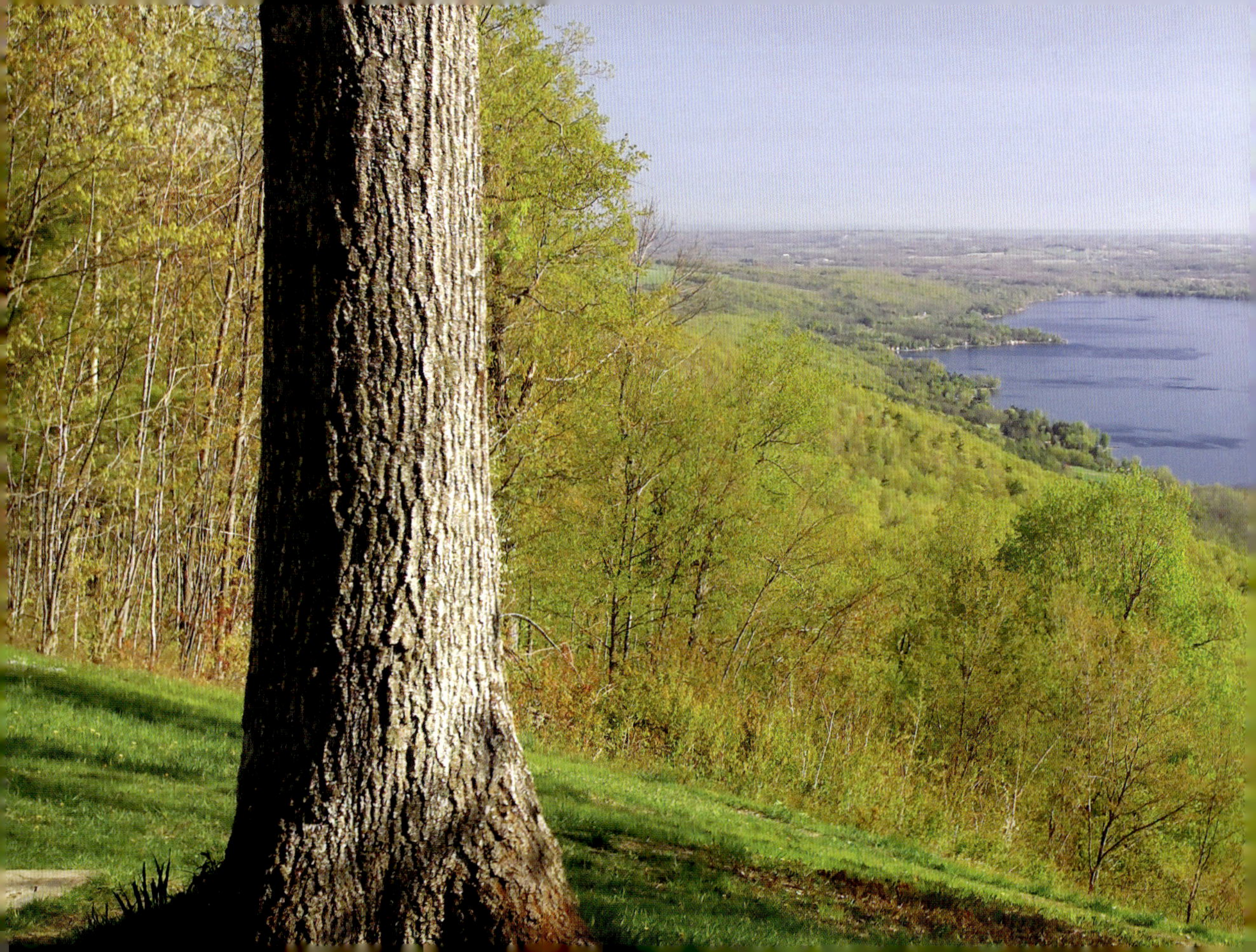

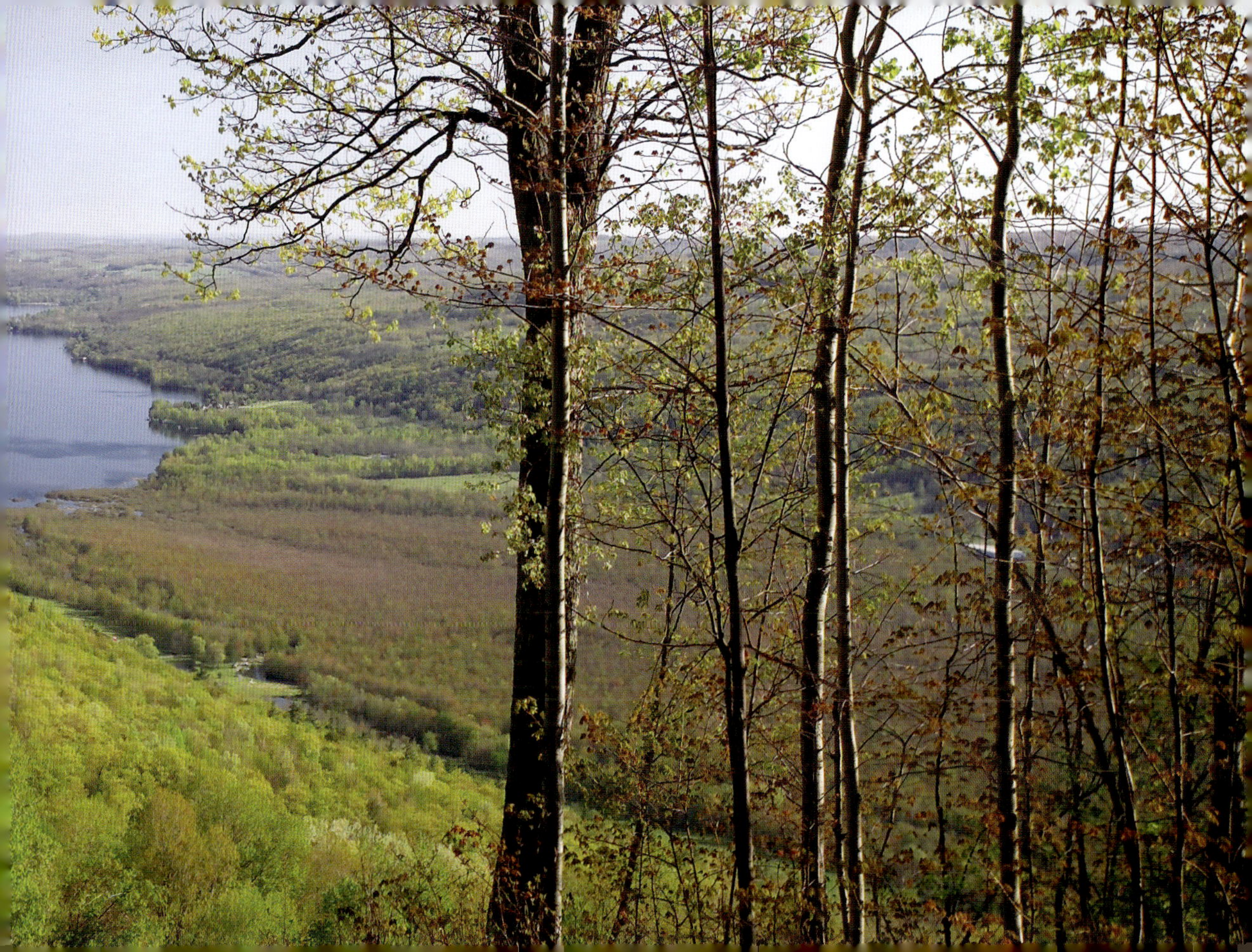

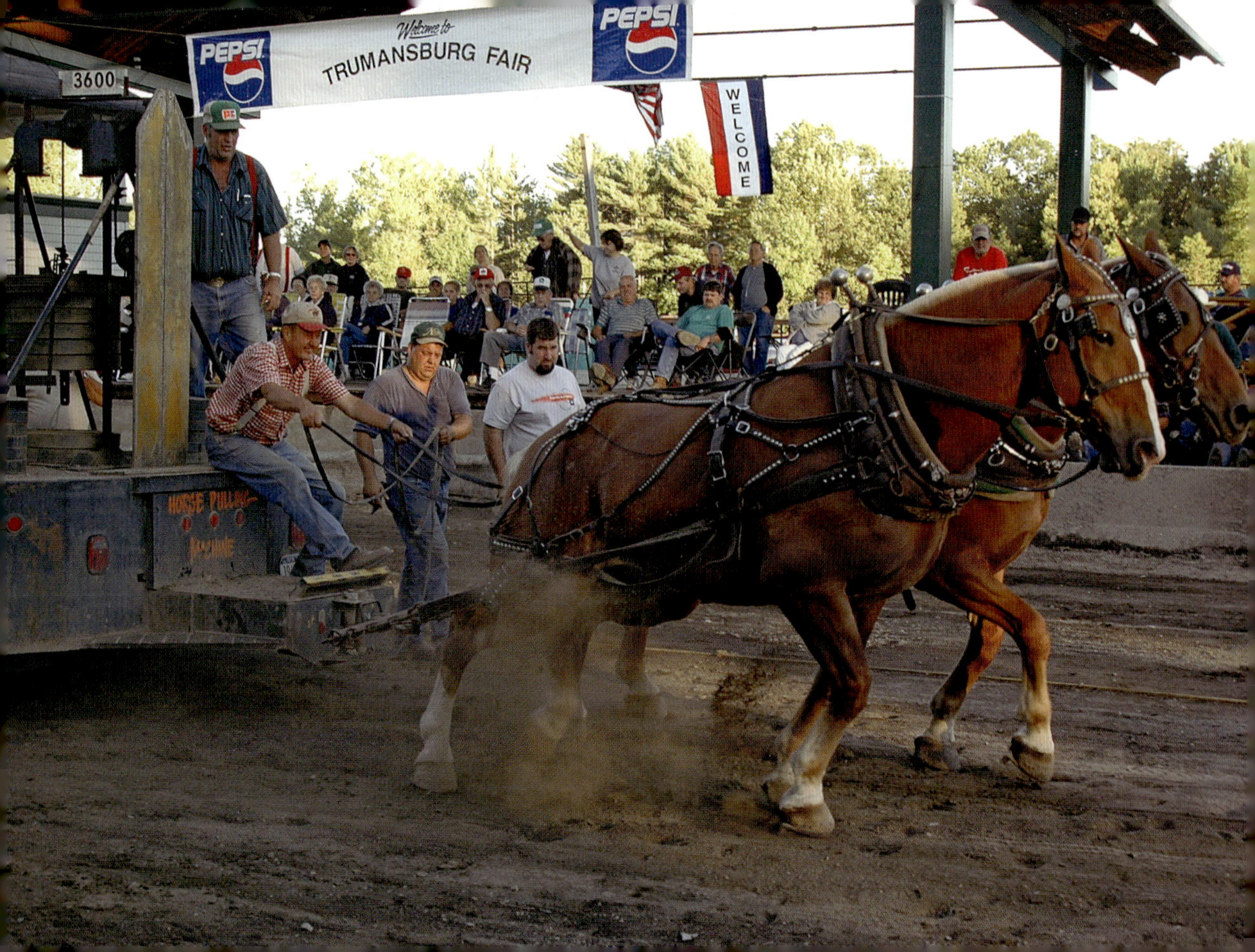
PEPSI
Welcome to
TRUMANSBURG FAIR
PEPSI
3600
WELCOME
HORSE PULLING
MACHINE

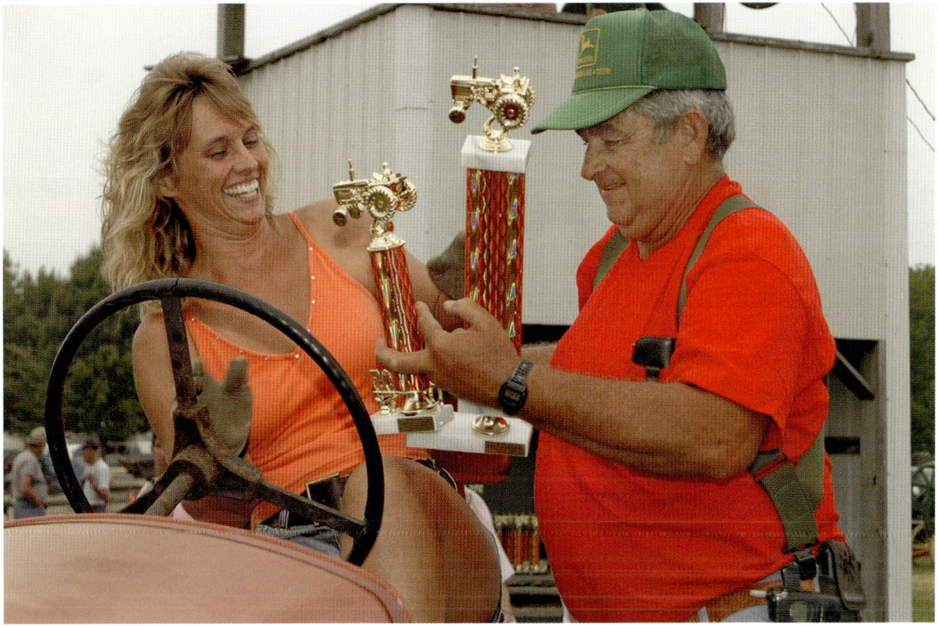

aboveThe winner of the tractor pull at the Trumansburg Fair. leftThe draft horse pull at the Trumansburg Fair. previousHoneoye Lake as seen from Harriet Hollister State Park, Route 36. nextSunday afternoons in August see the Skaneateles Polo Club taking to the field. page after nextRacing crews abound on the Erie Canal and the south end of Cayuga Lake.

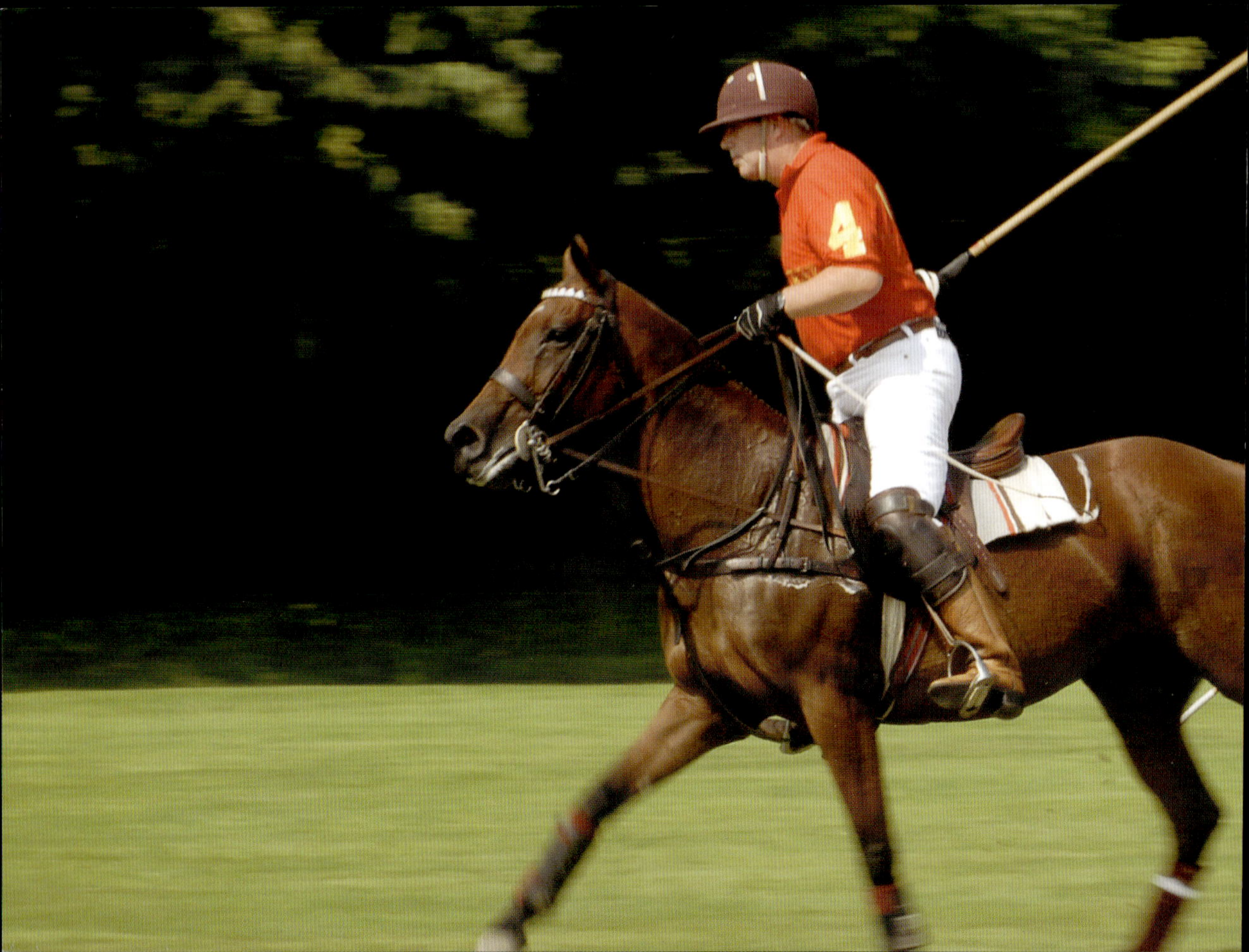

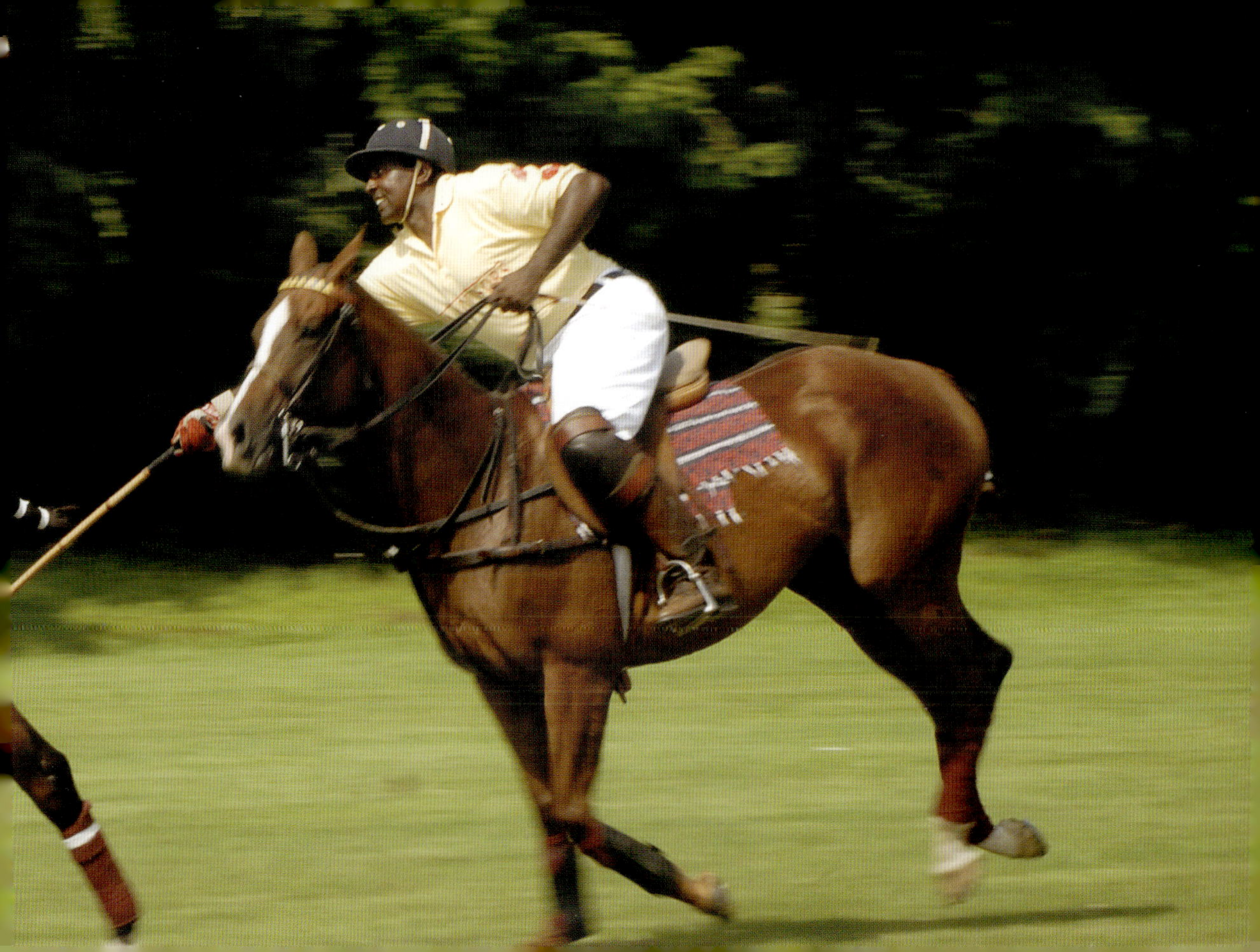

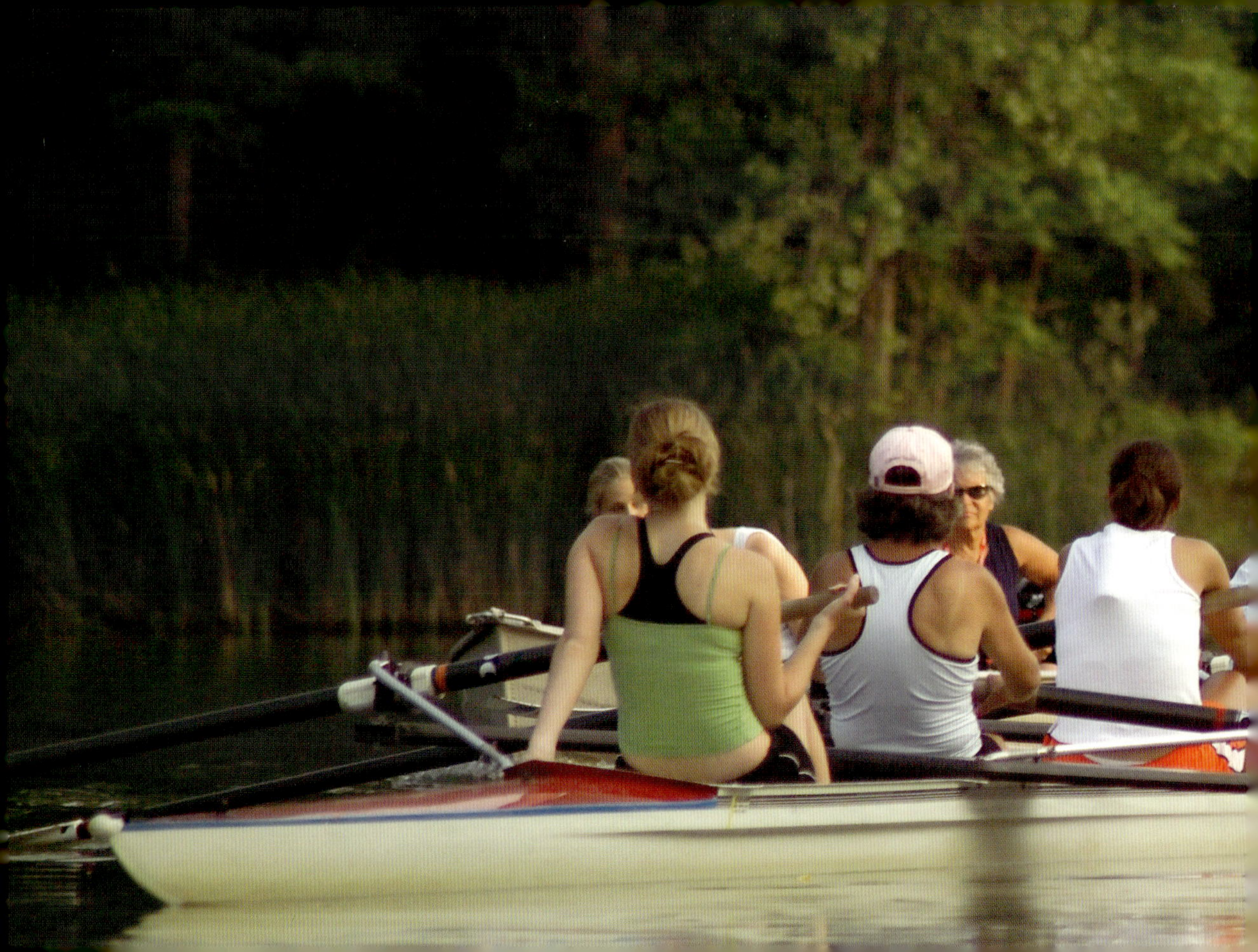

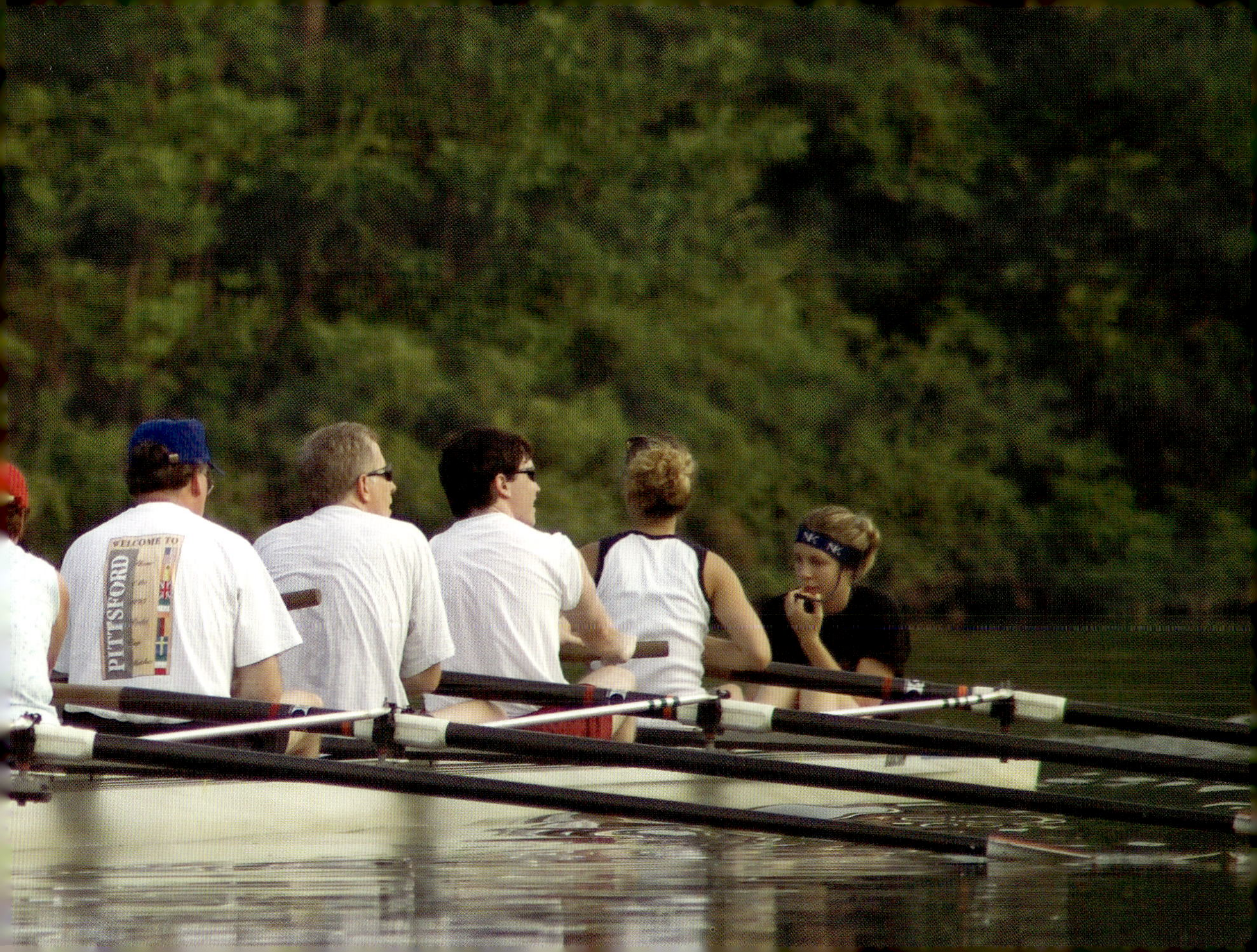
WELCOME TO
PITTSFORD

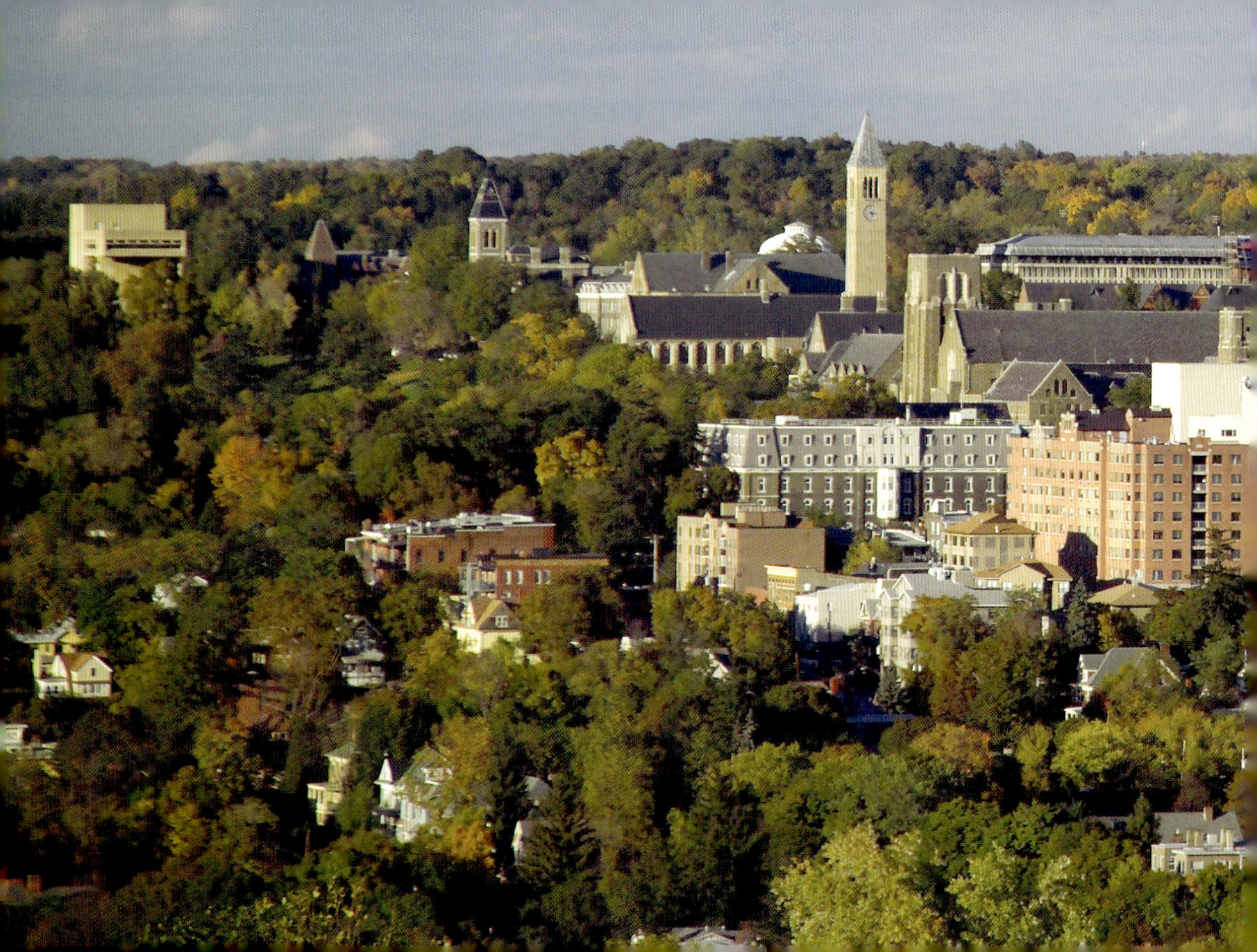

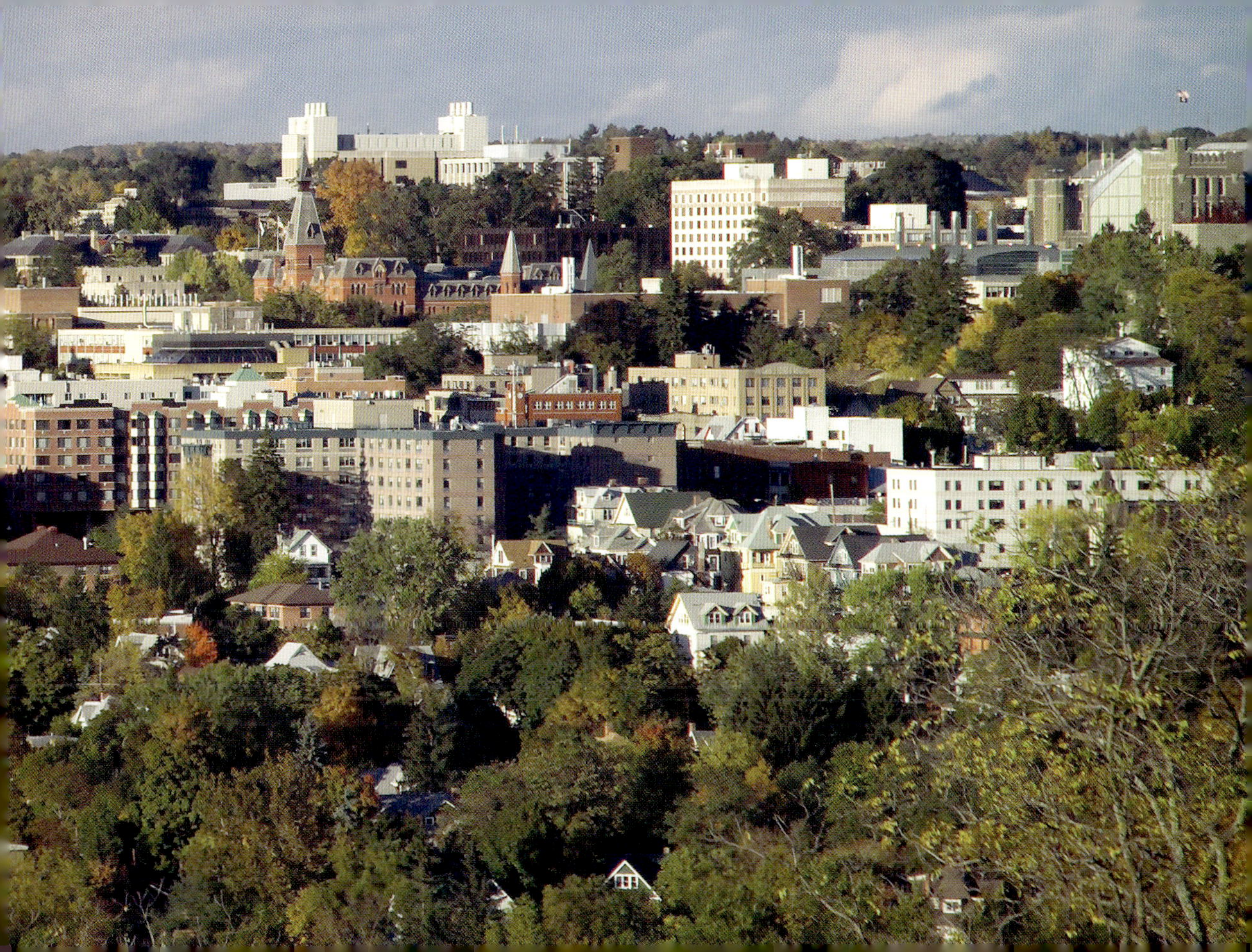

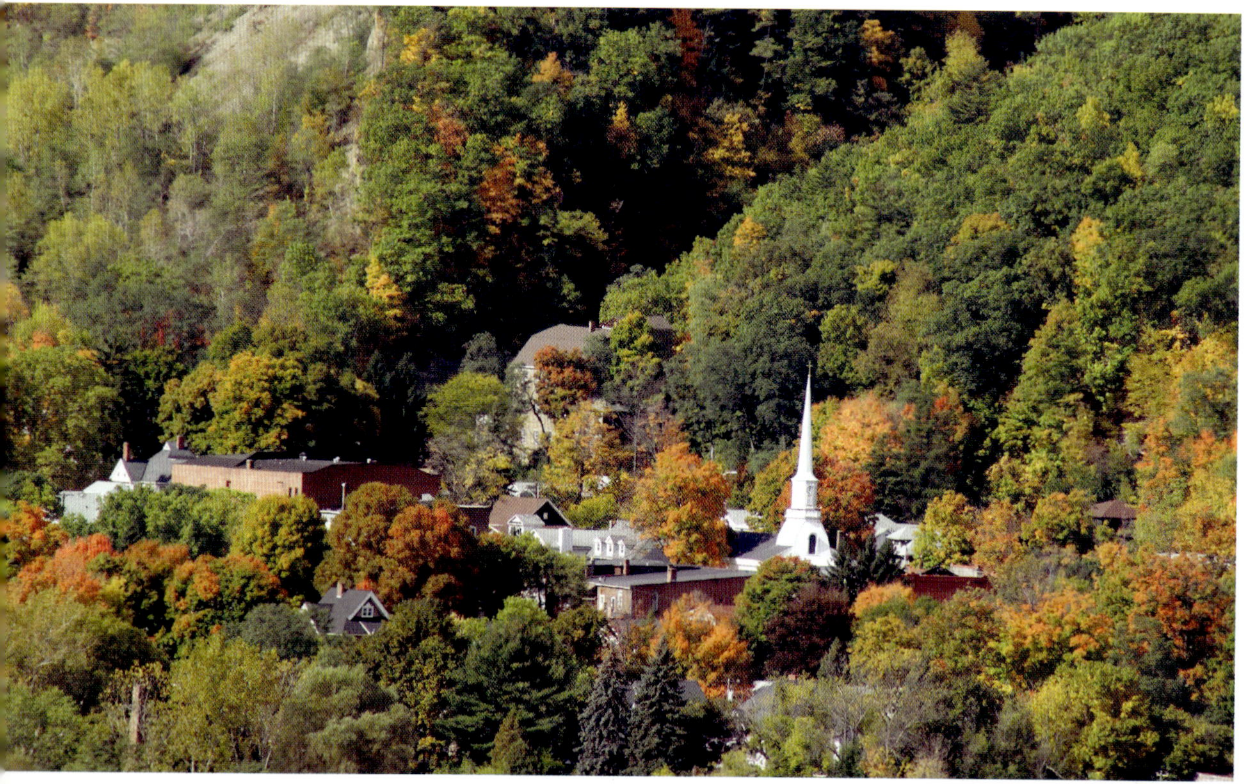

above Hammondsport, from the hills to the northeast. right and next Competitors at the Cayuga Lake Triathalon at Taughannock Falls State Park must swim, bike, and run. previous Cornell University stretches across the hills of Ithaca above Cayuga Lake.

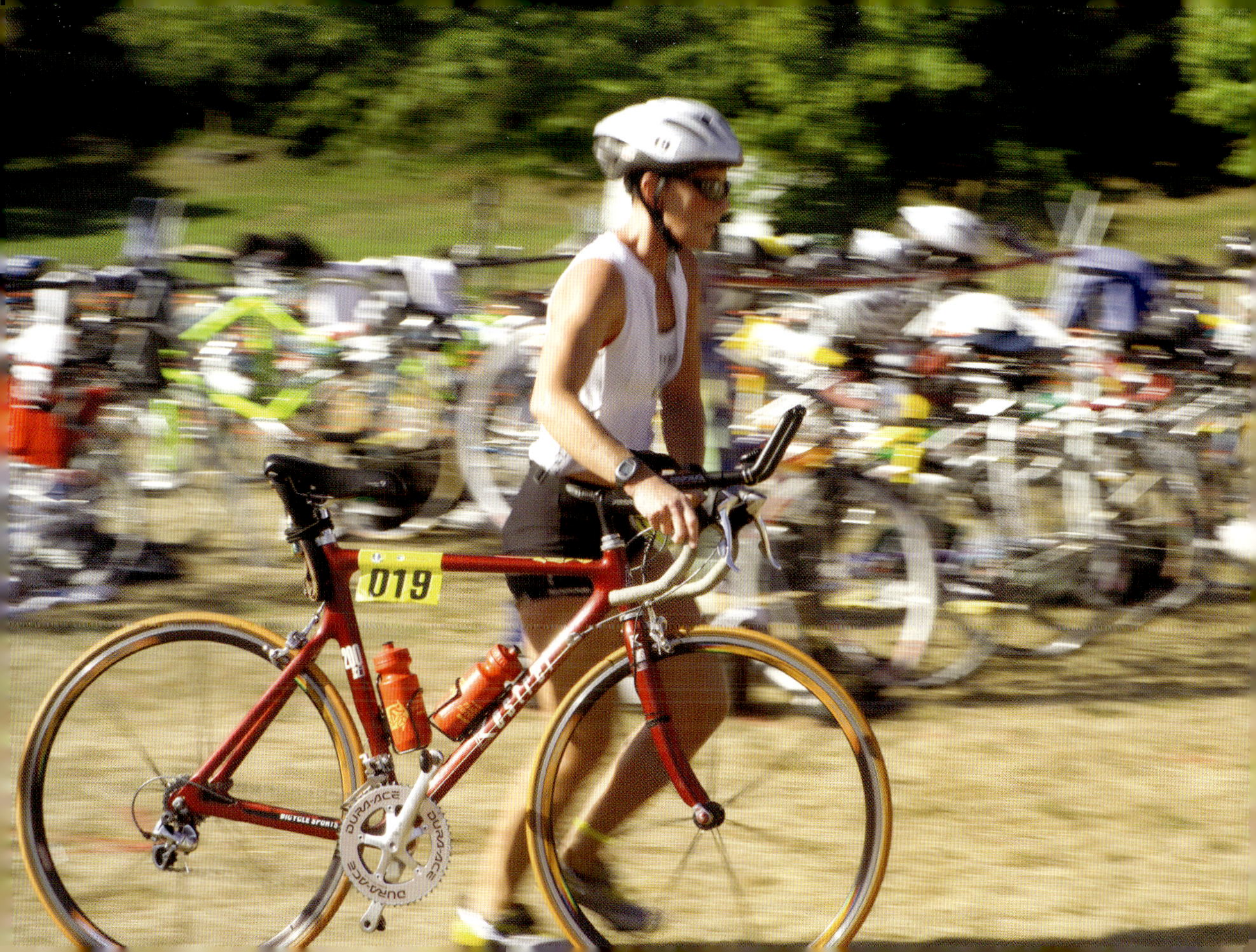
019
DURA-ACE

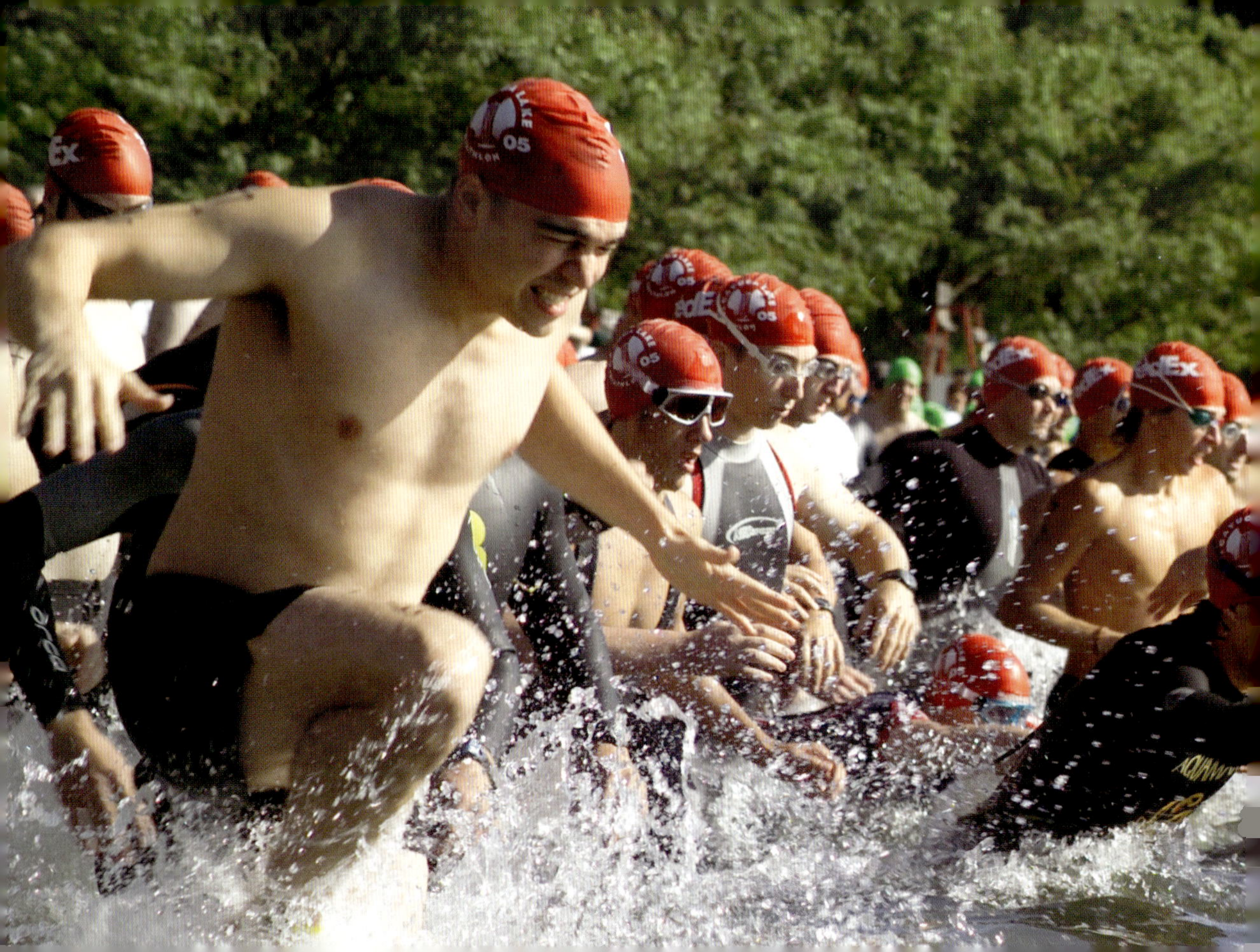
LAKE
05
orca

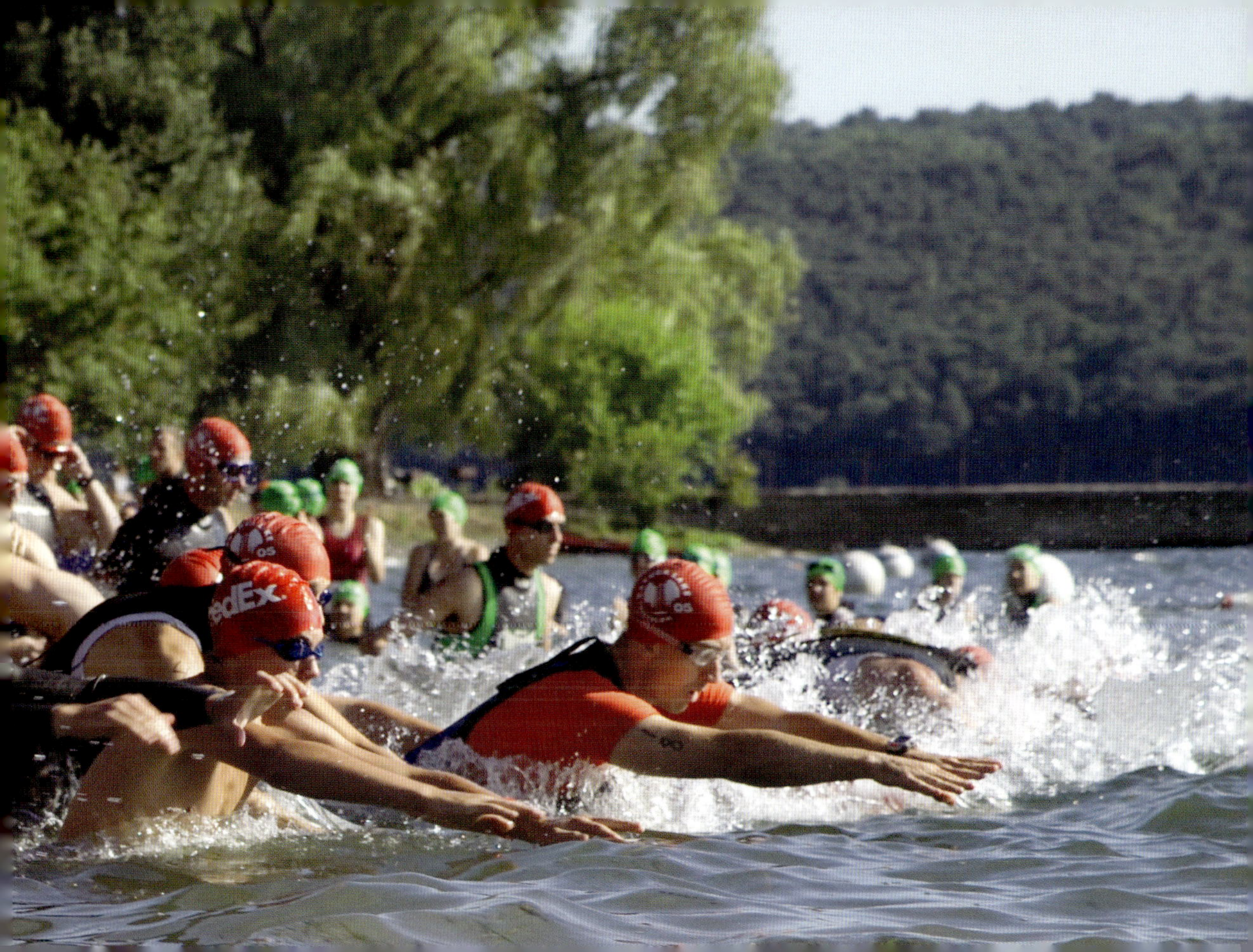

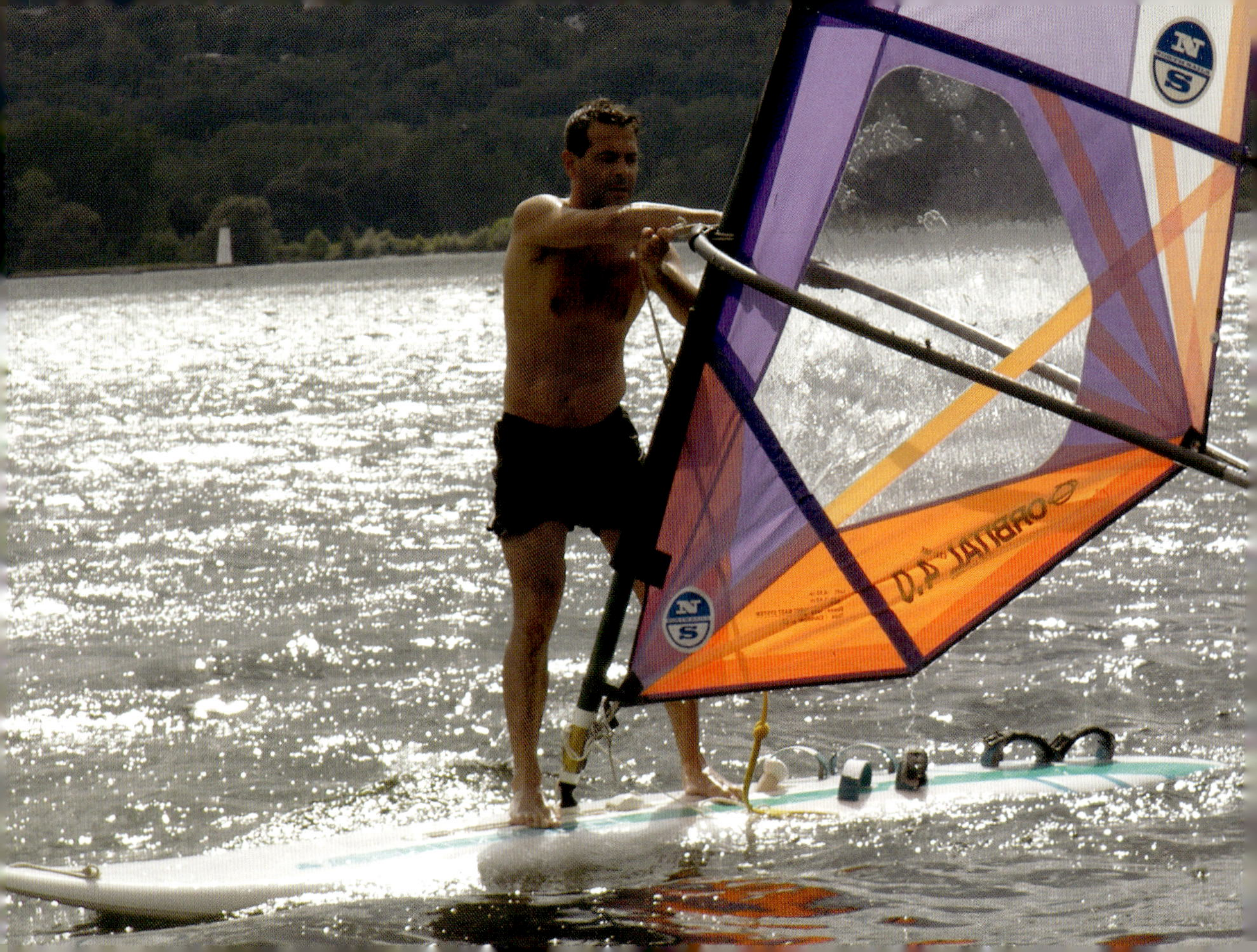

left Windsurfing on Cayuga Lake, just north of Stewart Park. next A kayaker plies Keuka Lake, which splits into two branches like a giant Y.

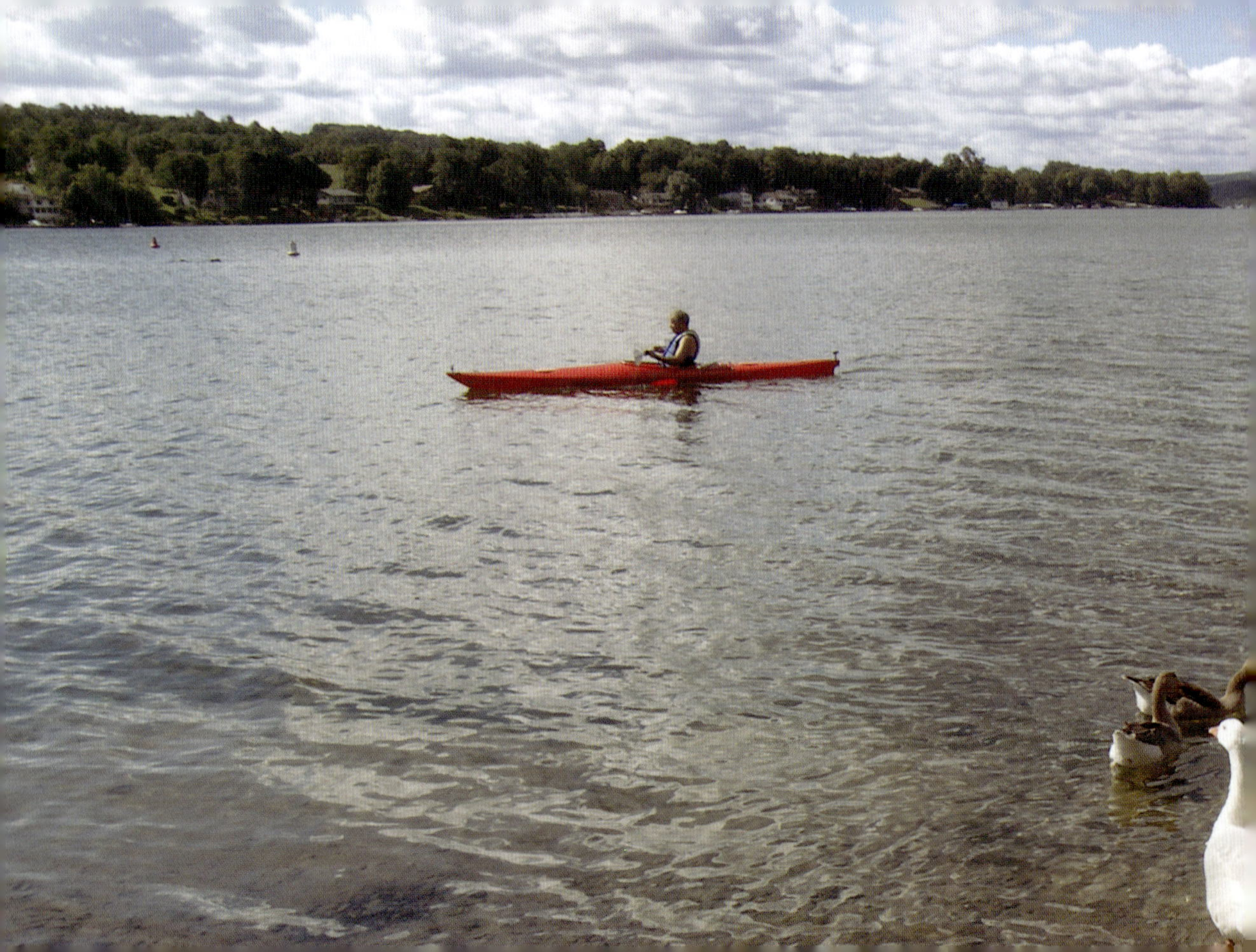

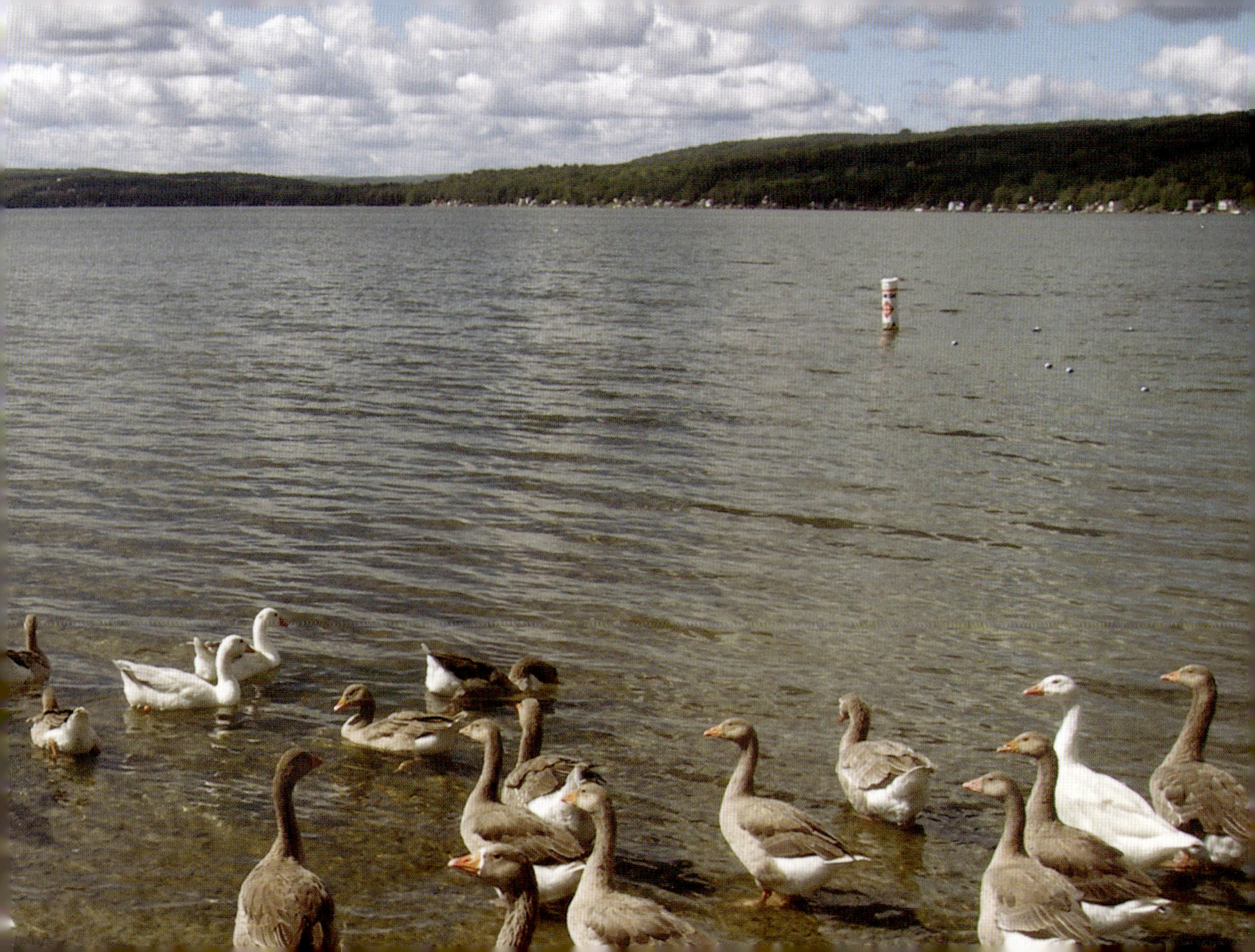

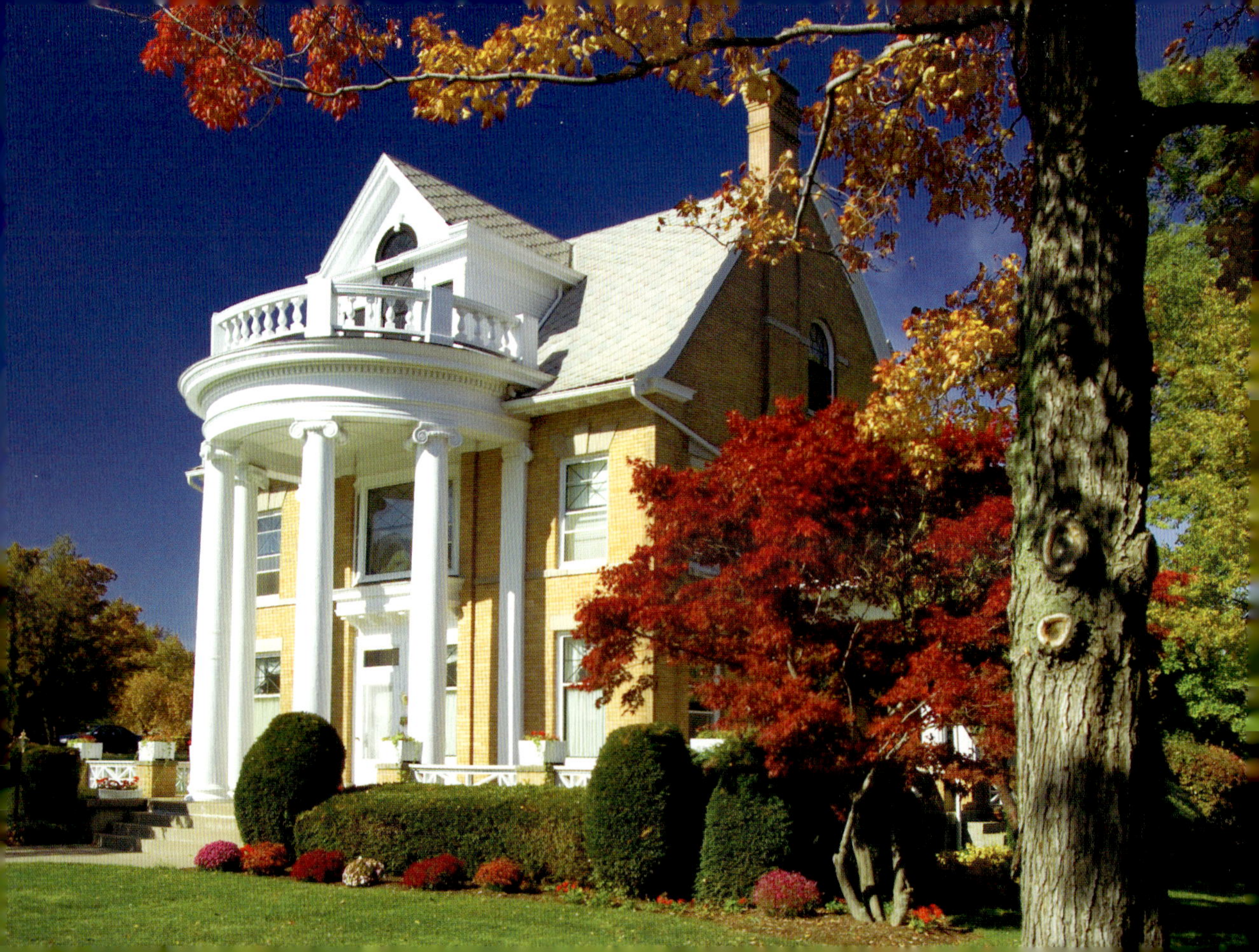

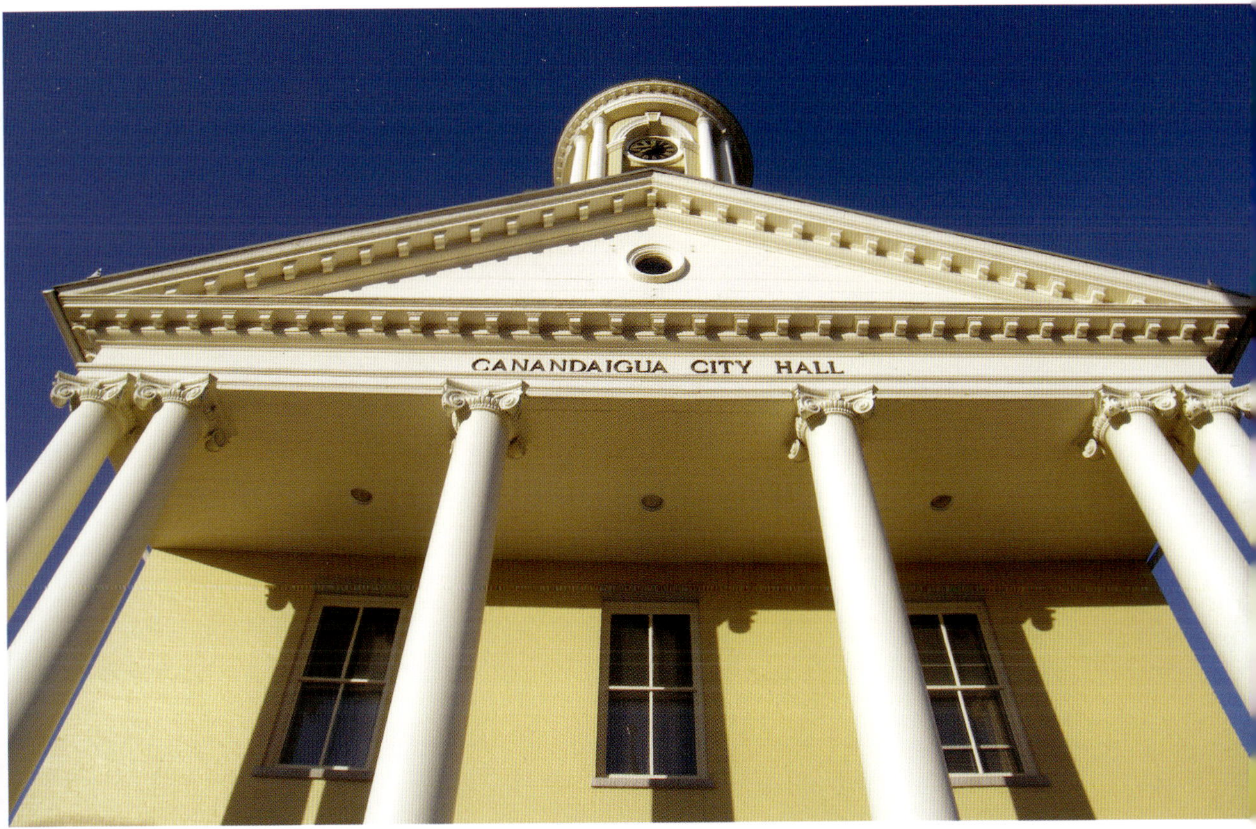

above Canandaigua City Hall. left The Lucina, the president's house, Keuka College. next A lakeshore gate in Skaneateles.

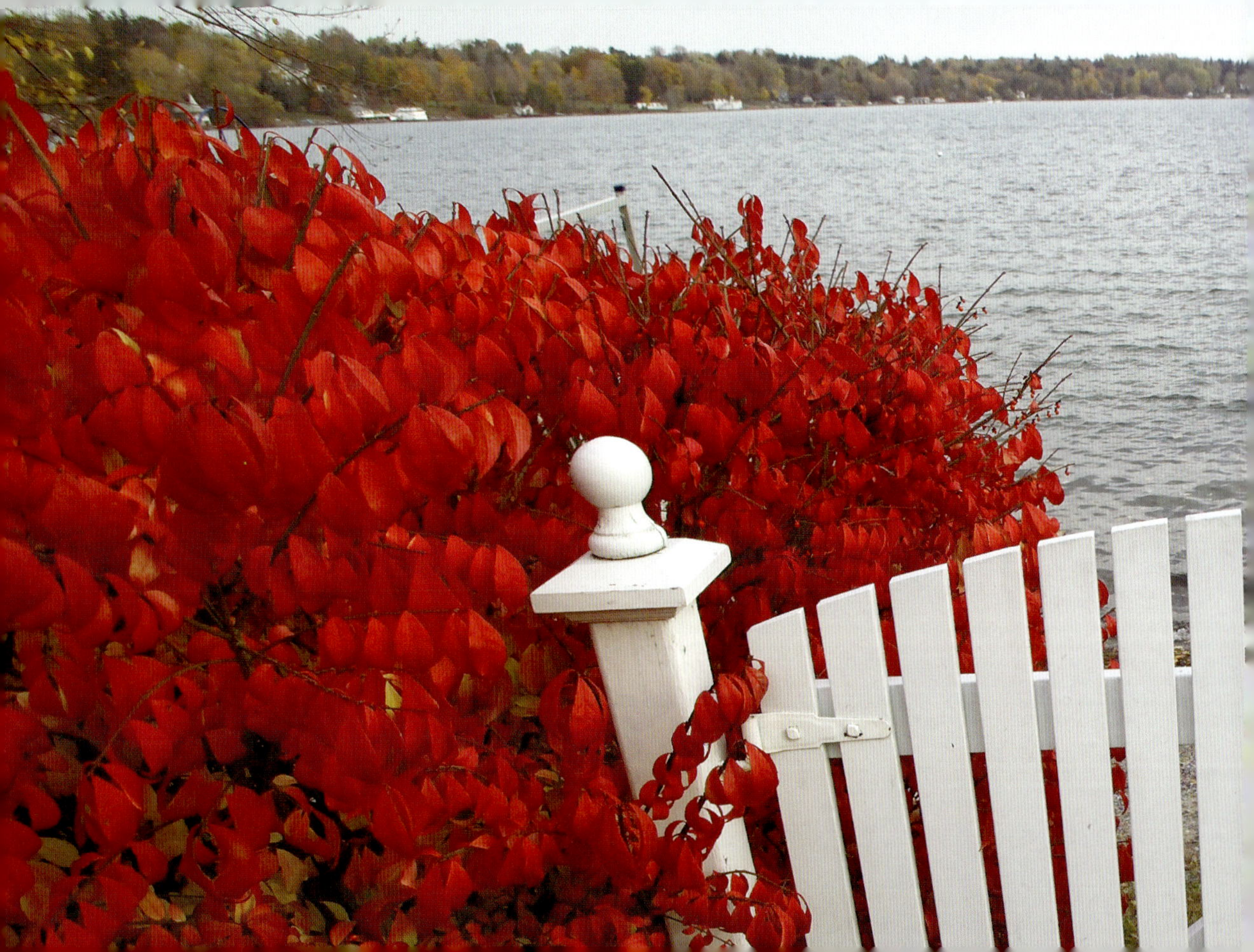

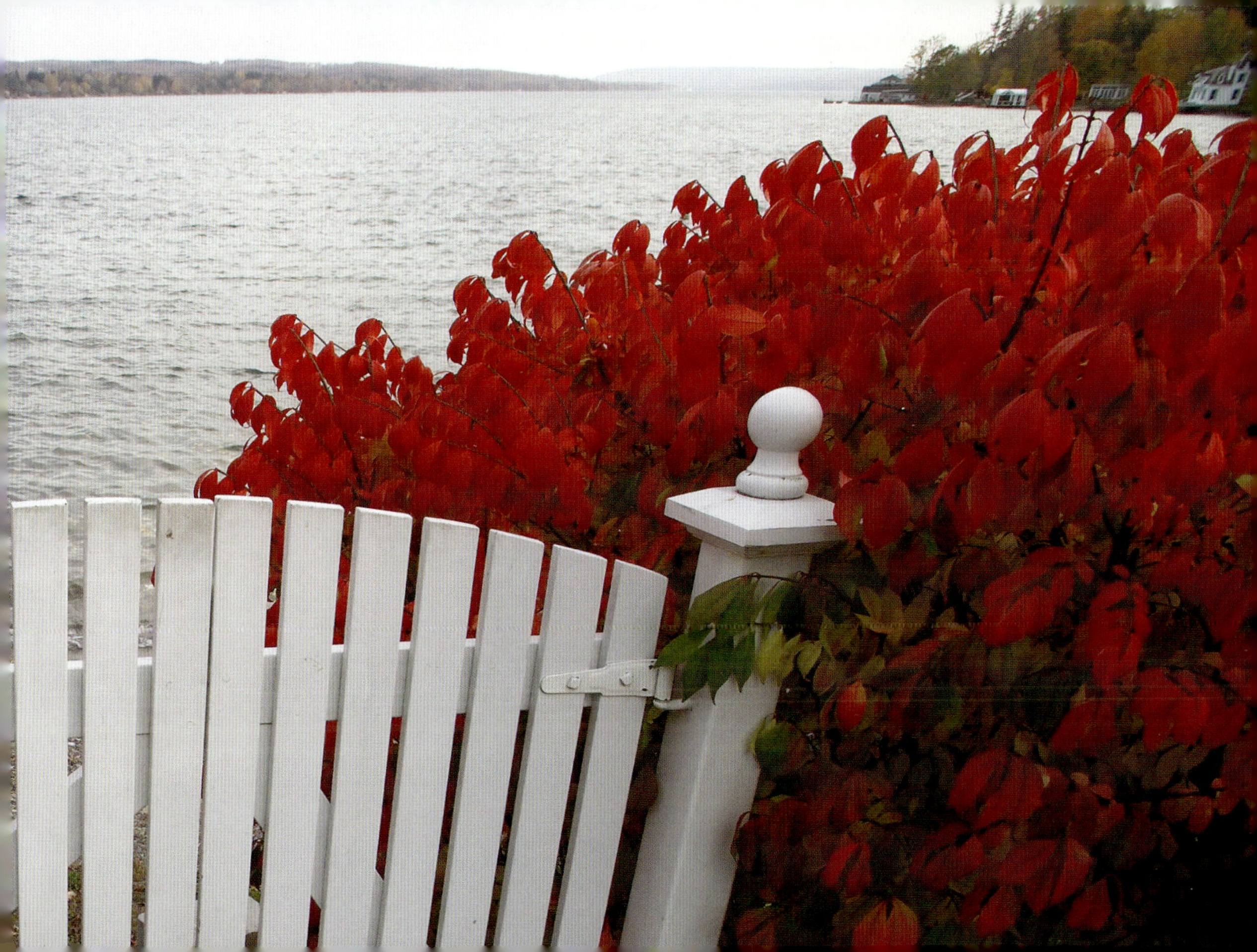

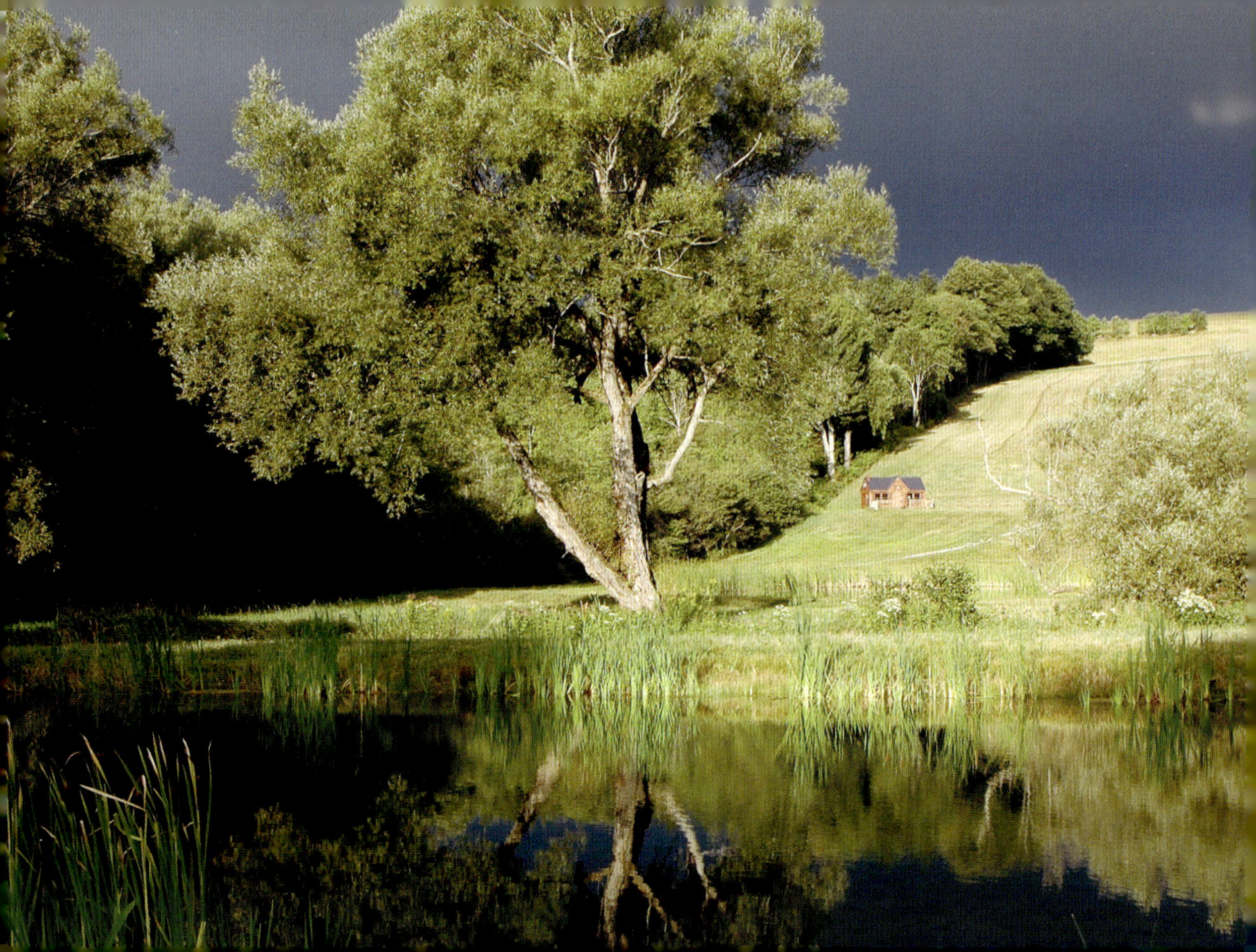

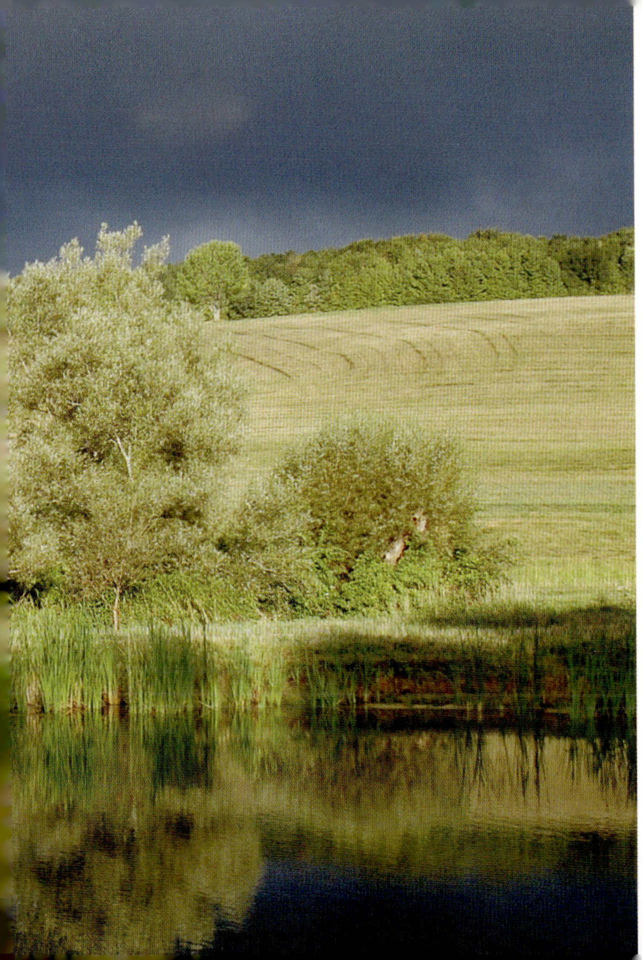

left A child's playhouse exaggerates the size of the landscape near Springwater. next Campers at Sampson State Park enjoy the sunset on Seneca Lake.

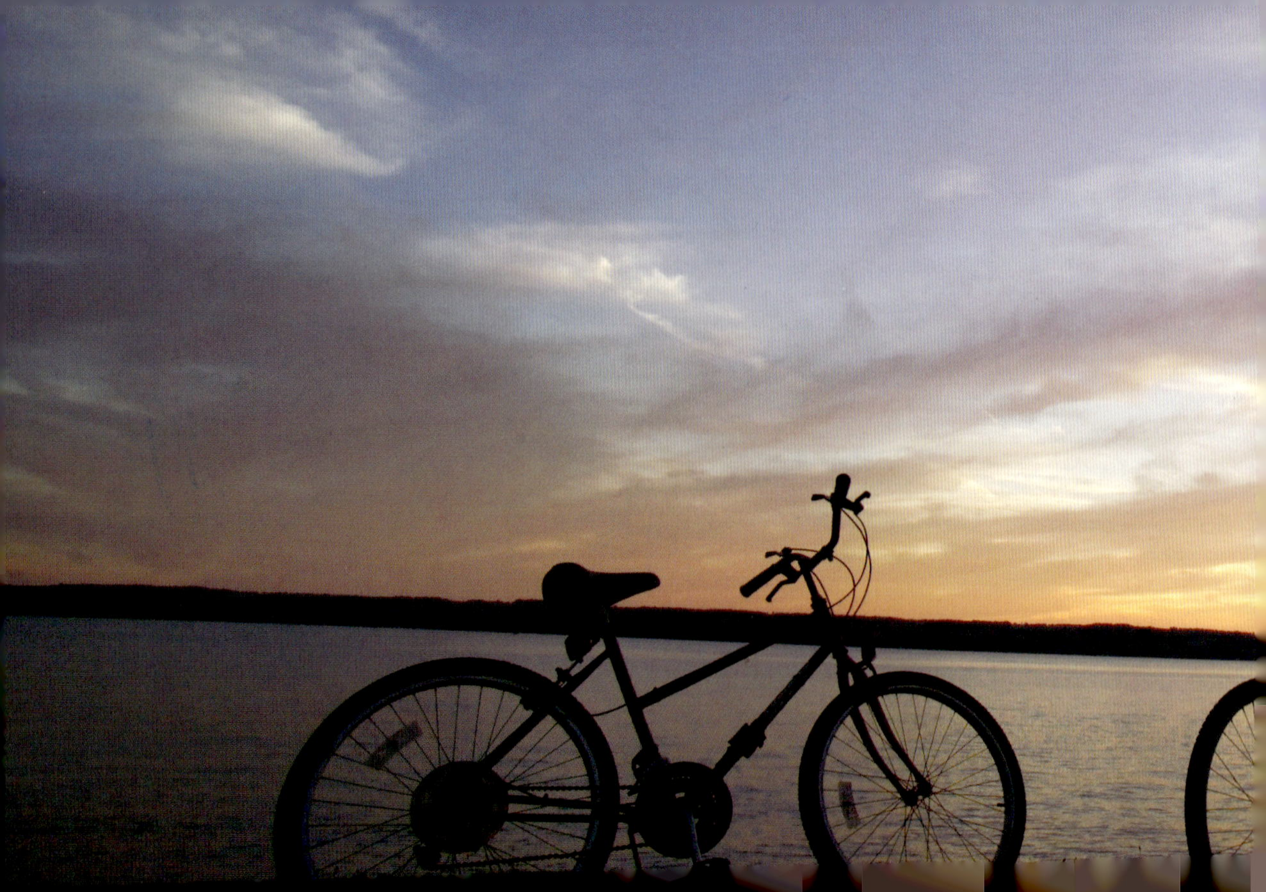

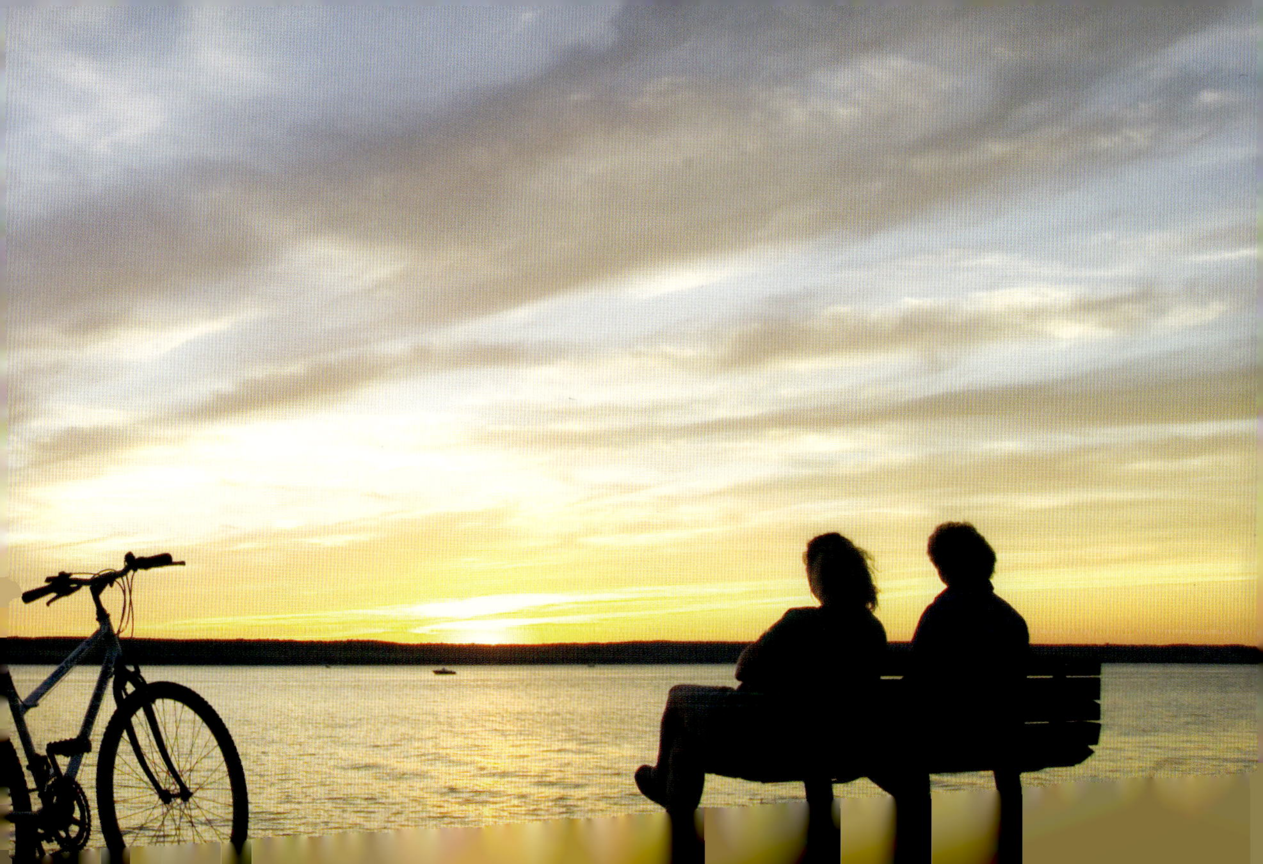

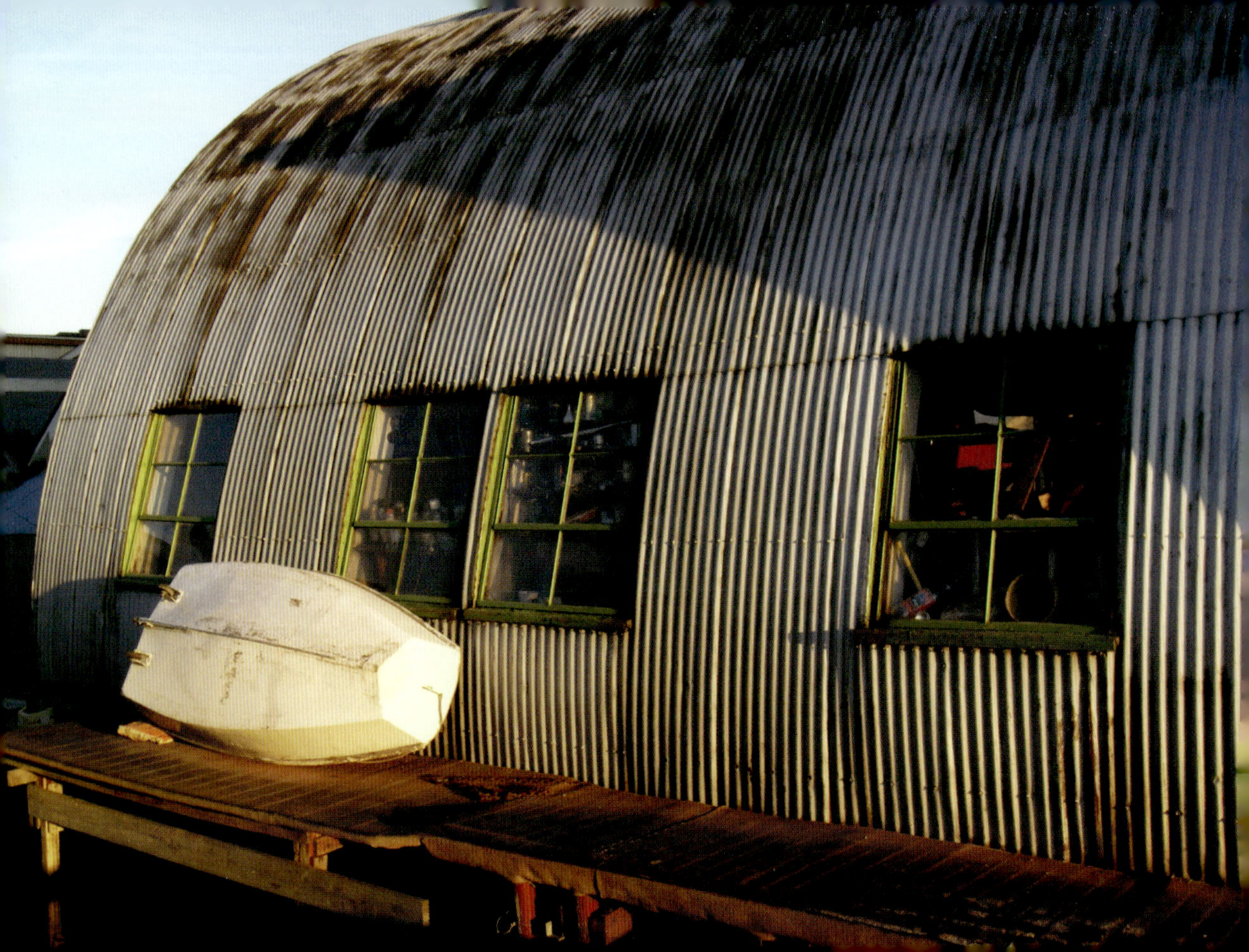

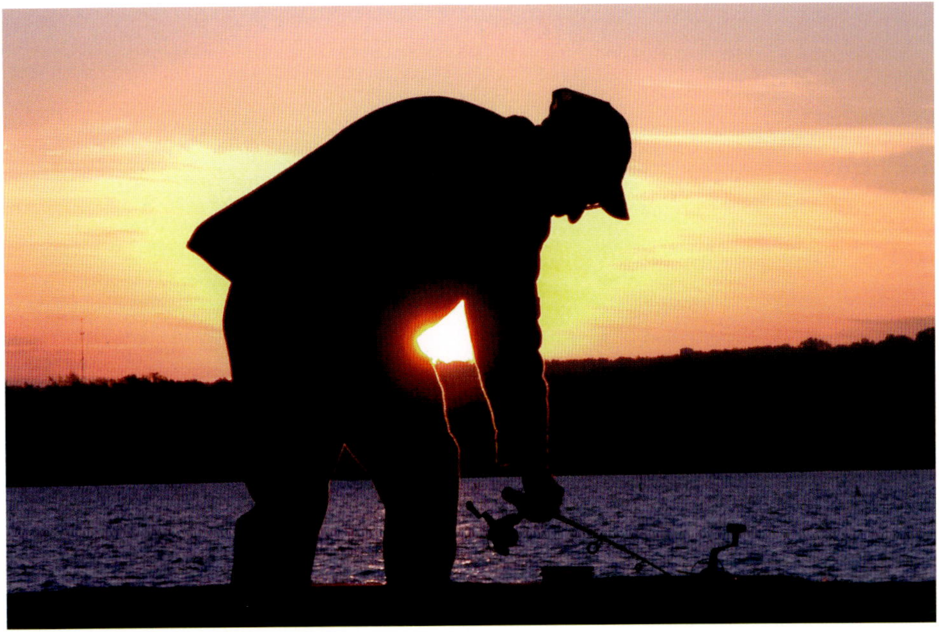

above and left The Canandaigua pier mixes cottages and bait shops, and offers a good spot to throw out the line. next The two-masted schooner *Malabar X* plies the waters of Seneca Lake from Watkins Glen. page after next A field of nearly ripe wheat near Seneca Lake.

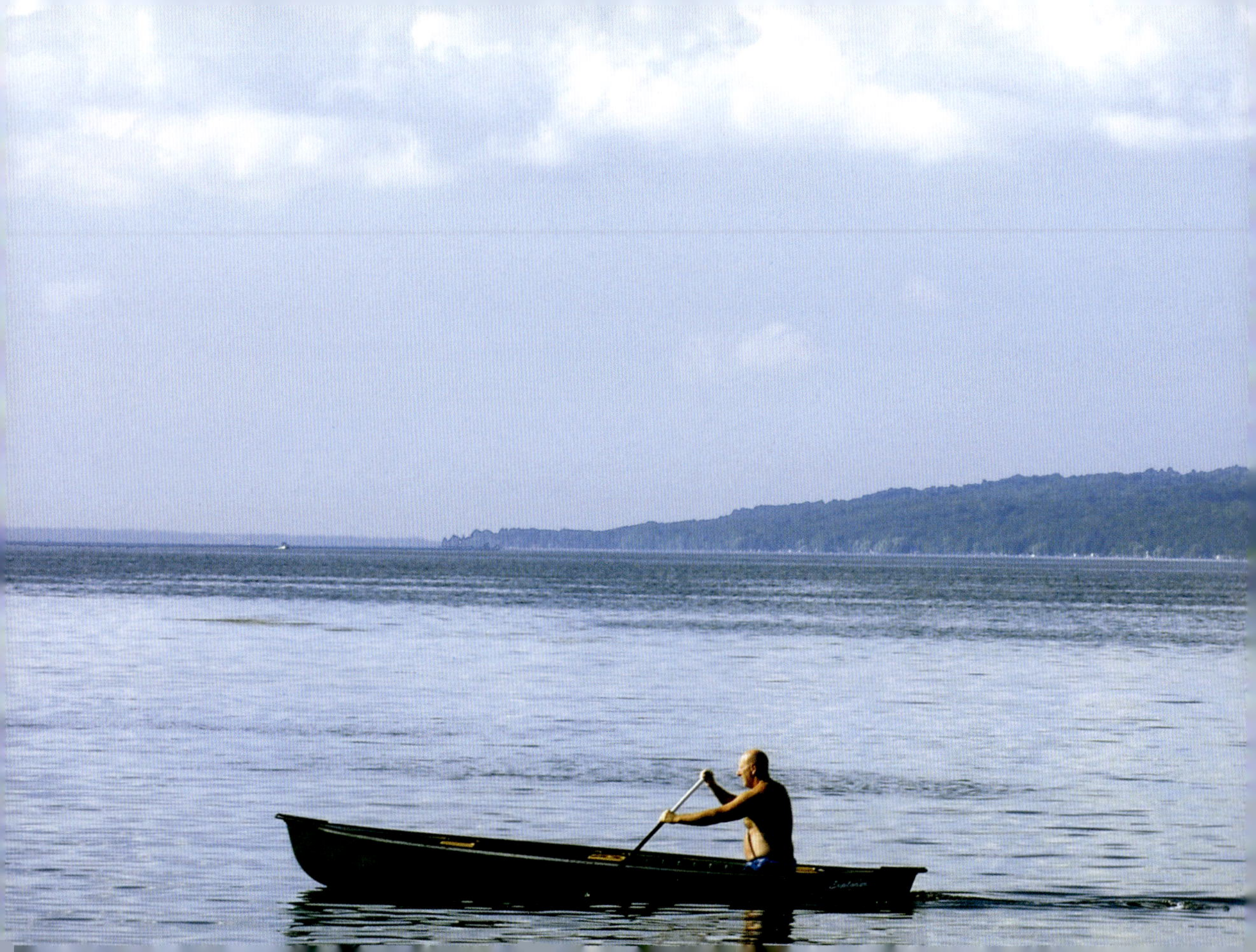

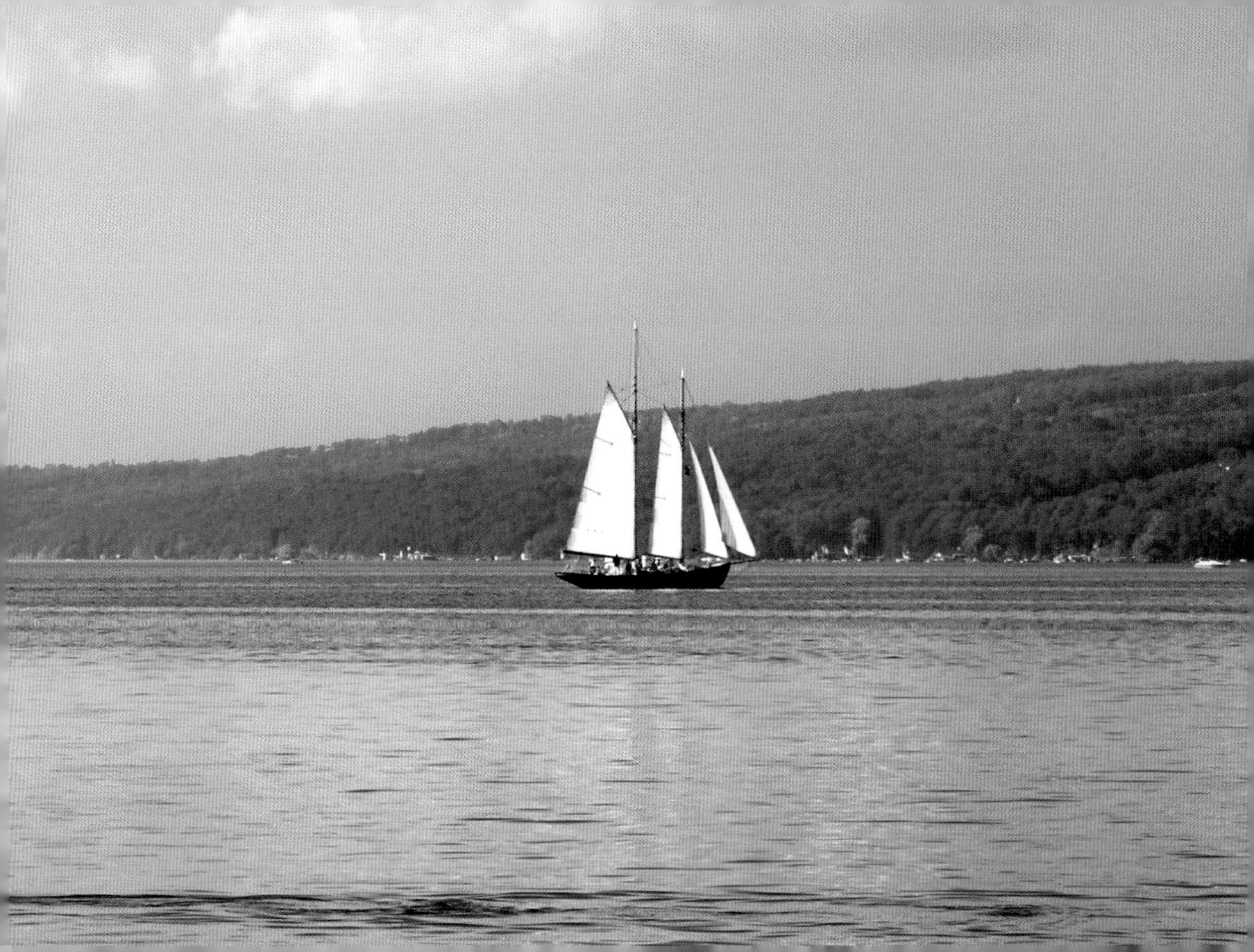

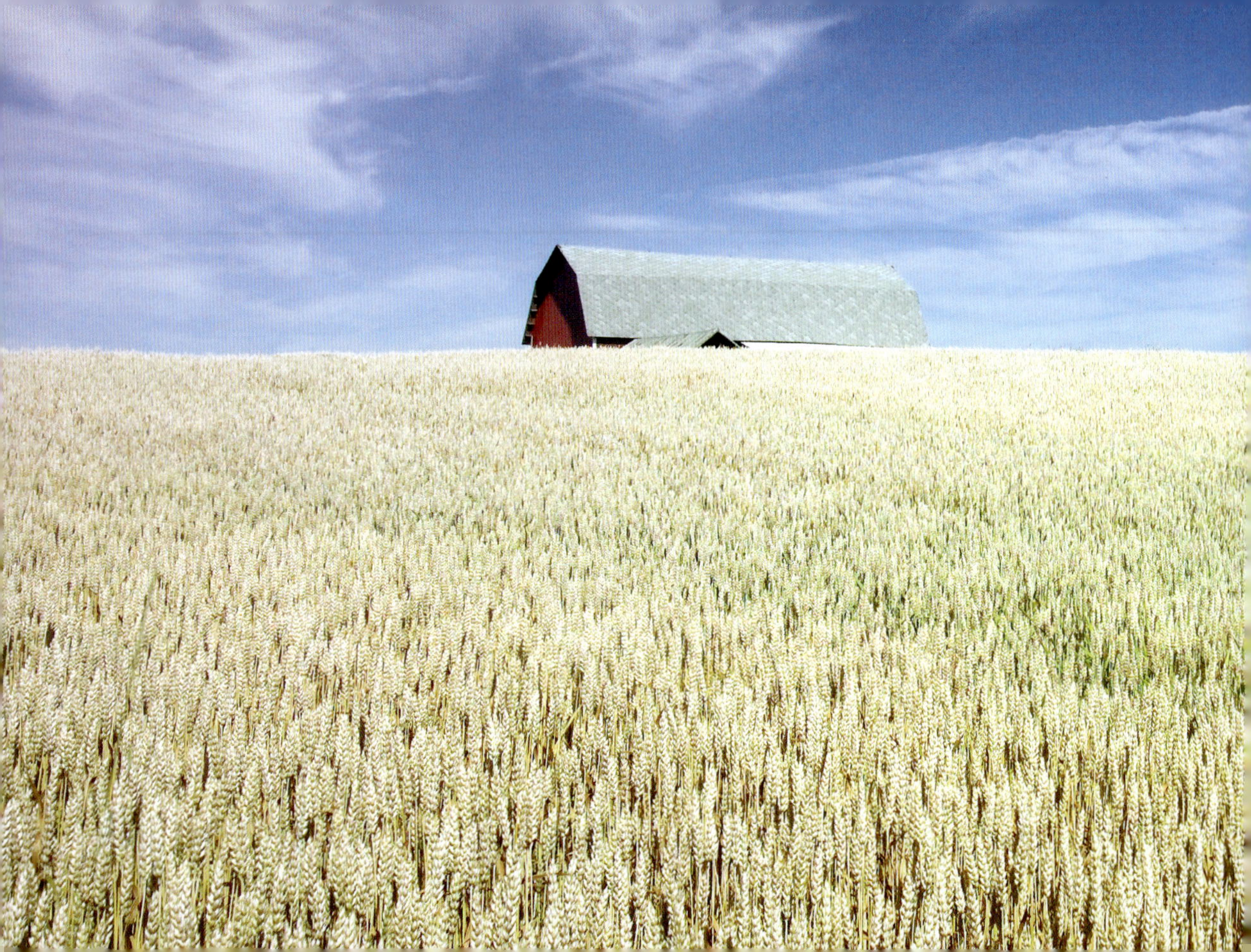

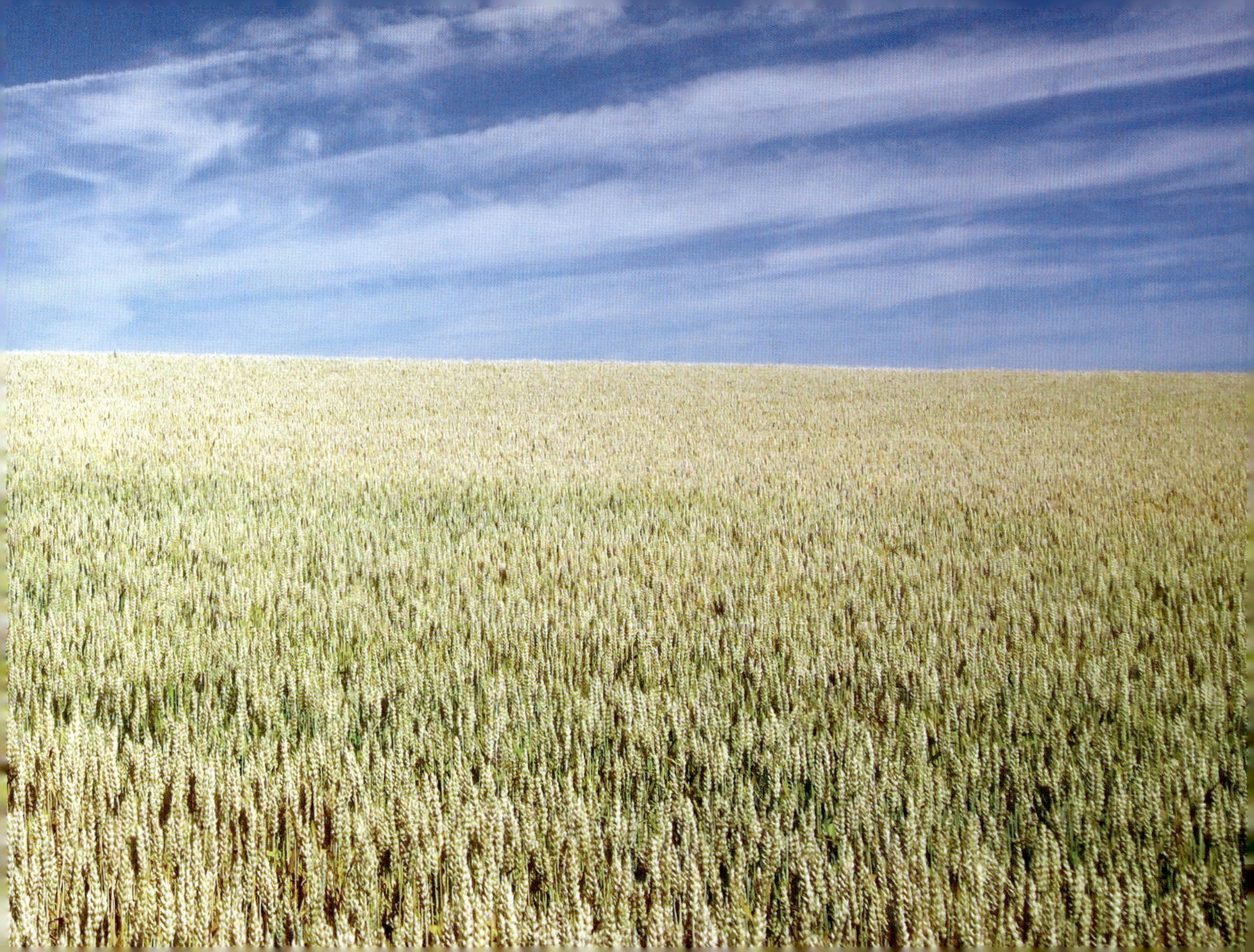

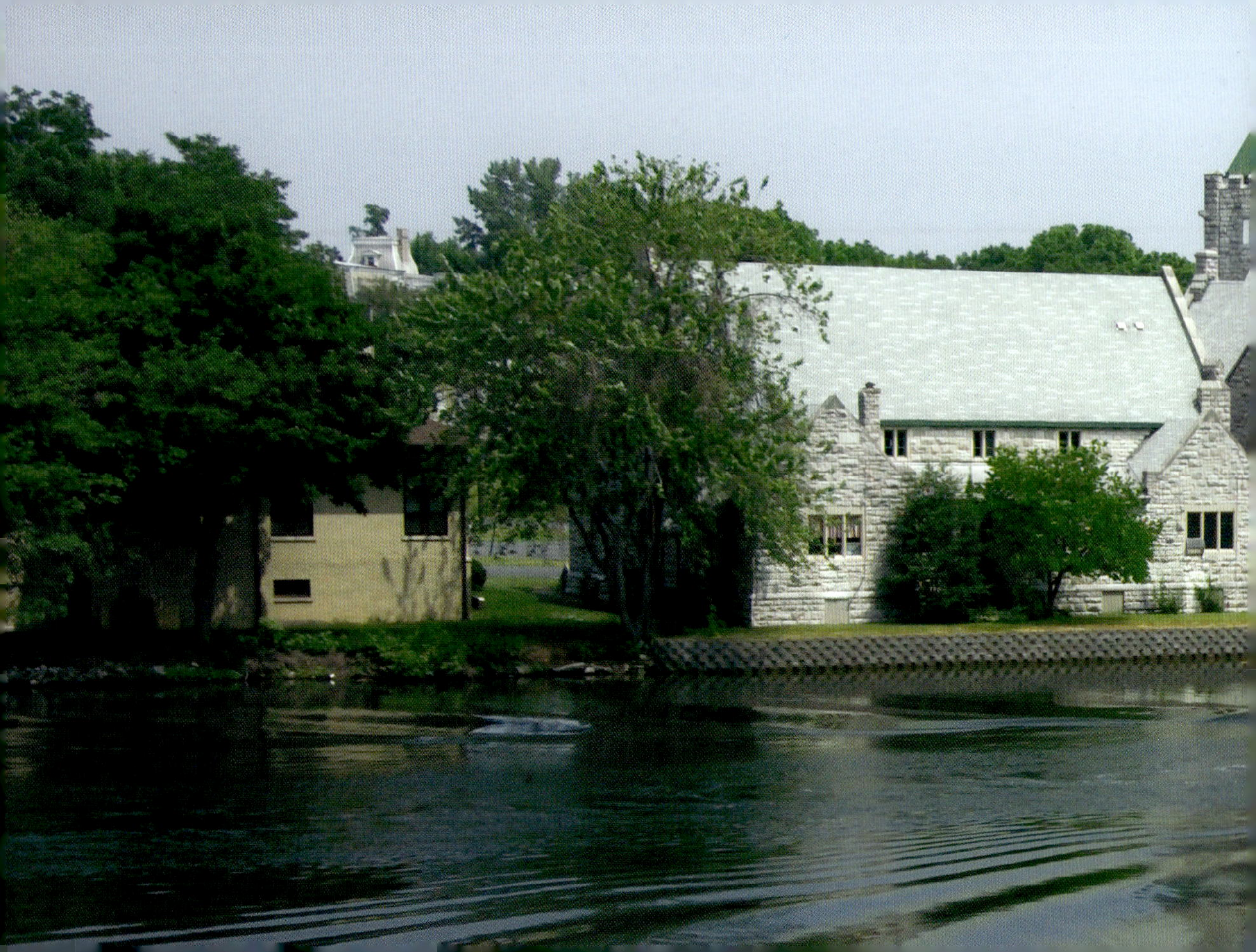

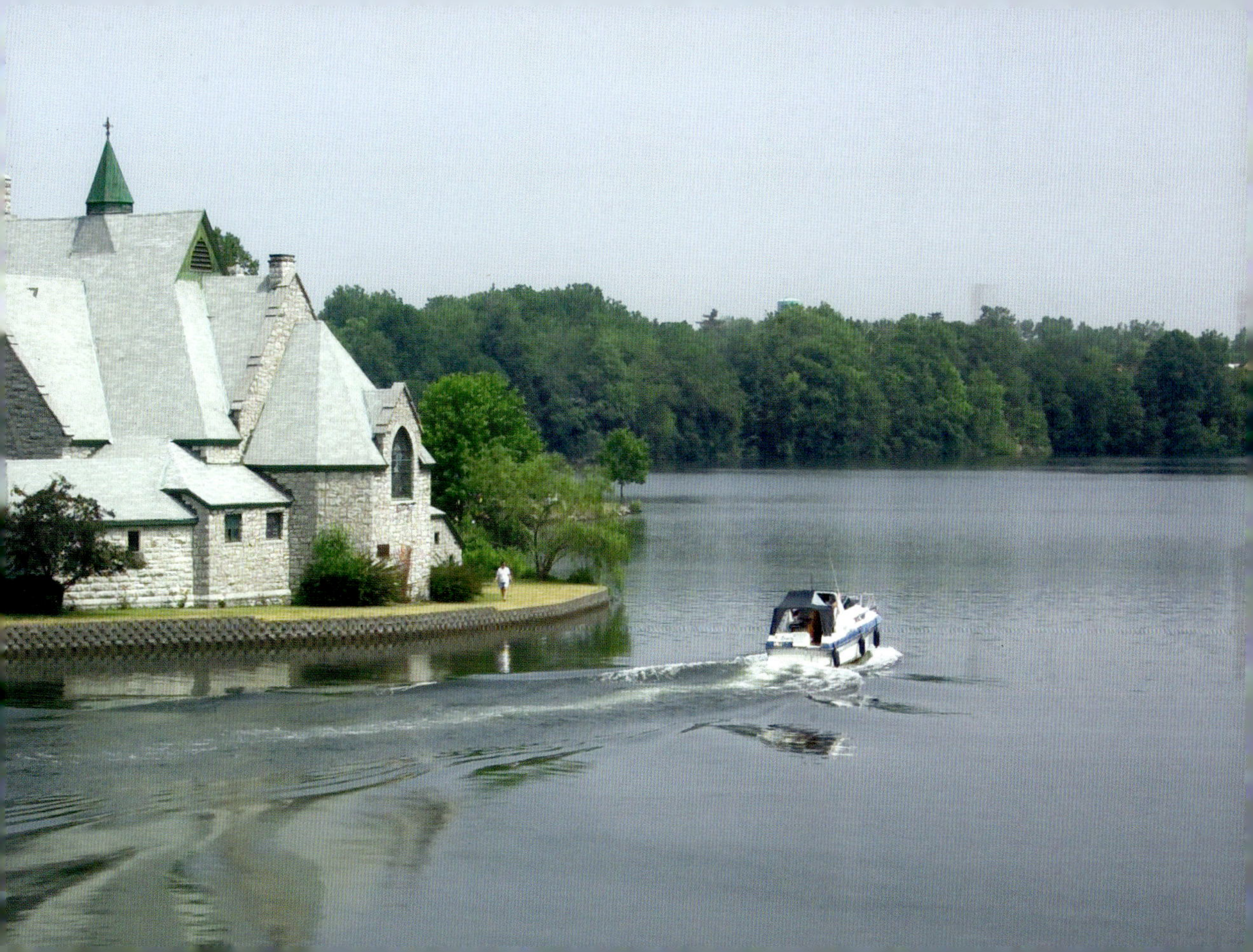

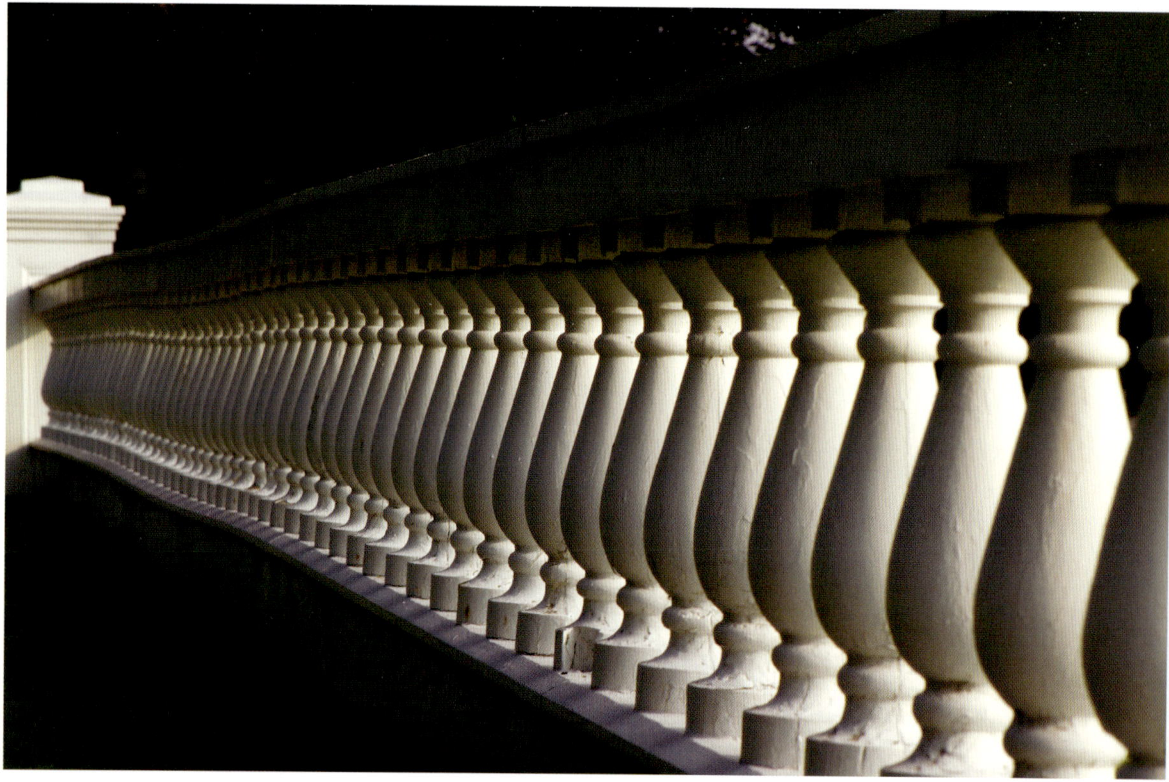

above Balustrade from Rose Hill Mansion, Geneva. right Just east of Branchport, Esperanza Mansion overlooks Keuka Lake. previous Built in 1885, the Trinity Episcopal Church of Seneca Falls sits on the bank of the Erie Canal. next The landmark resort Geneva on the Lake, on the western shore of Seneca Lake in the town of Geneva.

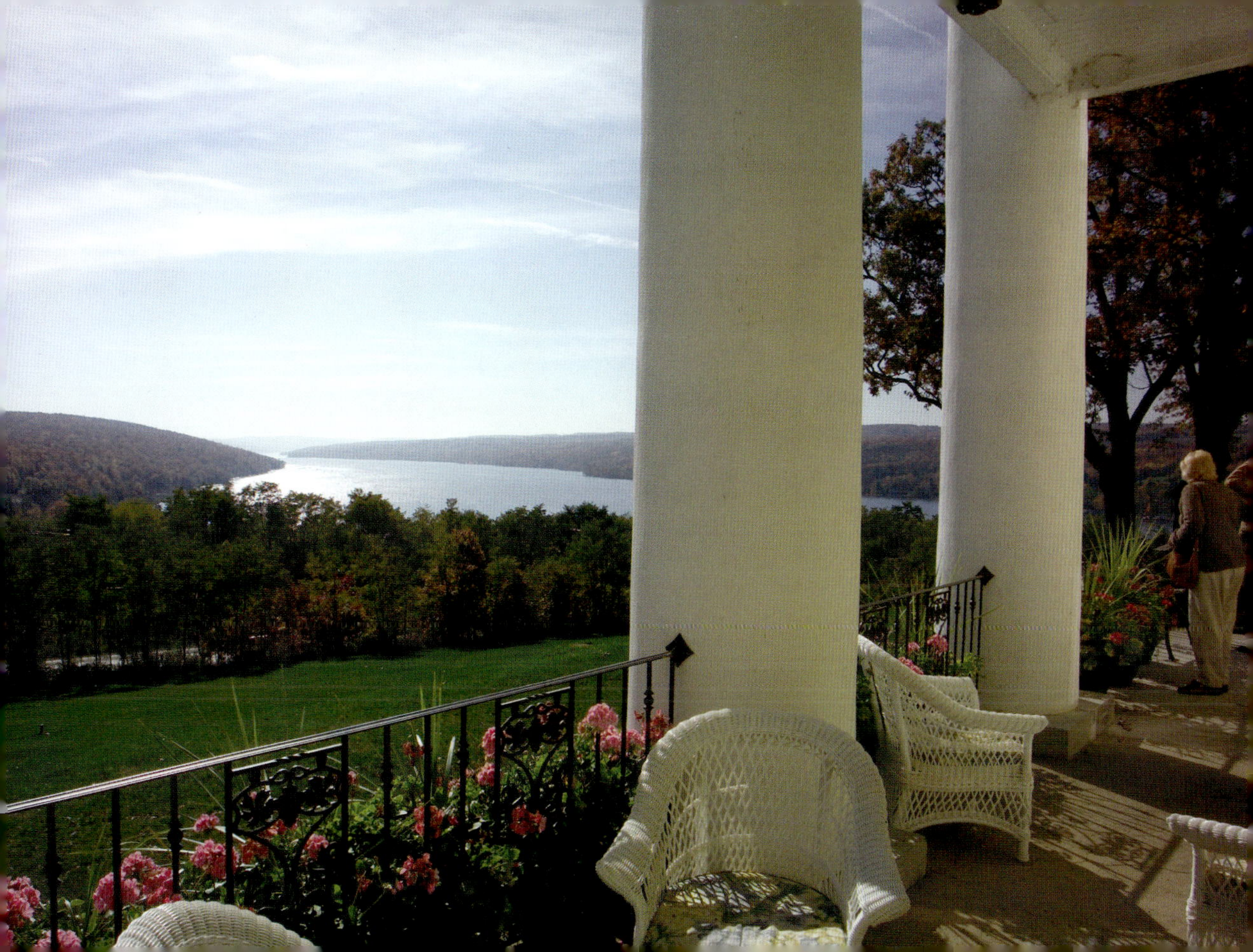

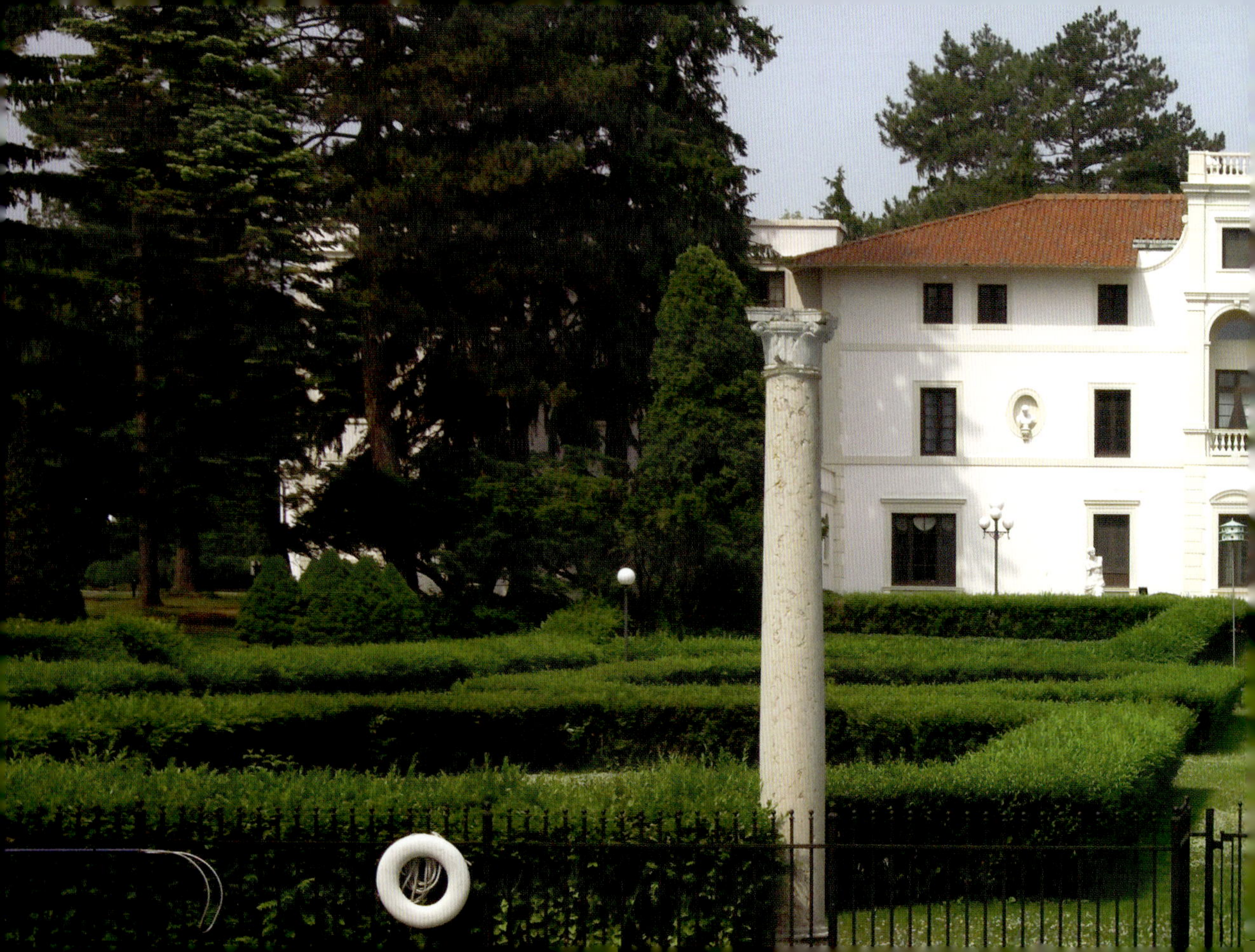

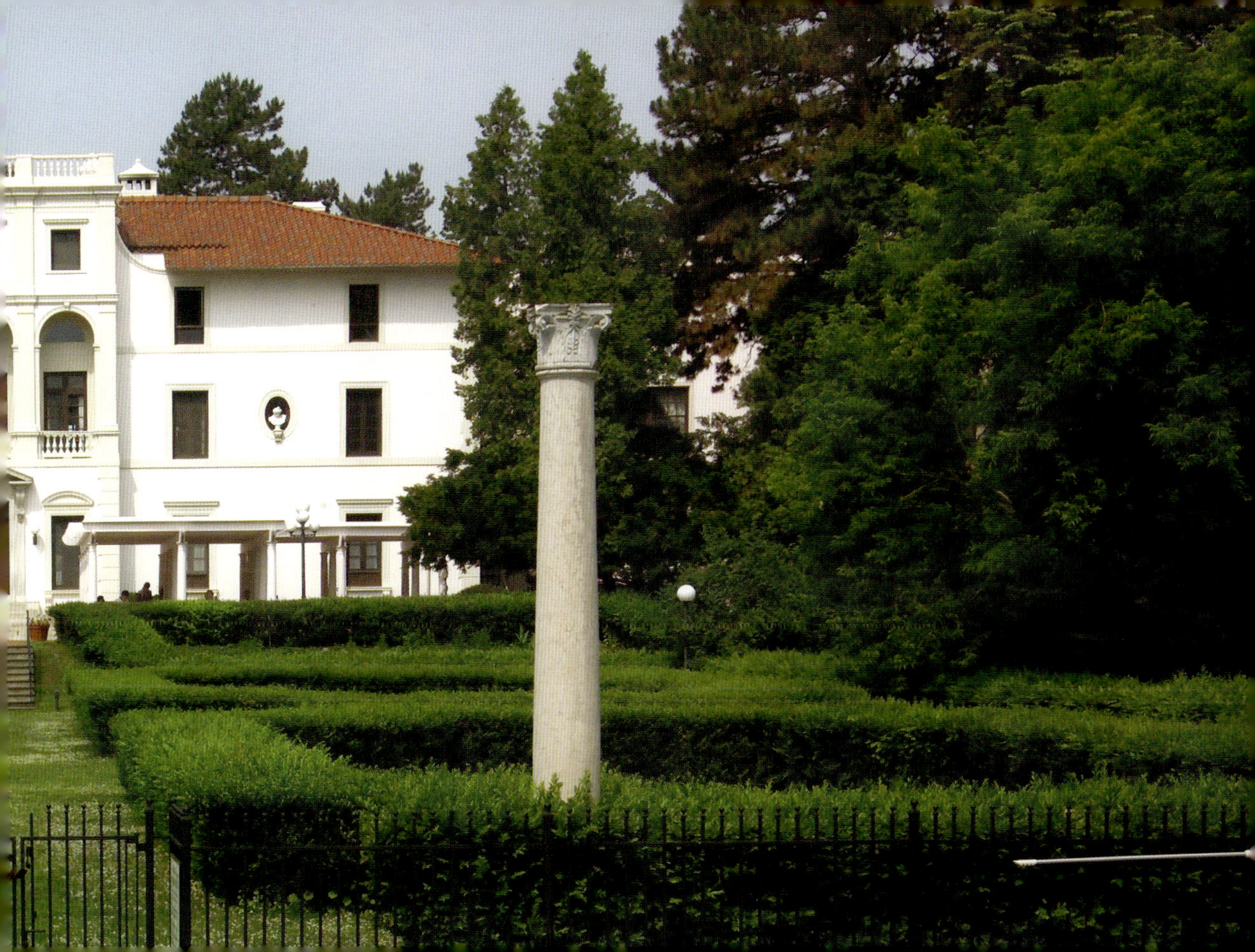

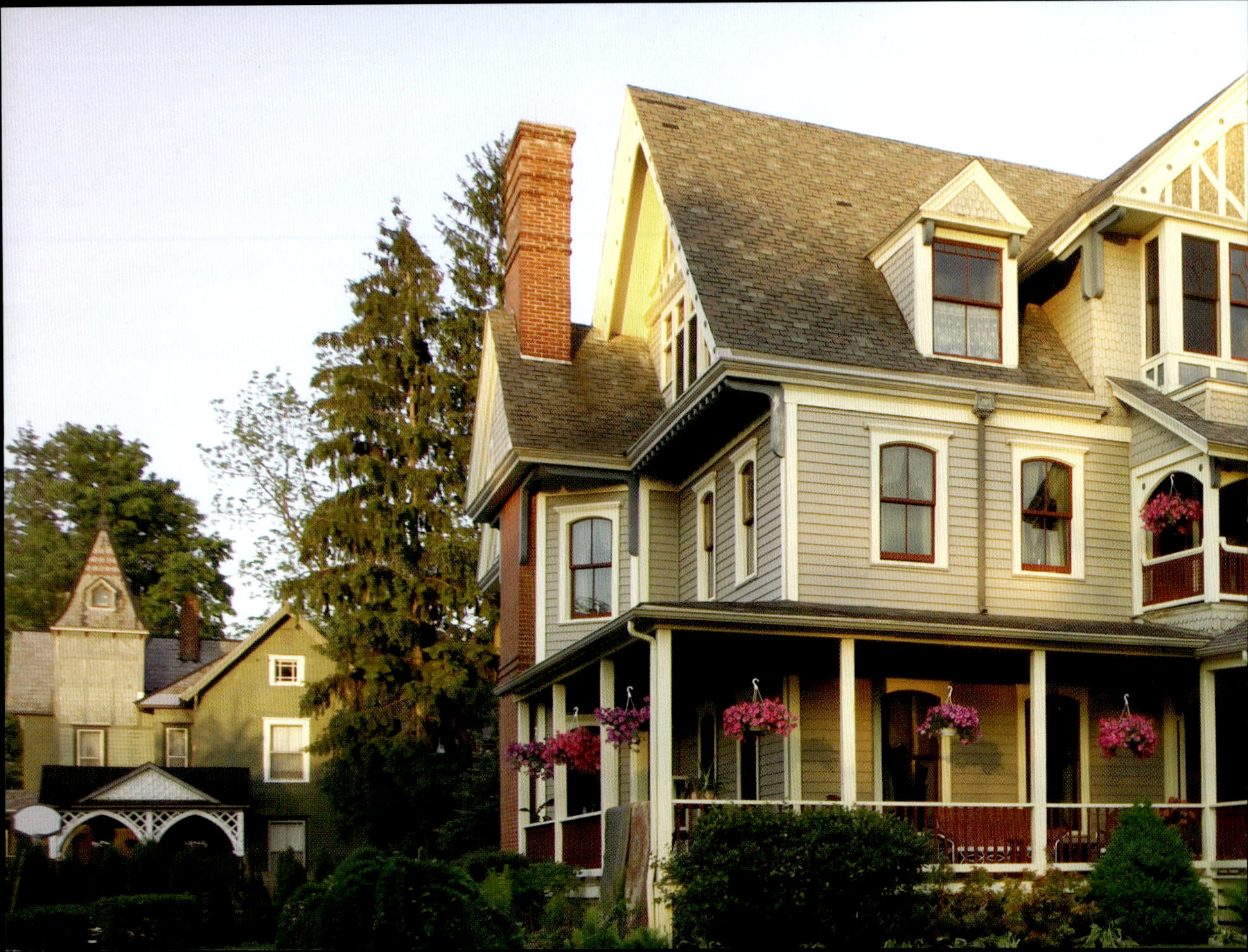

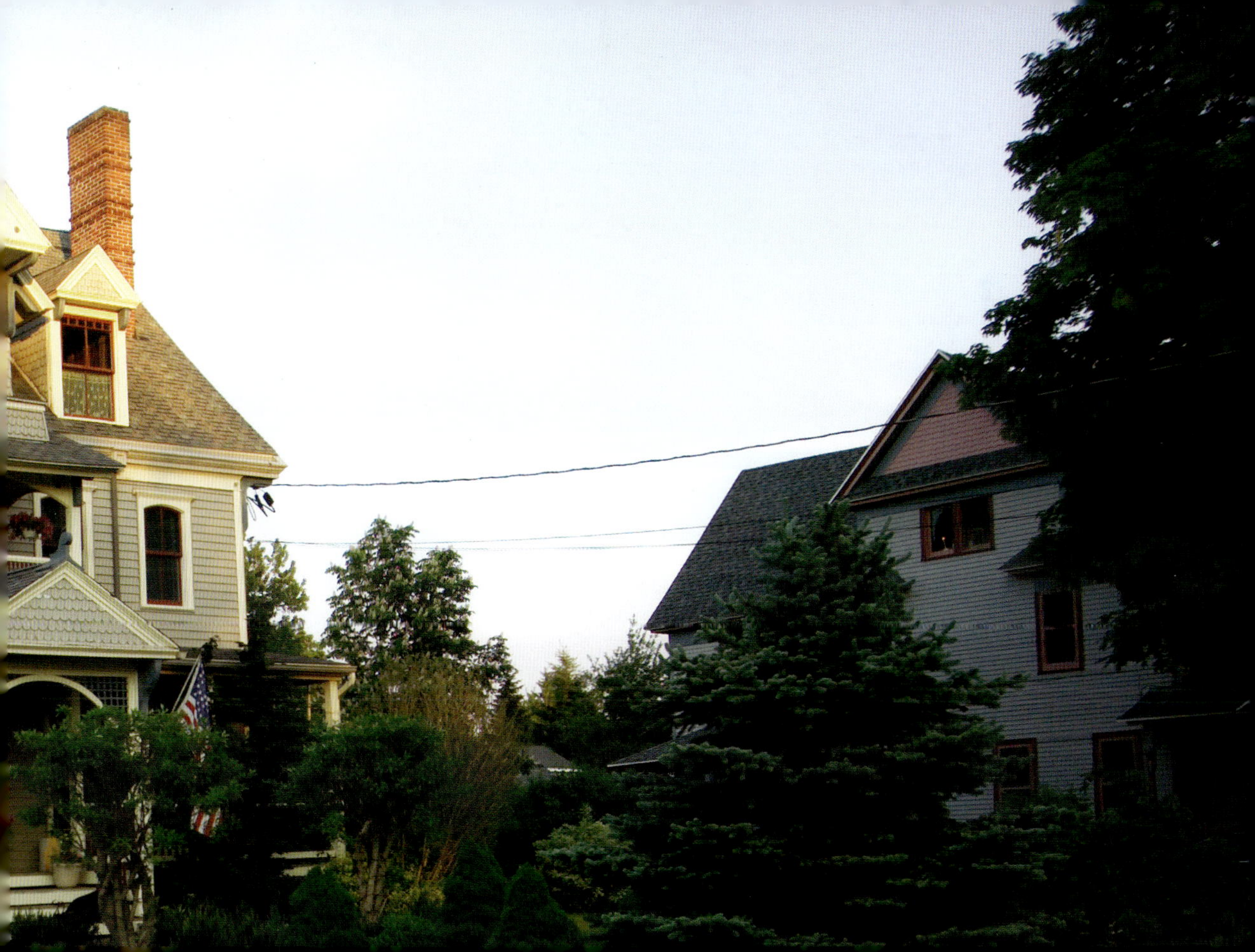

right and next two From Cazenovia to Lima, antique shops line Routes 5 and 20, the original New York turnpike. previous Painted Ladies and other Victorian homes adorn the stately streets of Clifton Springs.

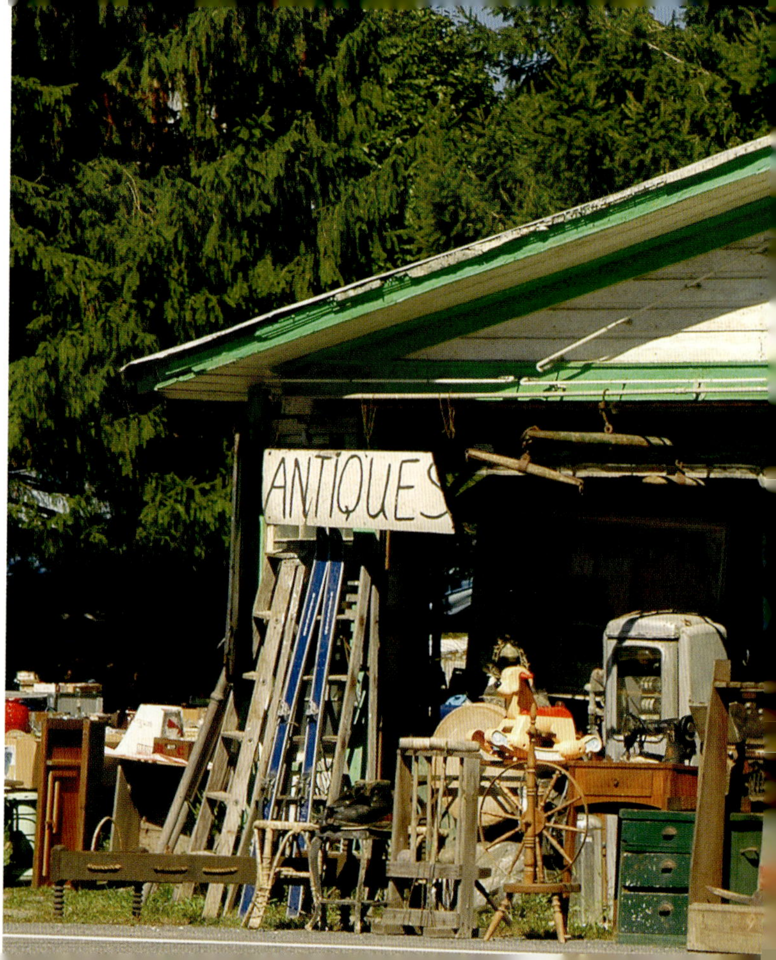

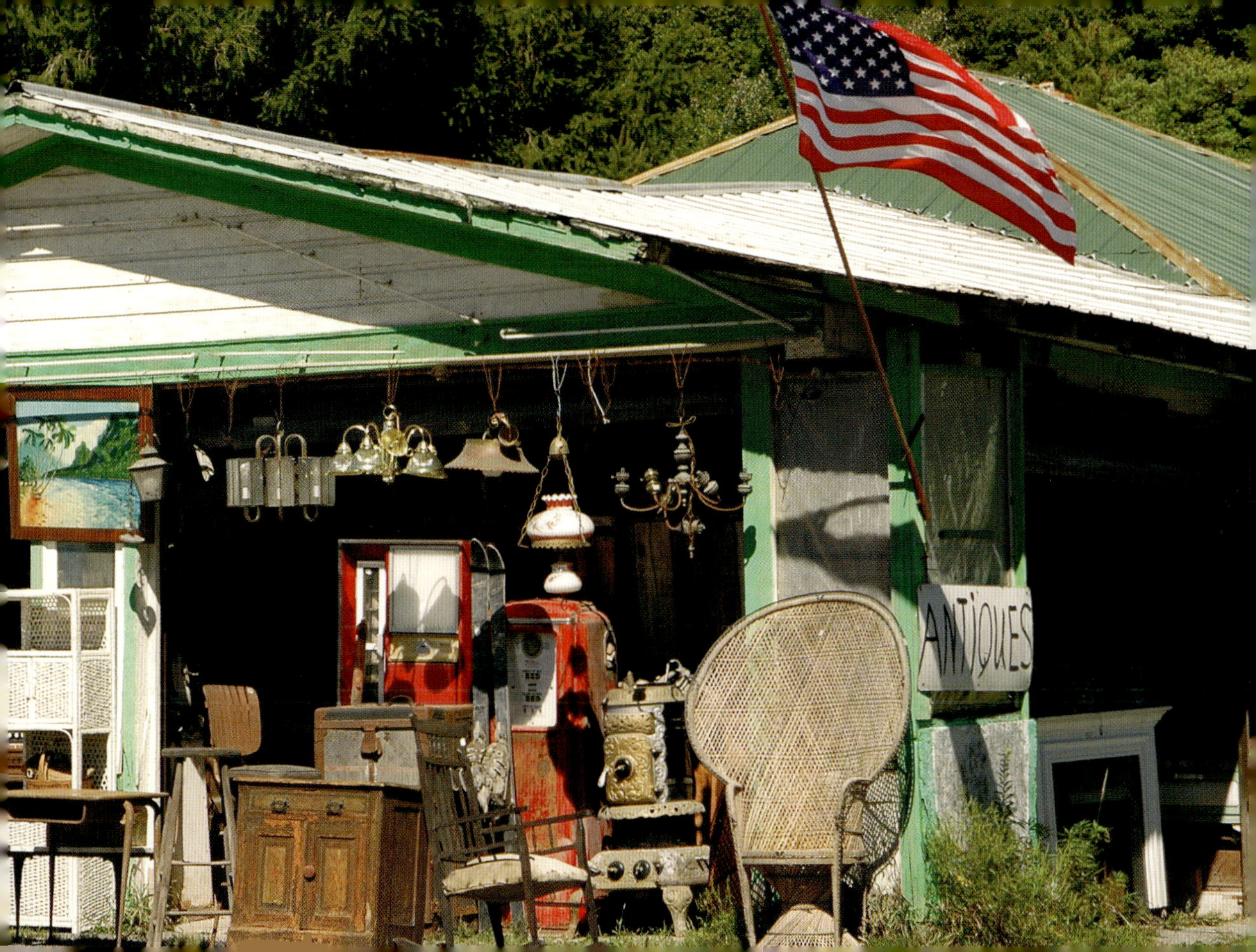
ANTIQUES

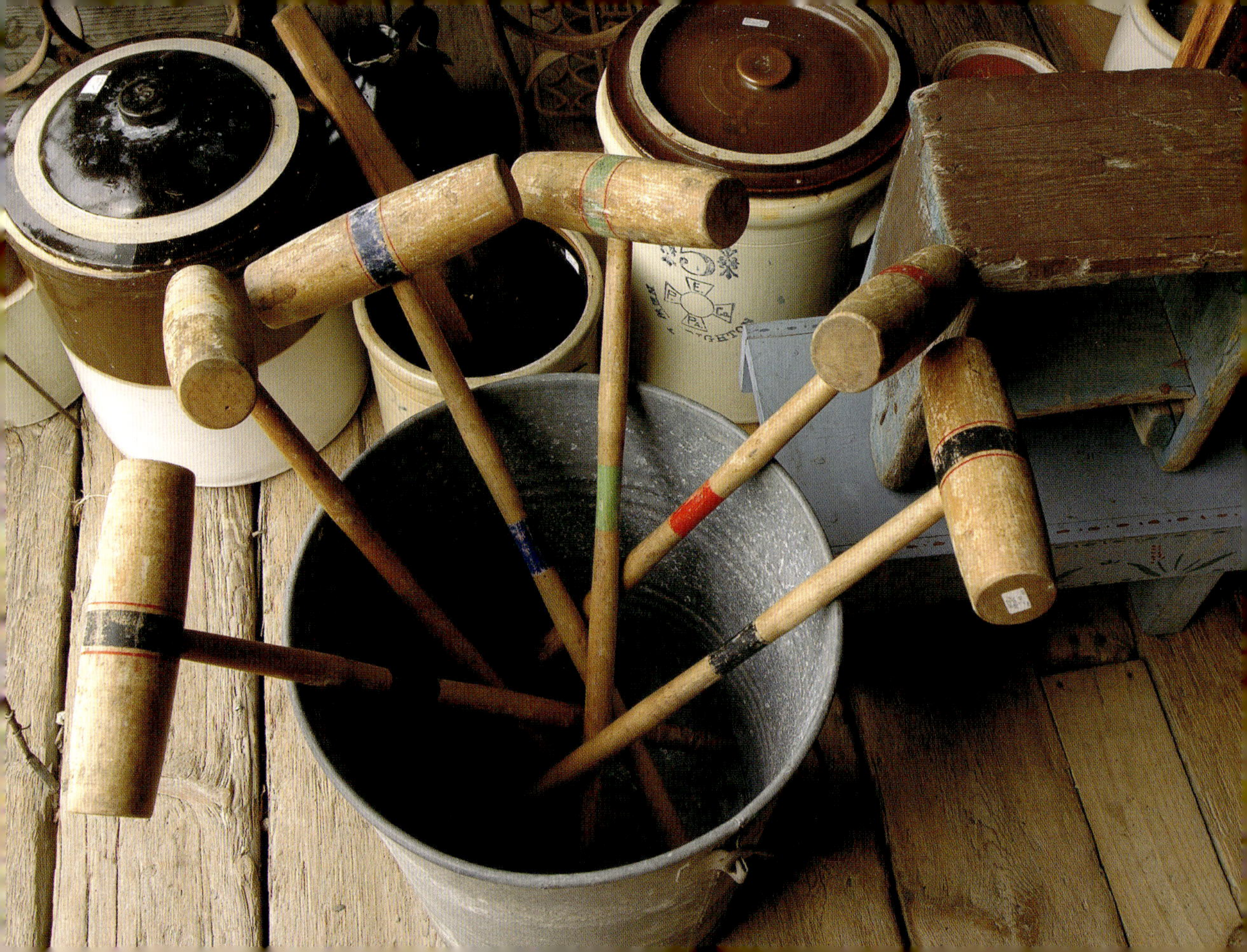

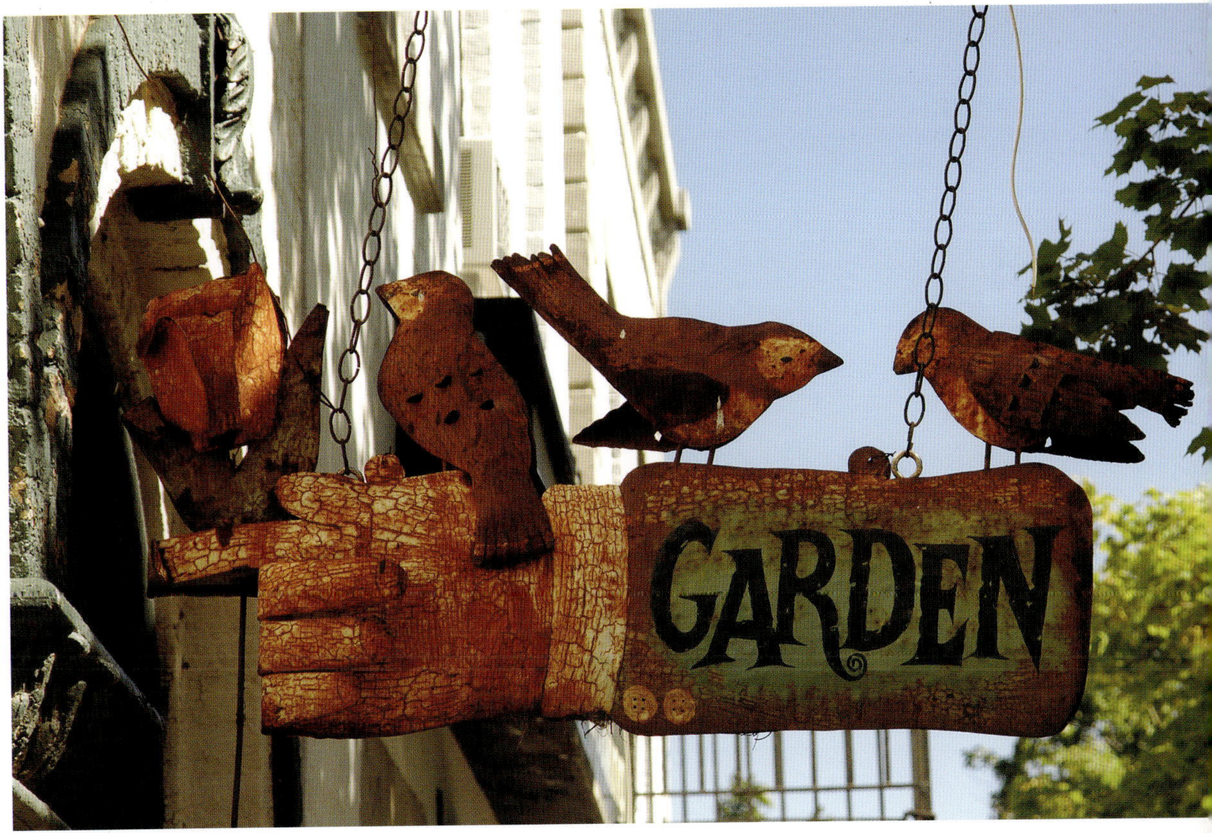
GARDEN

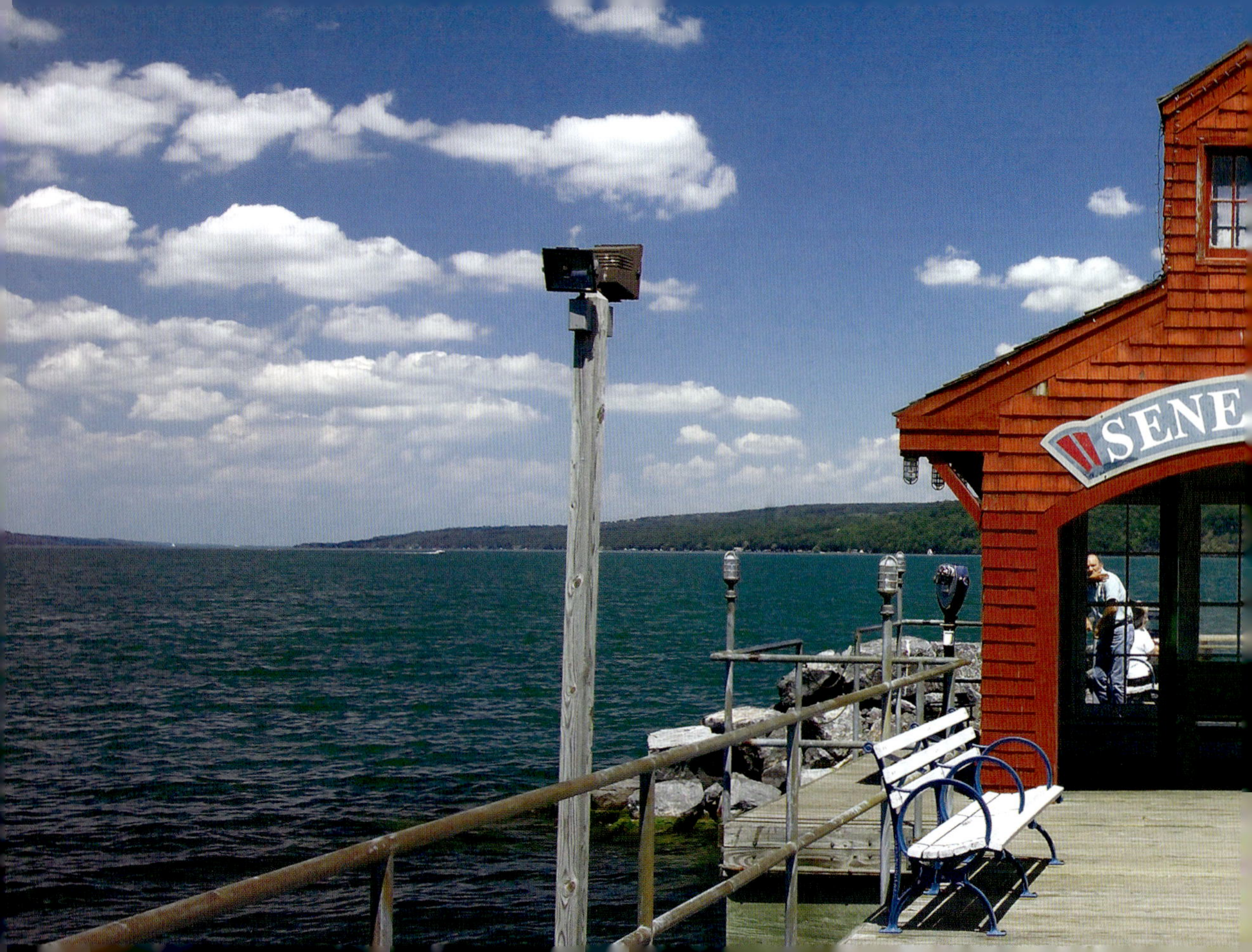
SENE

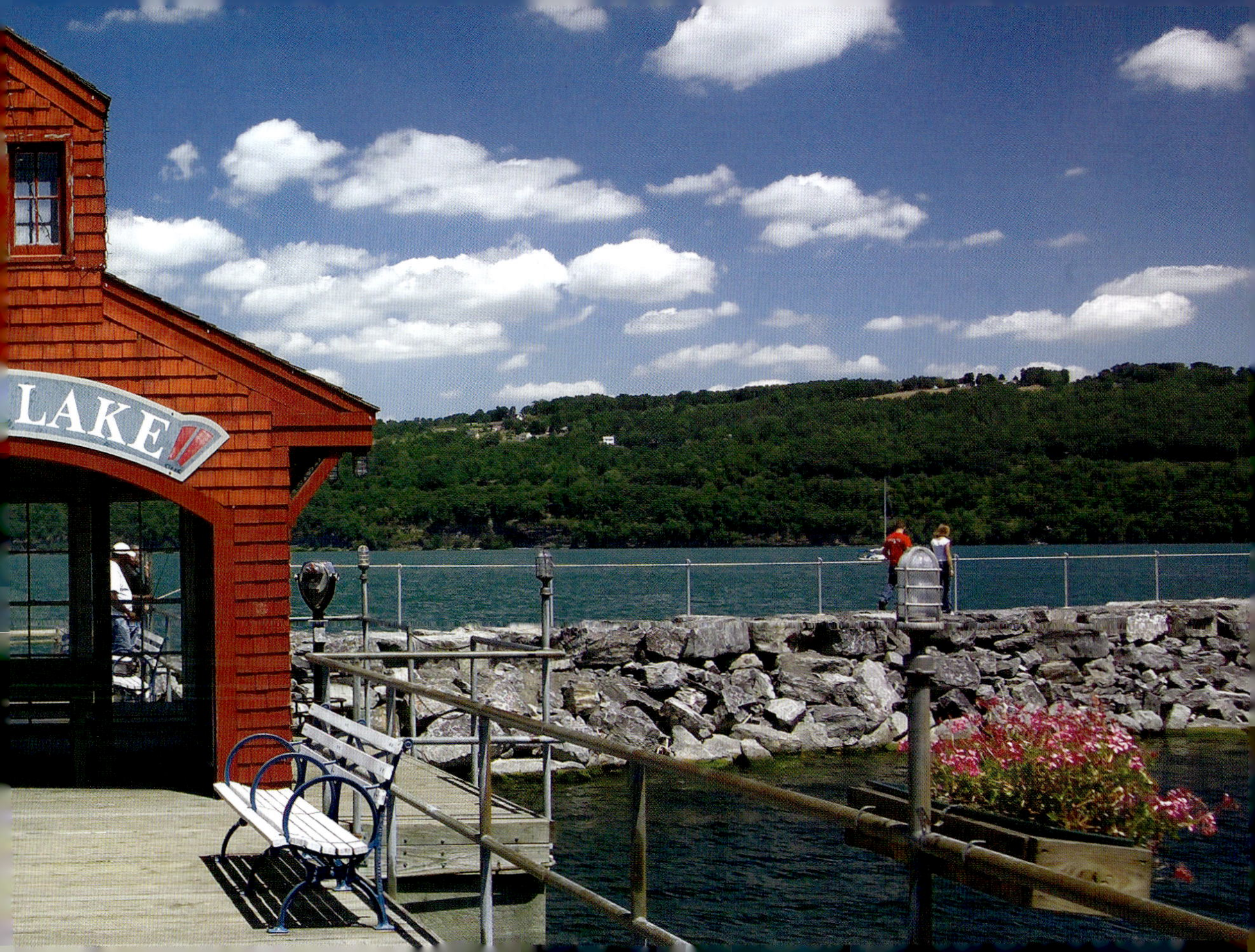
LAKE

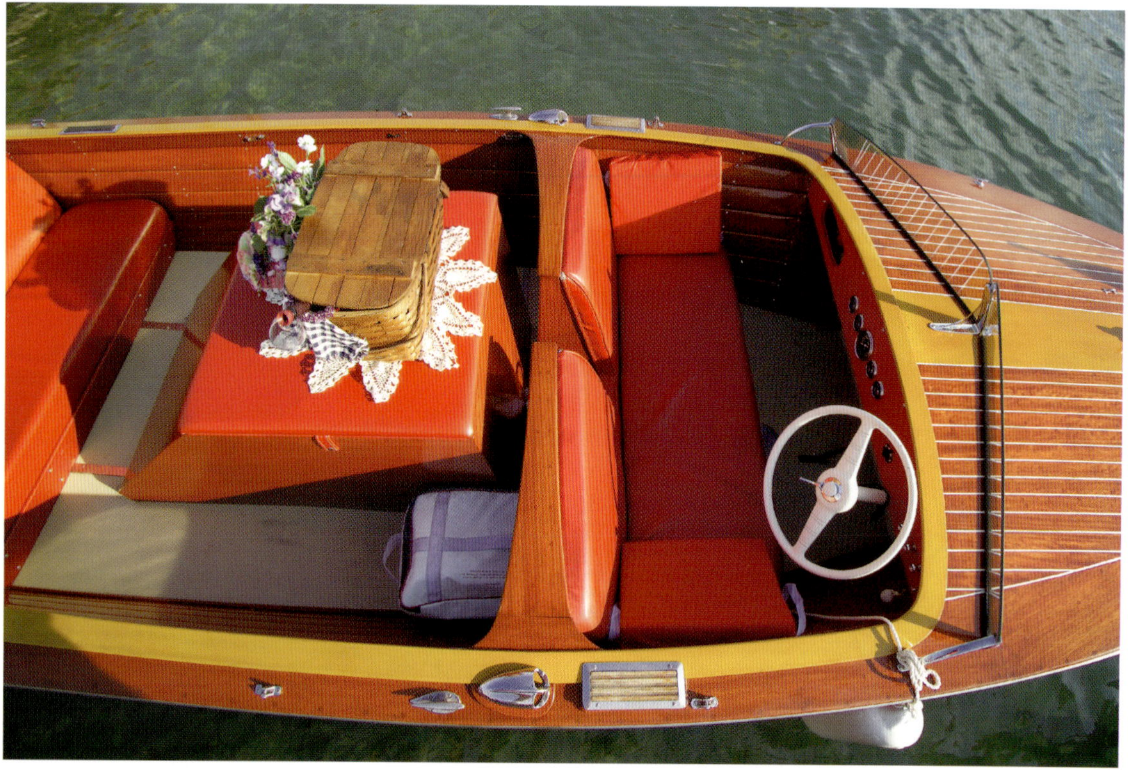

above and next three Antique and classic boat shows draw large crowds to the towns of Hammondsport and Skaneateles.
previous The fishing pier at Seneca Harbor Park, Watkins Glen.

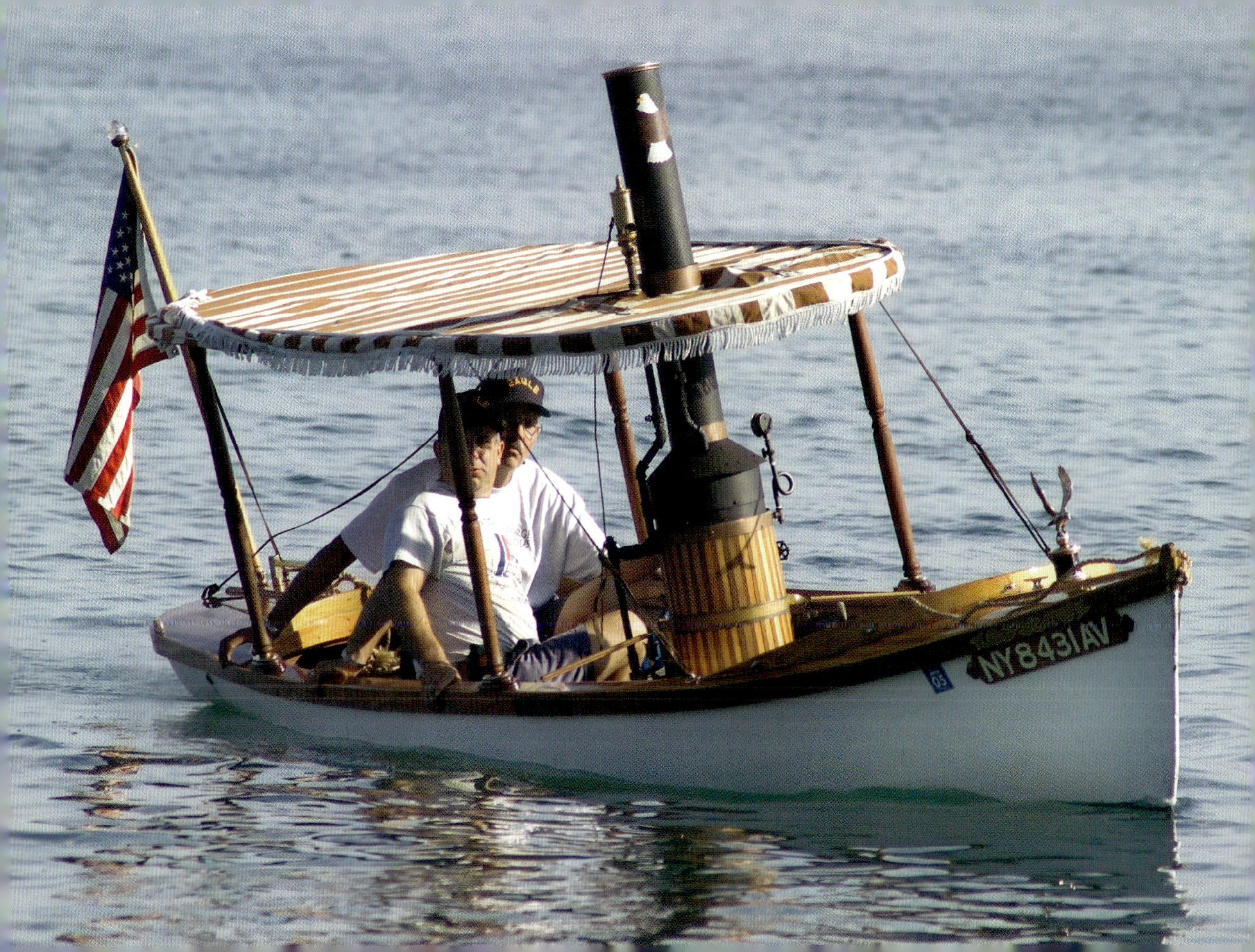
EAGLE
NY8431AV

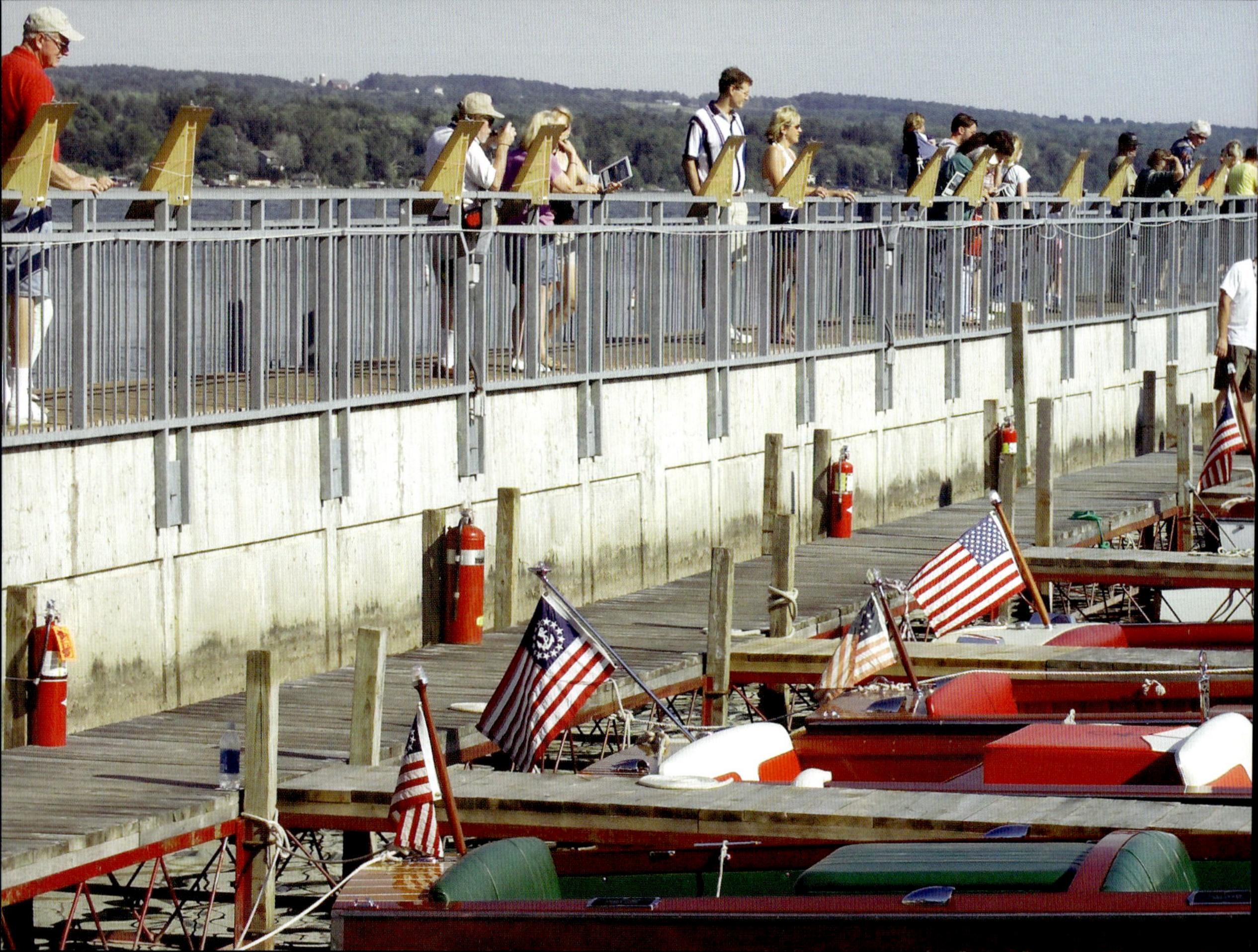

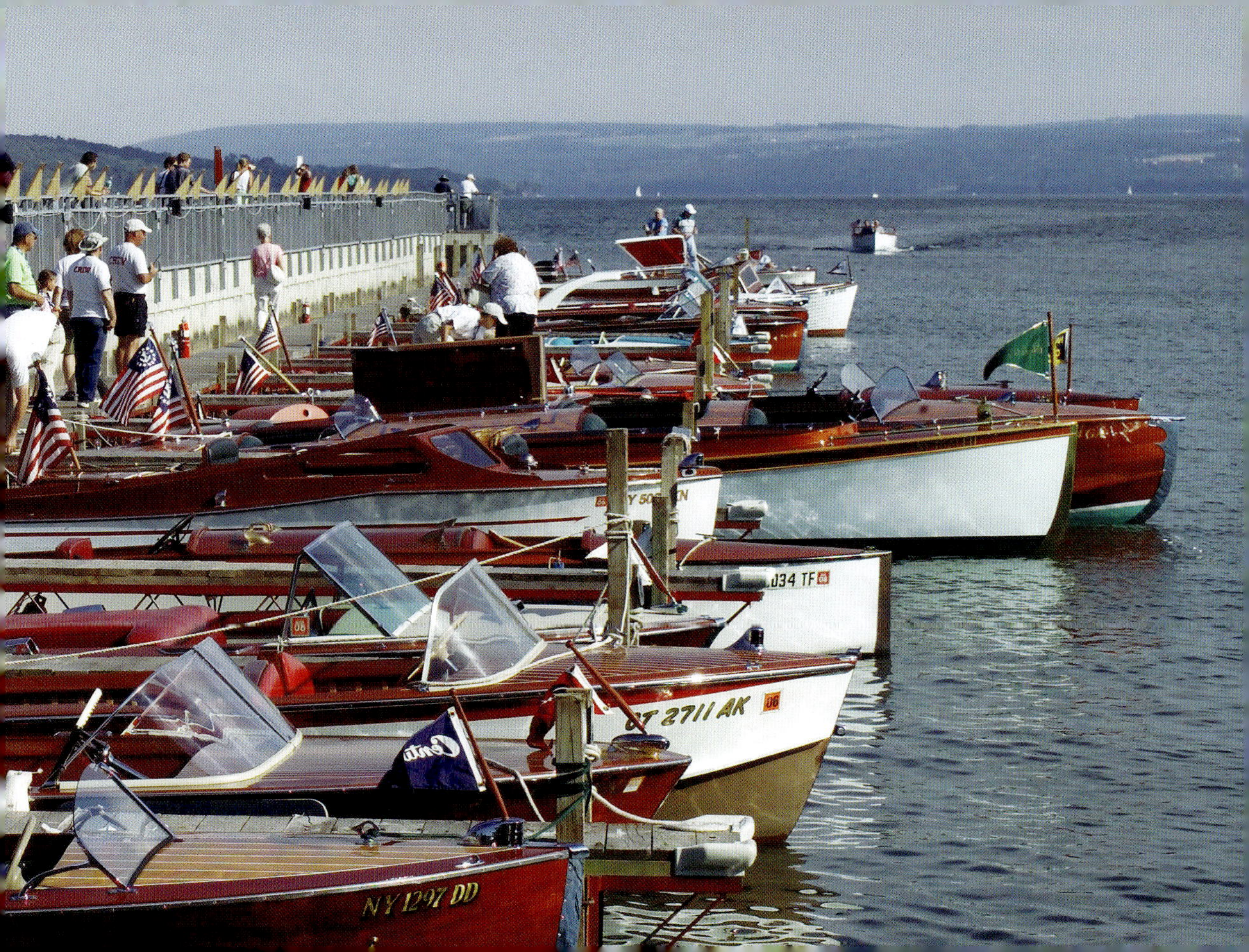
NY 1297 DD
CT 2711 AK
034 TF

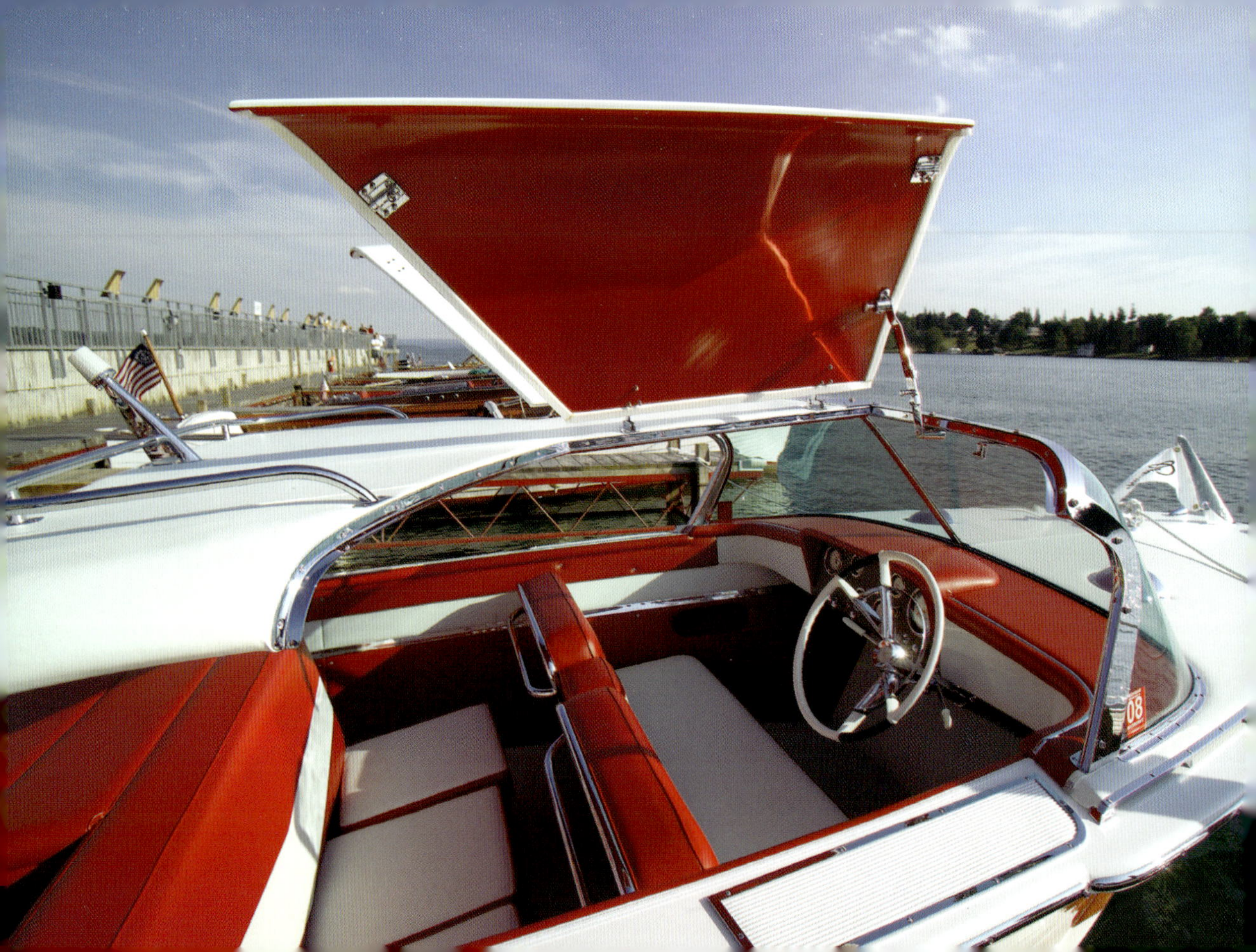
08

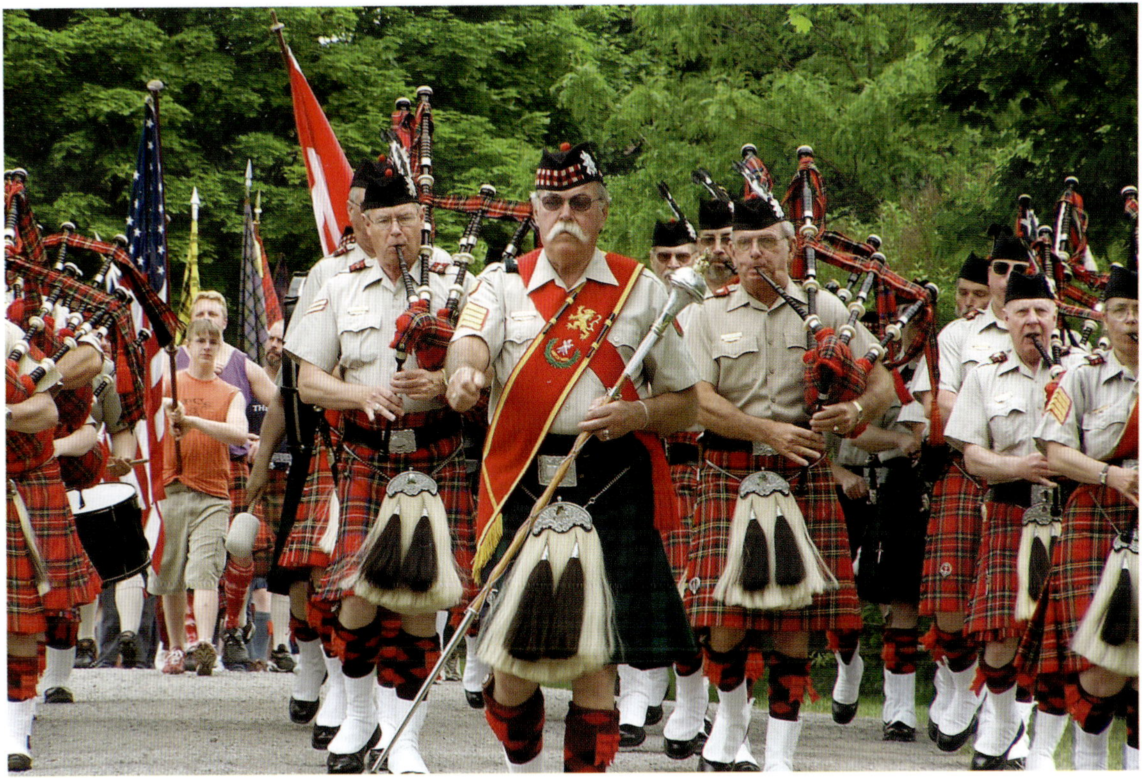

above Bagpipers perform at the Genesee Highland Gathering, Genesee Country Village & Museum. next An evening volleyball game at Honeoye Lake.

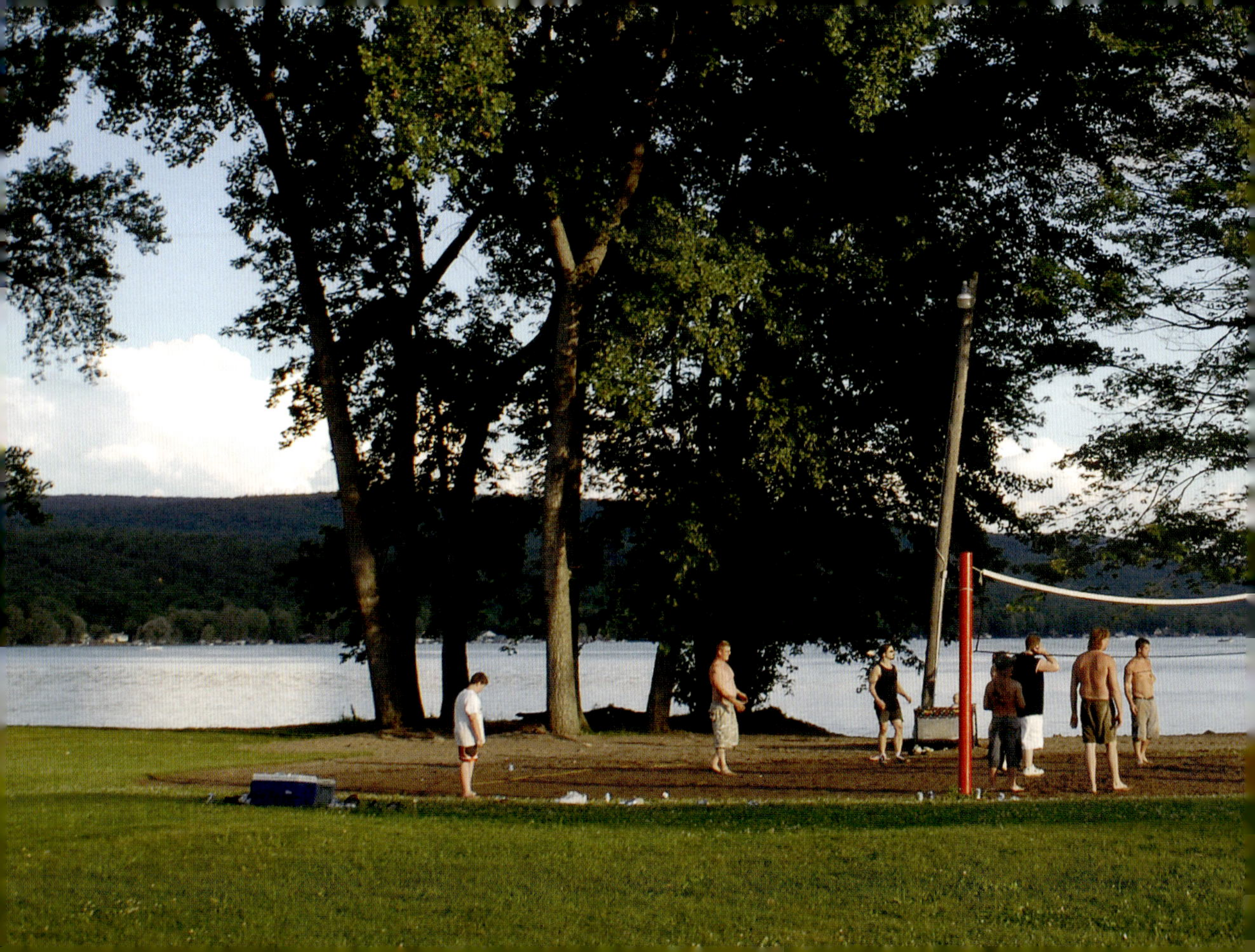

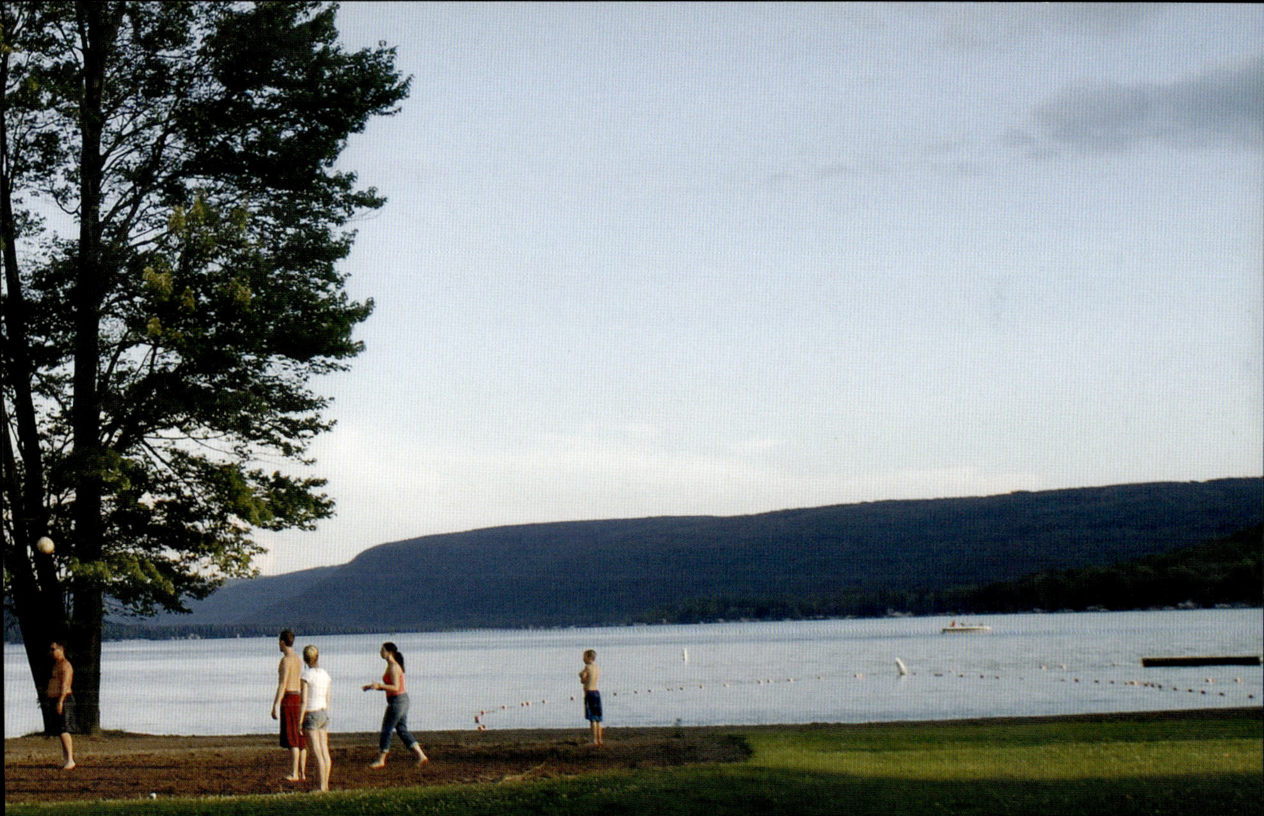

right Swimmers enjoy the lake at Taughannock State Park.
next Boathouses along the Canandaigua pier.

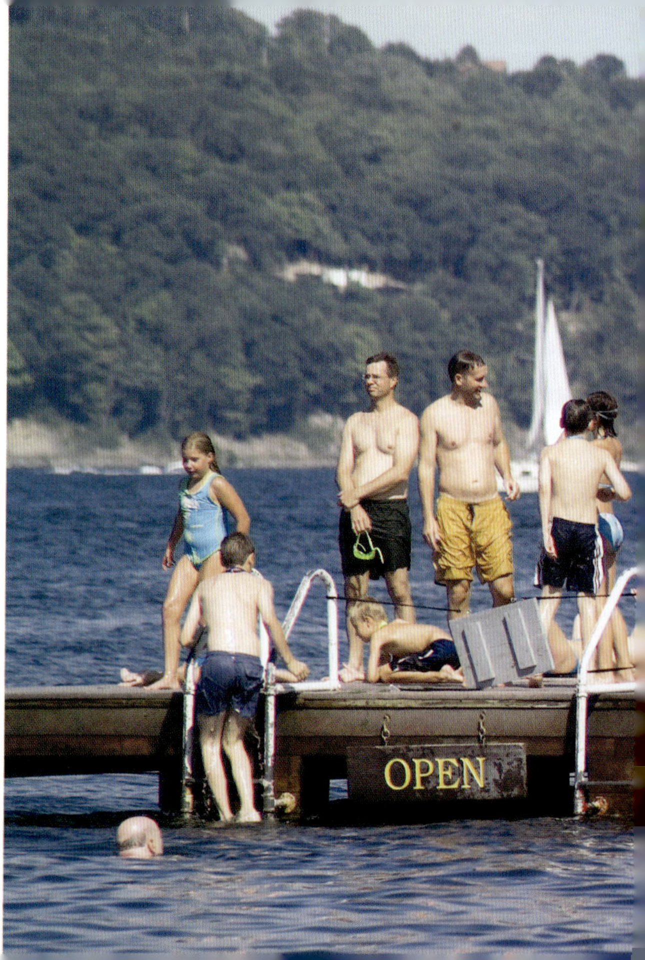

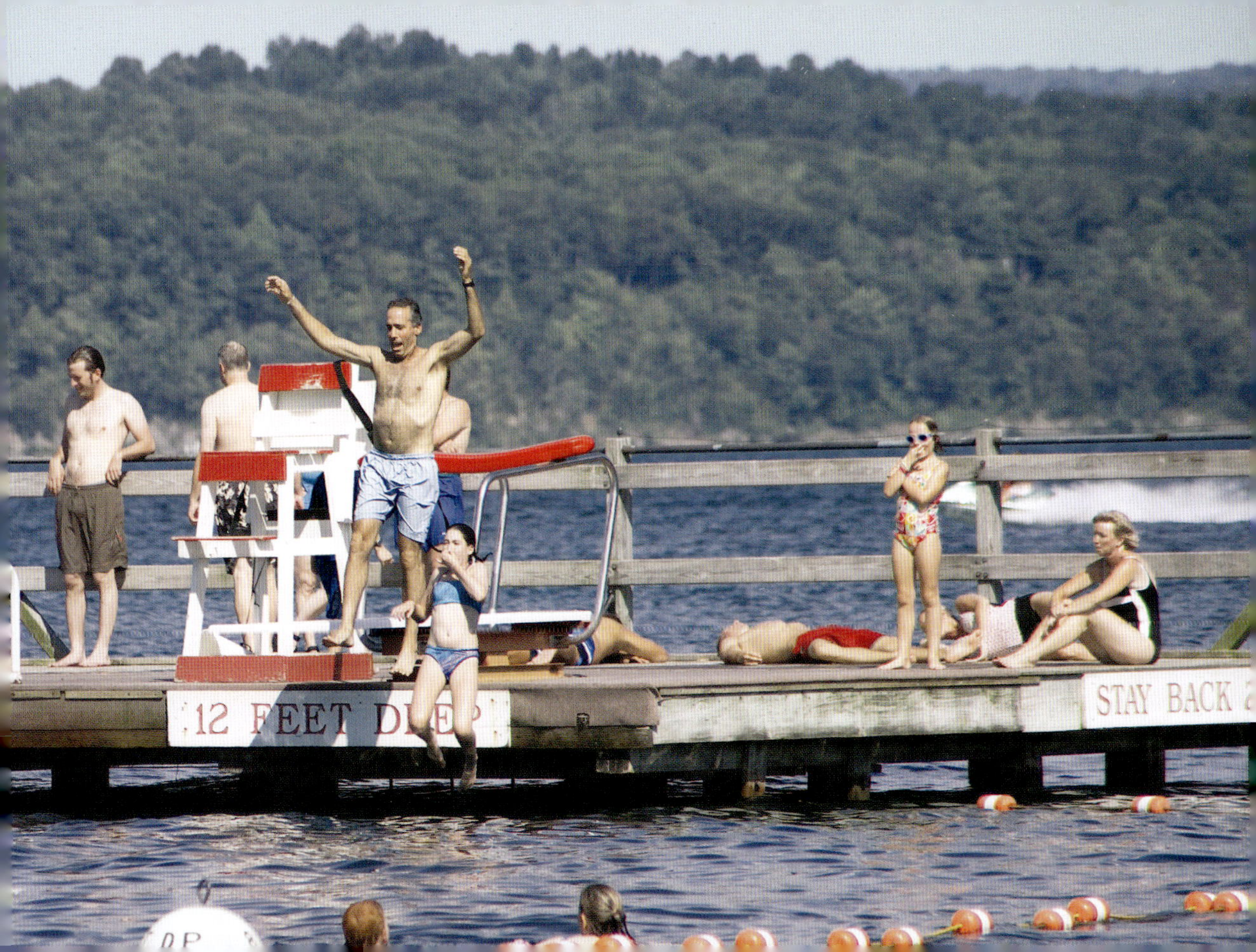

12 FEET DEEP
STAY BACK

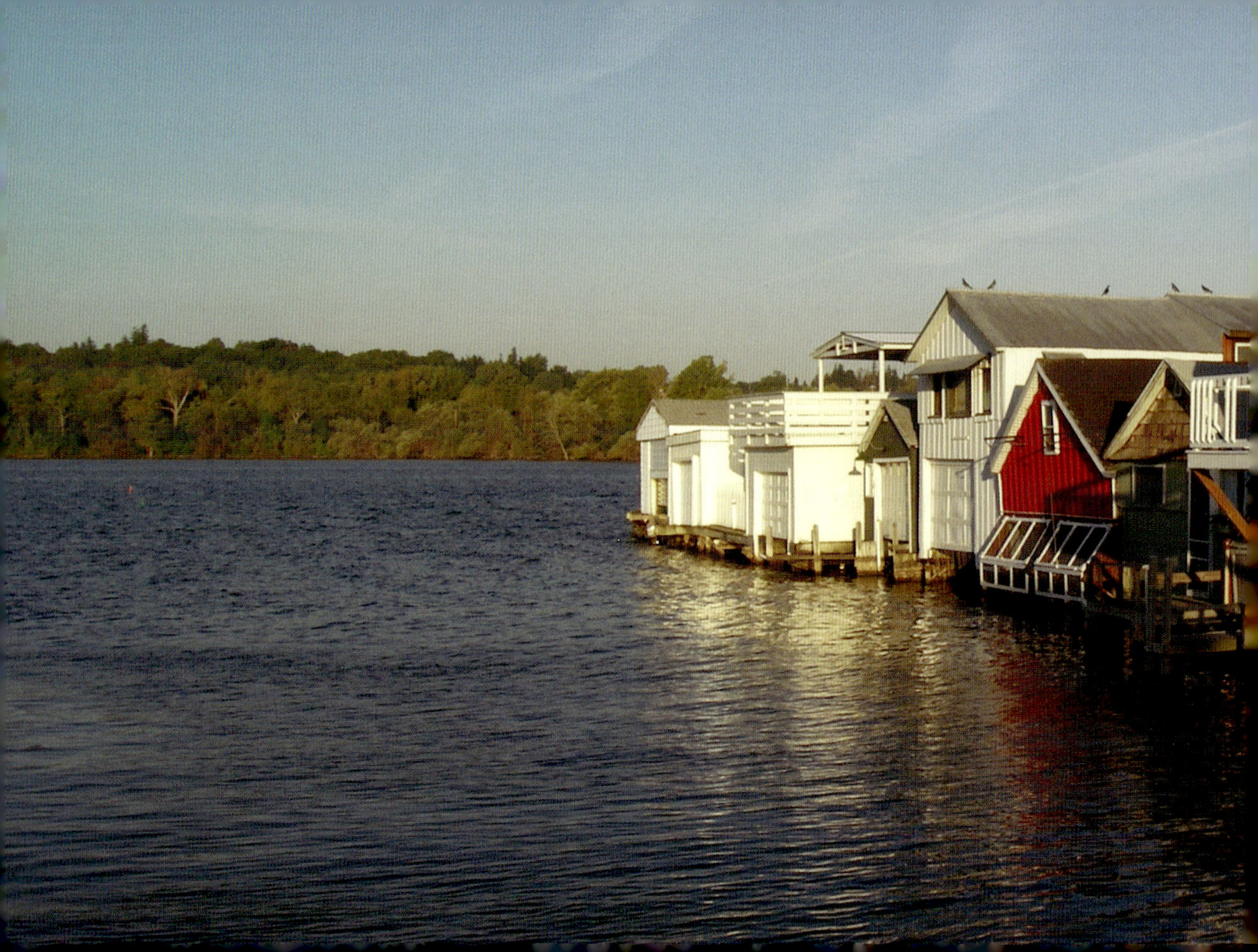

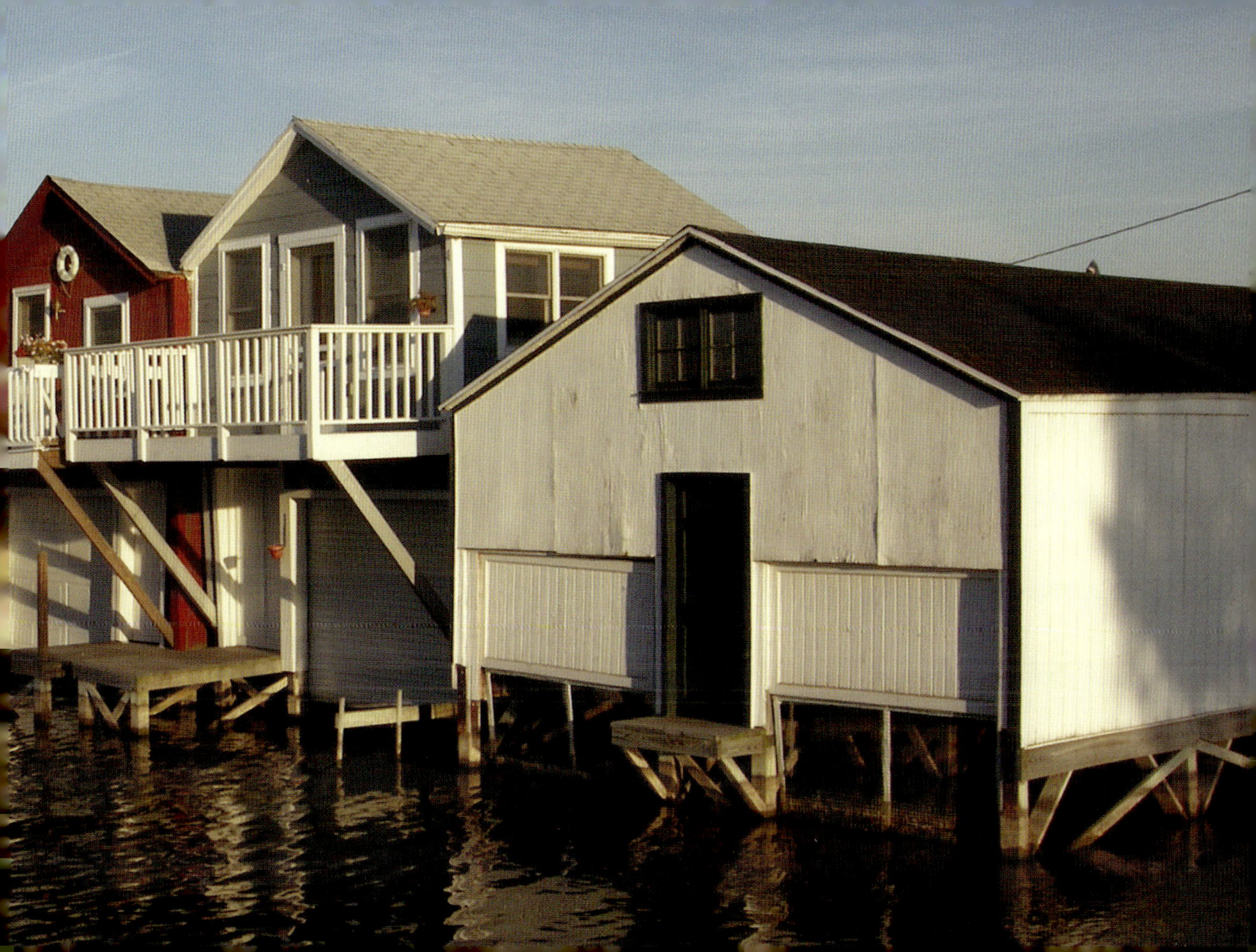

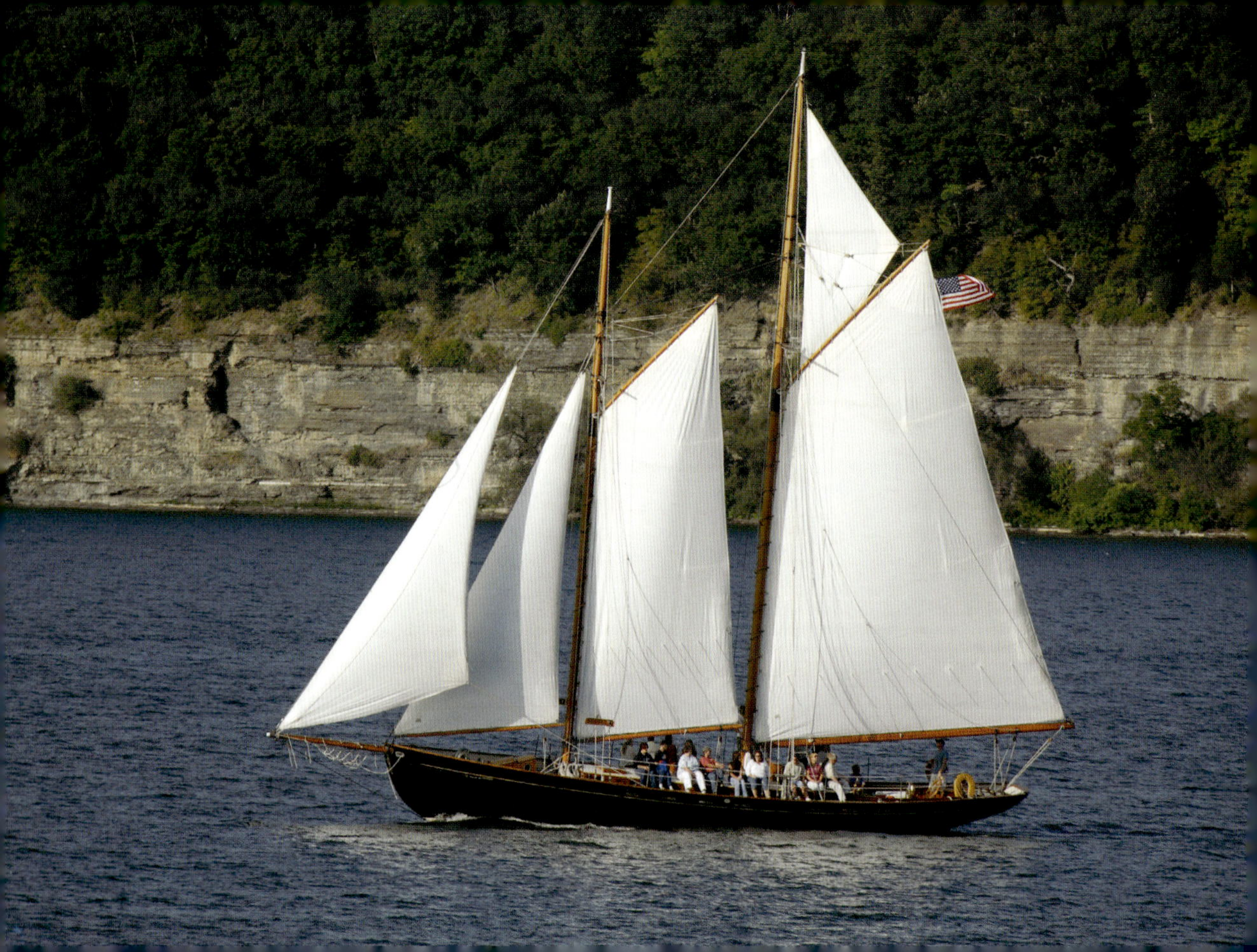

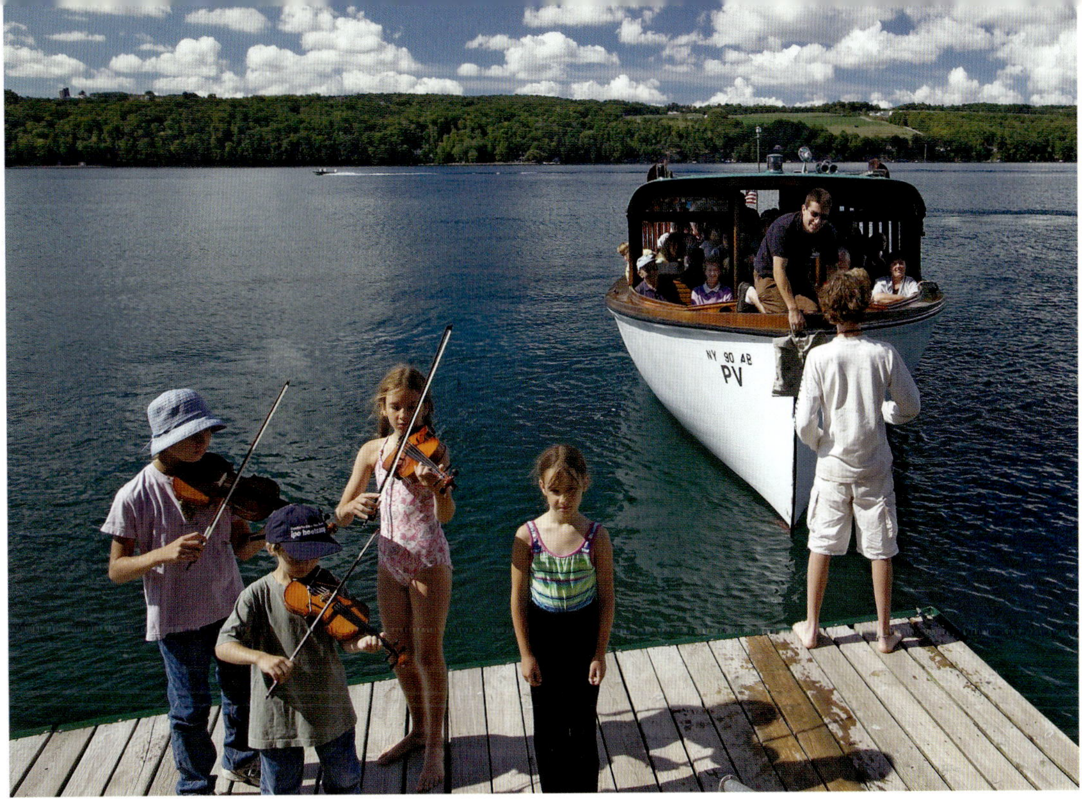

above Dockside musicians greet the Skaneateles mailboat. left Built in 1930, the *Malabar X* gives tourist rides from the port of Watkins Glen.

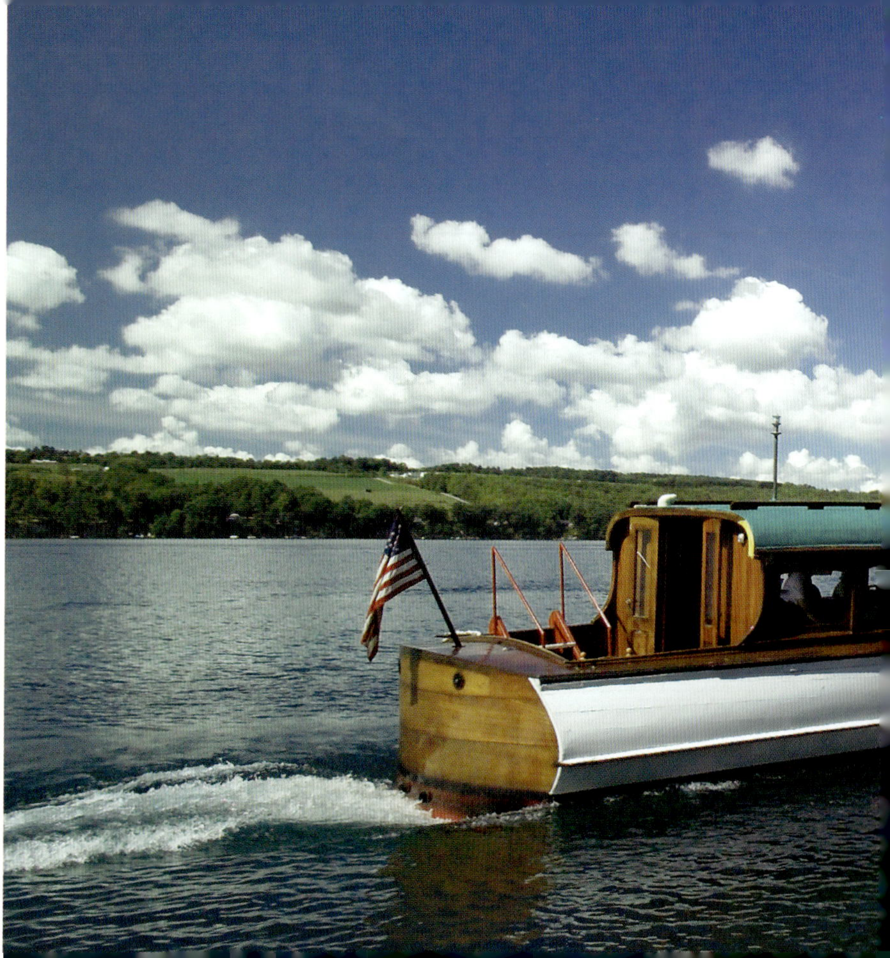

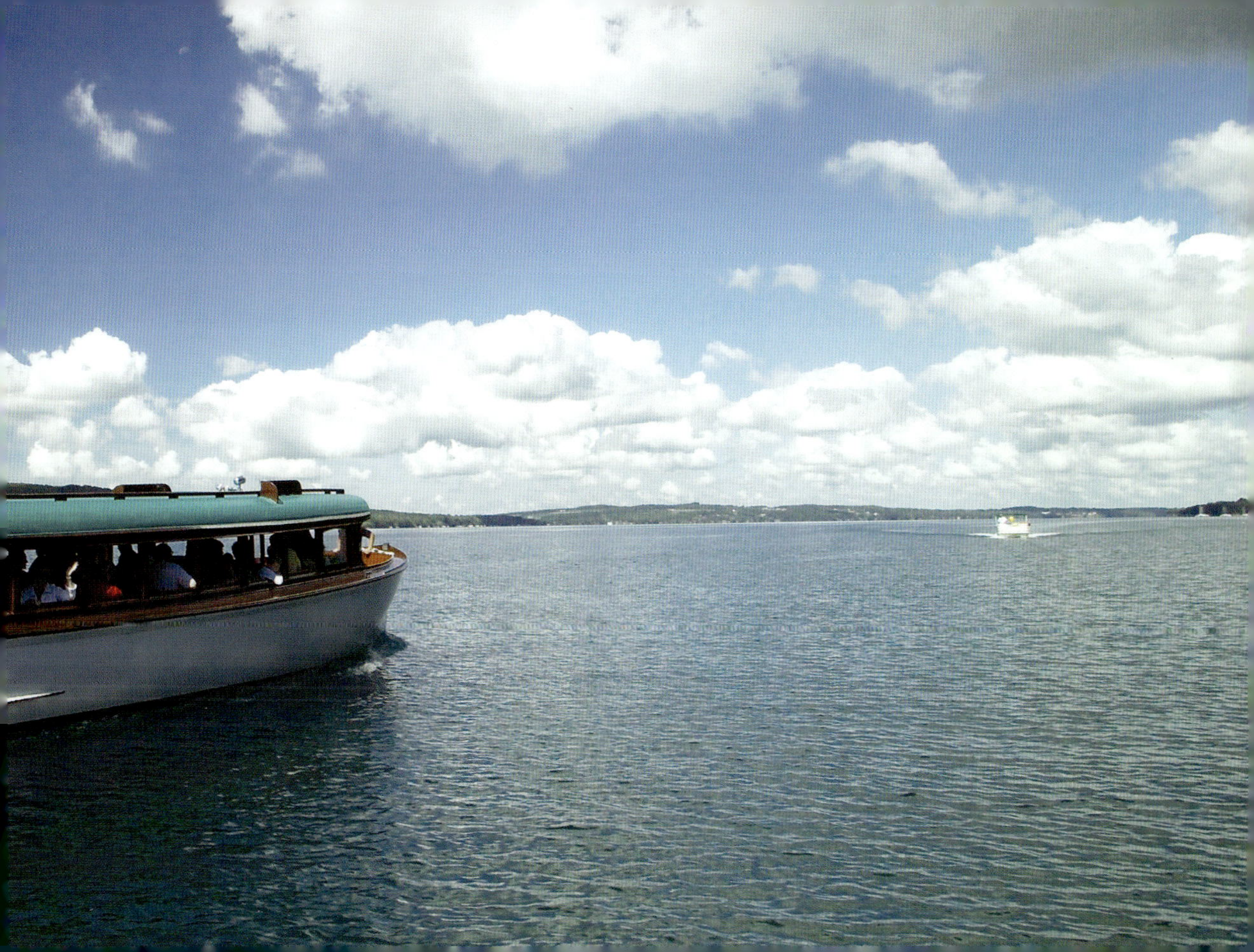

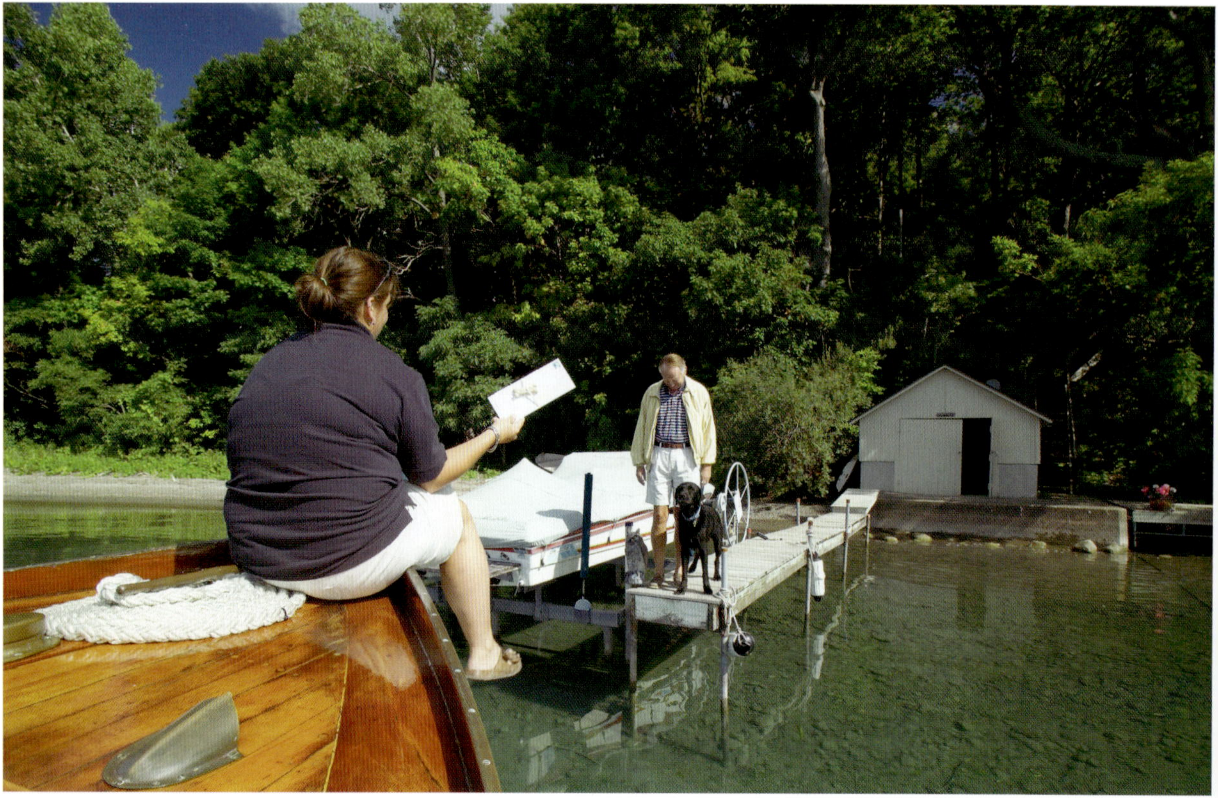

above, right, and previous The mail boat delivers to summer cottage dwellers on Skaneateles Lake.
next Waterloo observed the first Memorial Day on May 5, 1866, to honor the Civil War dead.

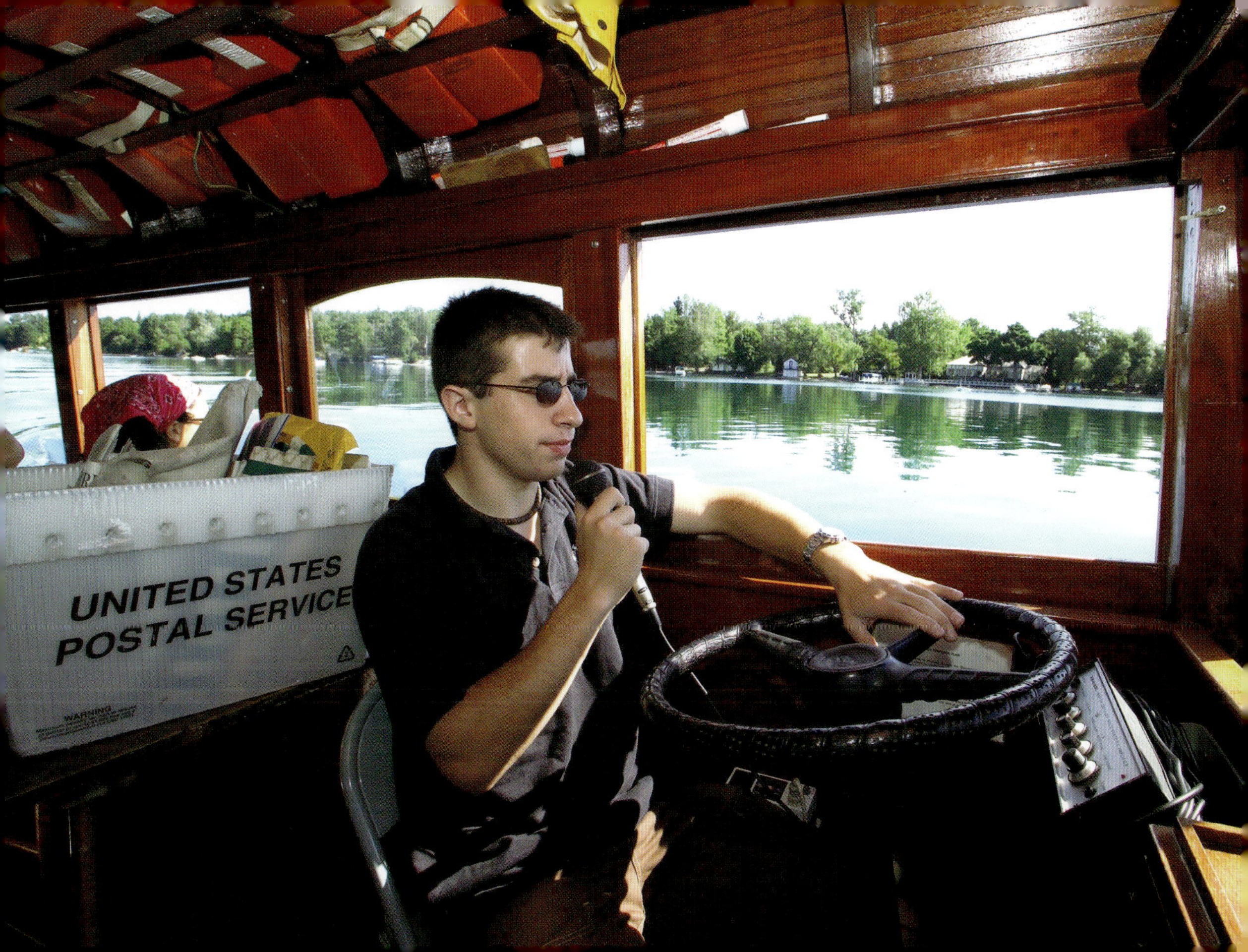
UNITED STATES
POSTAL SERVICE
WARNING

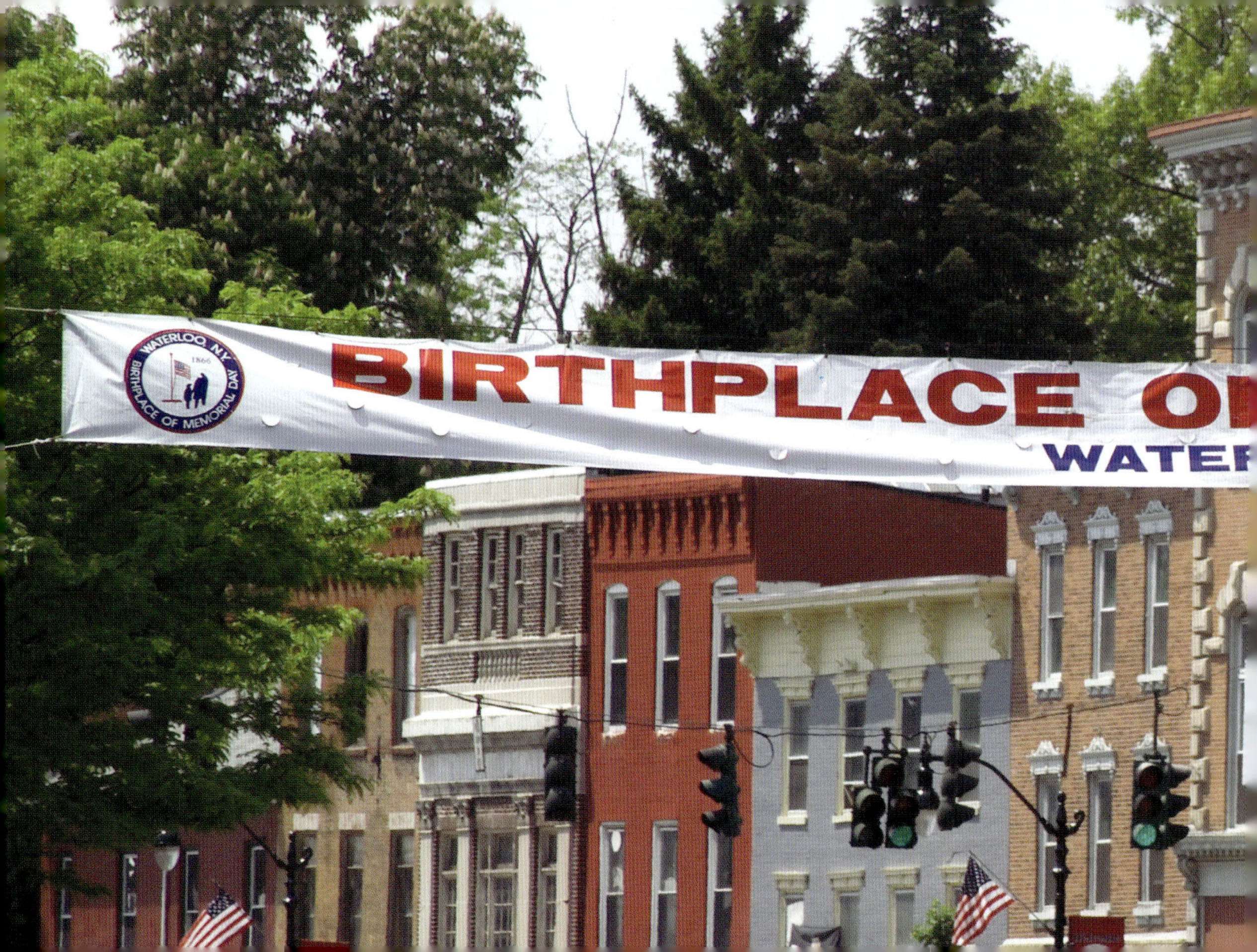
WATERLOO, N.Y.
1866
BIRTHPLACE OF MEMORIAL DAY
BIRTHPLACE

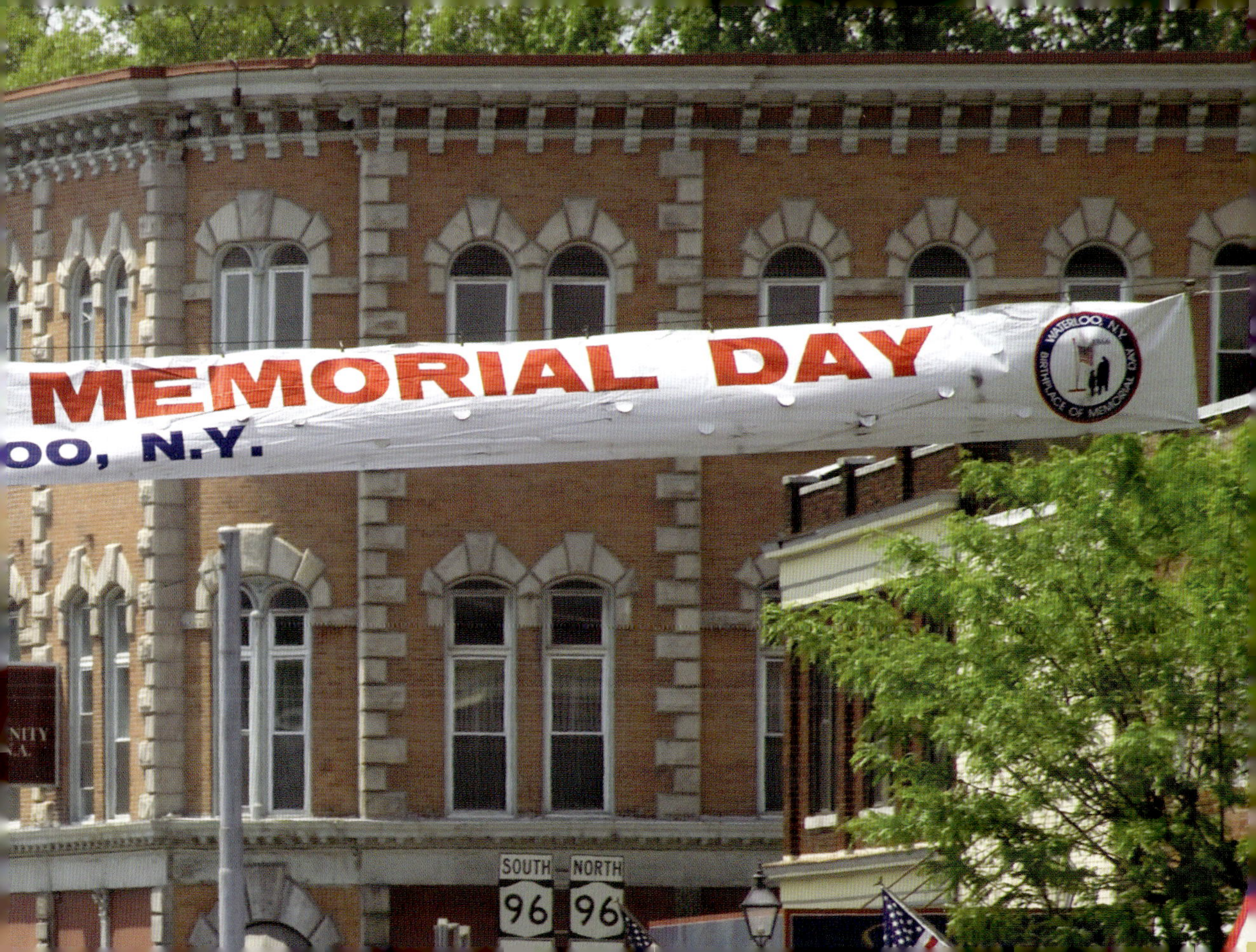
MEMORIAL DAY
OO, N.Y.
WATERLOO, N.Y.
BIRTHPLACE OF MEMORIAL DAY
SOUTH
96
NORTH
96

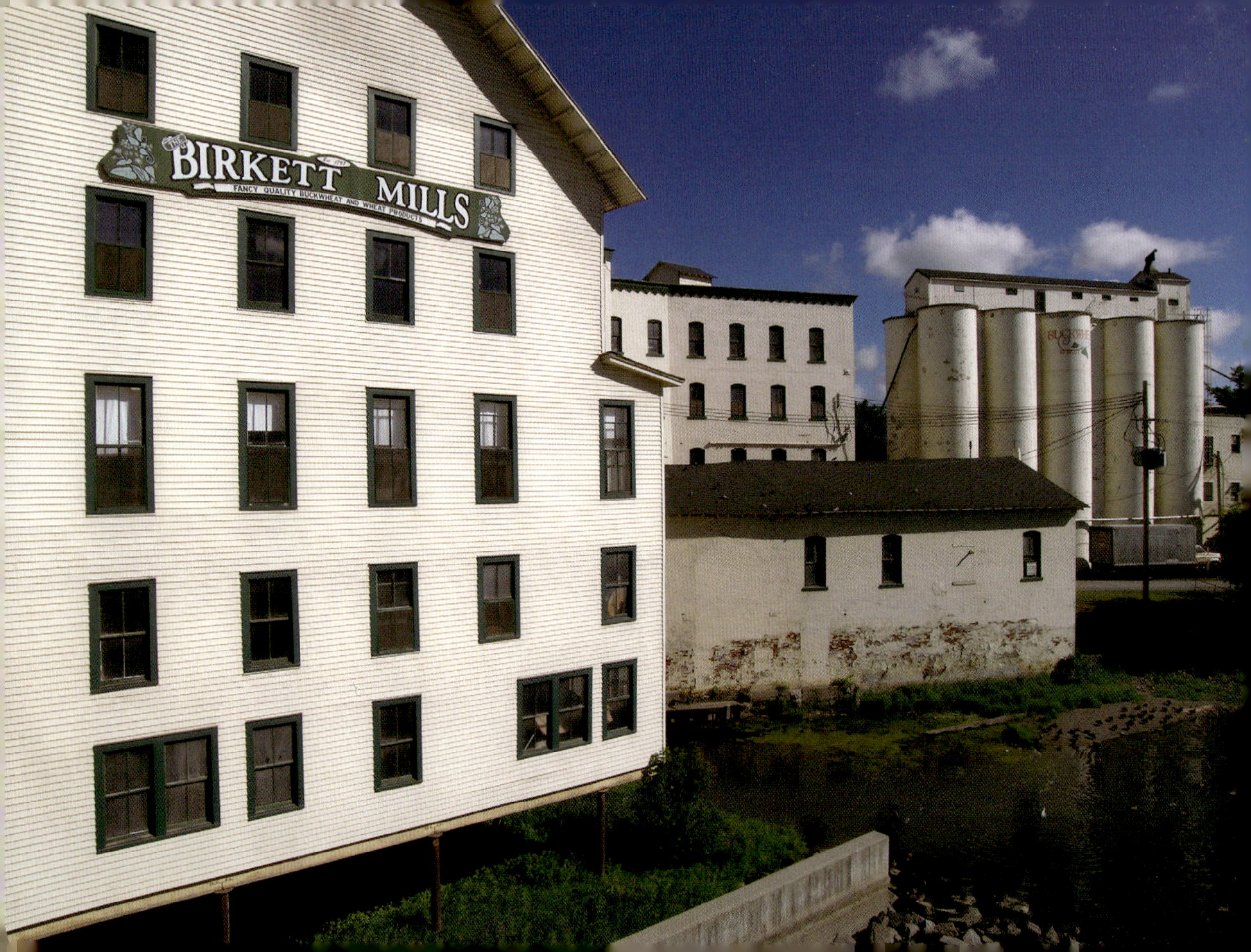
THE BIRKETT MILLS
Est. 1797
FANCY QUALITY BUCKWHEAT AND WHEAT PRODUCTS

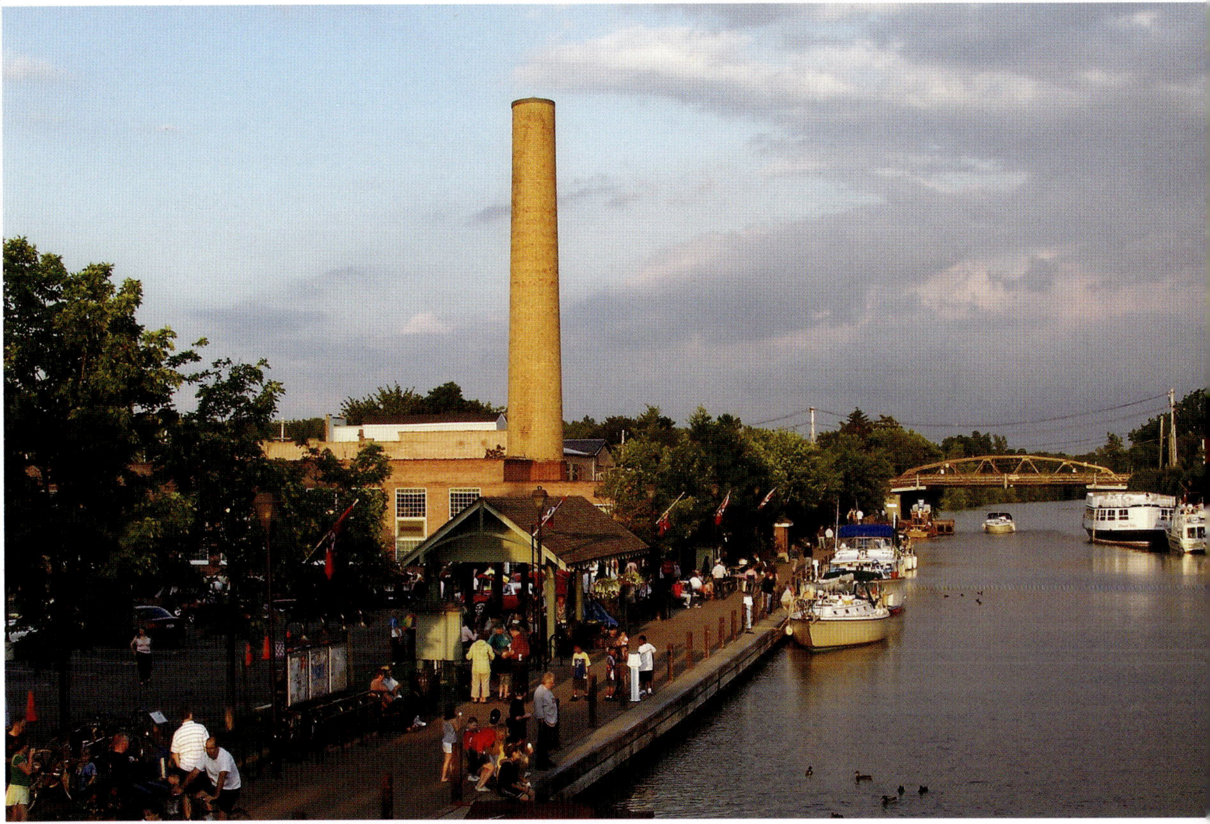

above Fairport Village offers docking facilities for those cruising the Erie Canal. left Operating since 1797, Birkett Mills in Penn Yan is among the world's largest producers of buckwheat products.

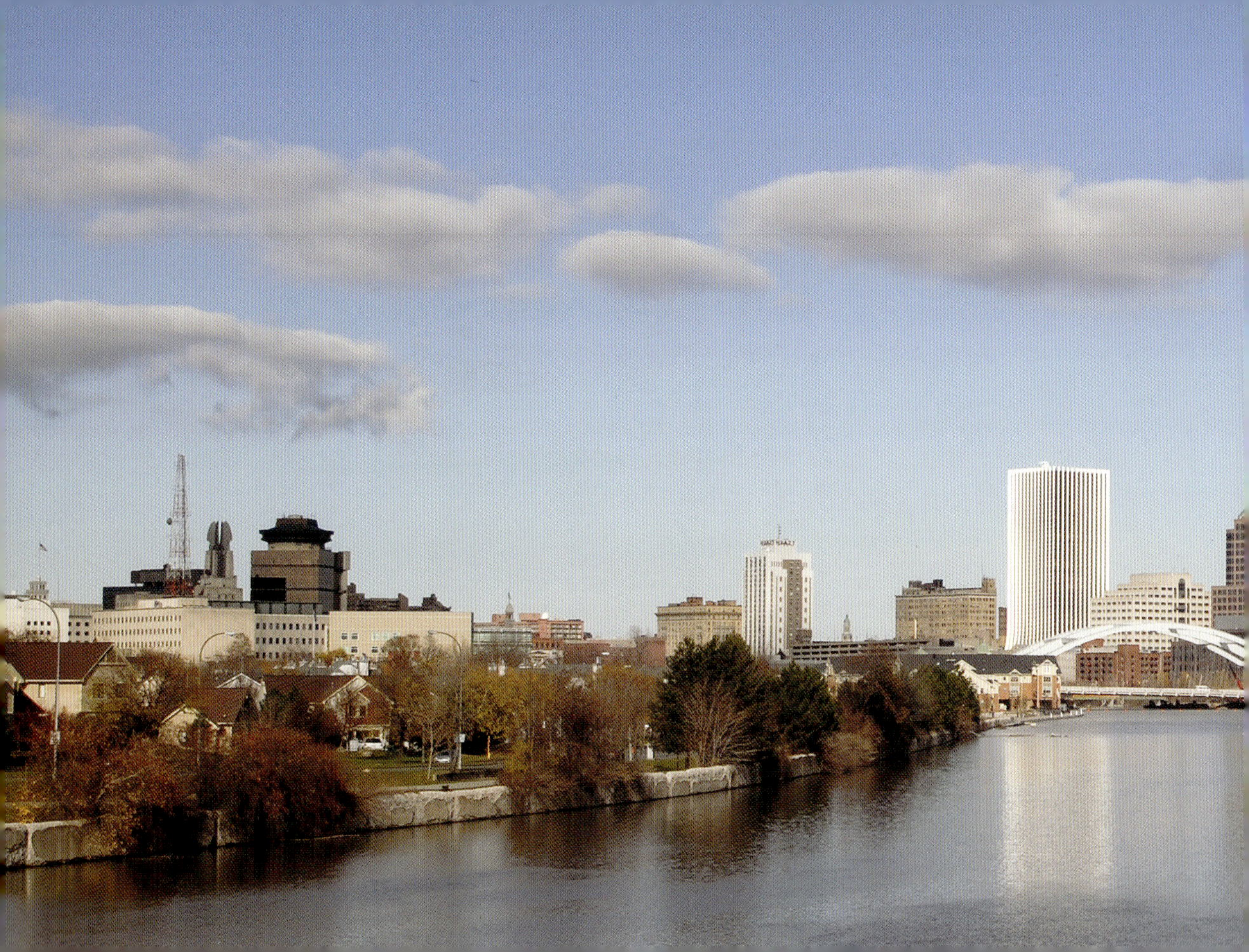

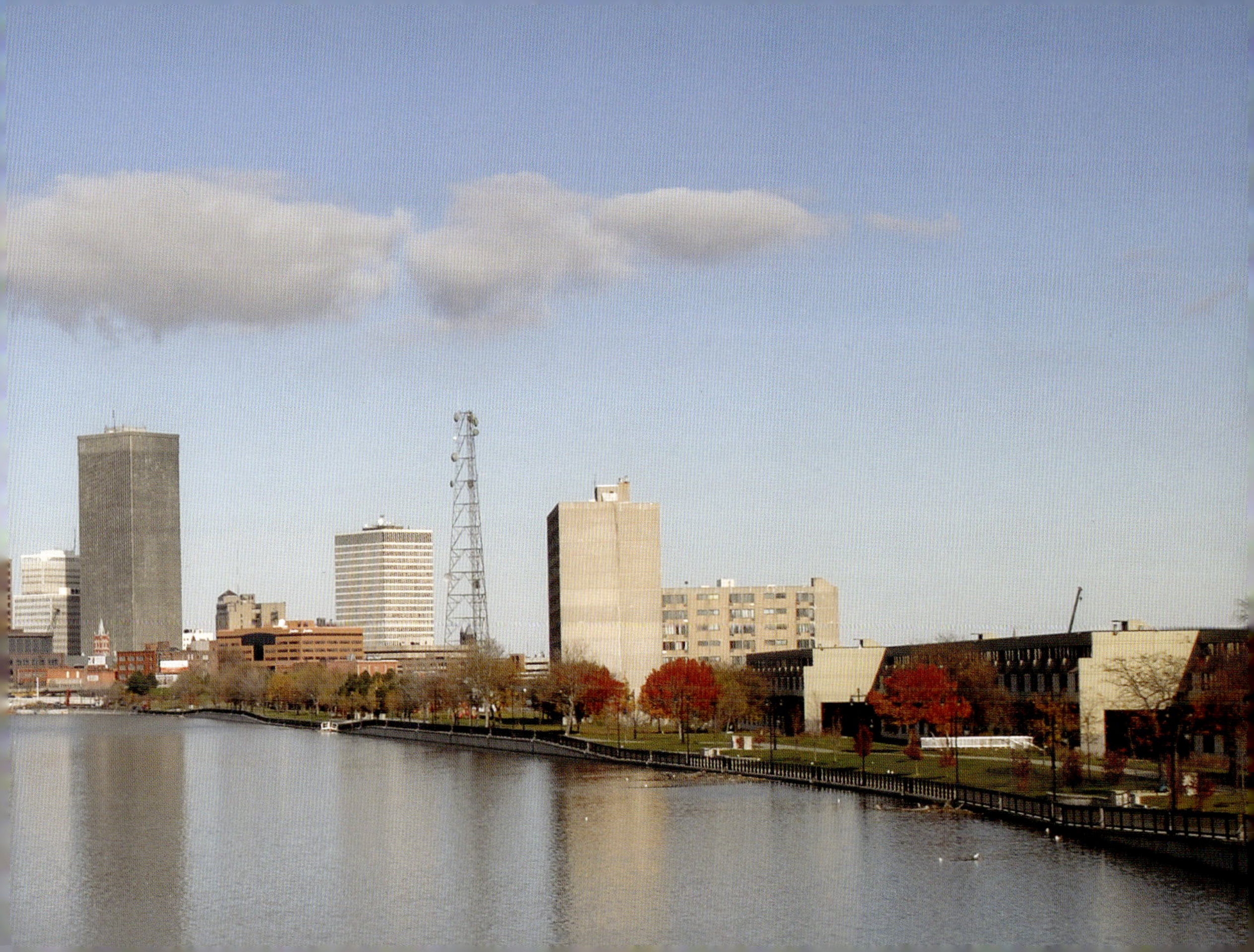

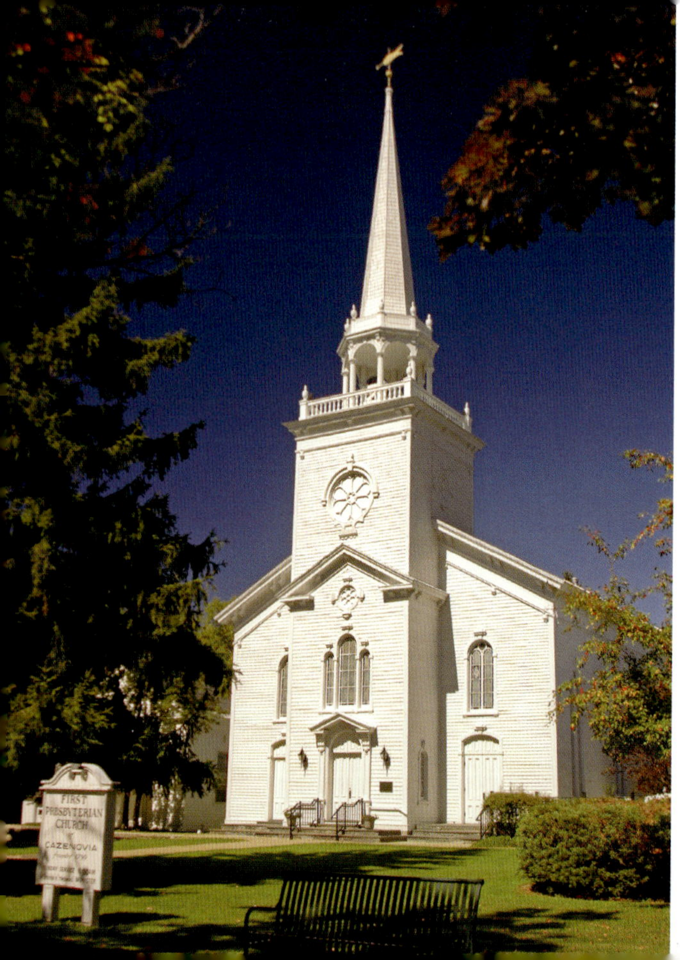

left The First Prebysterian Church of Cazenovia, founded in 1799. right The Palm House at Sonnenberg Gardens in Canandaigua, part of the original Lord and Burnham greenhouse complex. previous On the banks of the Genesee River, Rochester got its start as the center of a flourishing flour mill industry.

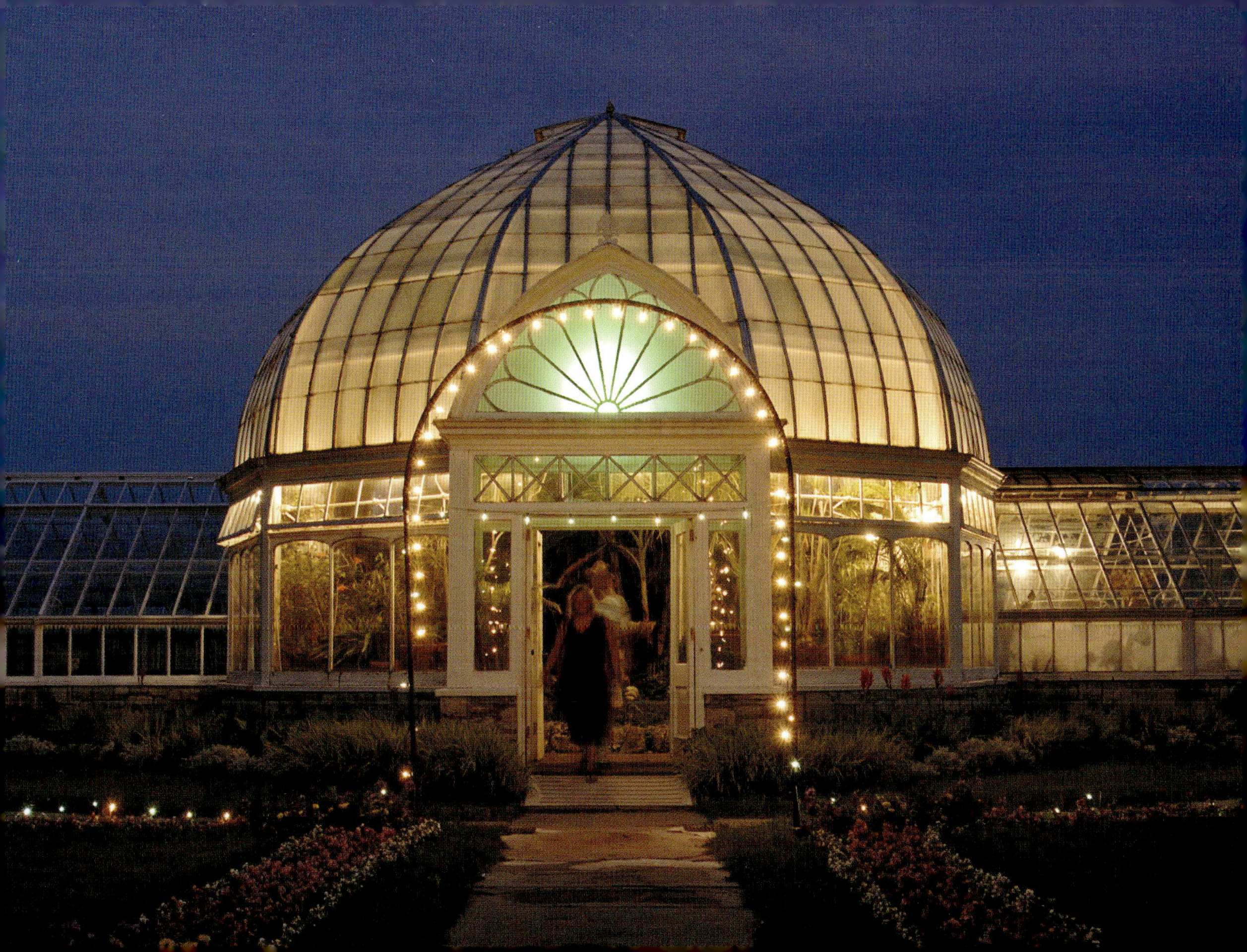

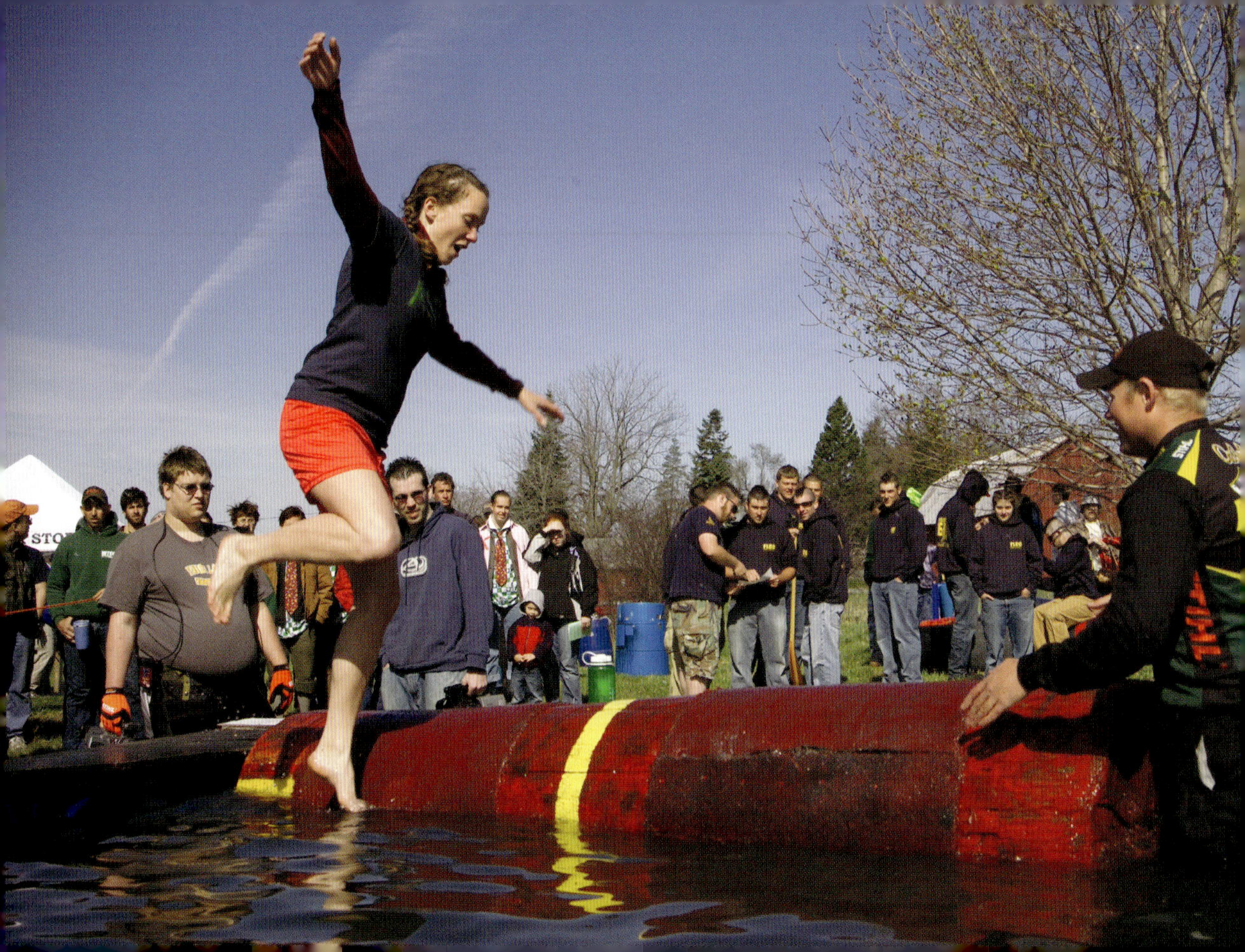

left A volunteer gives log rolling a try at the Finger Lakes Community College Lumberjack Festival. right A hot air balloon lifts off at the Letchworth State Park Festival in May. next A well-tended farm in Mennonite country near Bentley Corner.

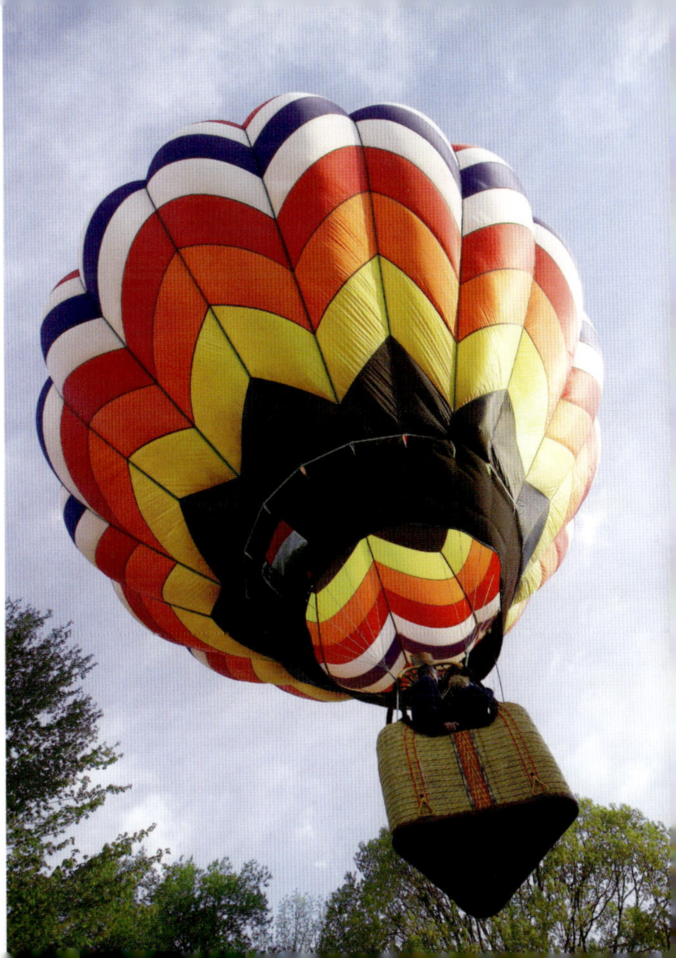

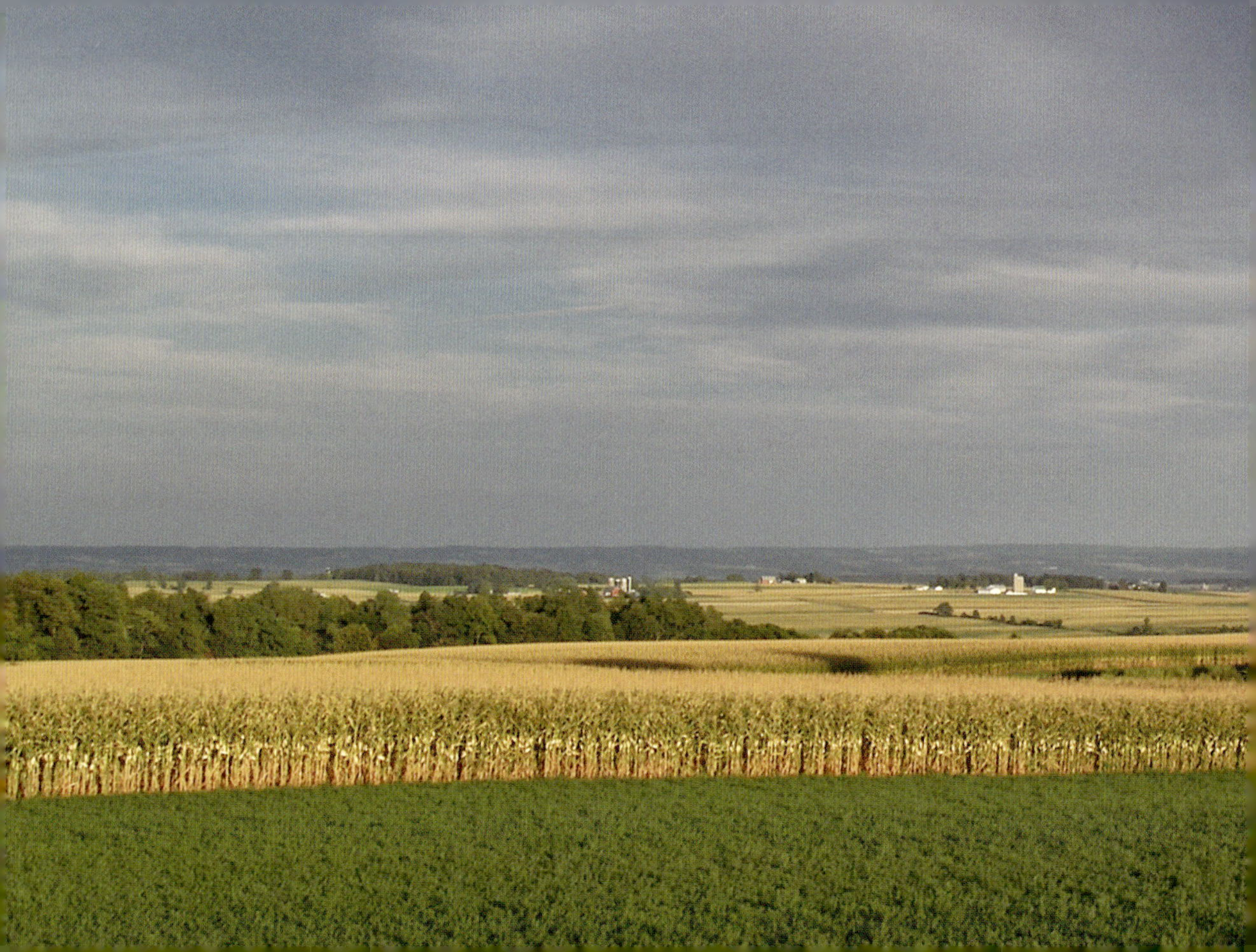

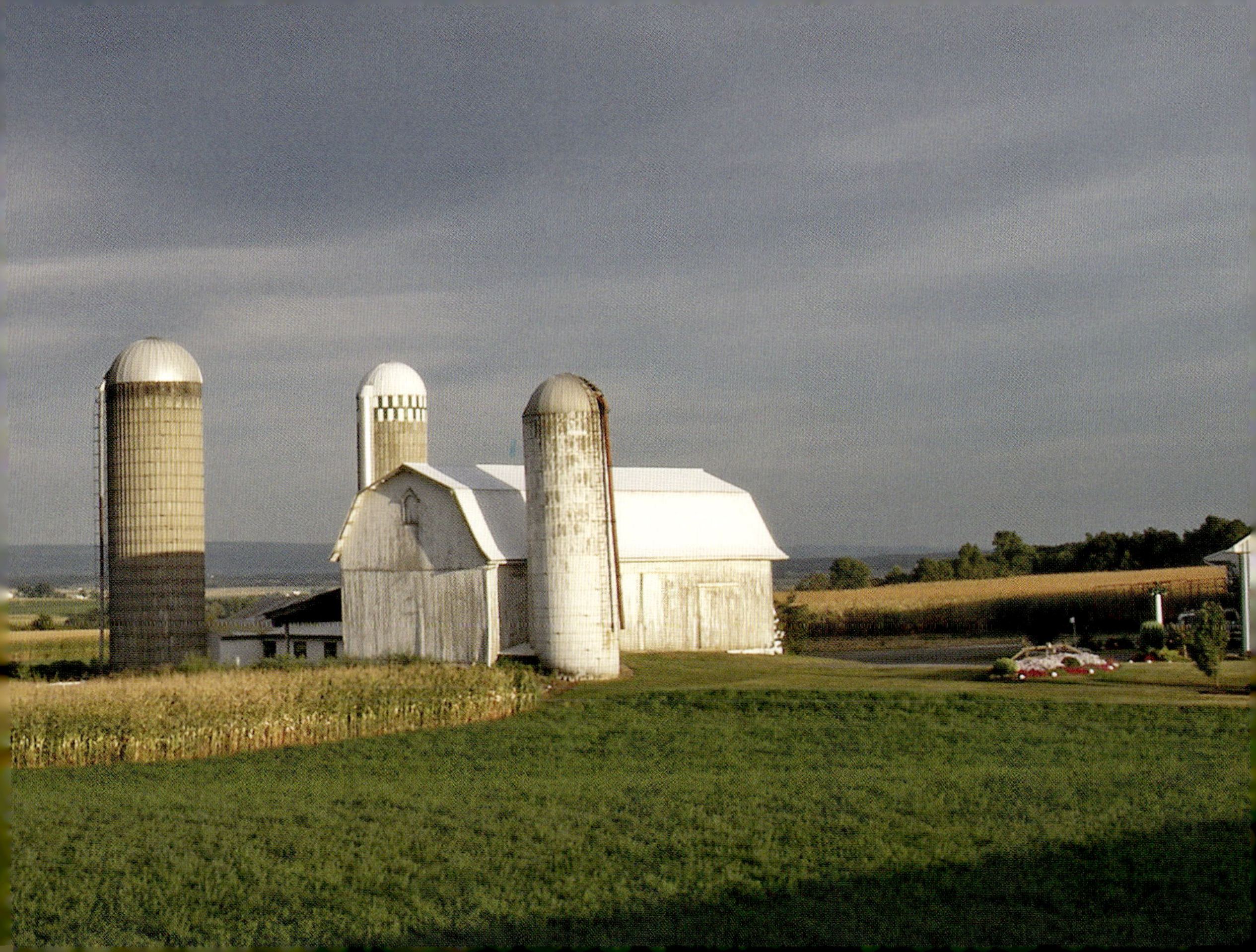

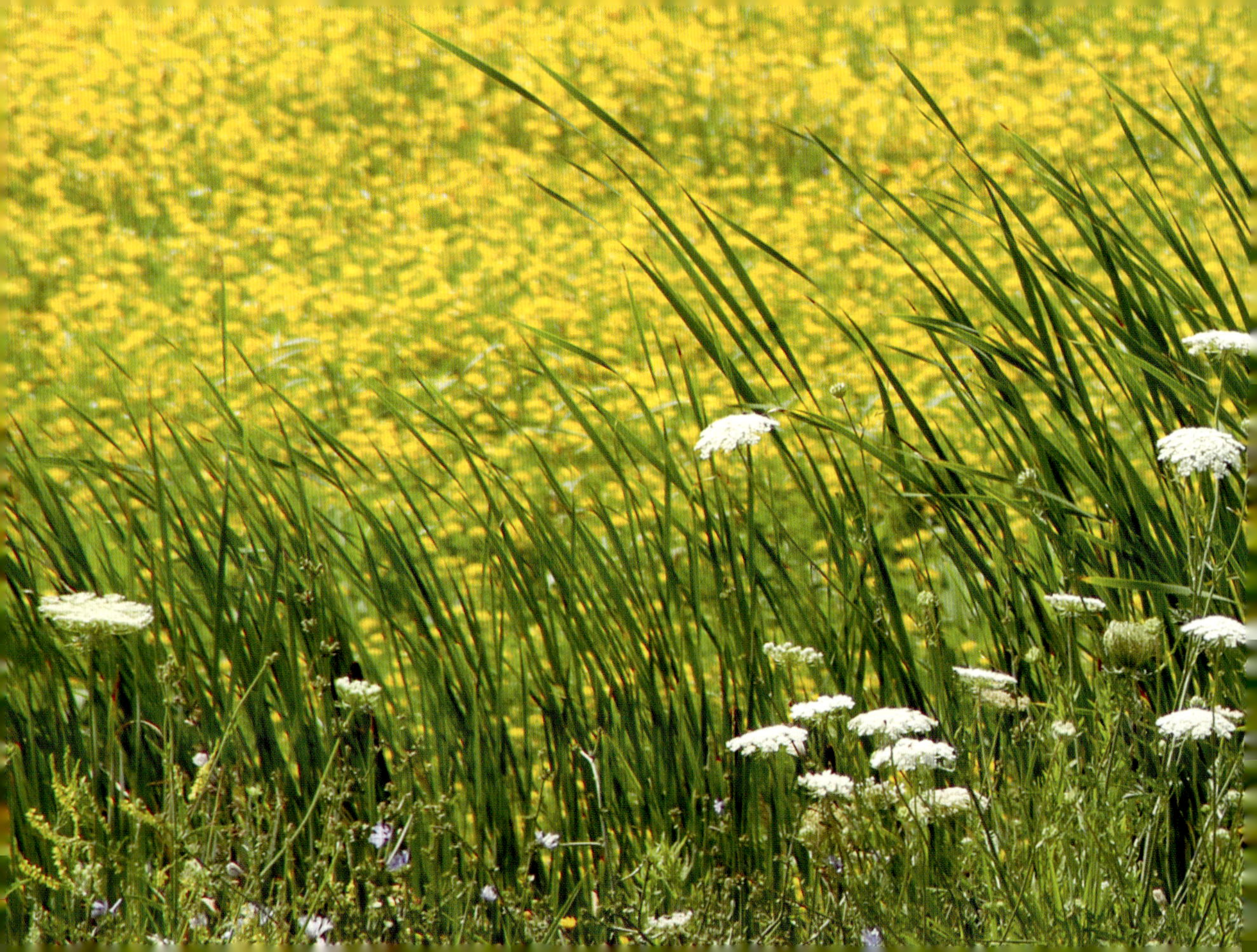

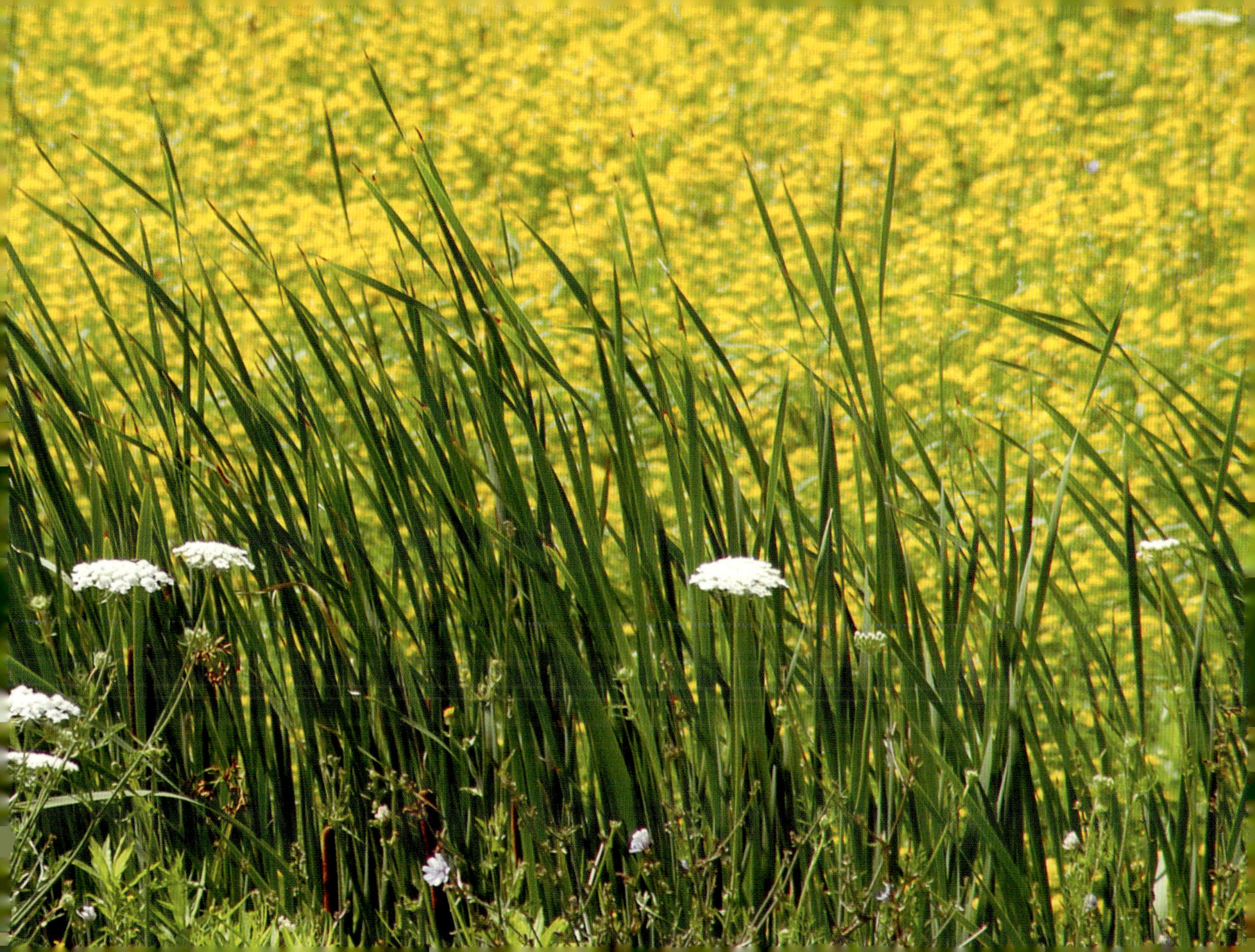

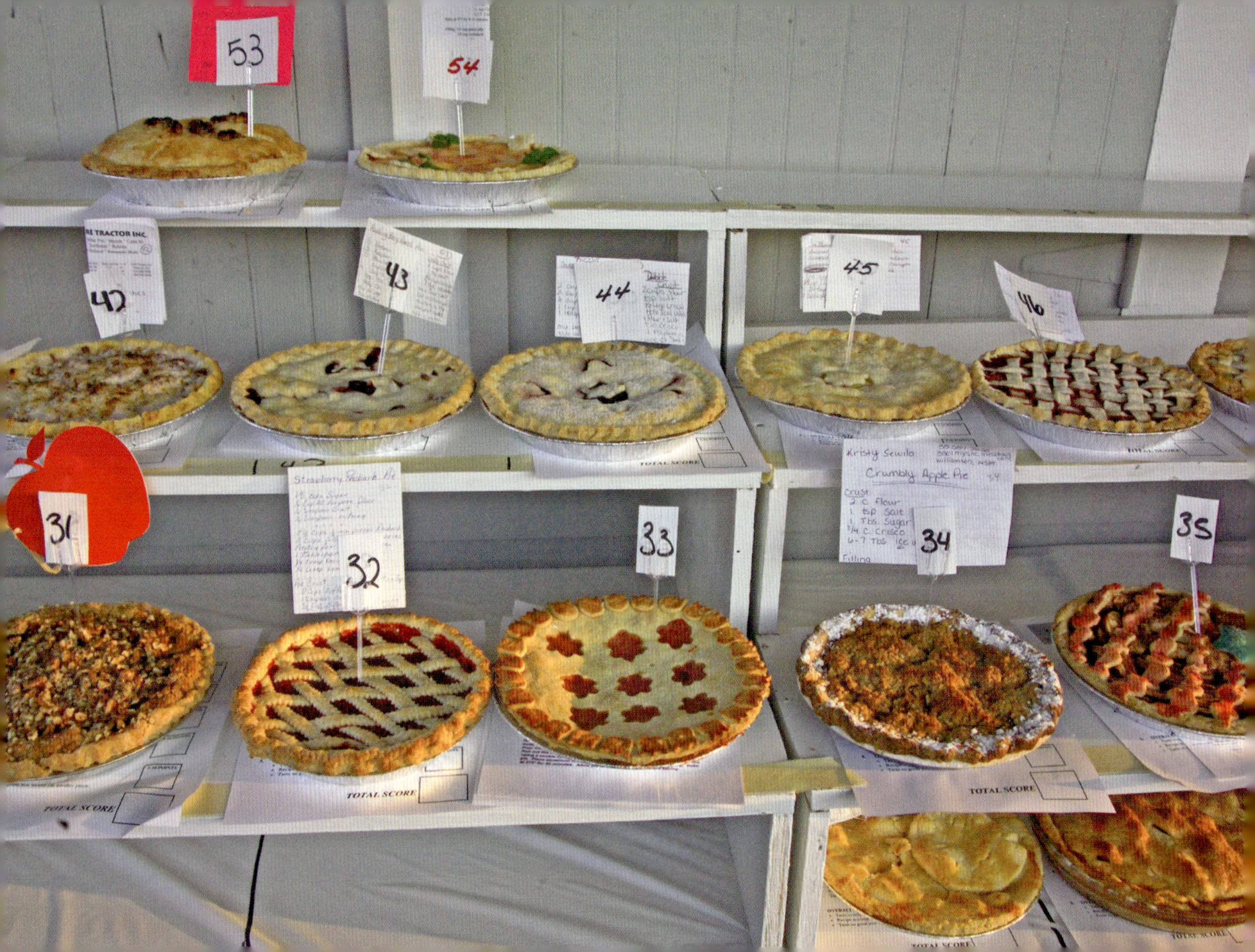
53
54
42
43
44
45
46
Kristy Sewilo
Crumbly Apple Pie
Crust
2 c flour
1 tsp salt
1 Tbs. Sugar
3/4 c Crisco
Strawberry Rhubarb Pie
31
32
33
34
35
TOTAL SCORE

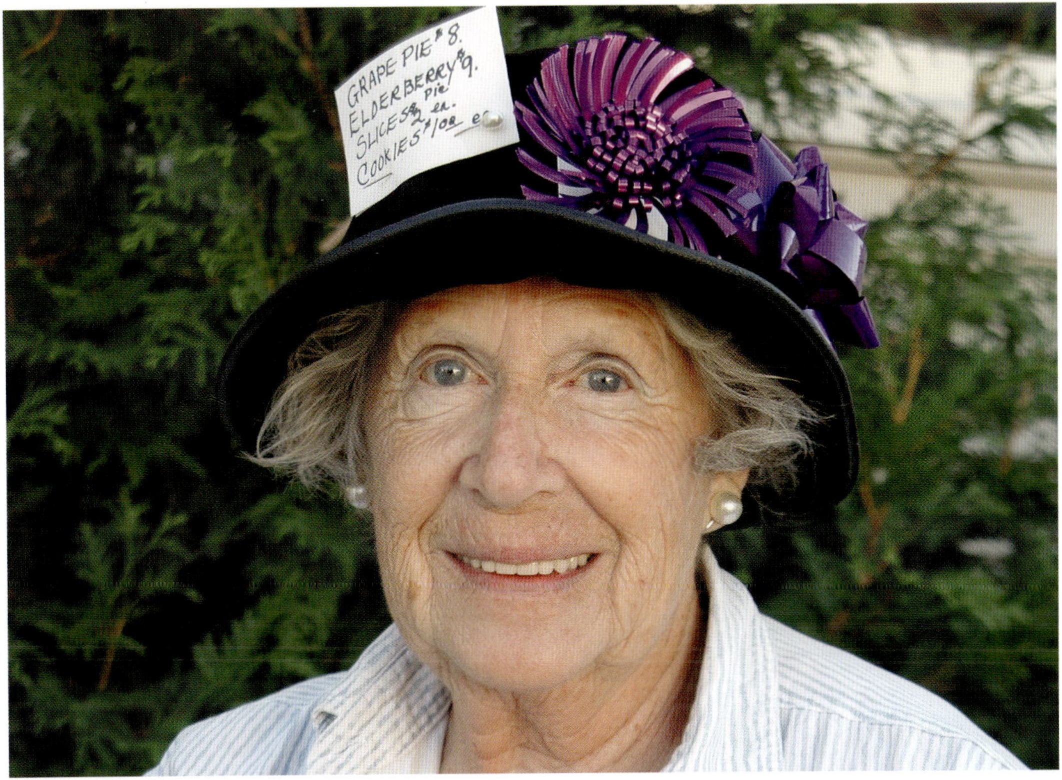

above A bakery vendor near Naples. left A pie contest at the Wayne County Fair. previous Cattail leaves and Queen Anne's lace in a roadside ditch.

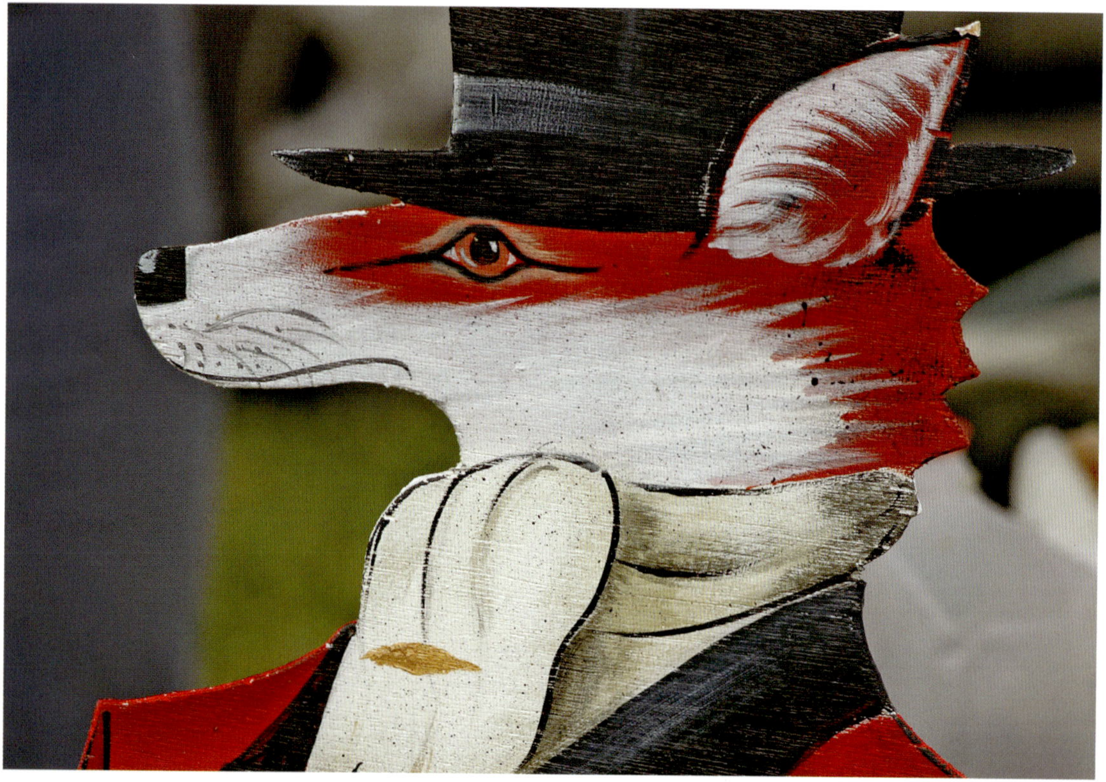

above, right, and next An annual event since 1928, the Genesee Valley Hunt races near Geneseo feature flat races and steeple chases, a dog jumping contest, and a tailgate competition.

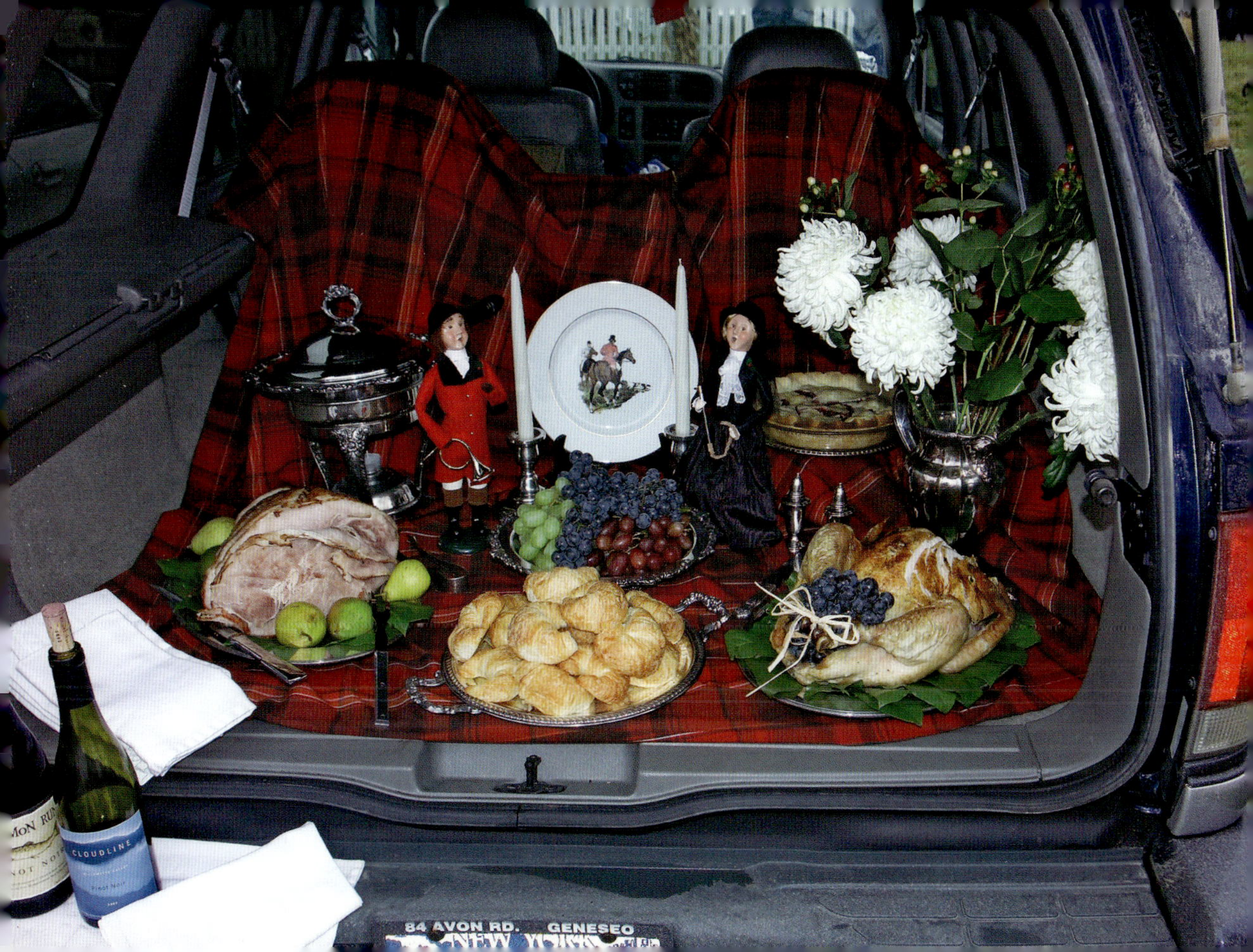
CLOUDLINE
Pinot Noir
84 AVON RD.
GENESEO

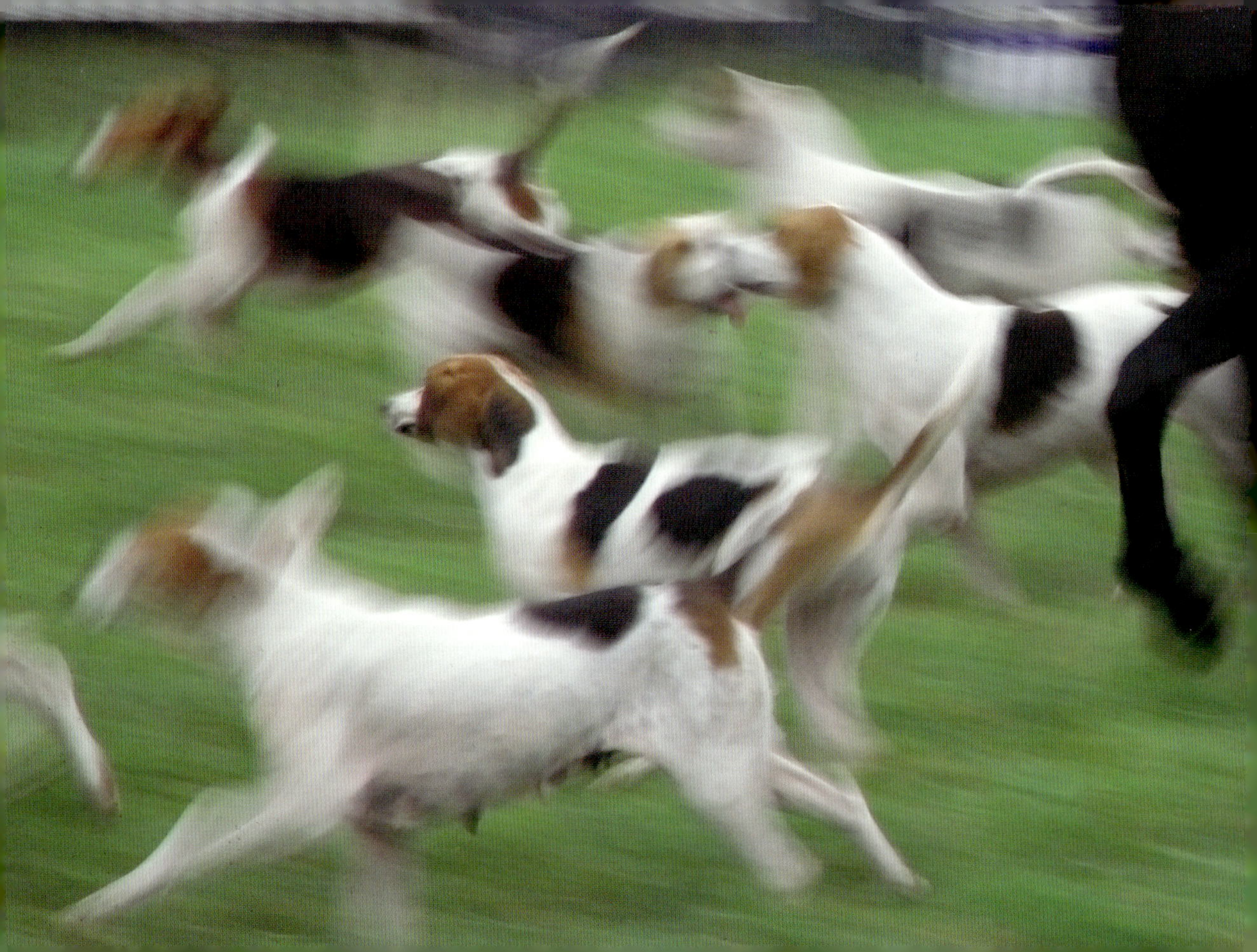

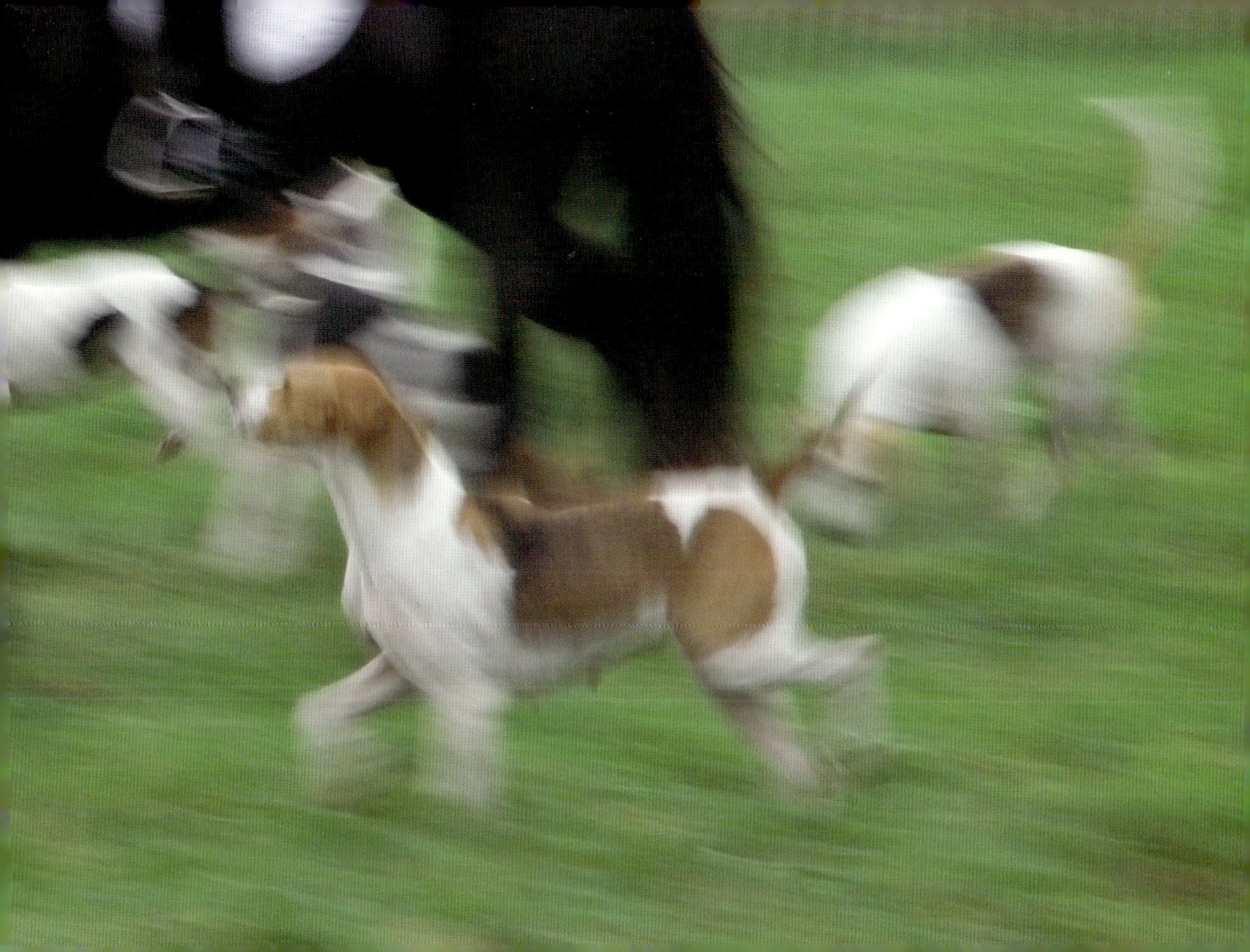

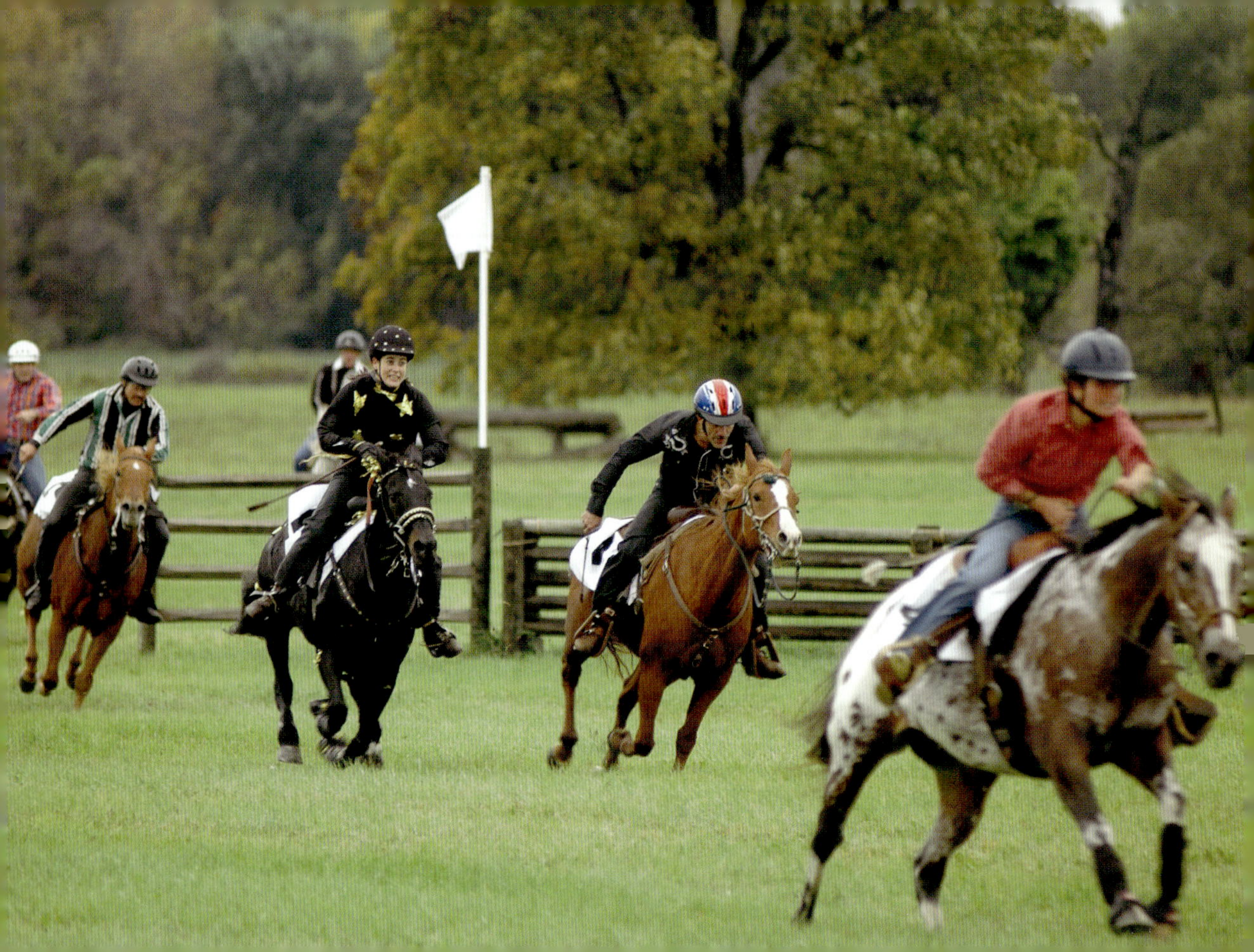

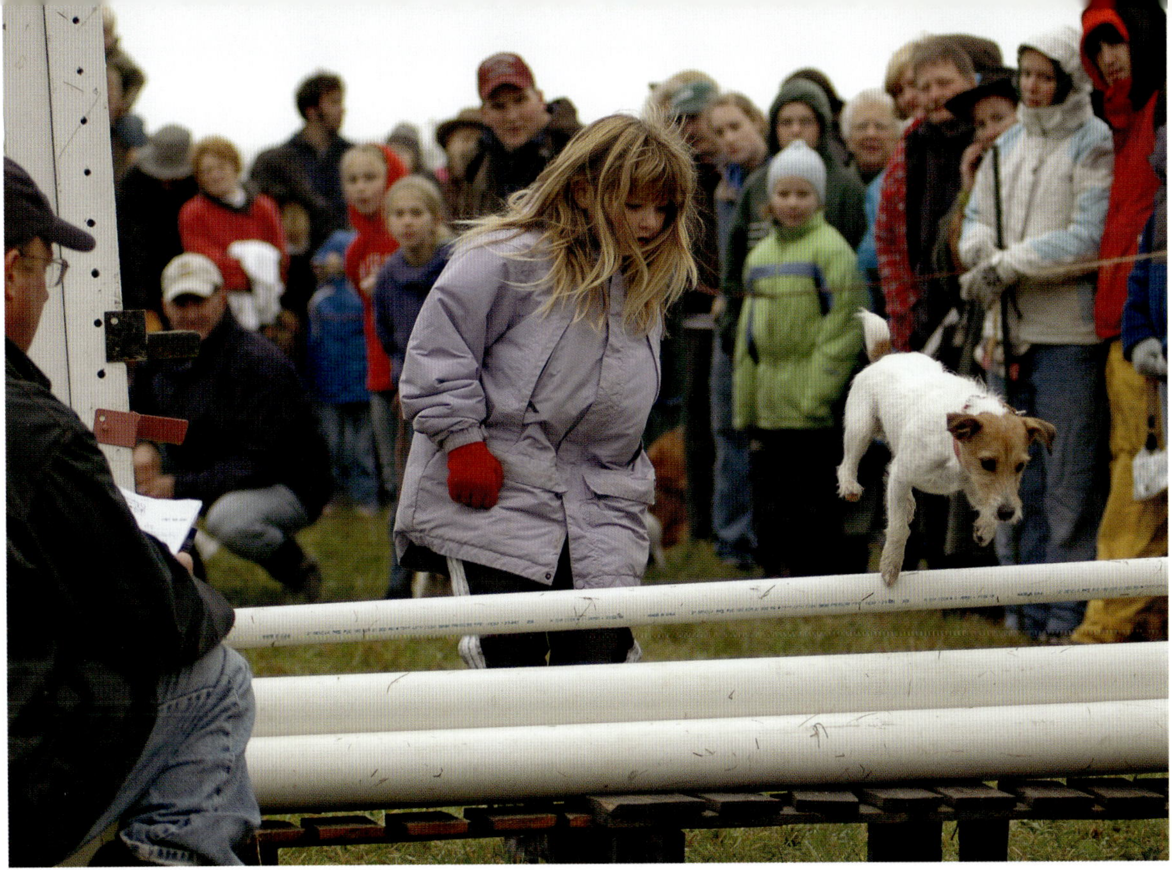

above and left Genesee Valley Hunt events. next The pleasing facades of Geneva include the Smith Opera House on the right.

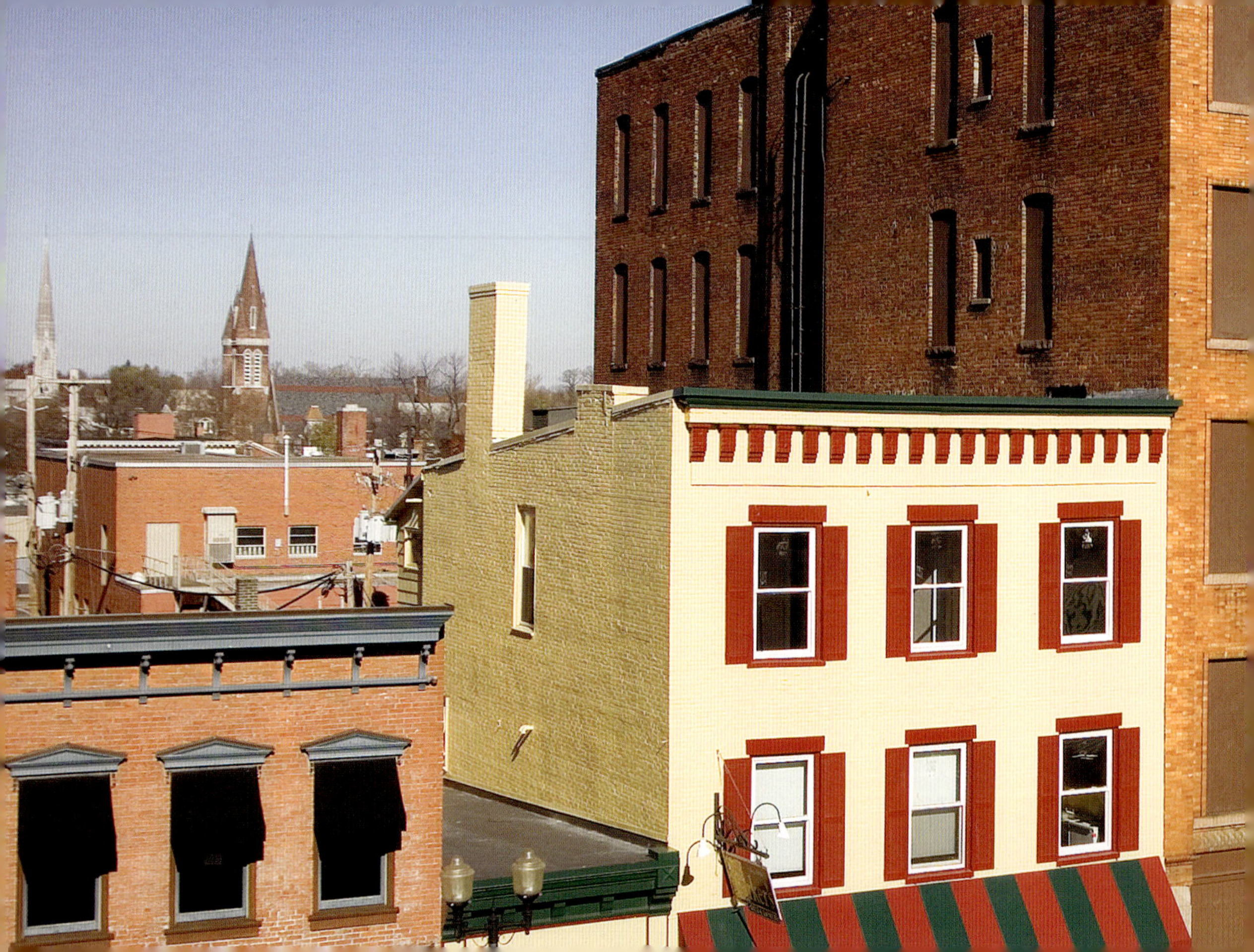

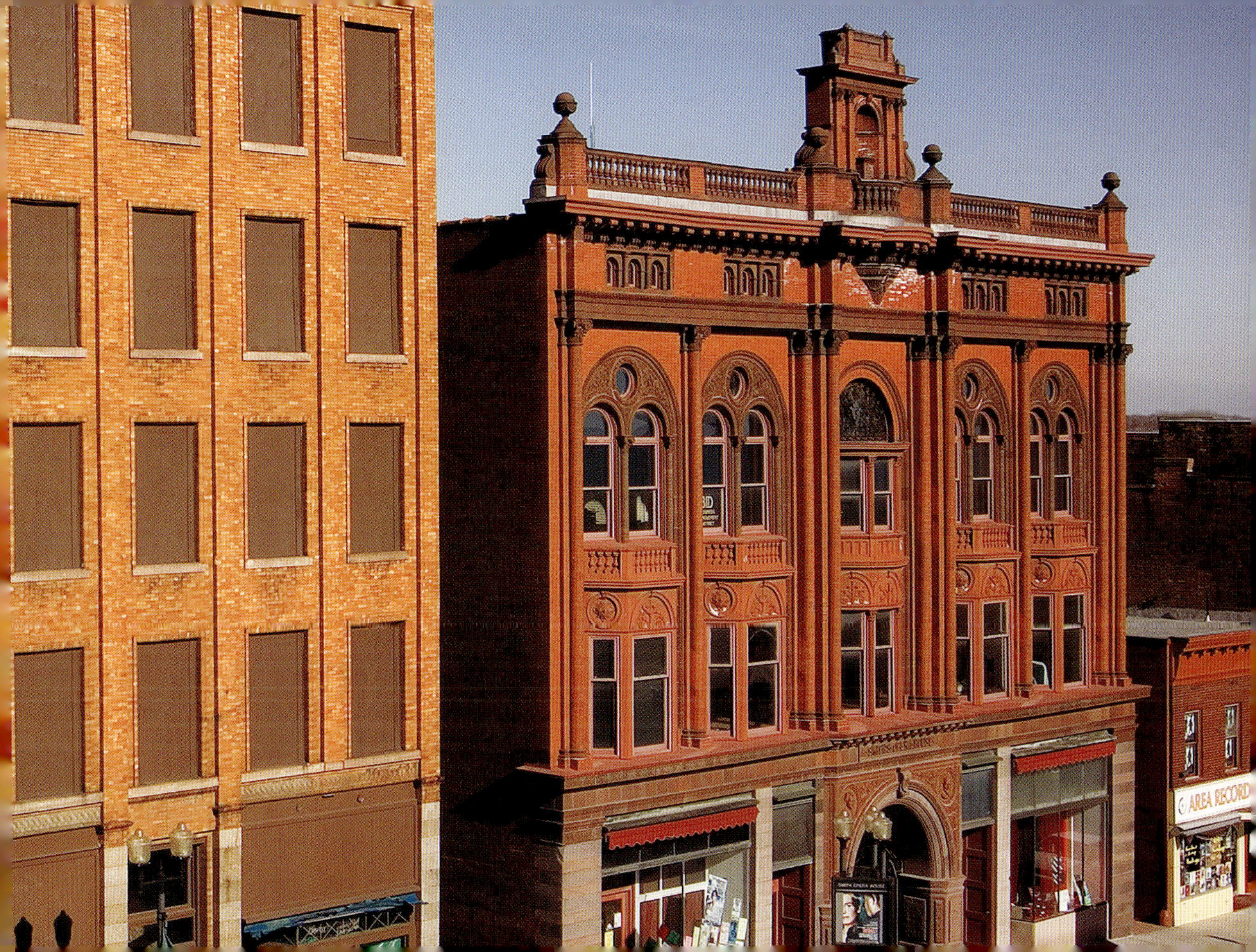
AREA RECORD

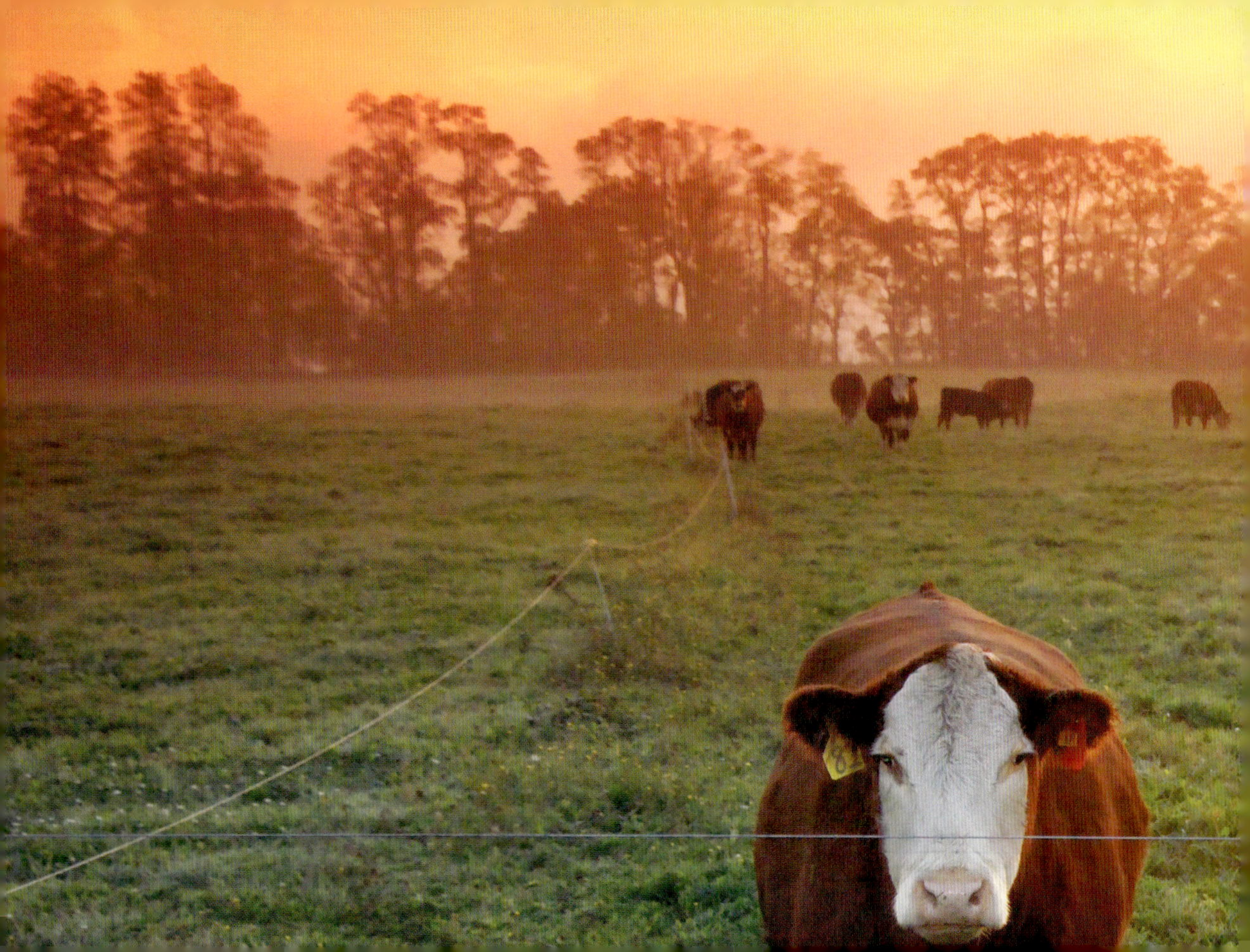

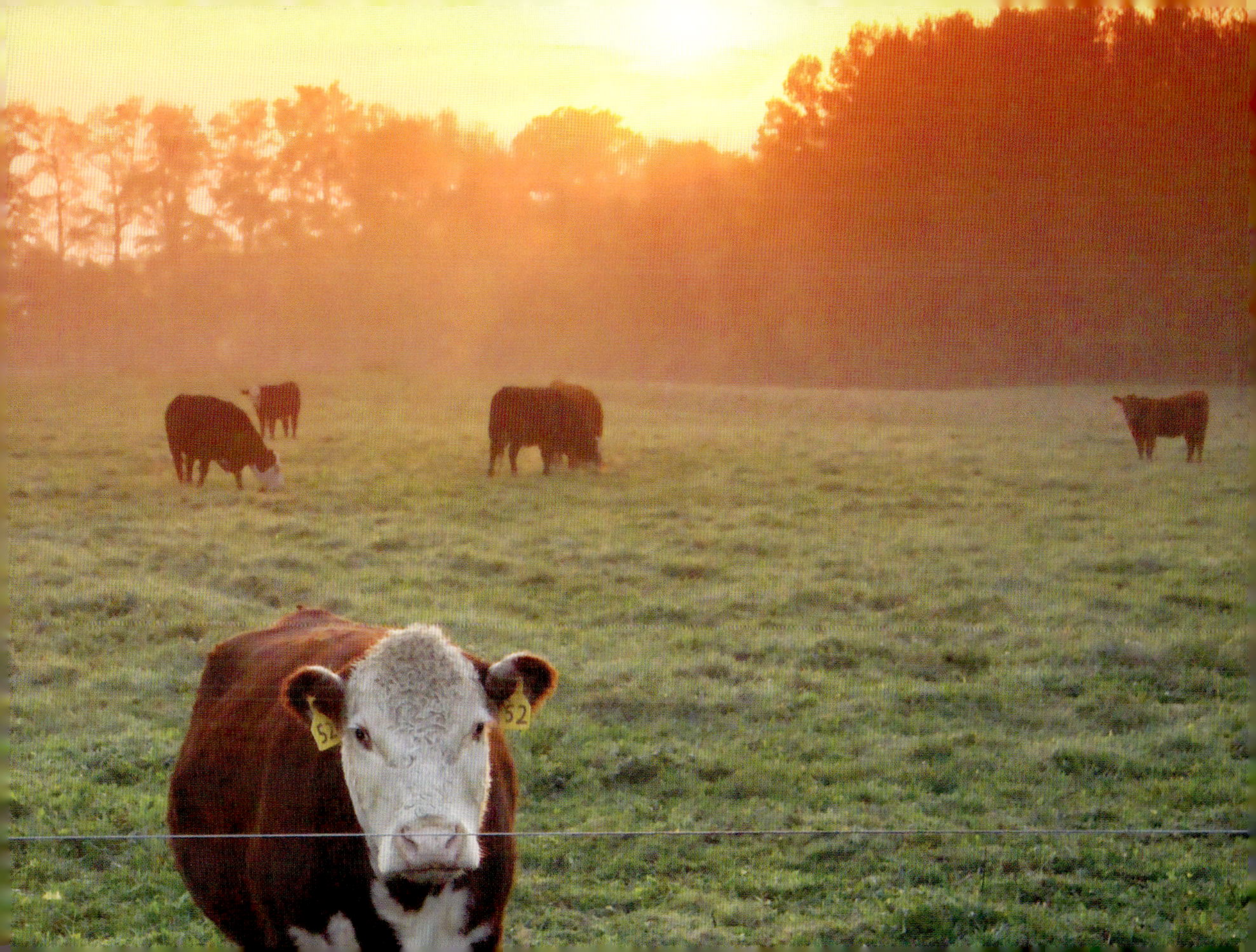
52

right and next The air thunders with Mustangs, Fokkers, Hurricanes, Spitfires and other warbirds at the Geneseo Airshow. previous Cattle are an important part of the Finger Lakes economy.

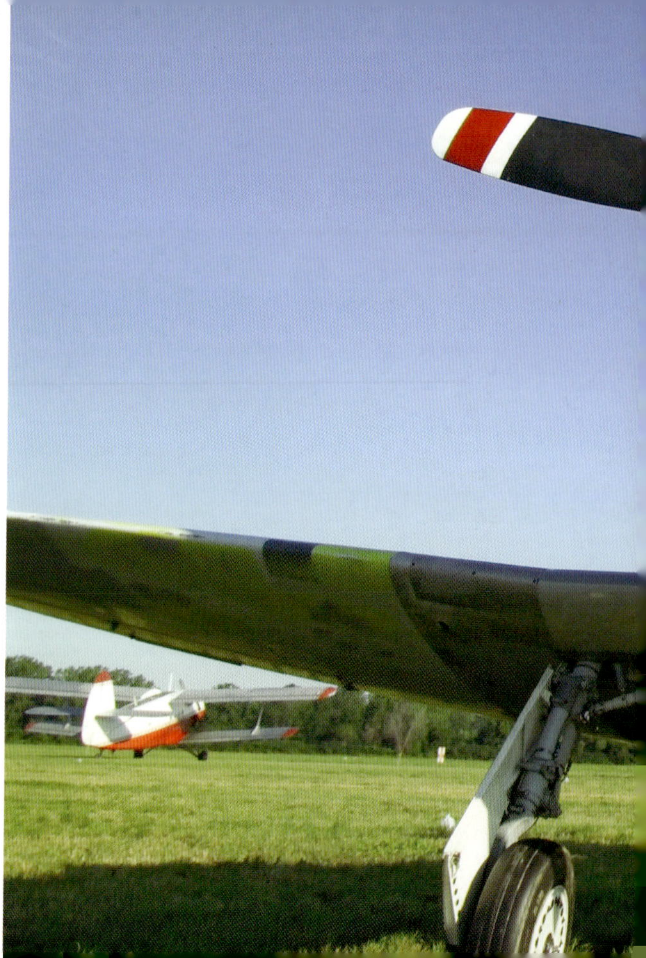

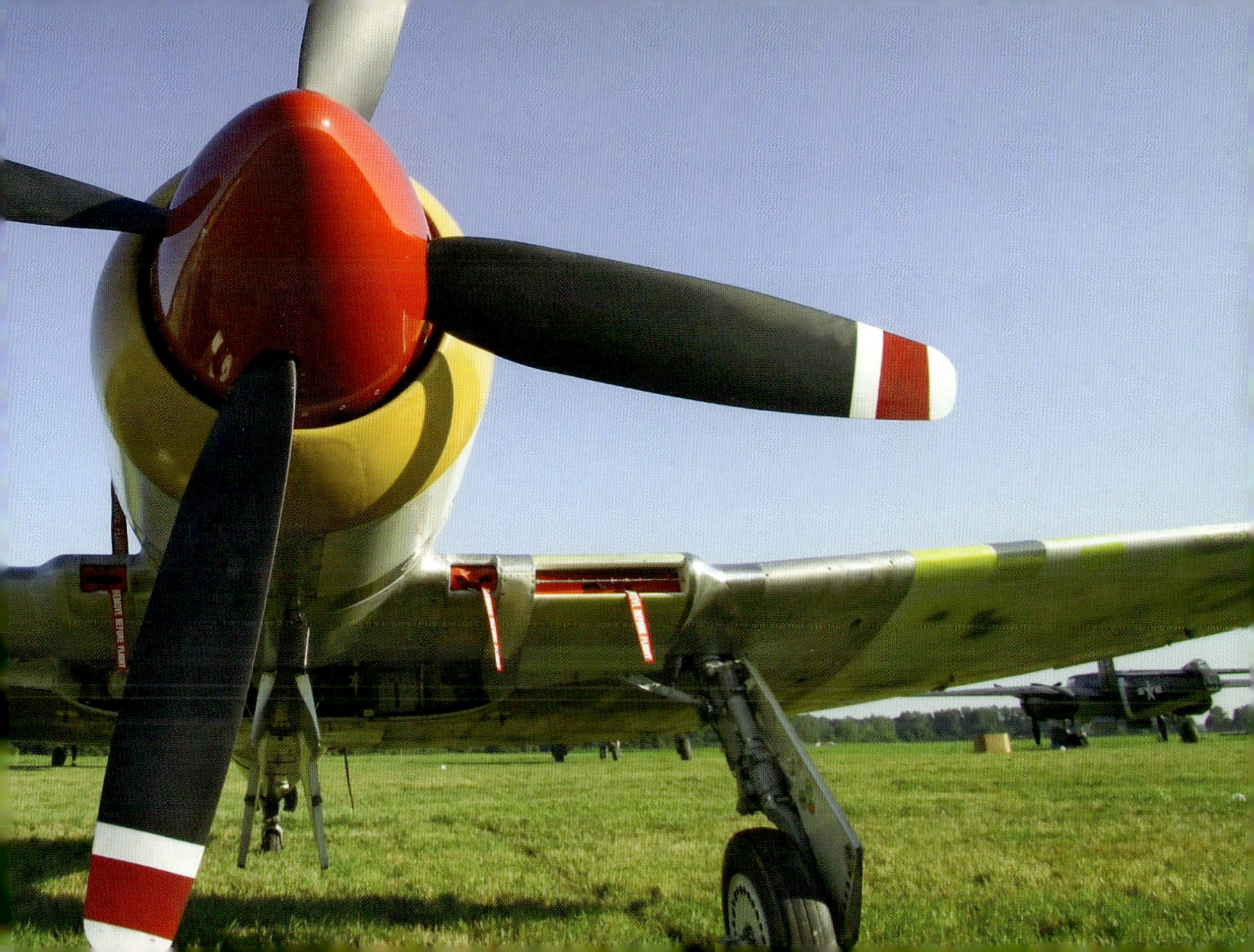

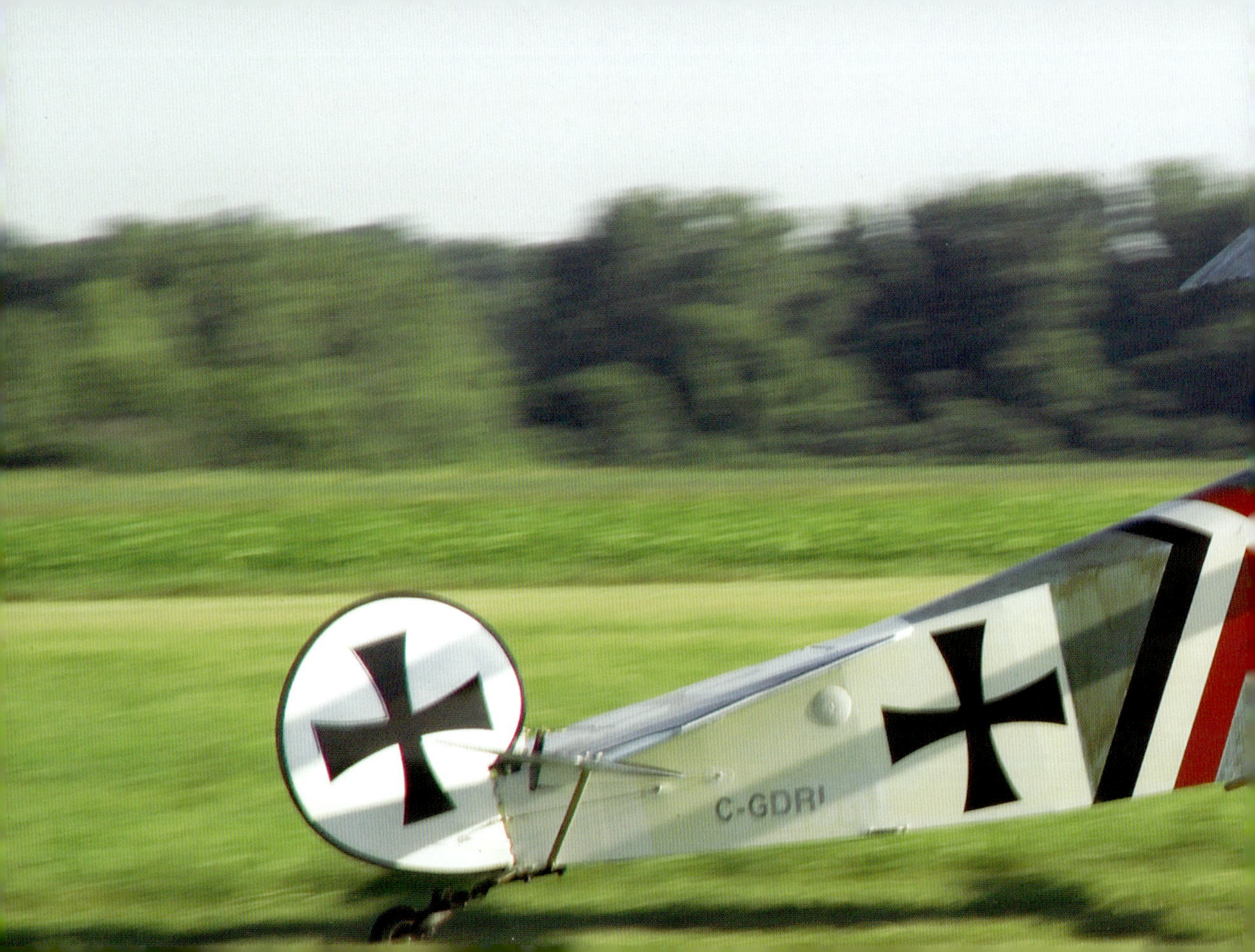
C-GDRI

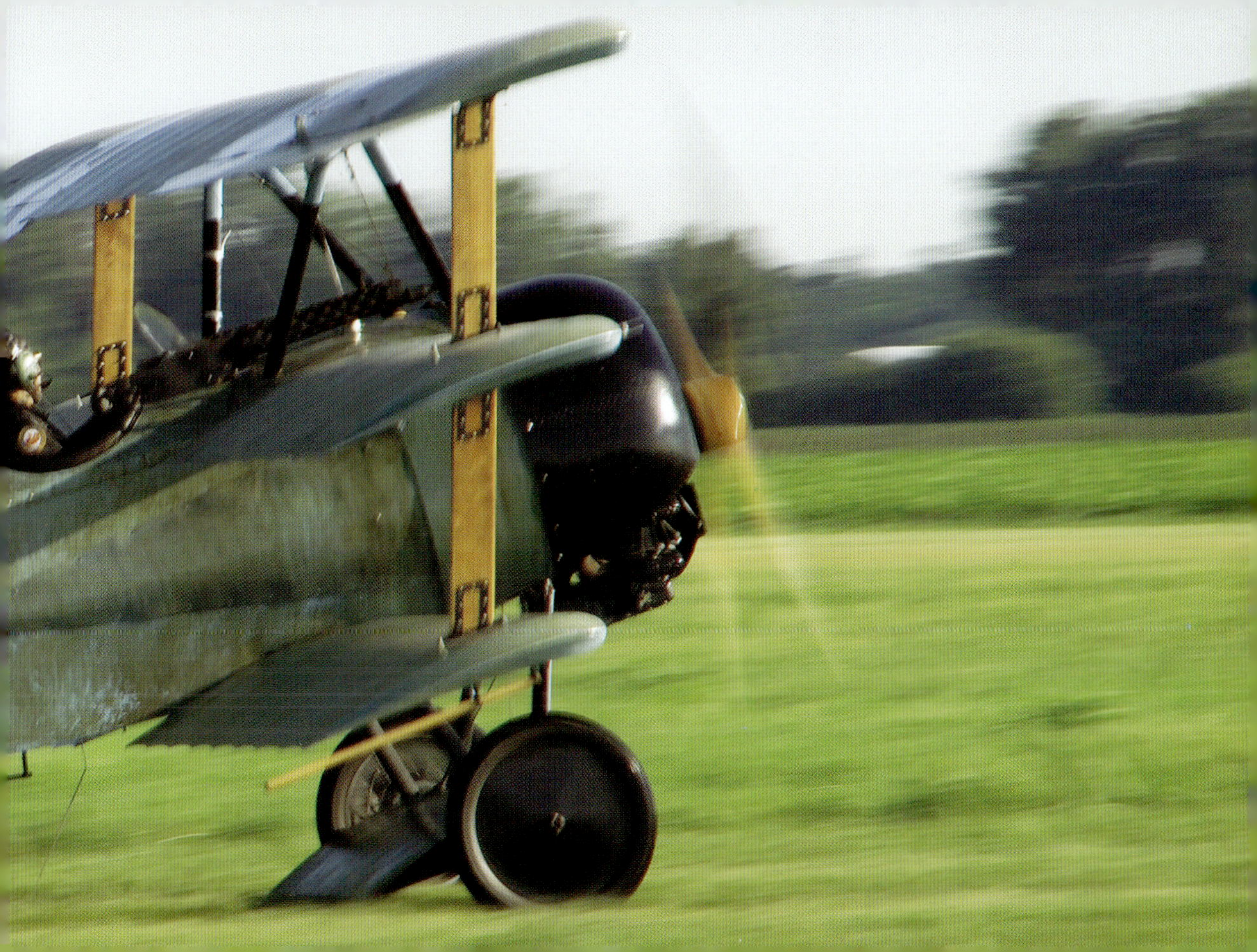

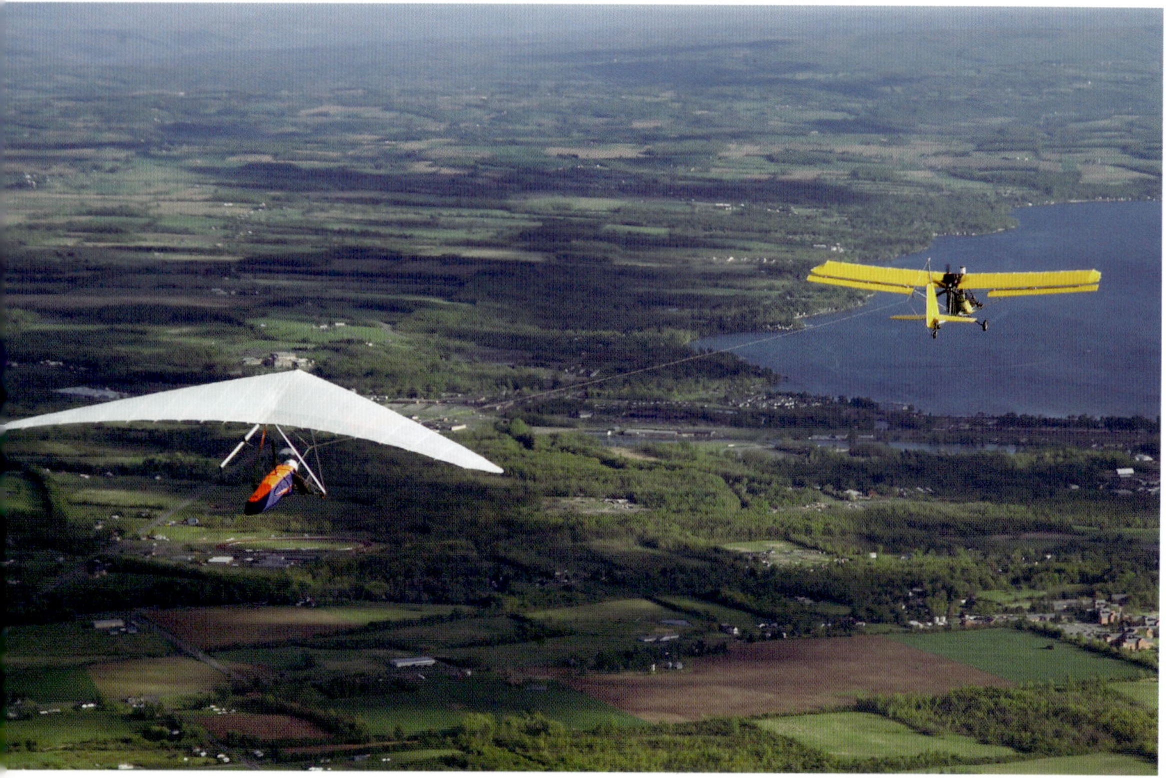

above and right Planes out of Finger Lakes Aerosports Park give hang gliders a boost, then release them onto summer thermals.

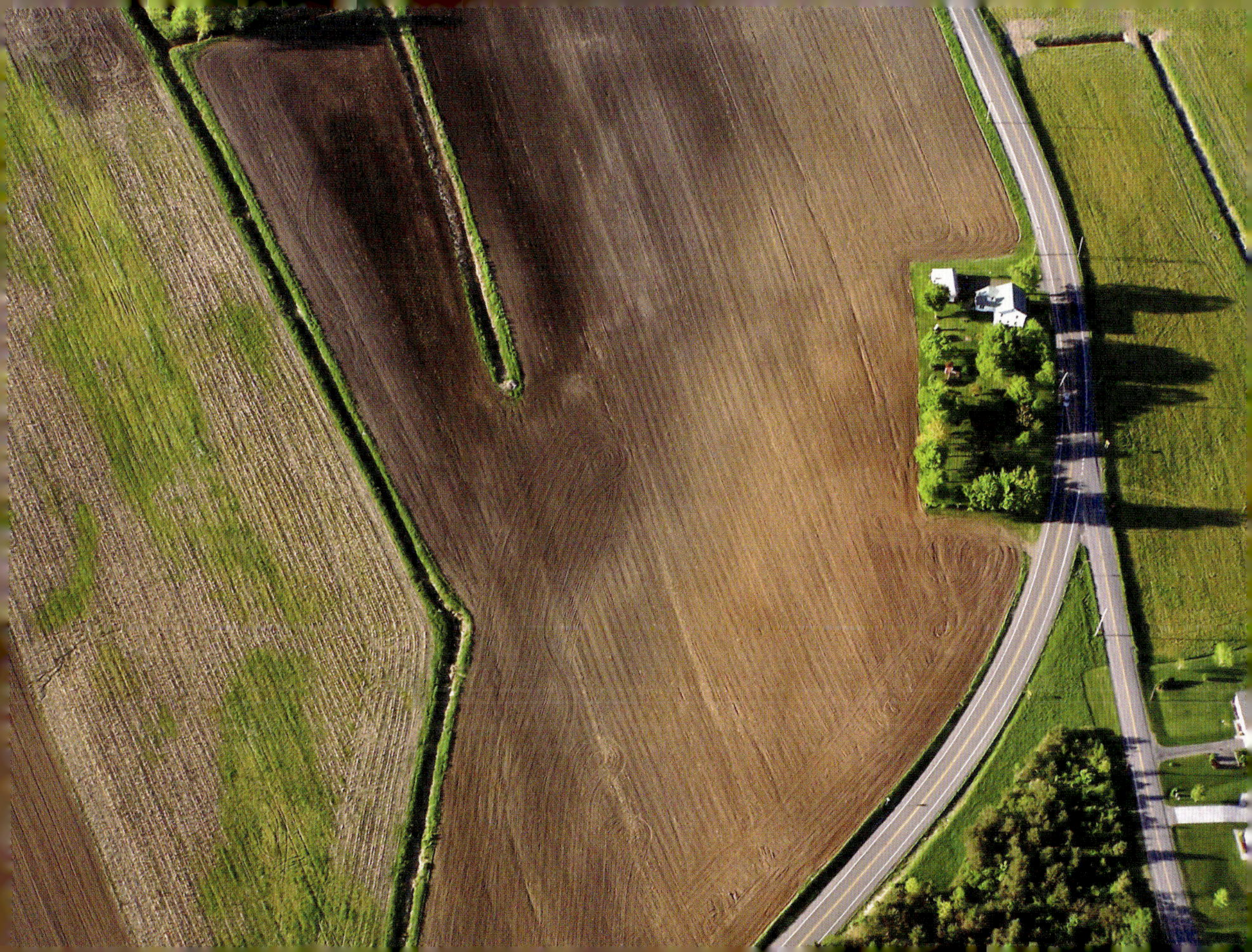

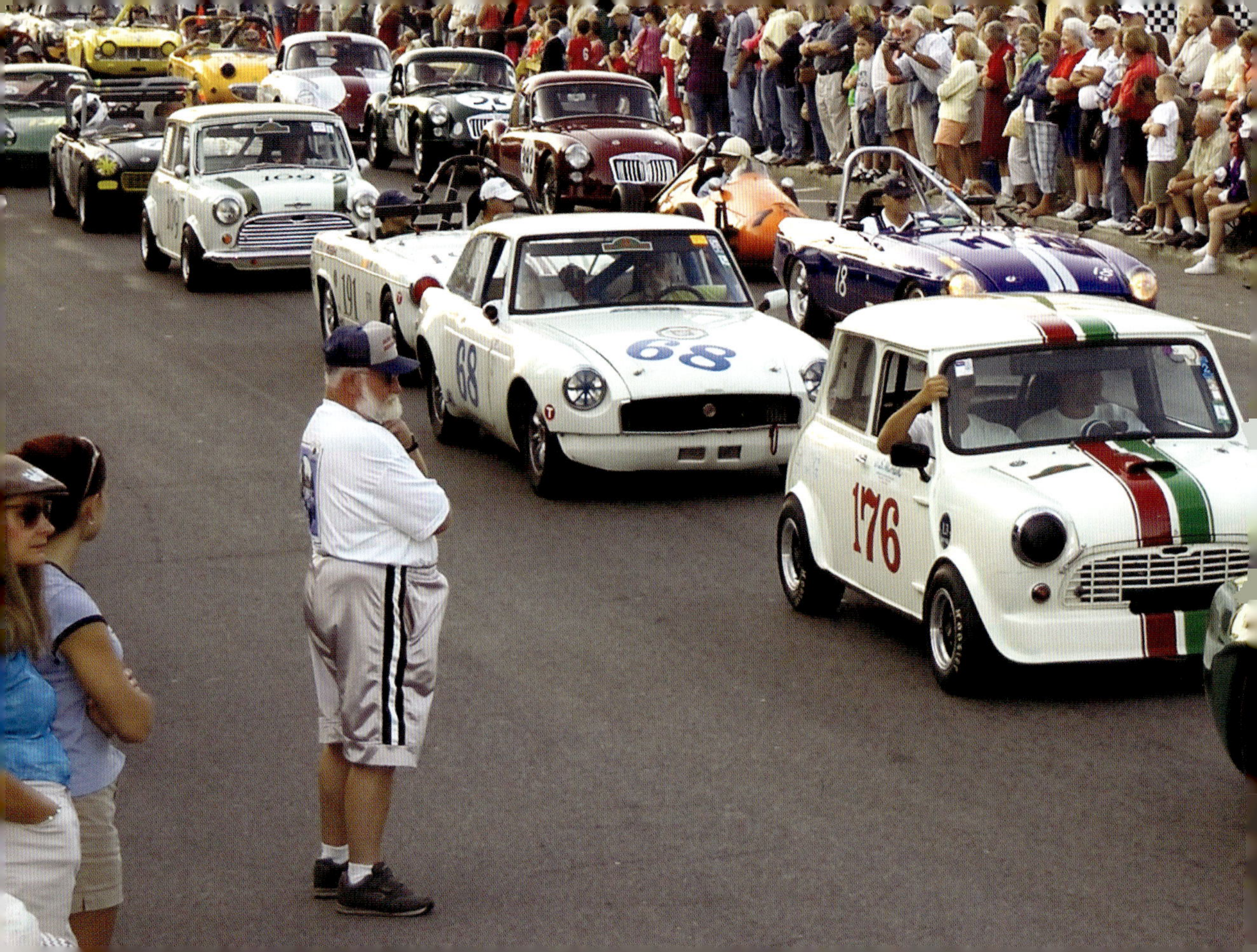
68
176
191

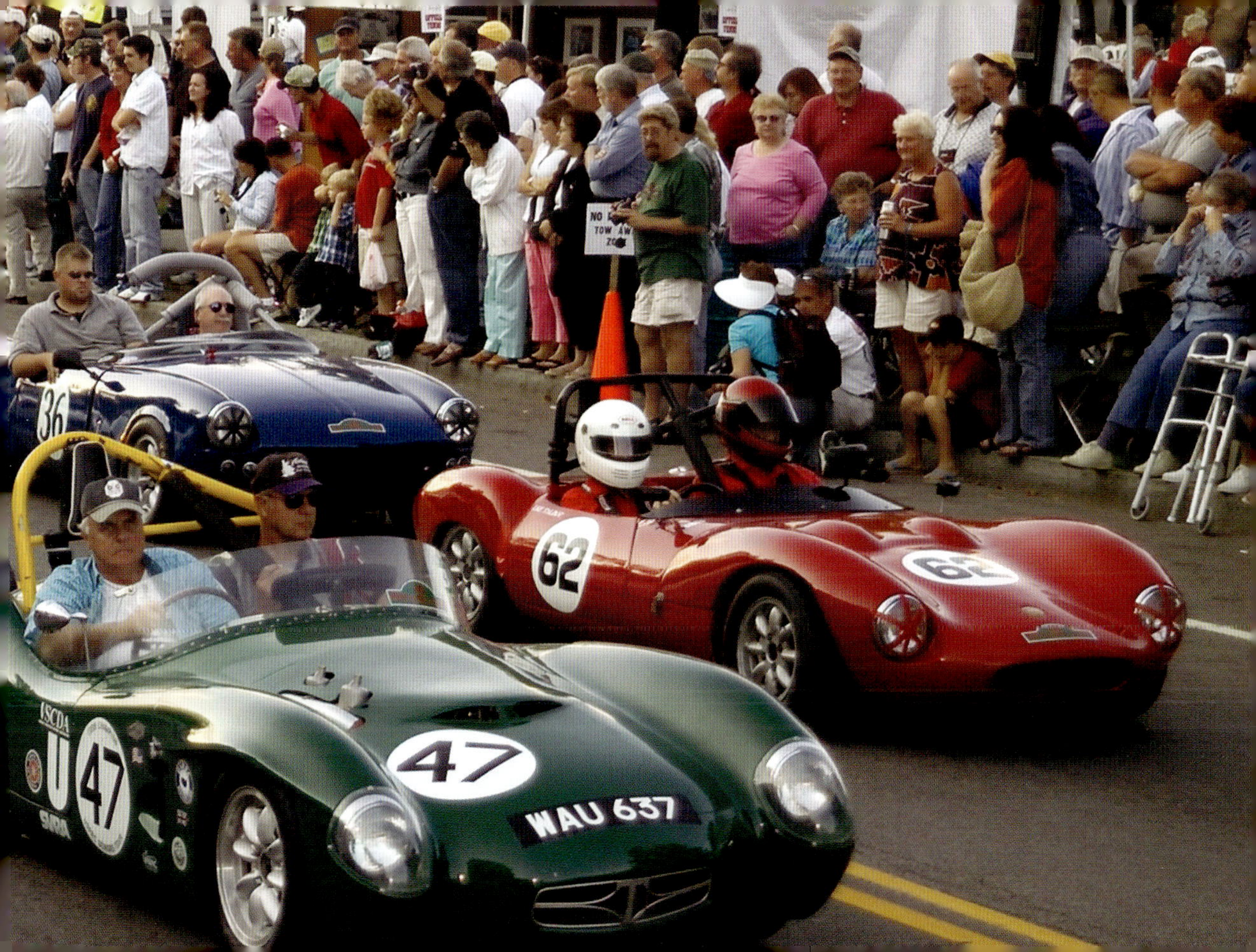
36
47
62
WAU 637

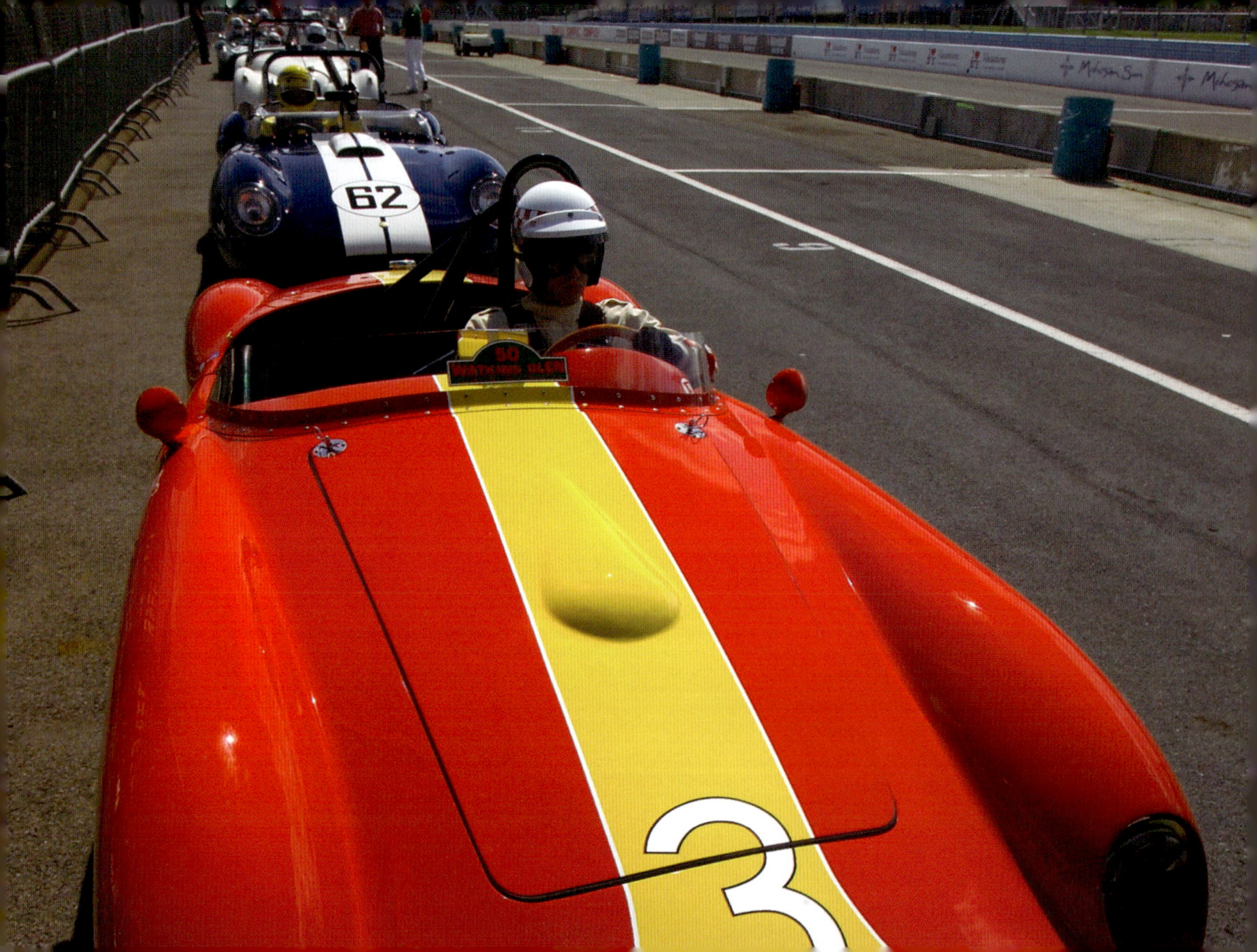
62
3

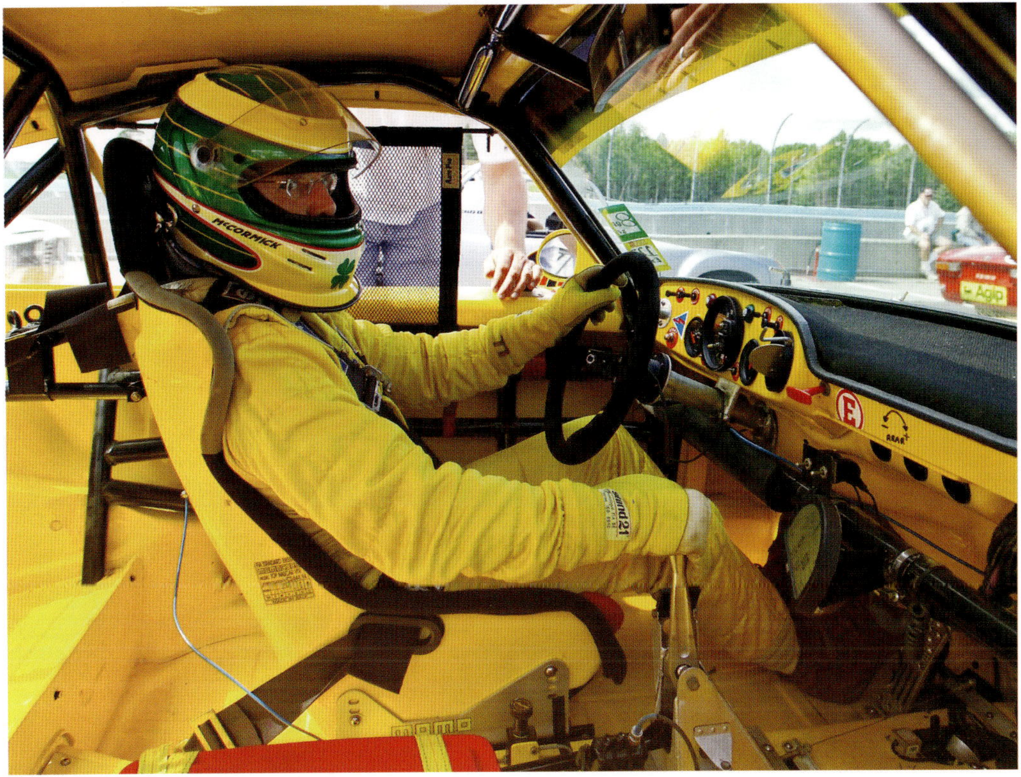

above and left The Watkins Glen International Speedway hosts NASCAR and SCCA races throughout the summer. previous Vintage race cars parade through Watkins Glen as part of the anniversary festivities of the Zippo U.S. Vintage Grand Prix. next two If it floats it can join the cardboard boat race at Seneca Falls.

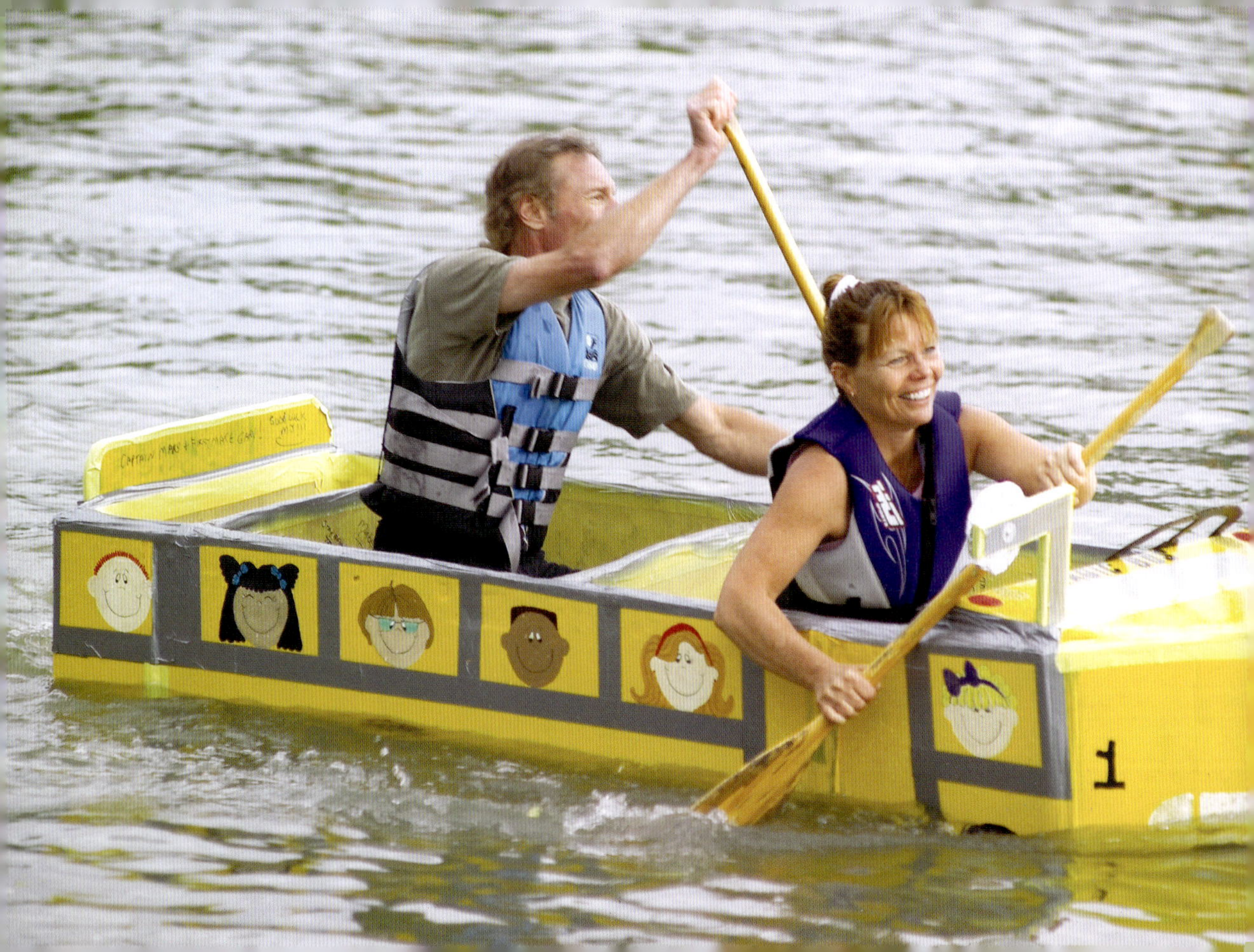
1

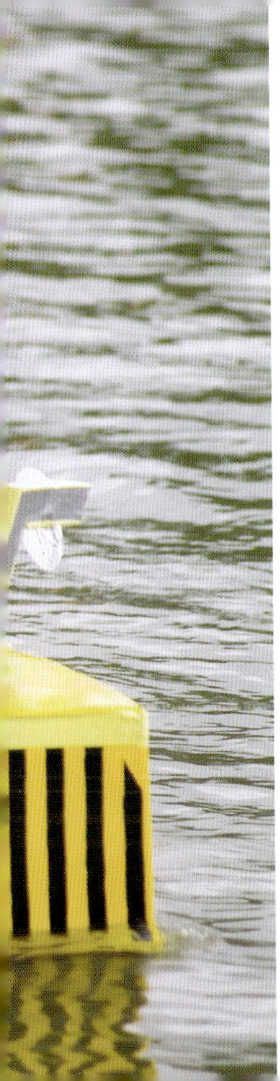

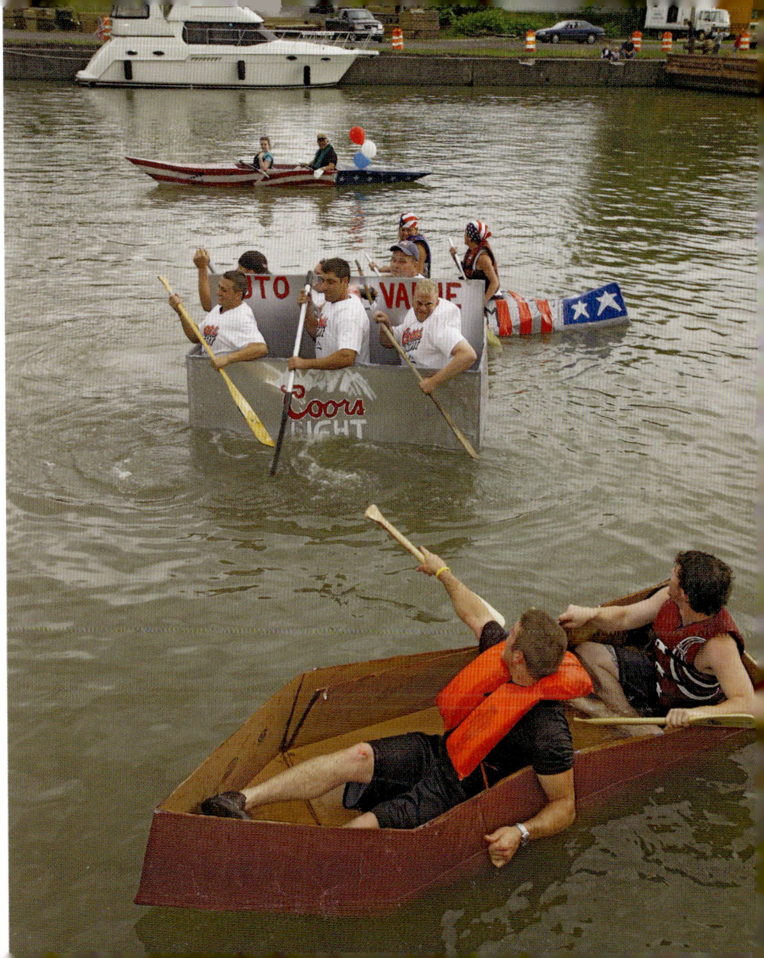
Coors

right On the northern tip of Skaneateles Lake, the upscale town of Skaneateles is a favorite tourist destination.
next Lamoreaux Landing, on the east shore of Seneca Lake, is one of over 100 wineries in the Finger Lakes.

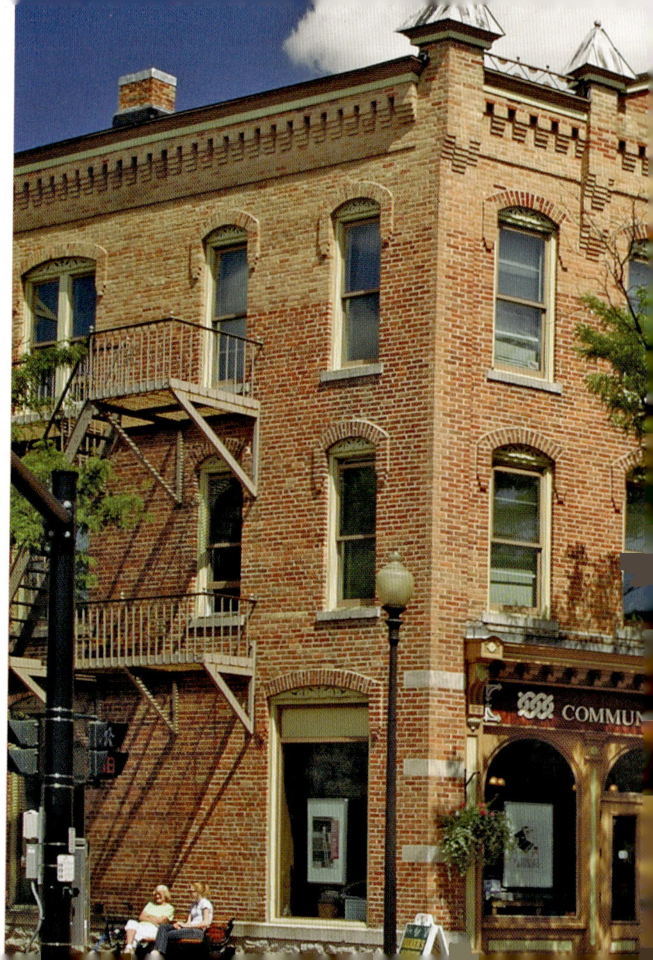

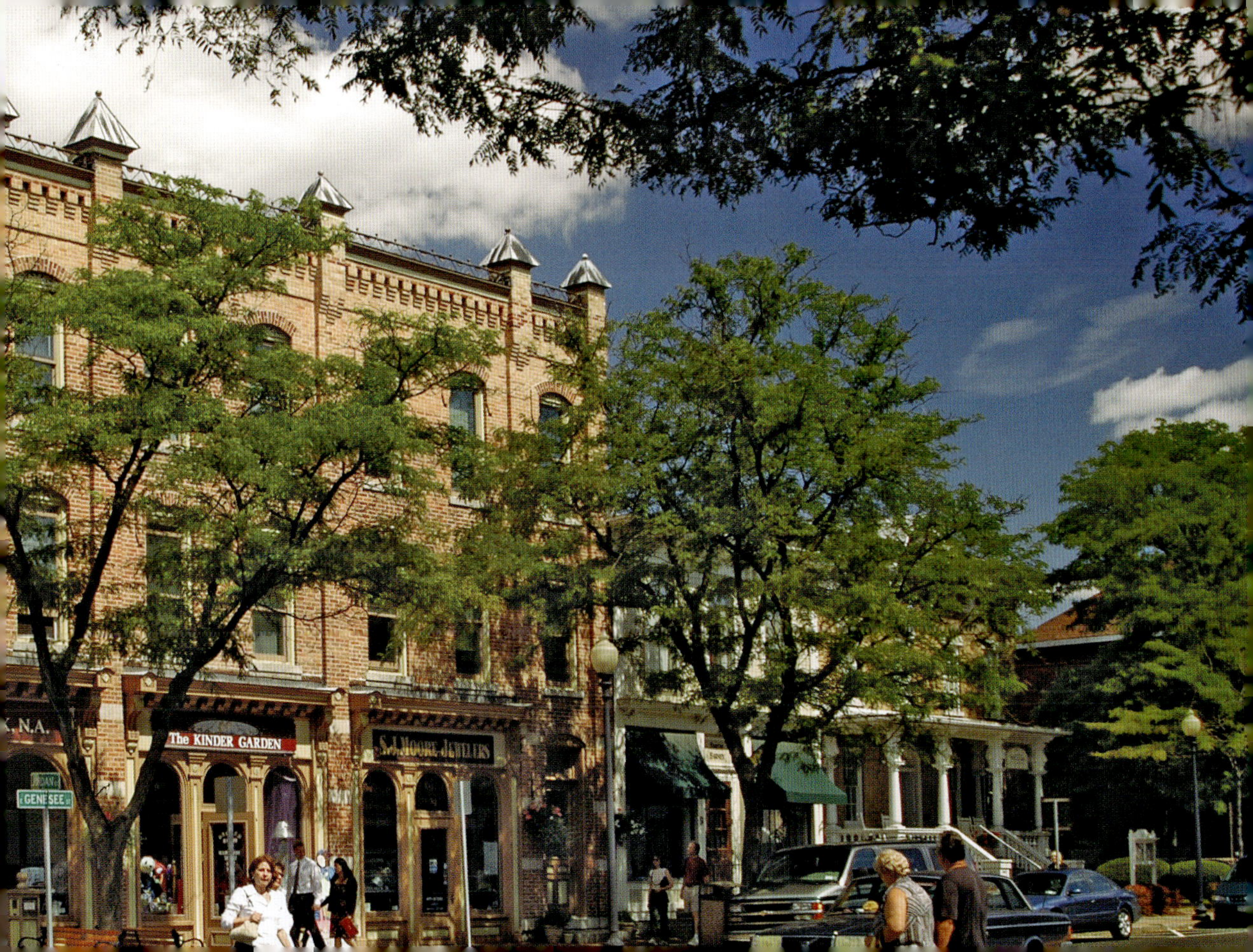
N.A.
The KINDER GARDEN
GENESEE

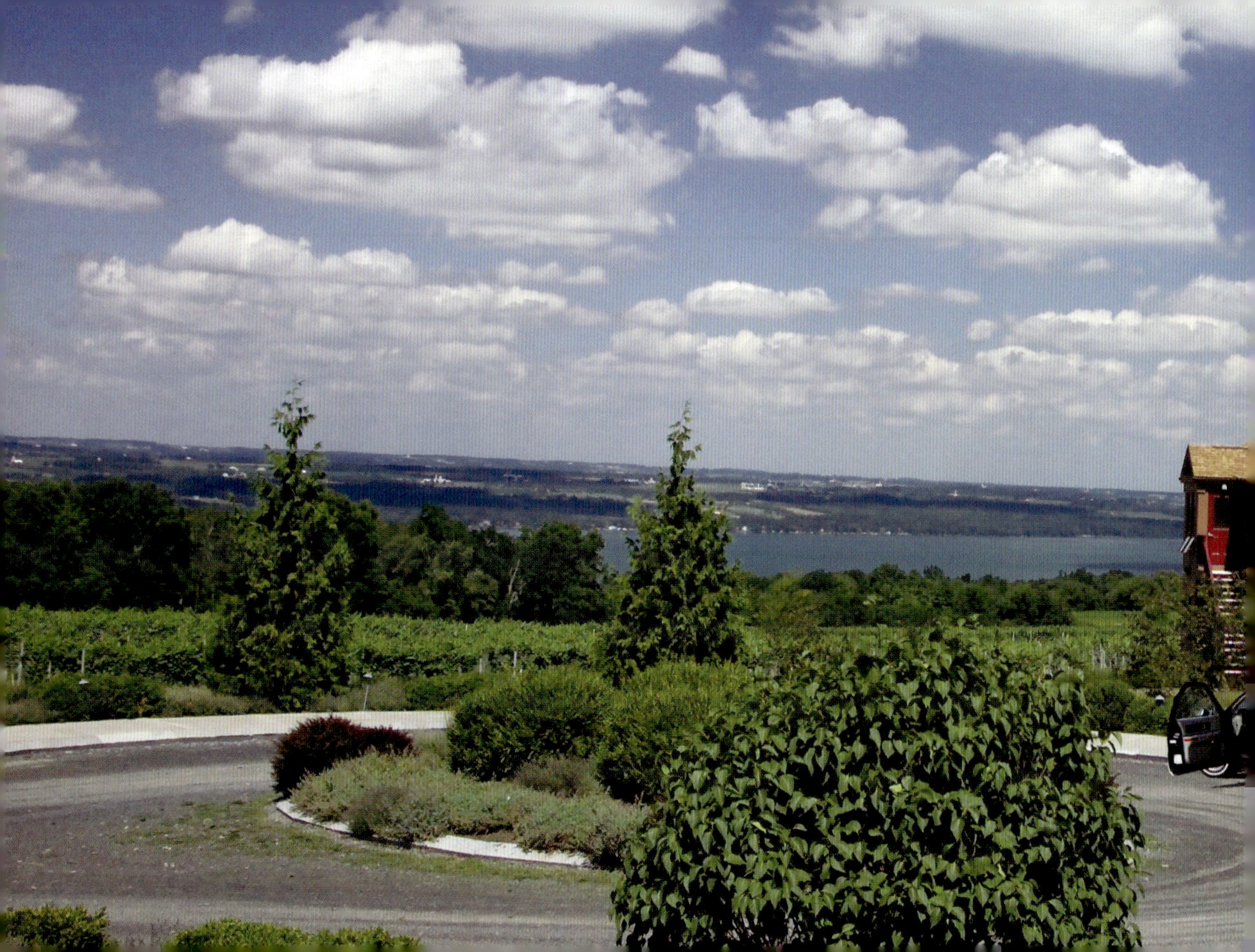

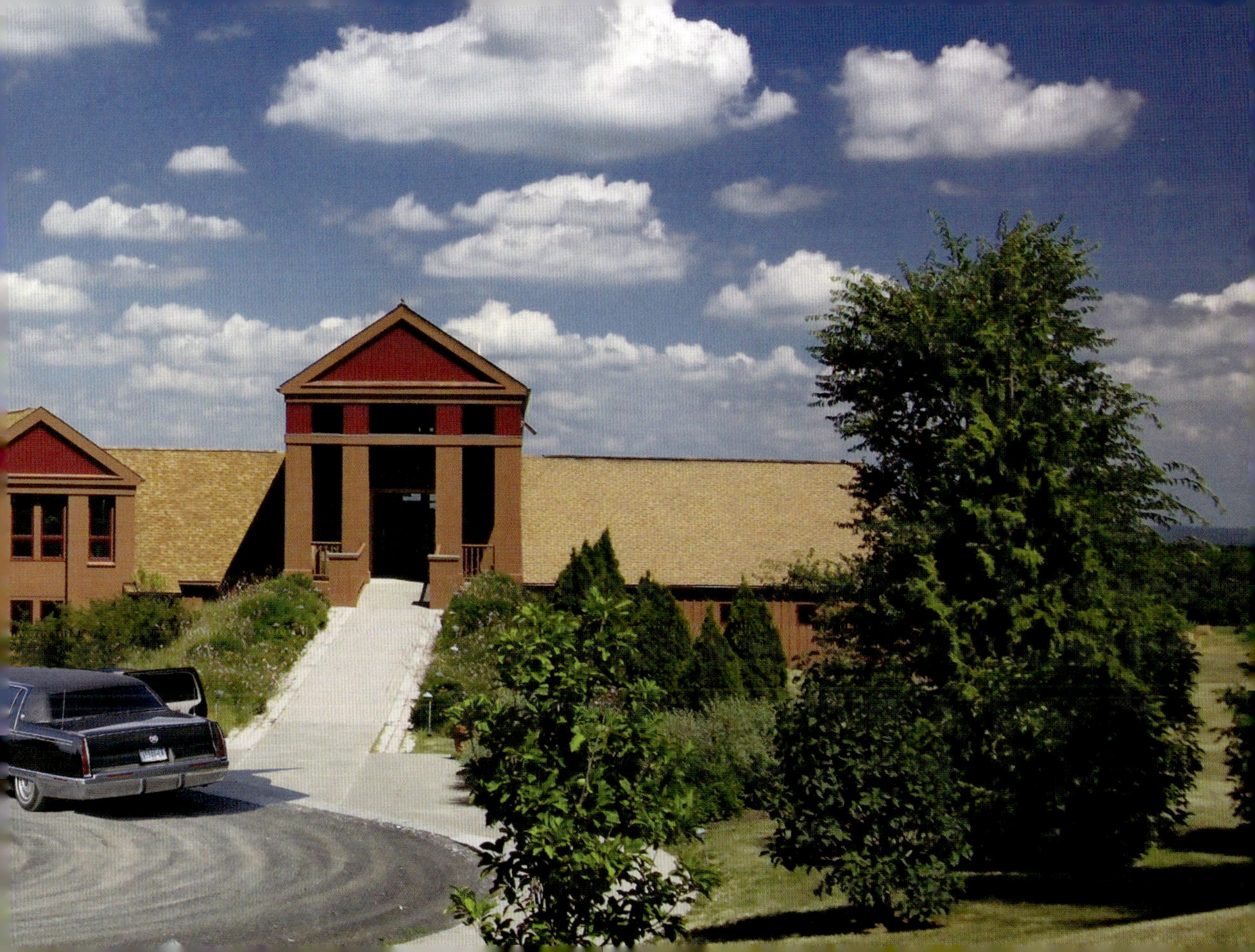

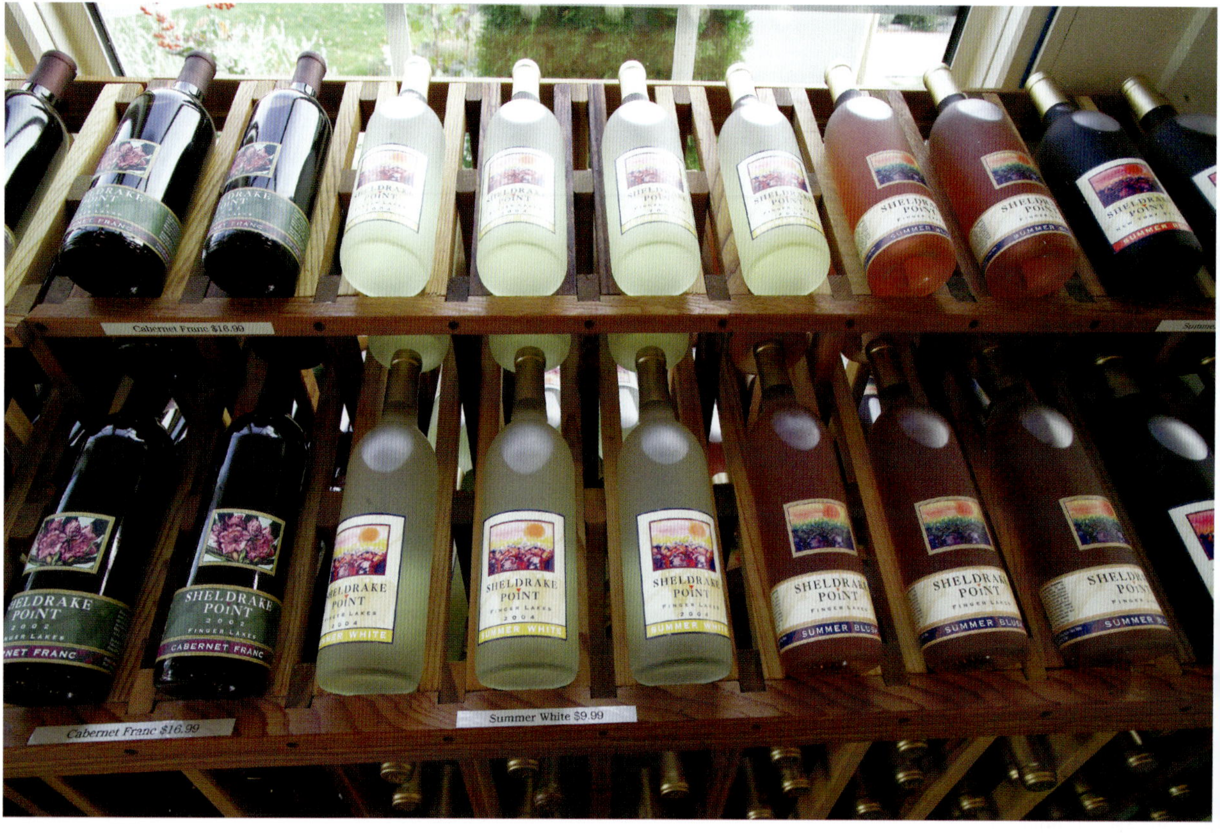
Cabernet Franc $16.99
SHELDRAKE POINT
2002
FINGER LAKES
CABERNET FRANC
SHELDRAKE POINT
FINGER LAKES
2004
SUMMER WHITE
Summer White $9.99
Cabernet Franc $16.99

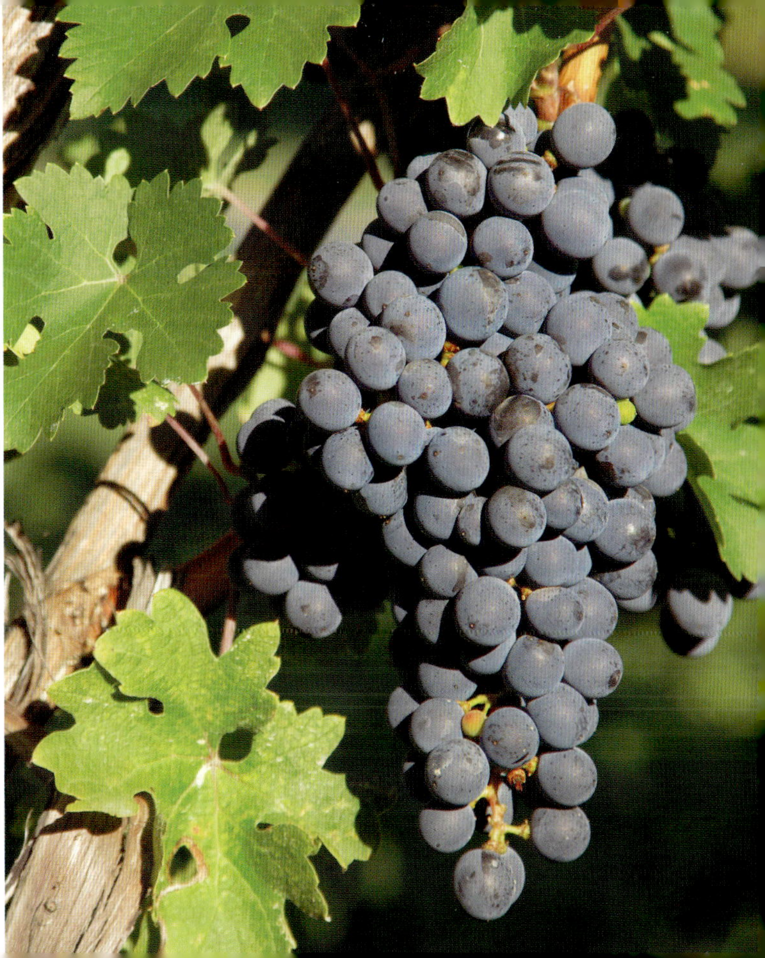

left and right In late summer, dry days and cool nights enrich the sugar content of the grapes, resulting in top quality wine. next Sixteen-mile-long Canandaigua Lake from Bare Hill where the Senecas hold a bonfire at summer's end.

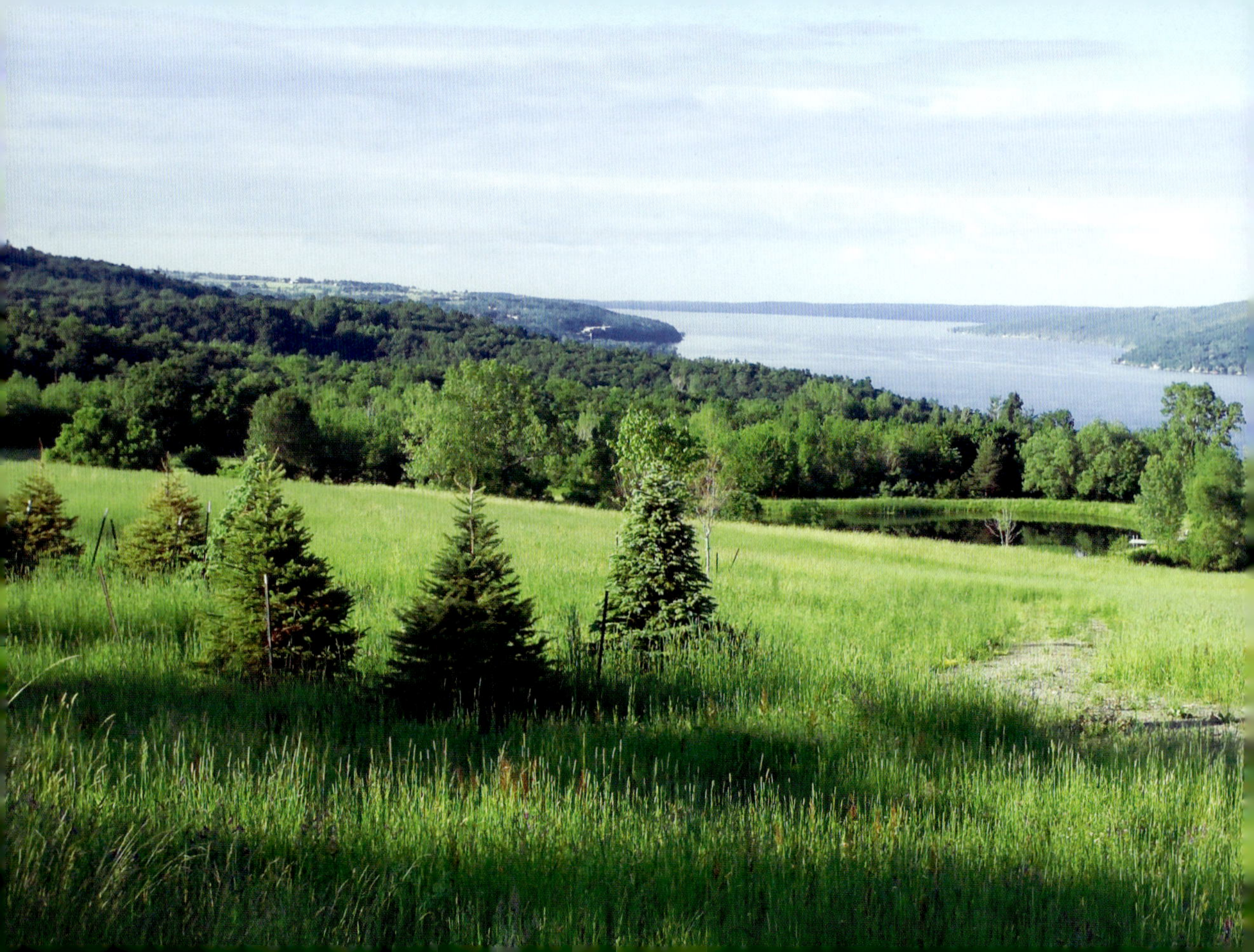

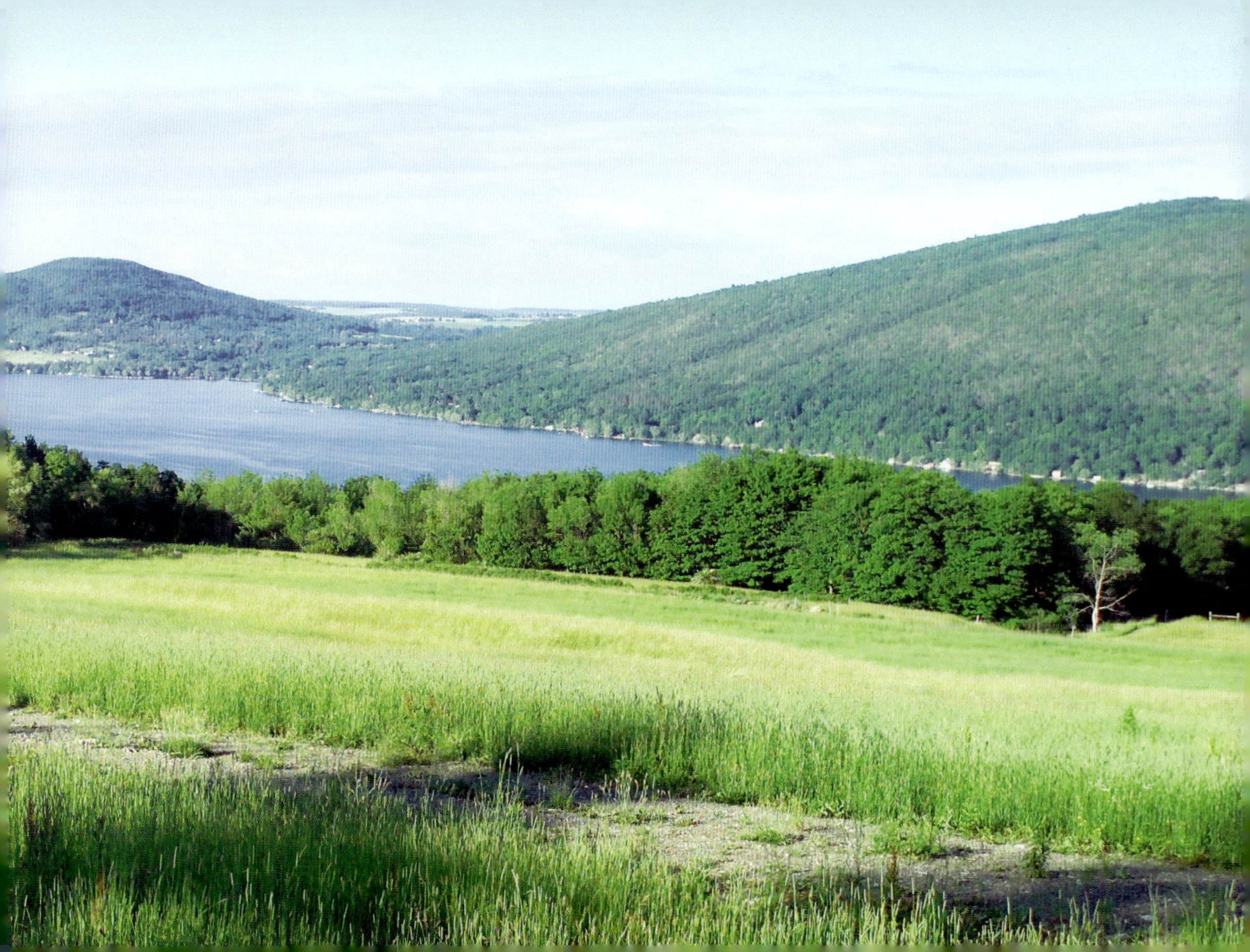

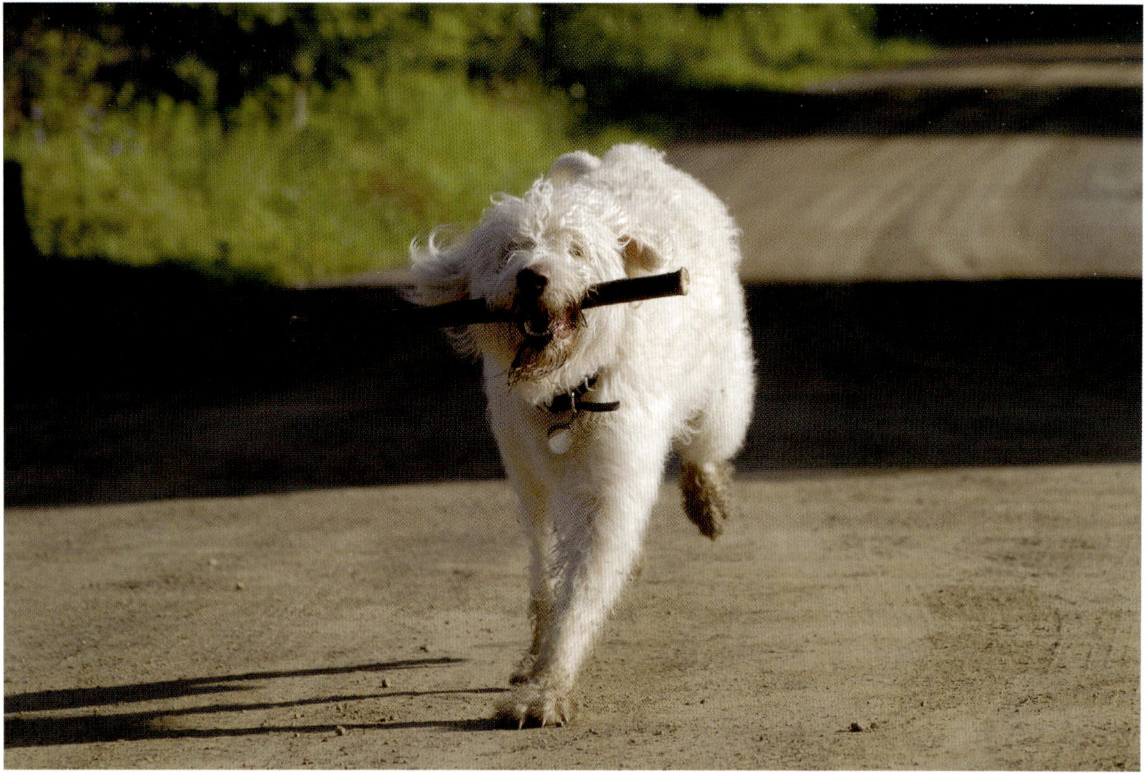

above Rufus, a rollicking labradoodle, runs on a farm road. right With no fuel-driven or electrical devices, the Mennonites live the farm life of a century ago. next A four-in-hand at the famous Walnut Hill Carriage Driving Competition in Pittsford.

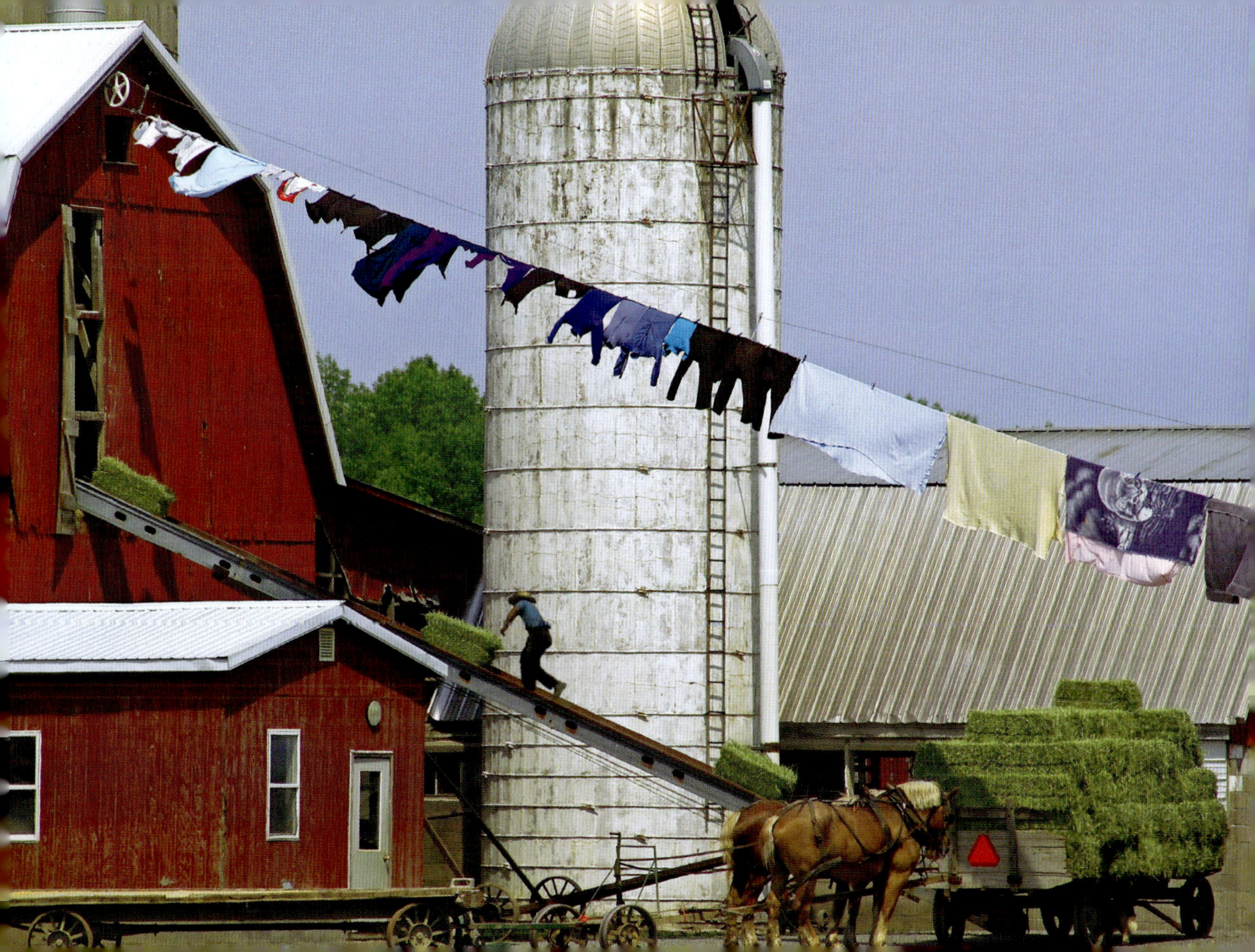

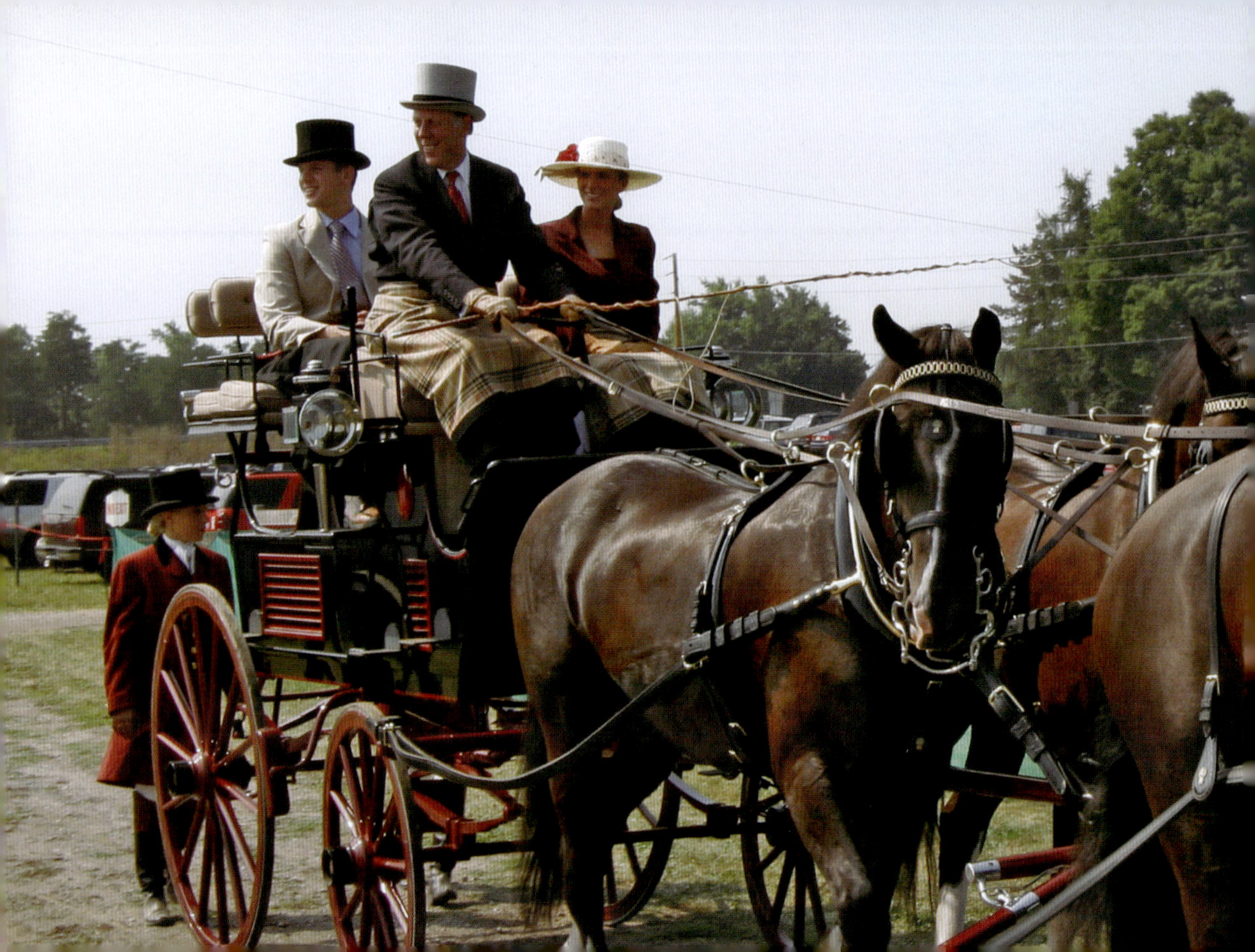

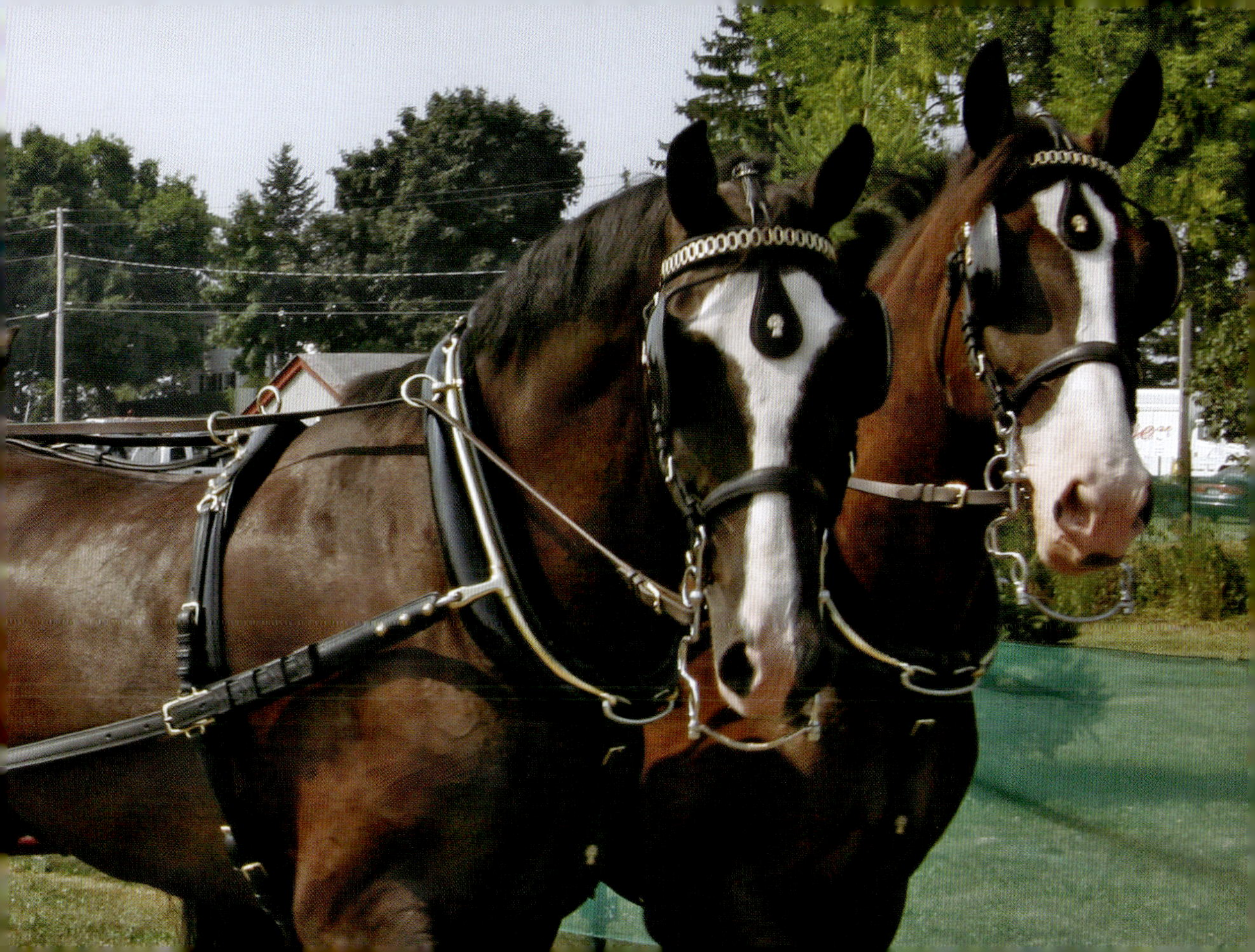

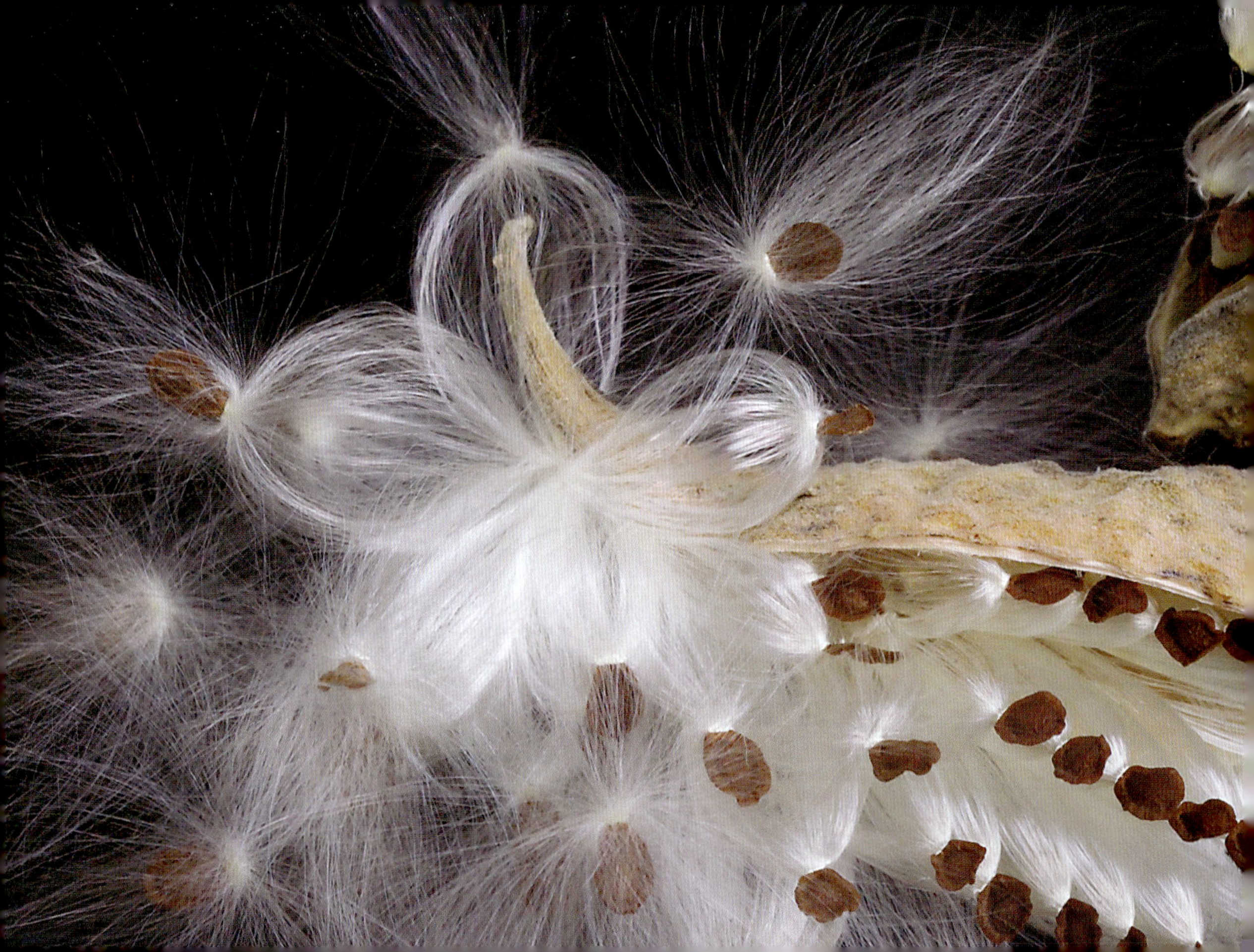

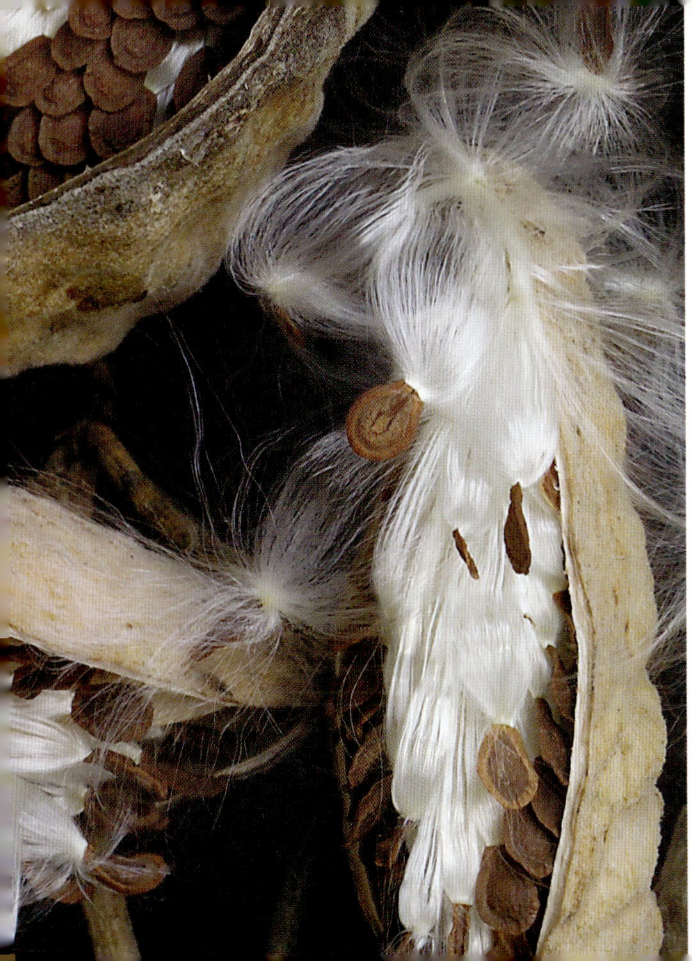

left Milkweed in late summer.

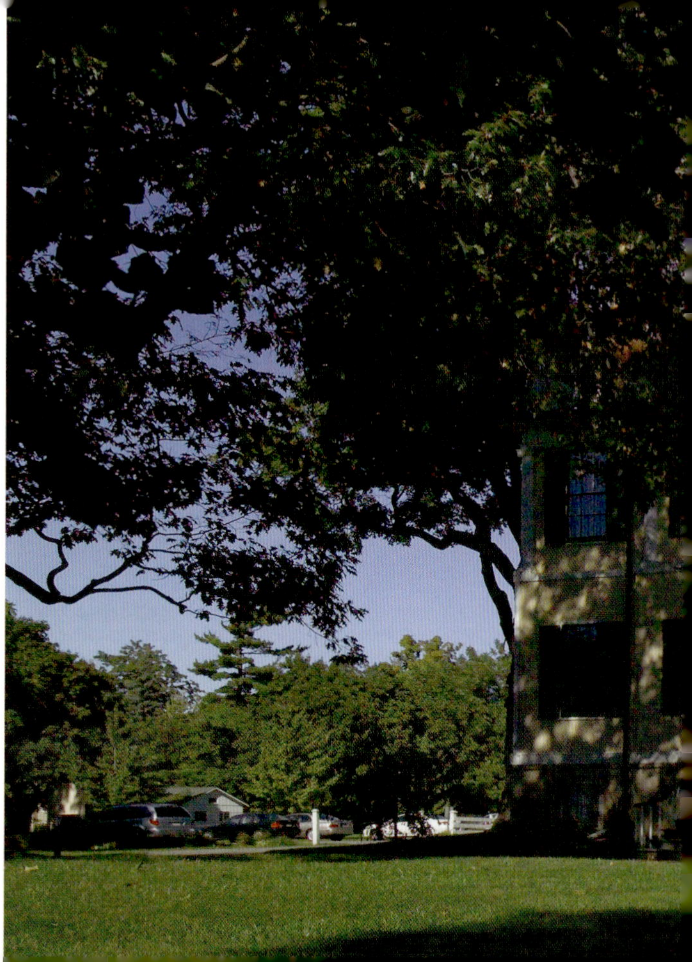

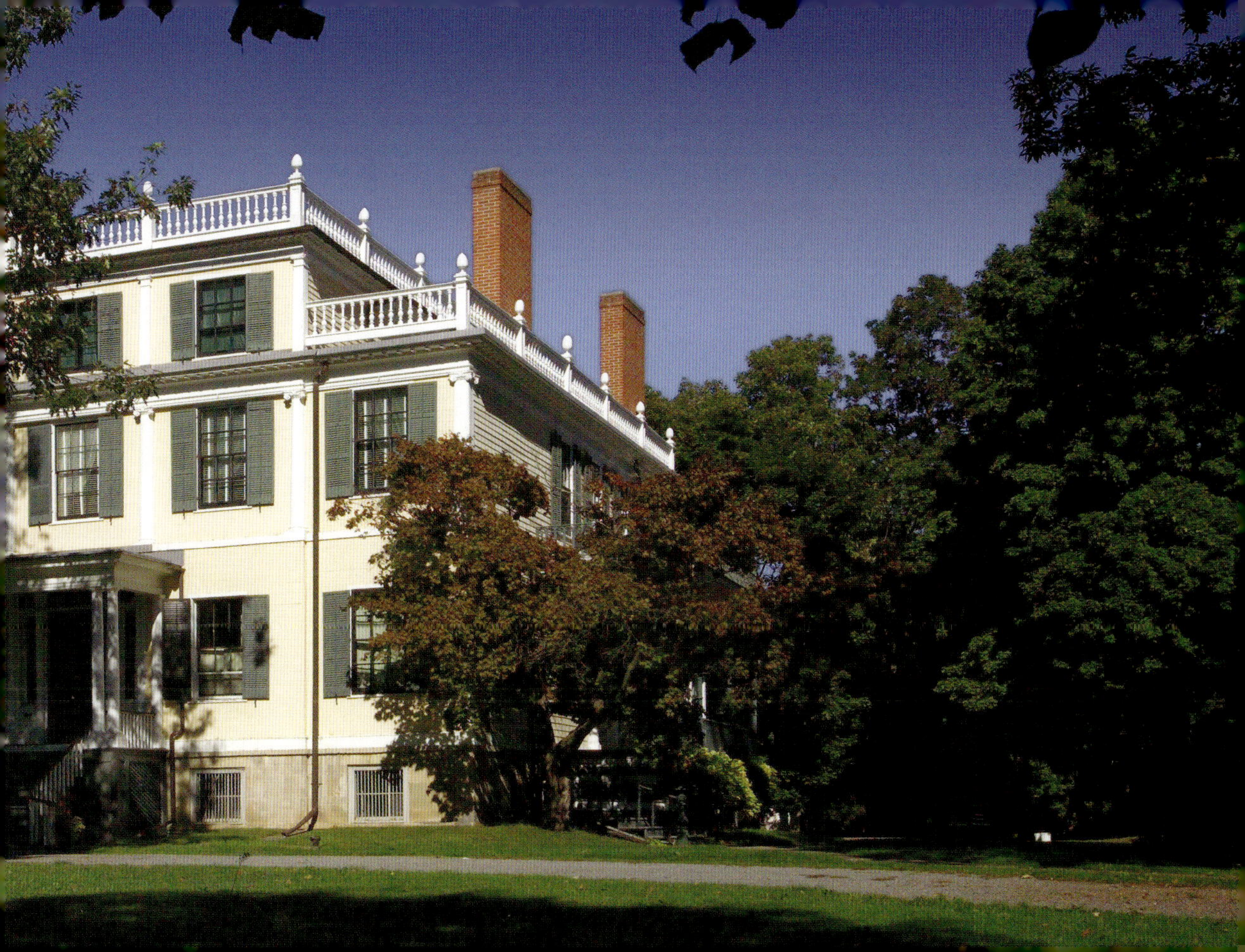

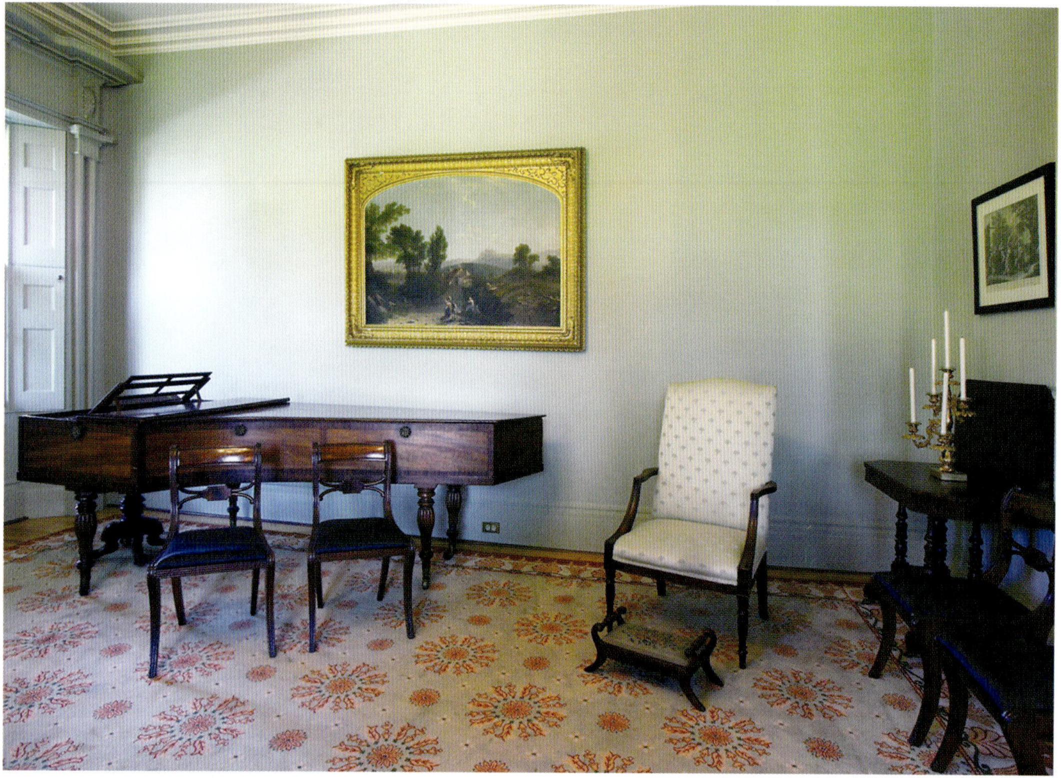

above, right, and previous Built in 1816, the federal-style Granger Homestead in Canandaigua also features a carriage museum.
next This sunflower farm near Clifton Springs grows over 20,000 plants per acre.

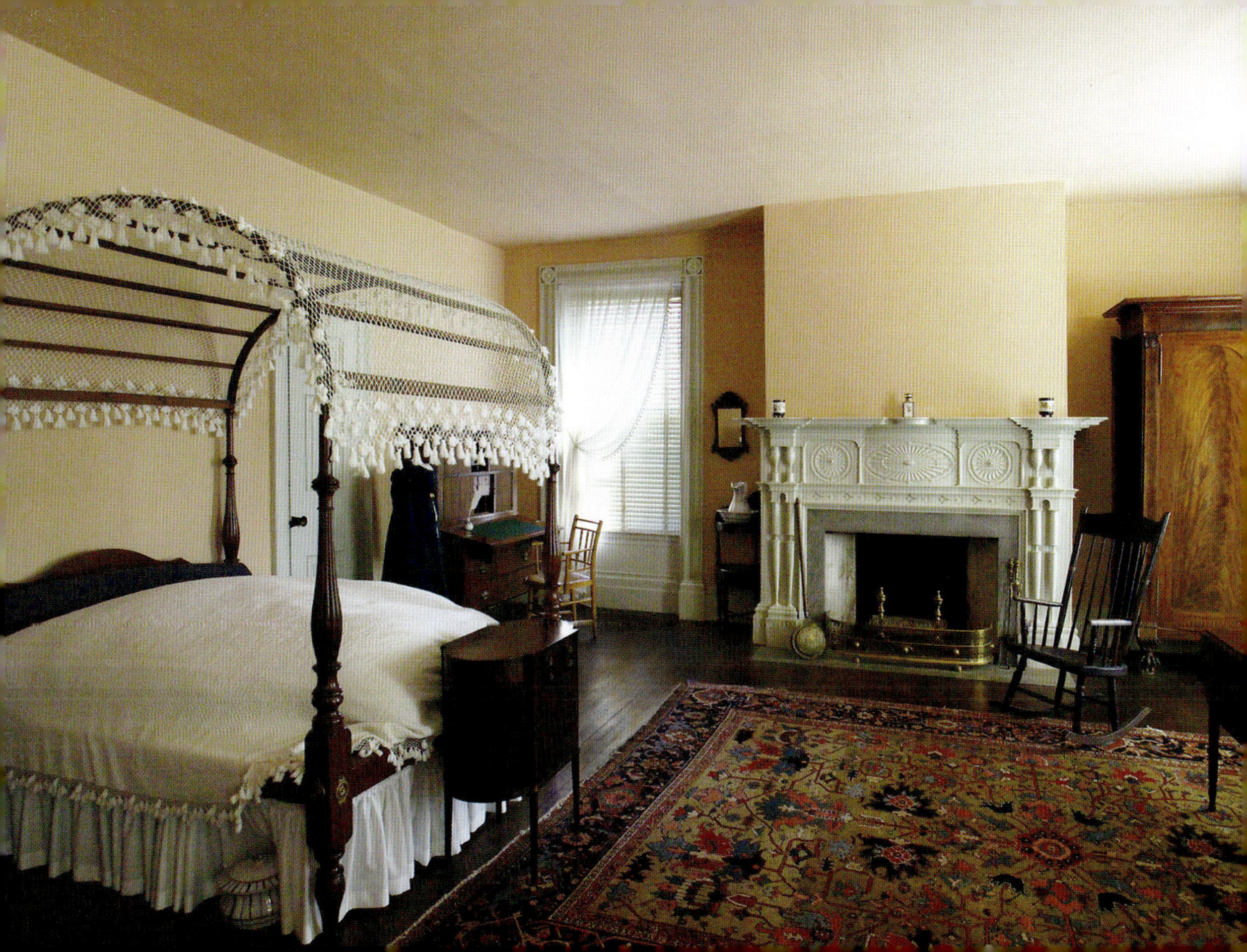

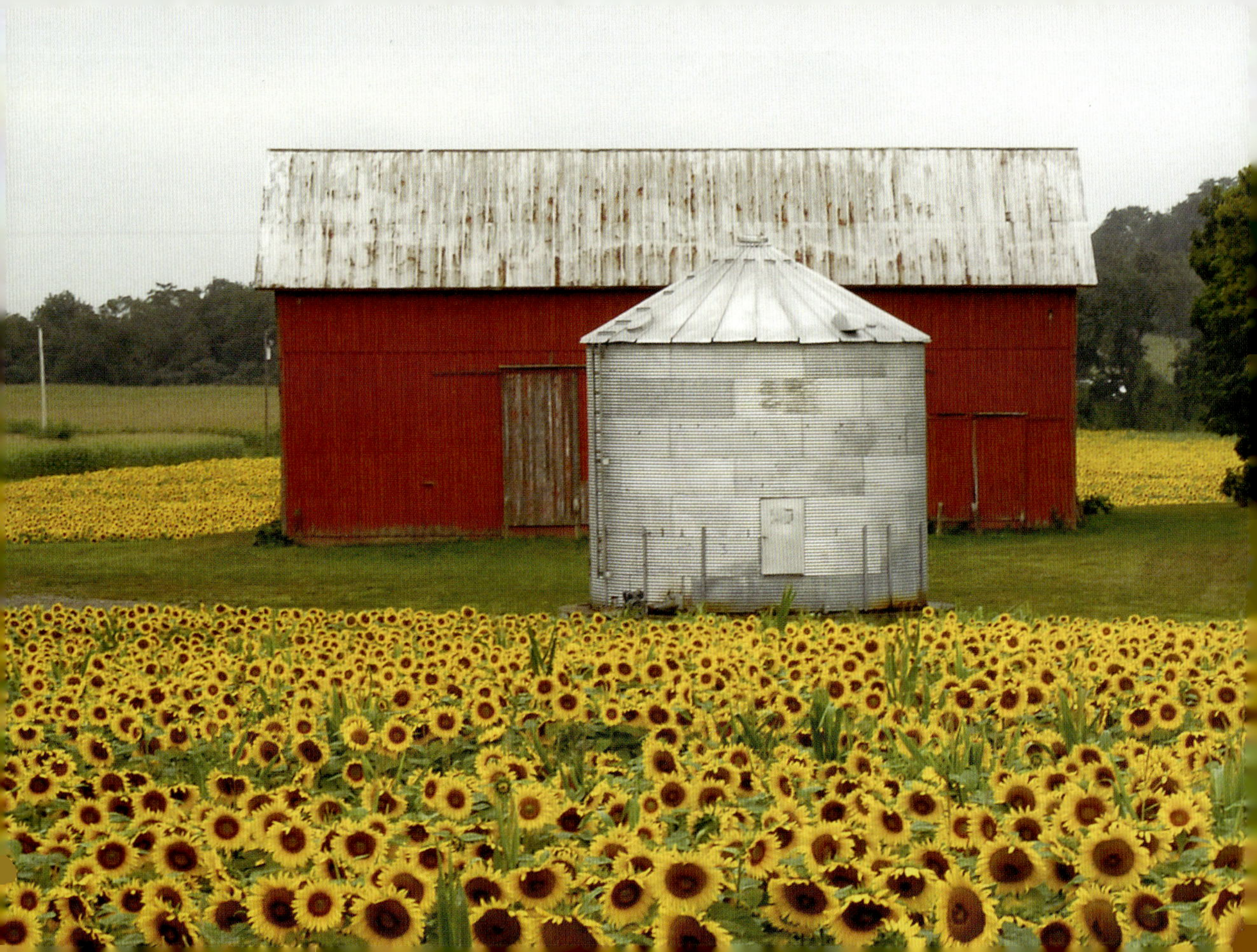

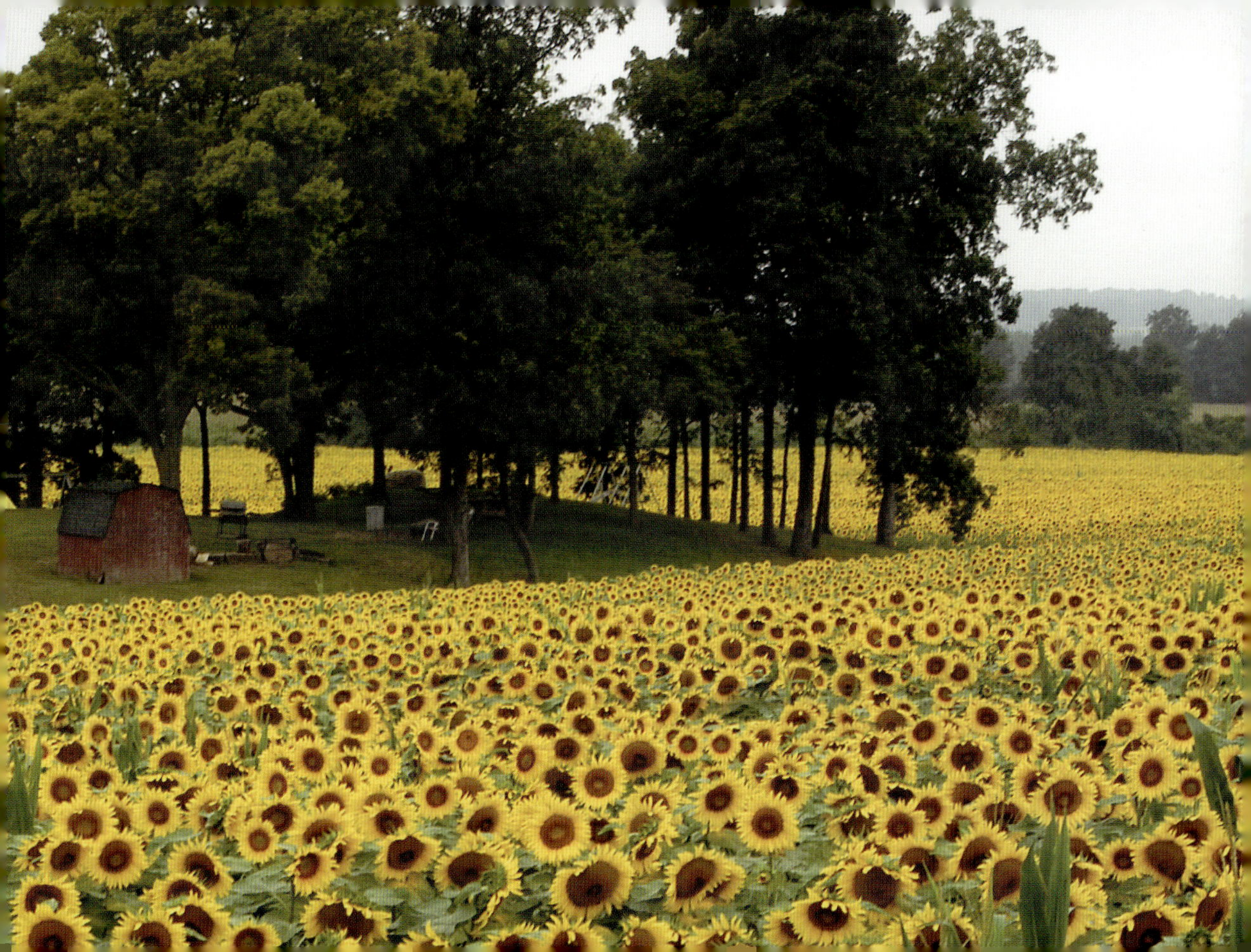

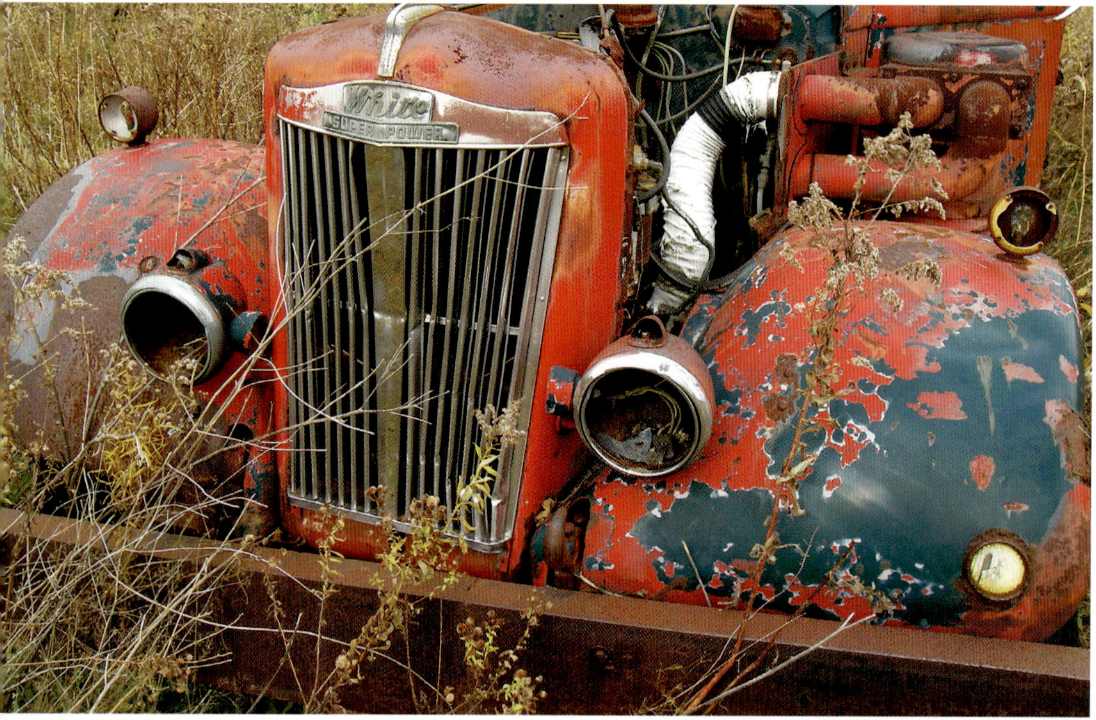

above An abandoned truck is artfully reduced by nature. right A reconstructed 1950's–era Texaco station in the hills above Penn Yan. next A Harley lover enjoys the annual New York State H.O.G. Convention.

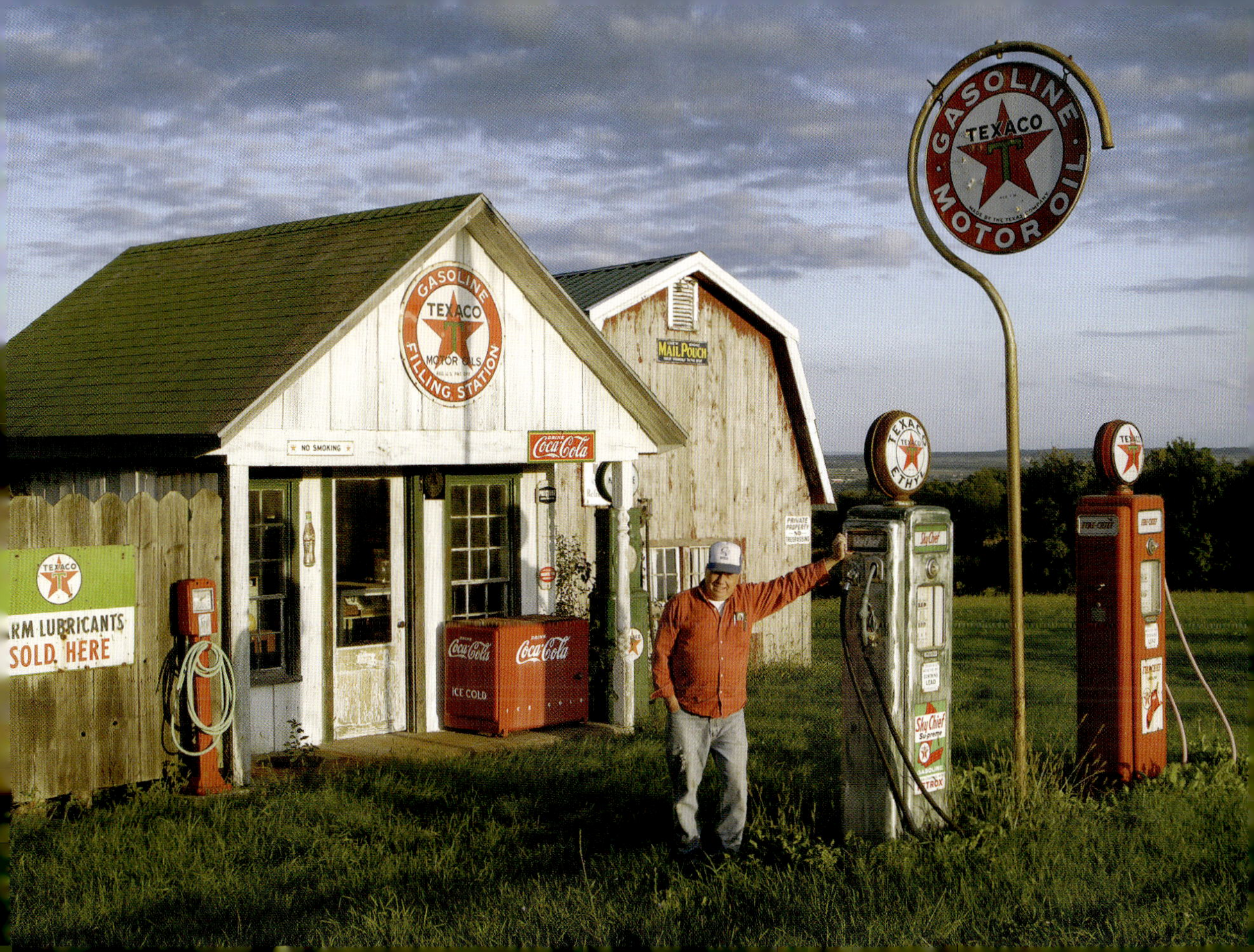
GASOLINE
TEXACO
MOTOR OIL
GASOLINE
TEXACO
MOTOR OILS
FILLING STATION
NO SMOKING
Coca-Cola
MAIL POUCH
RM LUBRICANTS
SOLD HERE
Coca-Cola
Coca-Cola
ICE COLD
TEXACO
ETHYL
Sky Chief

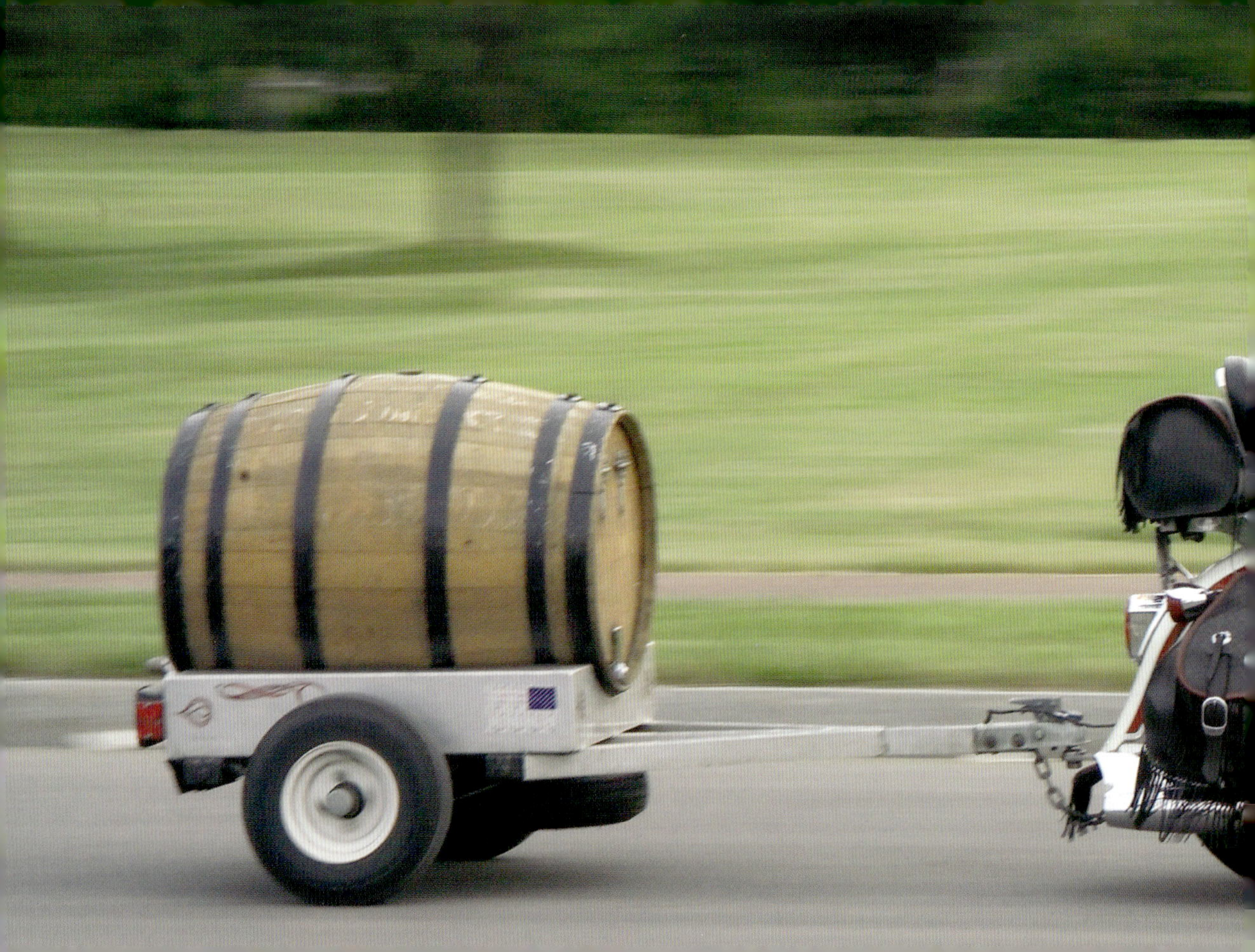

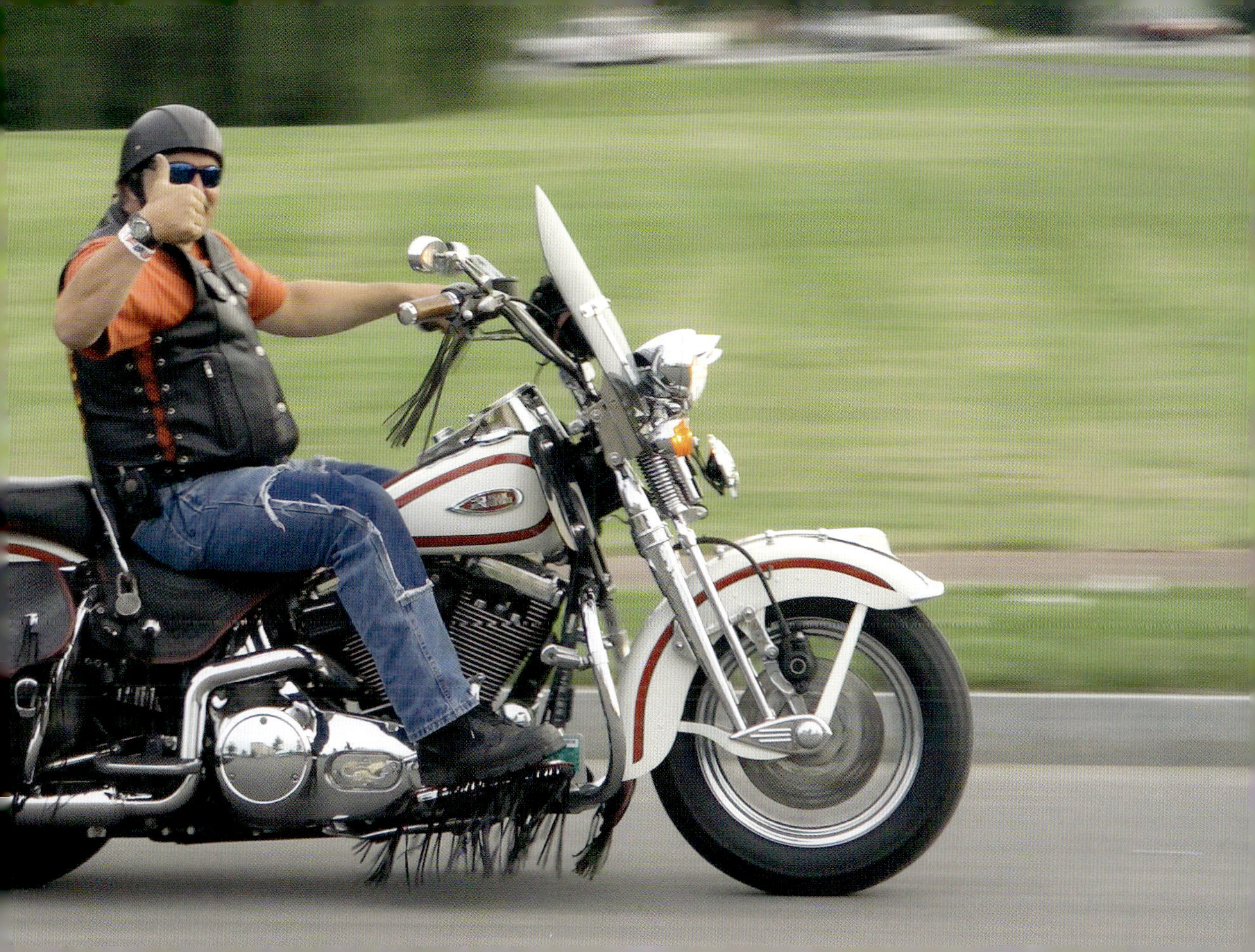

right A bed and breakfast near Sheldrake Point on 41-mile-long Cayuga Lake.

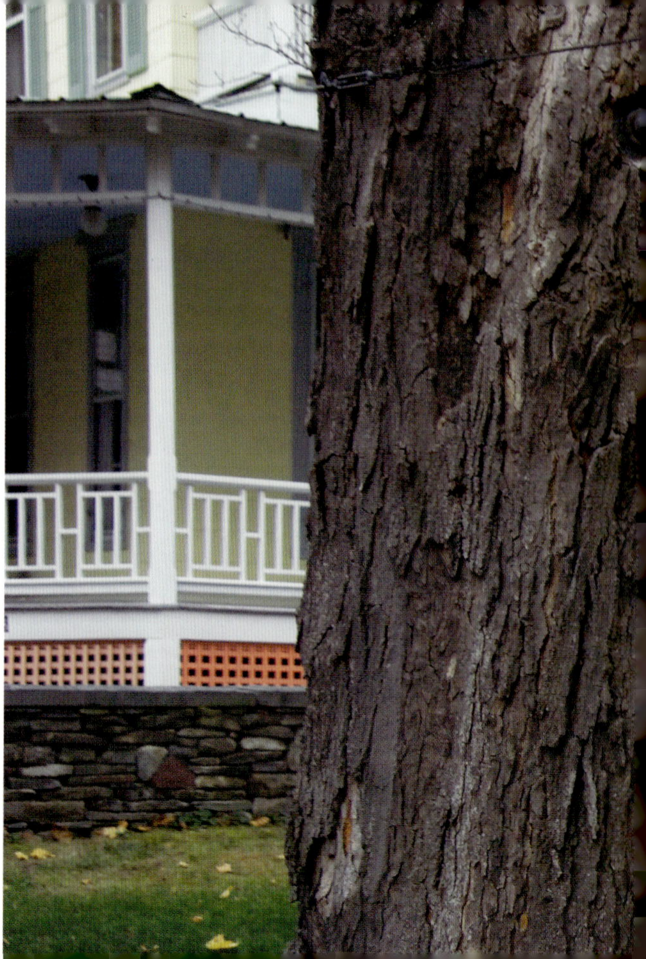

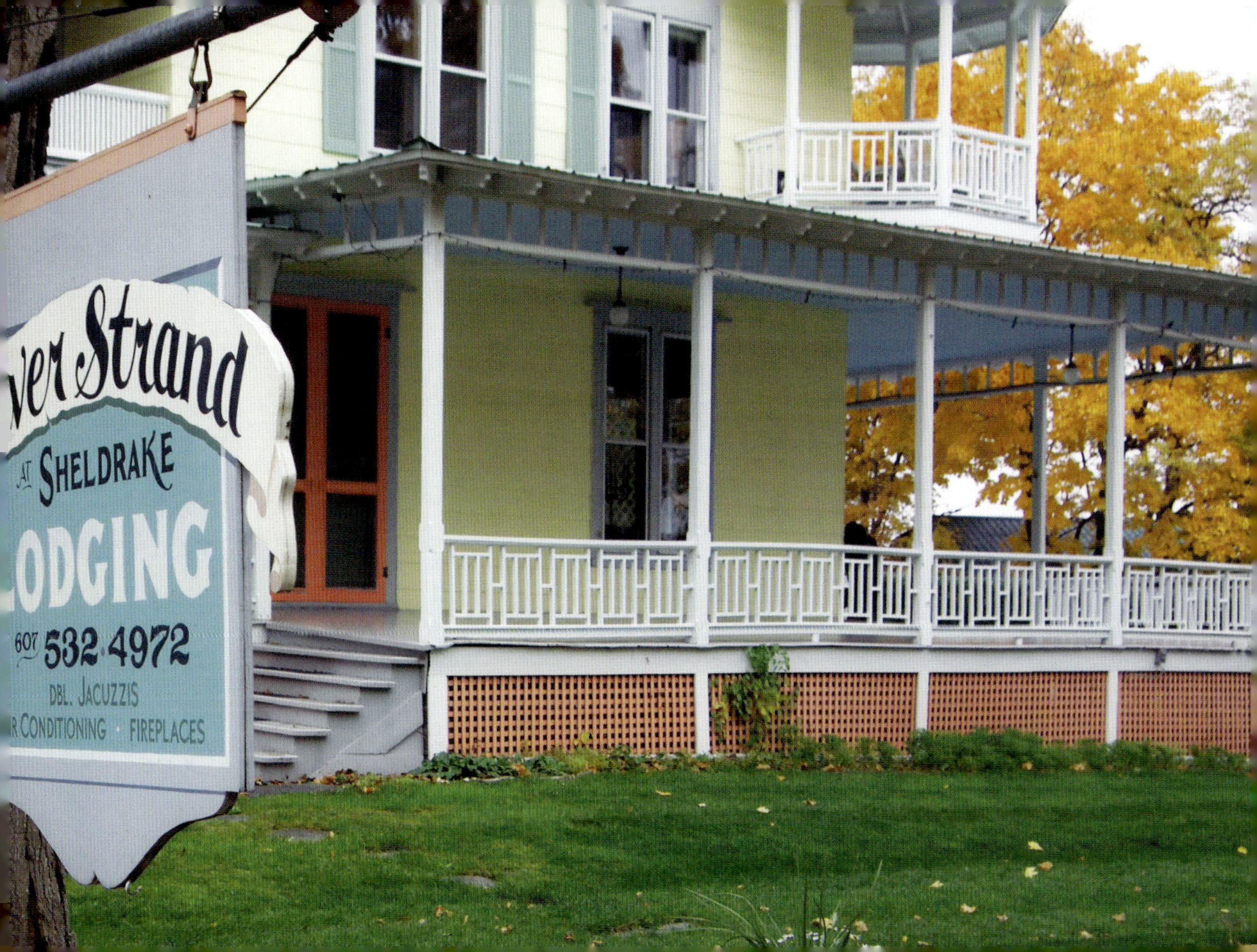

ver Strand
AT SHELDRAKE
LODGING
607 532-4972
DBL. JACUZZIS
R CONDITIONING · FIREPLACES

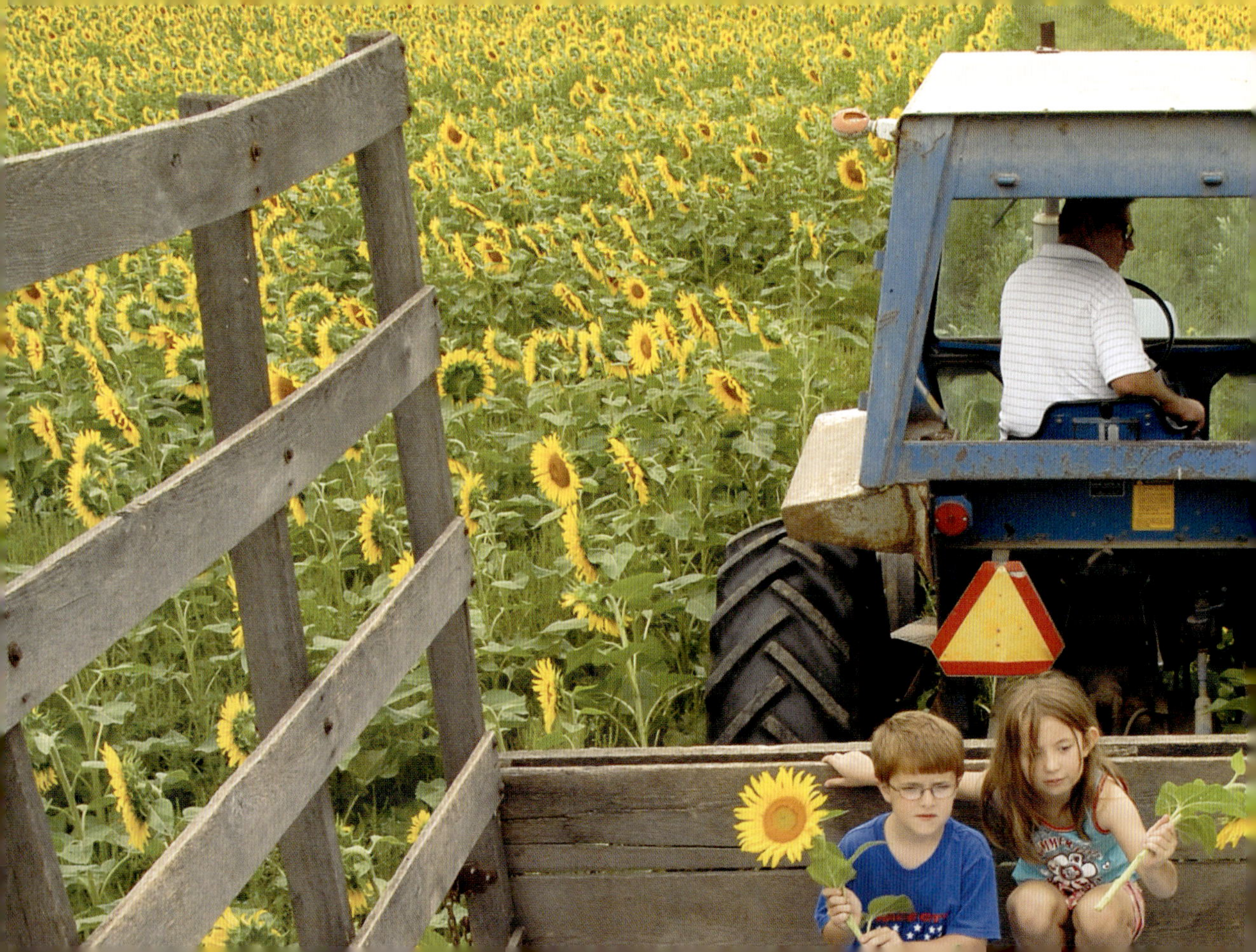

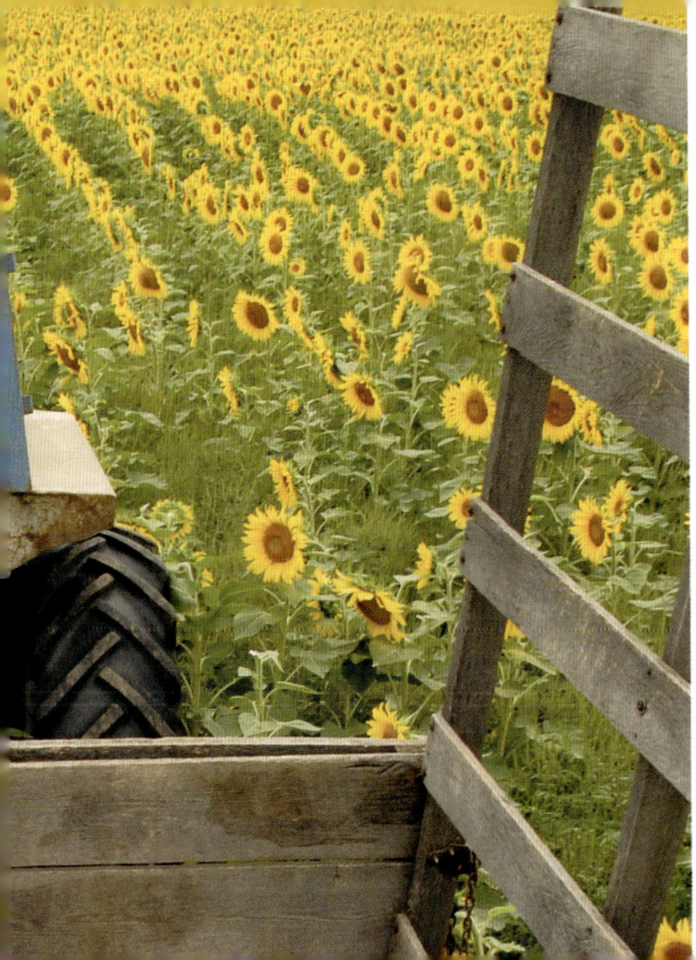

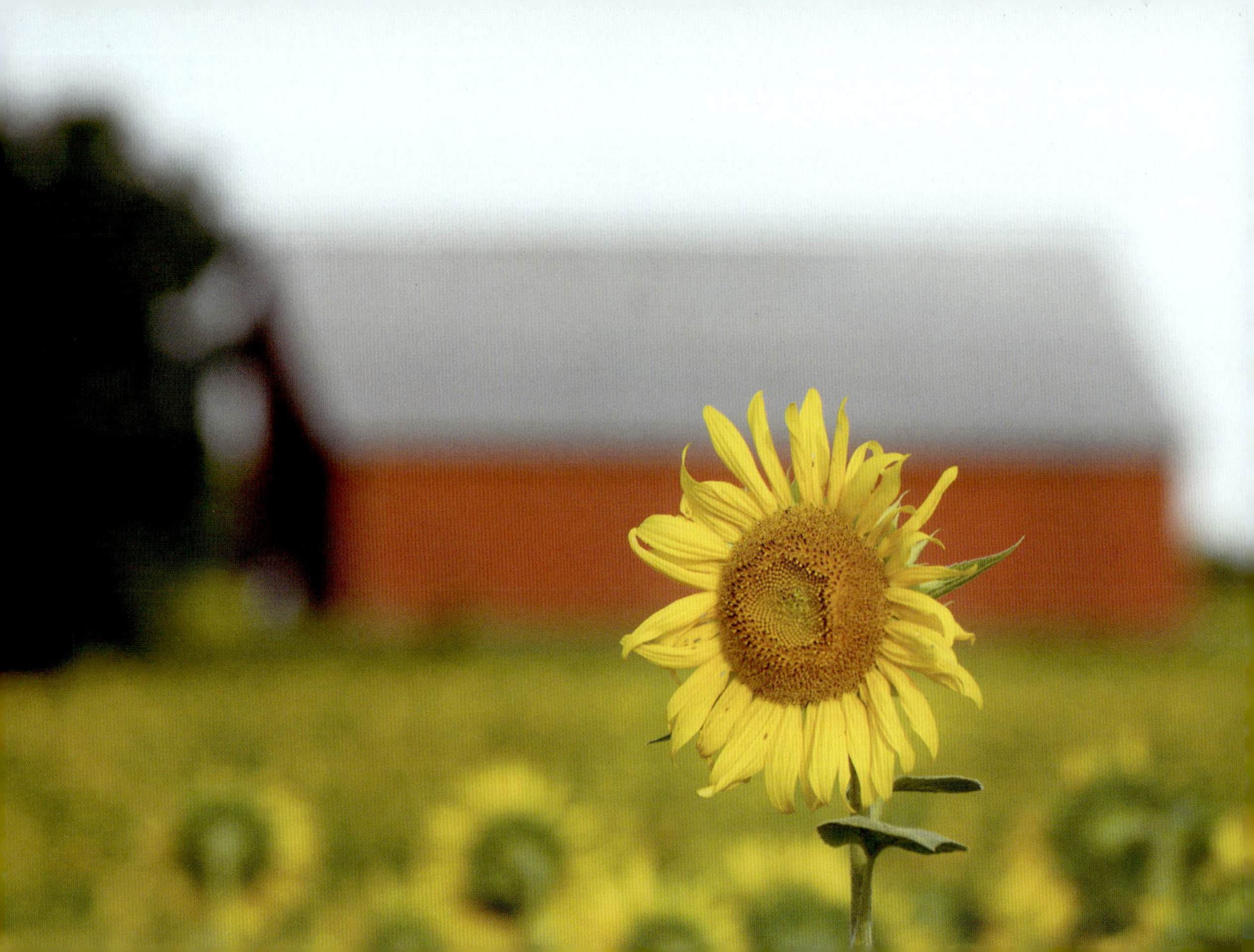

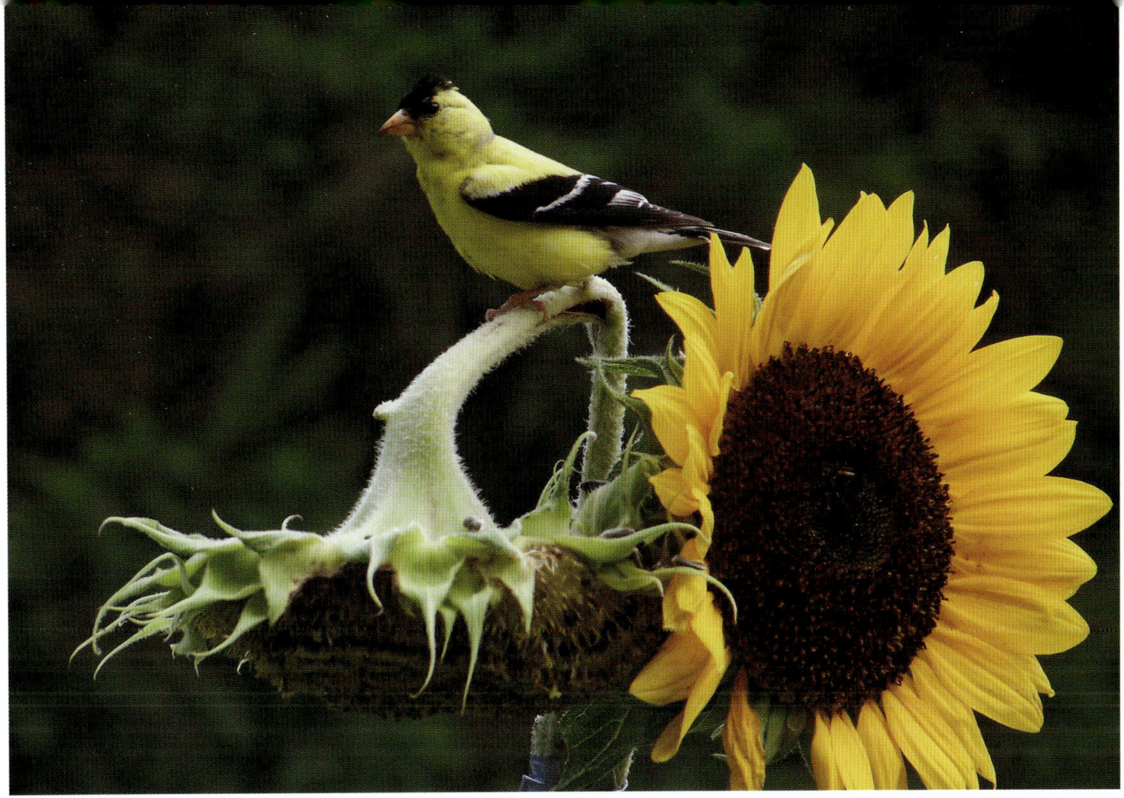

above and left As the finches know, this crop is for the birds. previous A farmer gives “hayrides” through his sunflower fields just before the harvest. next Winding roads and soaring hills make the Finger Lakes a favored destination for bikers. page after next On Cayuga Lake the counteracting forces of water currents carve a mystical spiral.

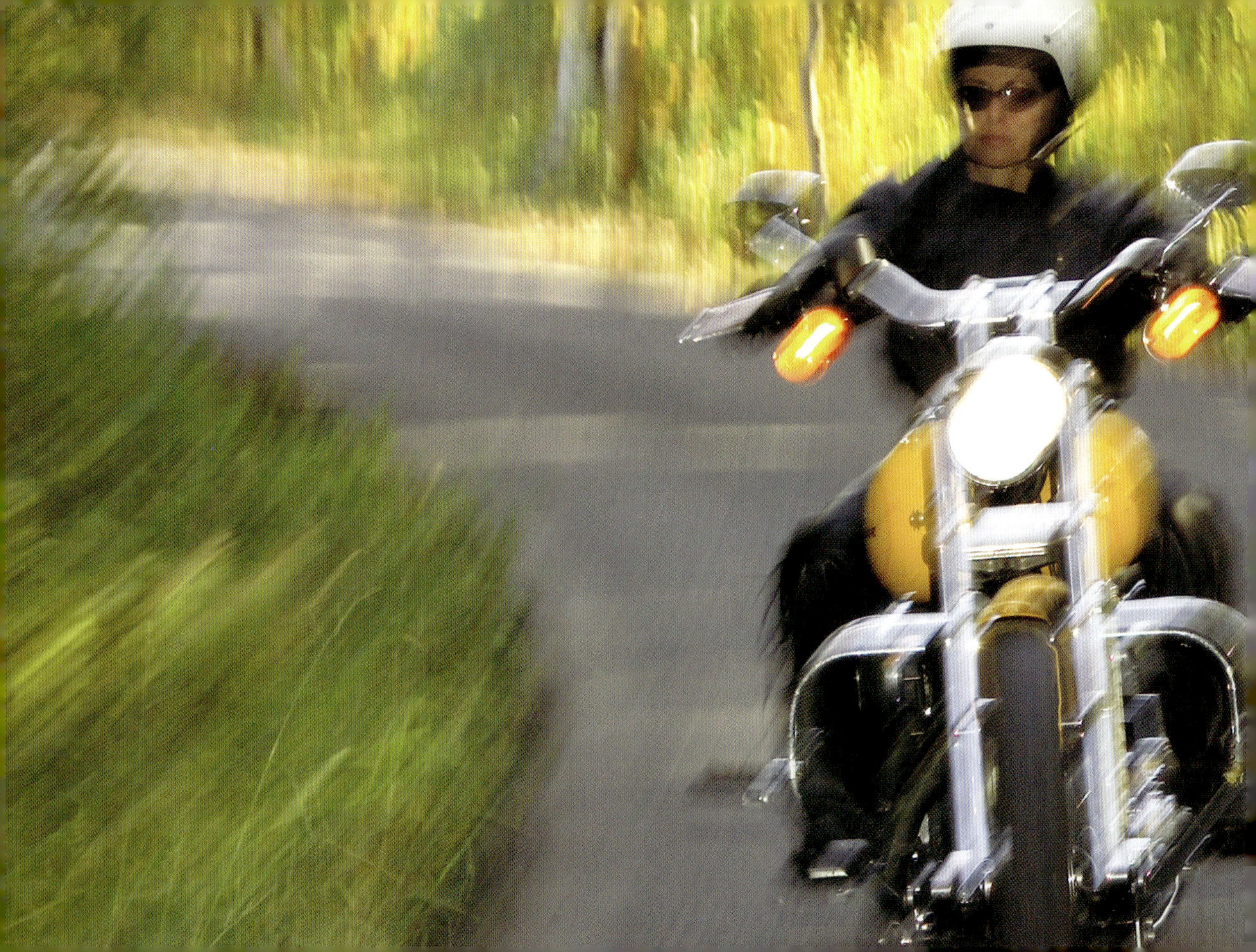

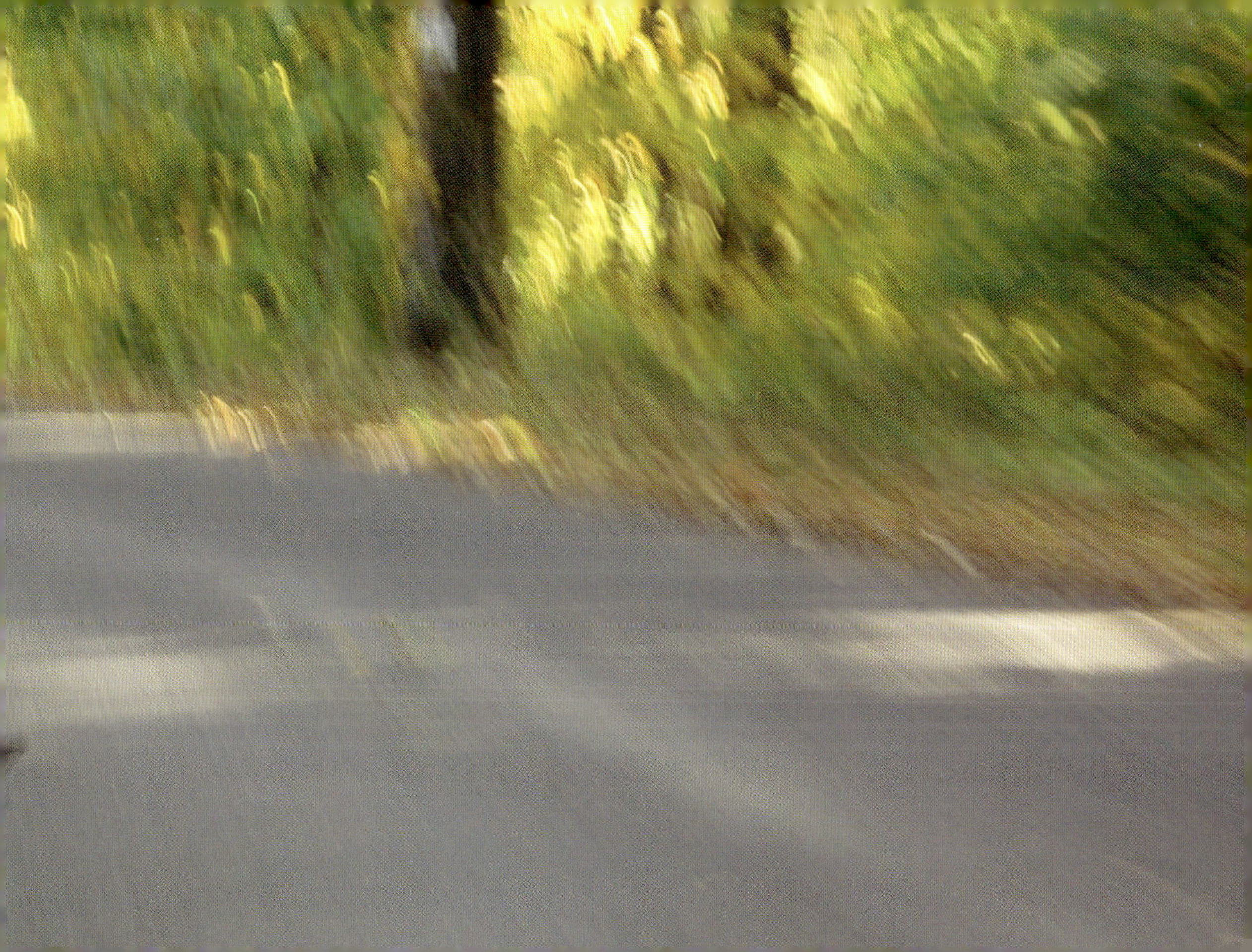

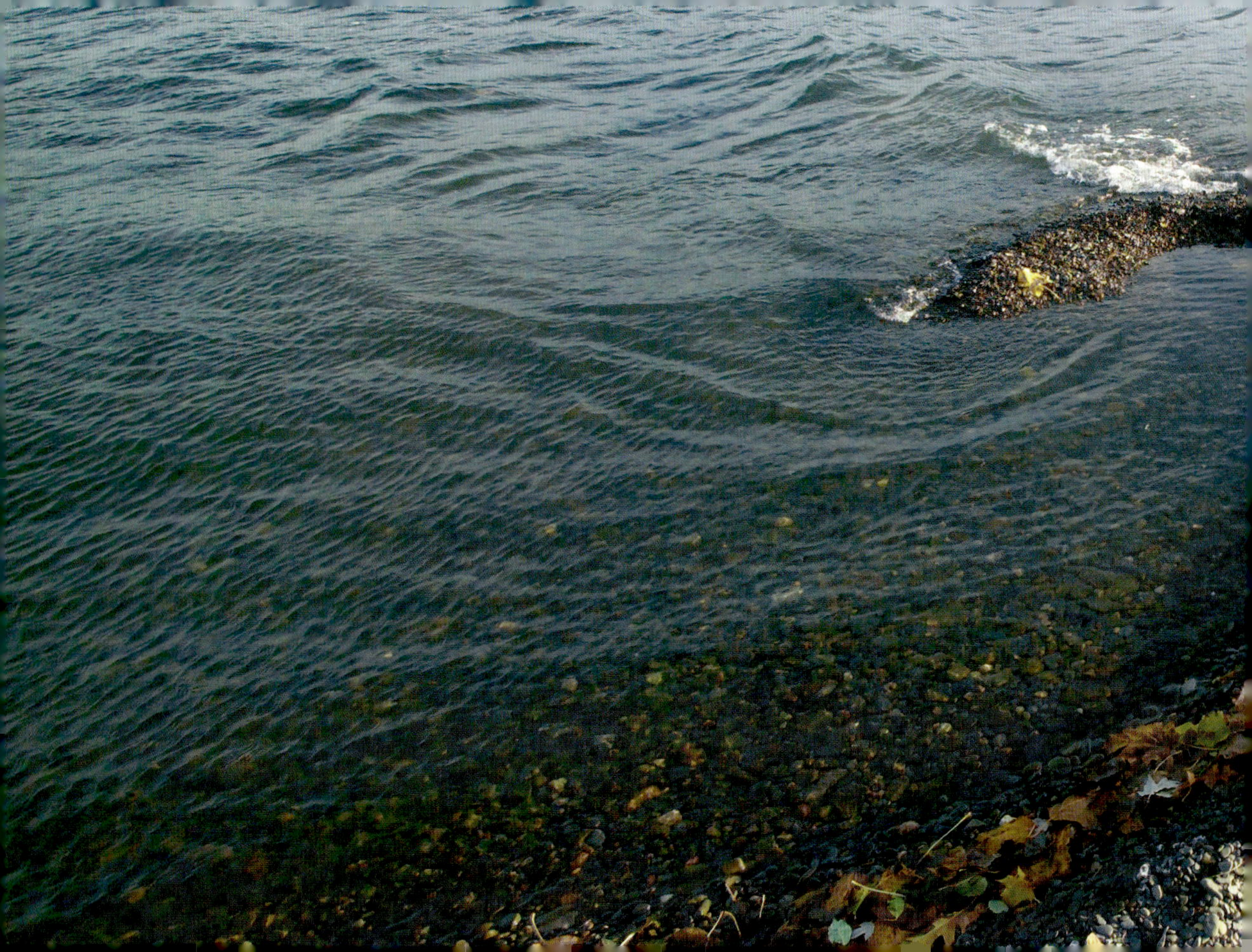

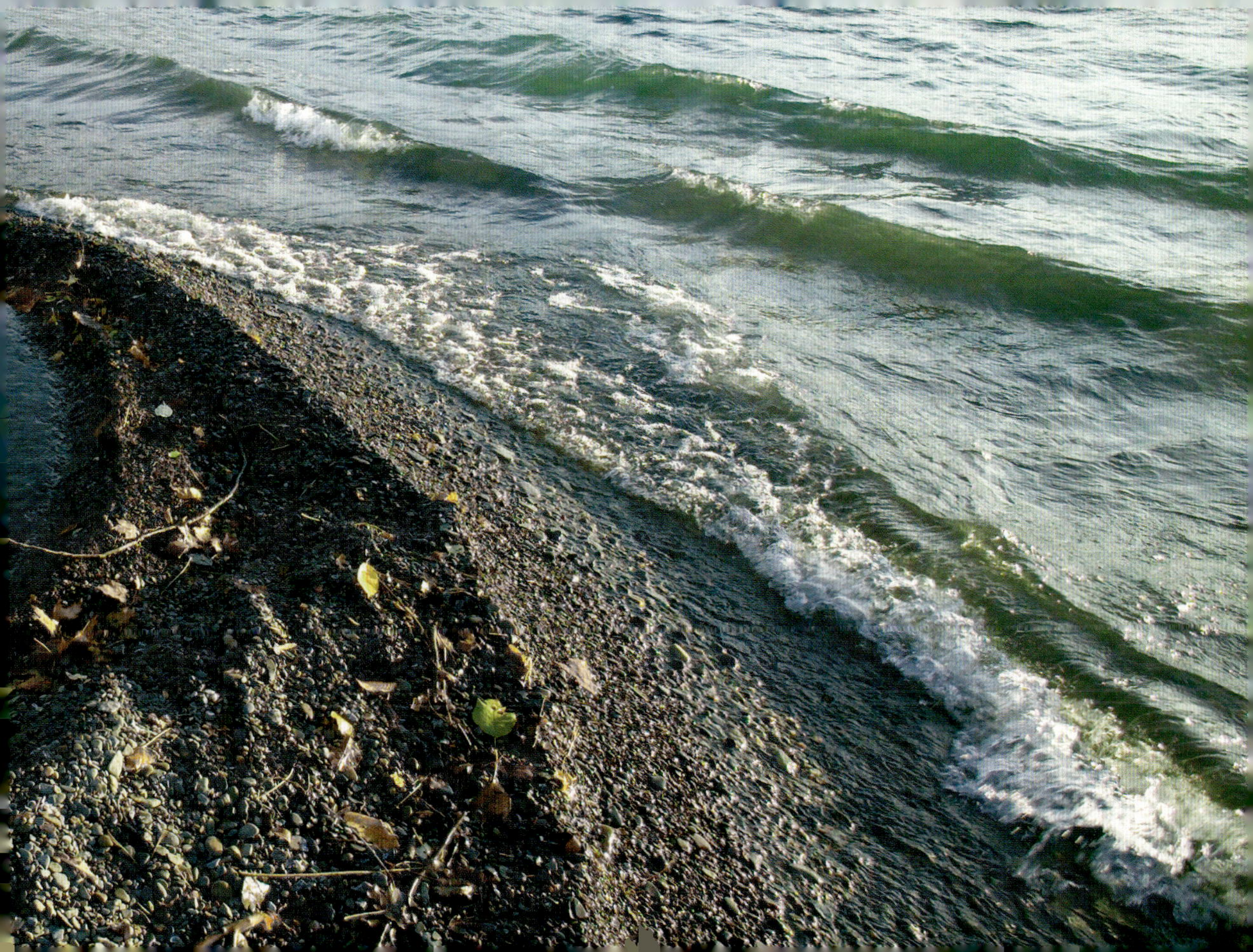

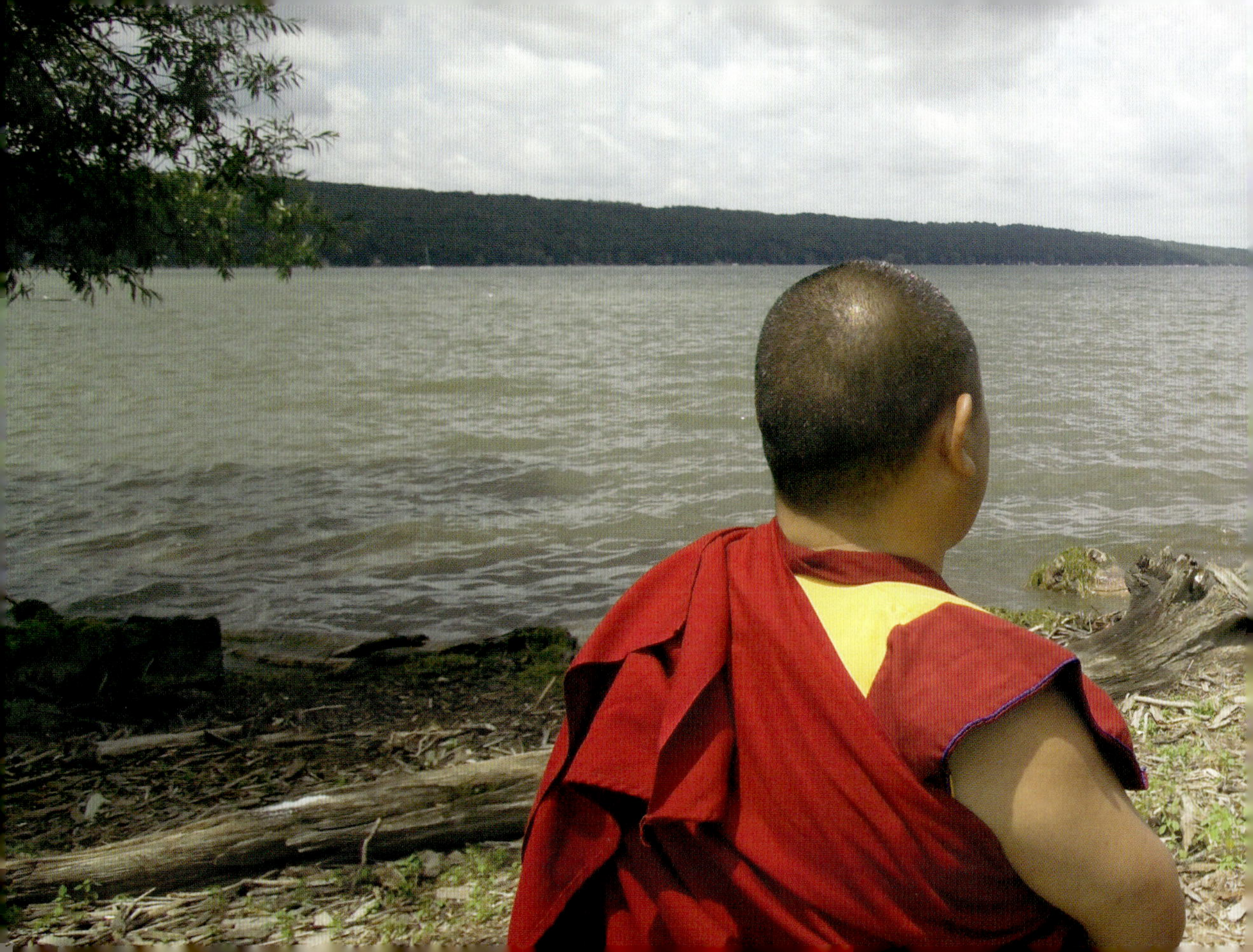

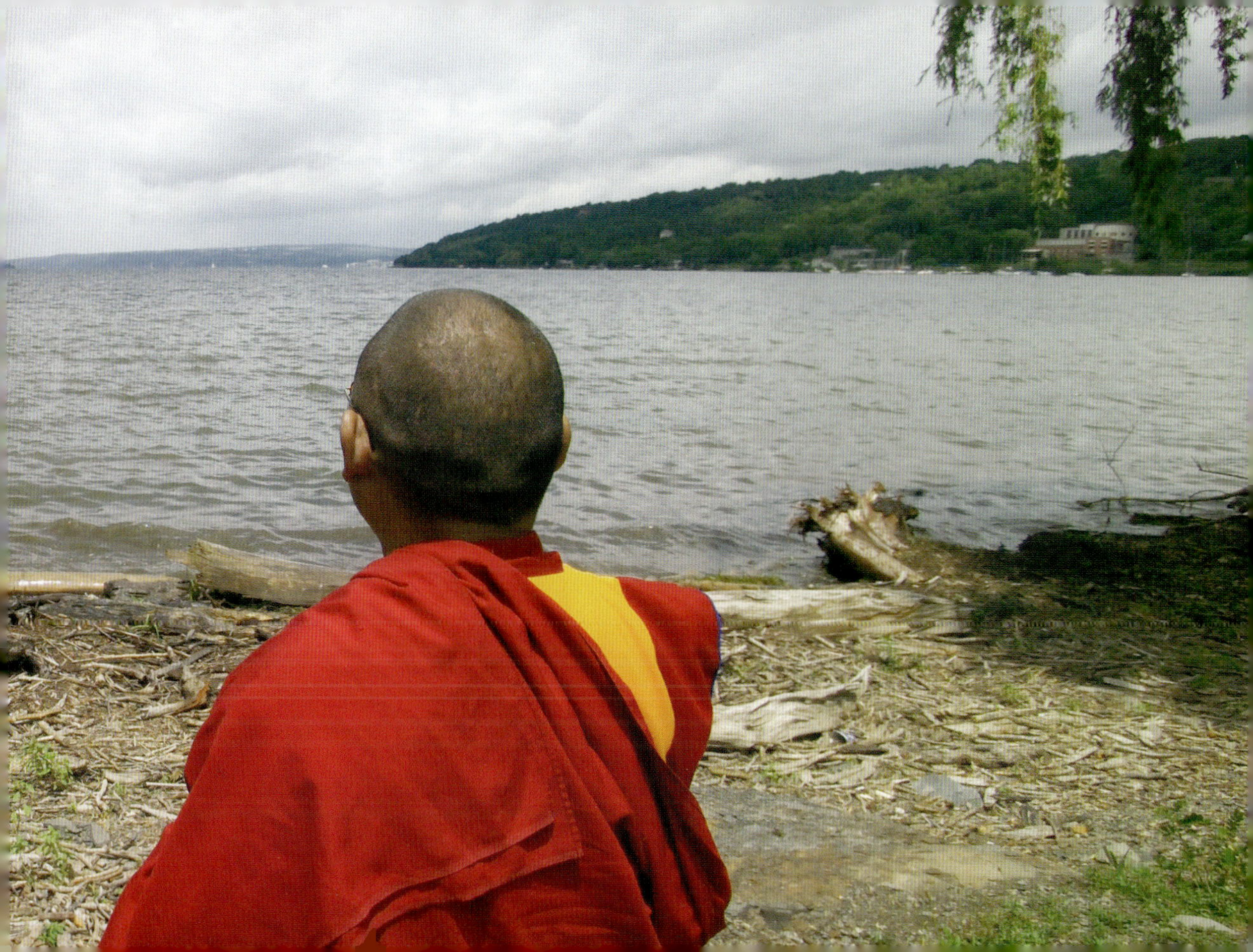

right Autumn starts early in the ravines, and by mid-October the world is golden. previous Tibetan monks from Ithaca's Namgyal Monastery, the North American Seat of the Dalai Lama.

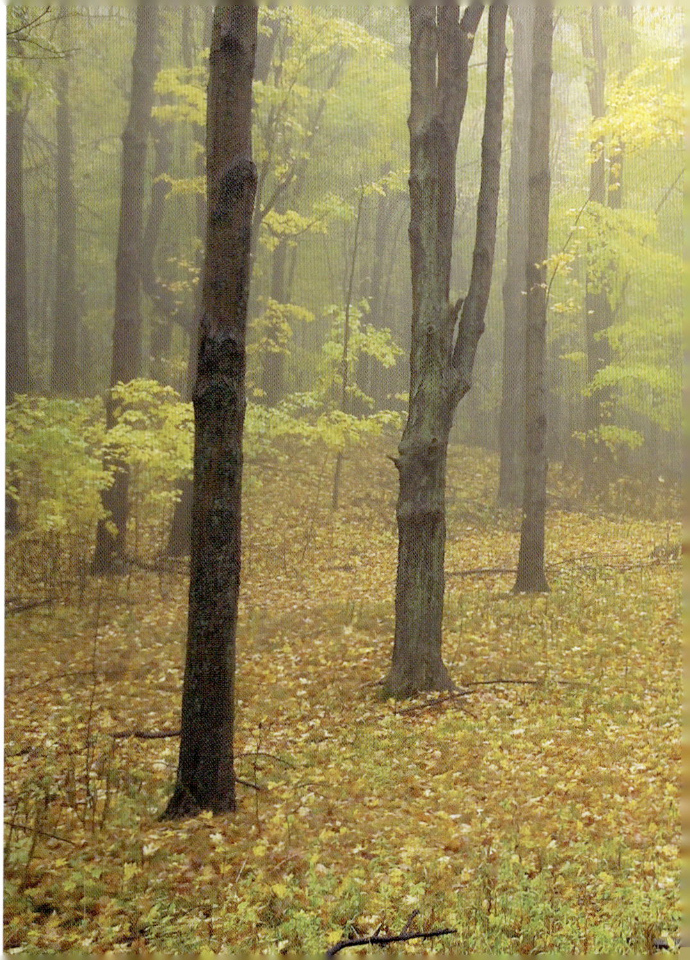

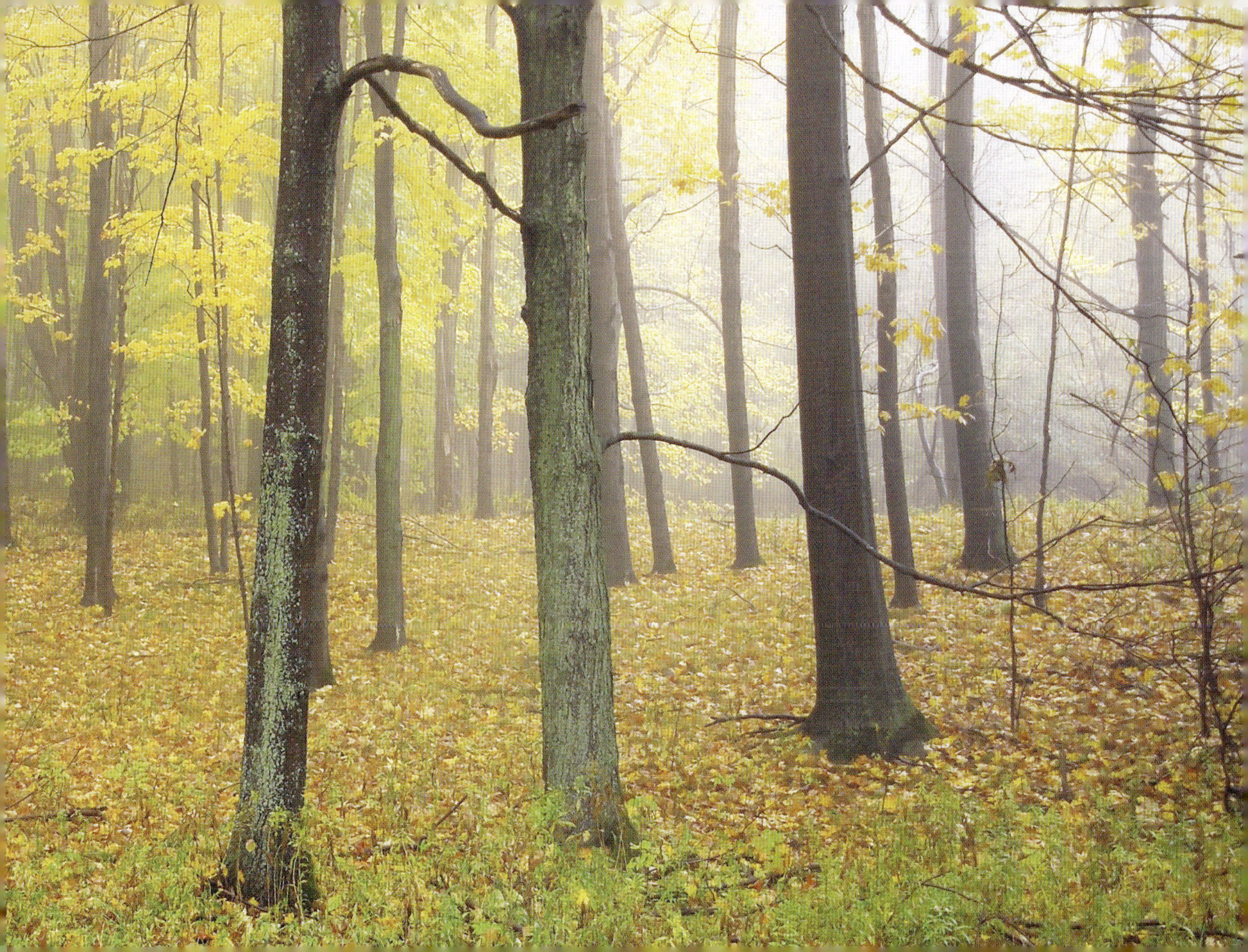

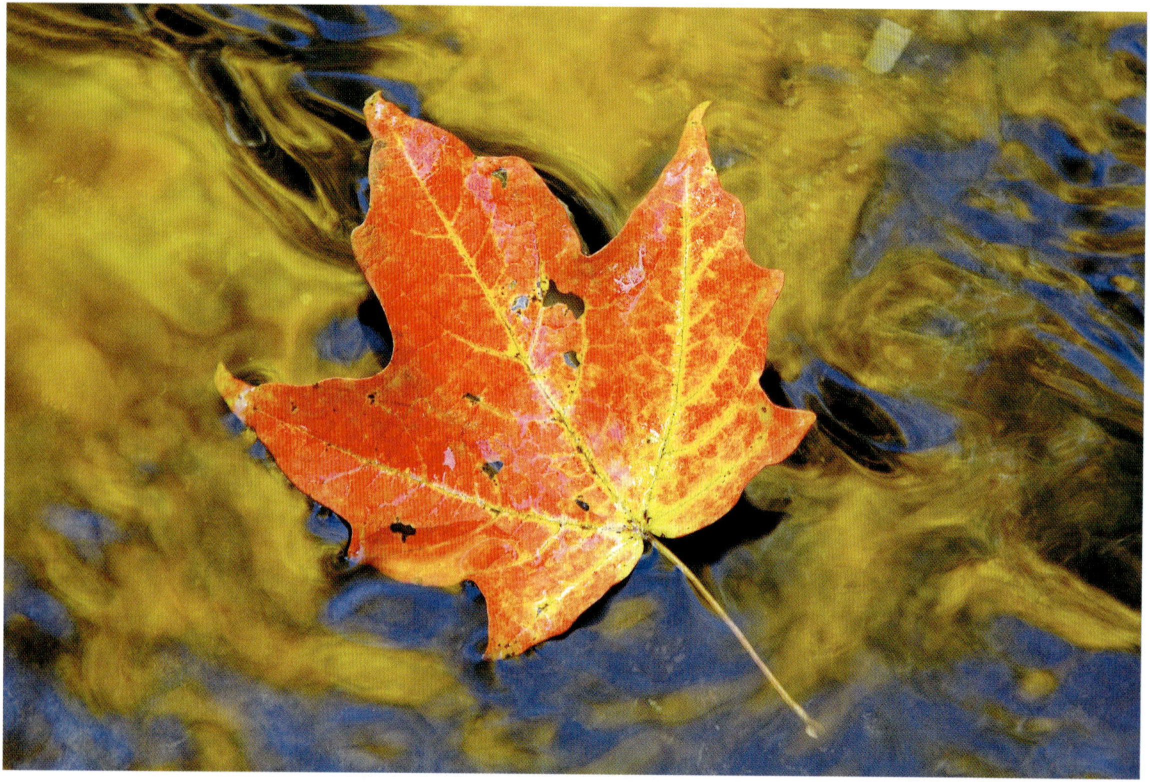

above and right Reflections on the restricted waters of Hemlock and Canadice Lakes. next Sunset at Sampson State Park on Seneca Lake. page after next The Senecas give thanks for the harvest each September on Bare Hill above Canandaigua Lake.

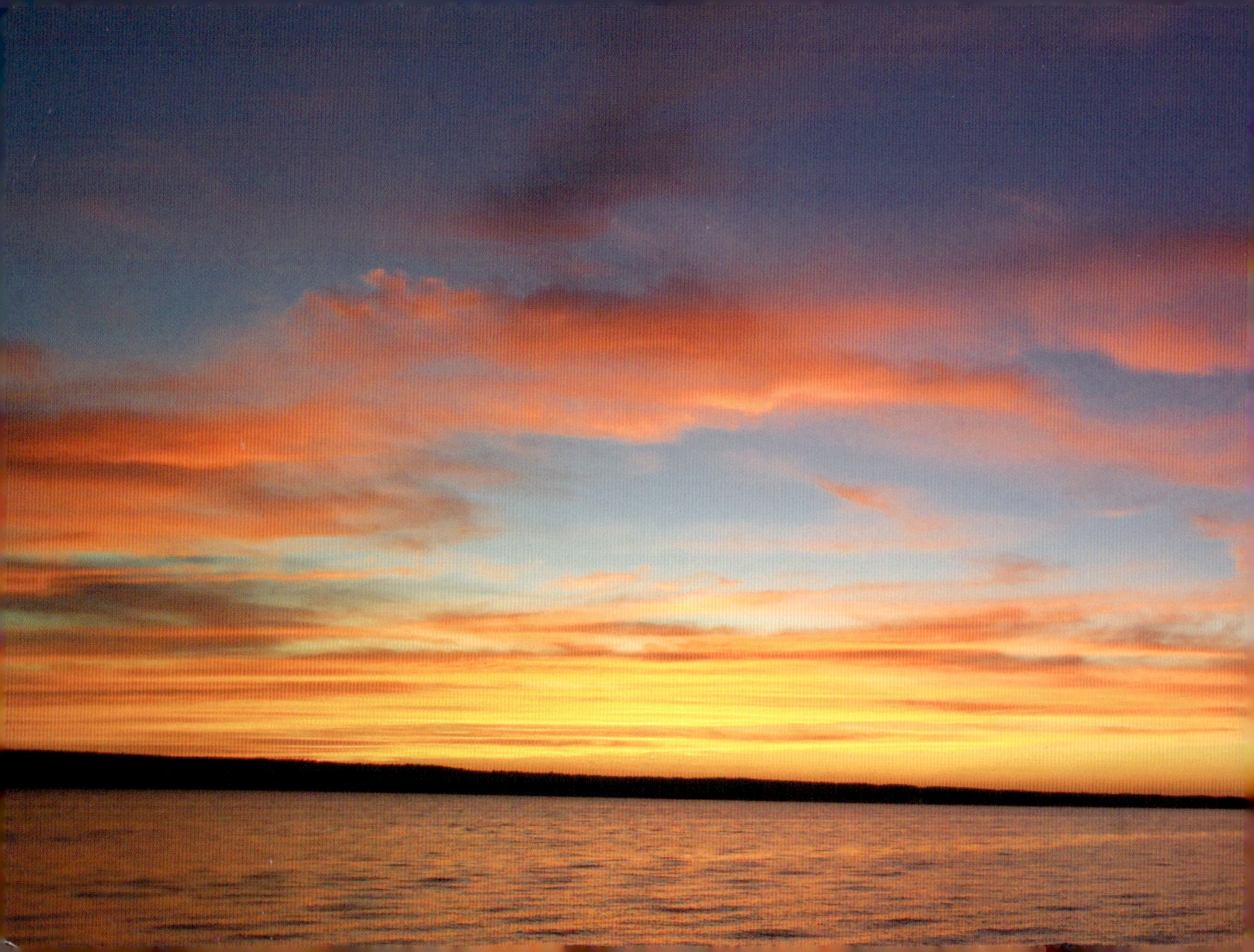

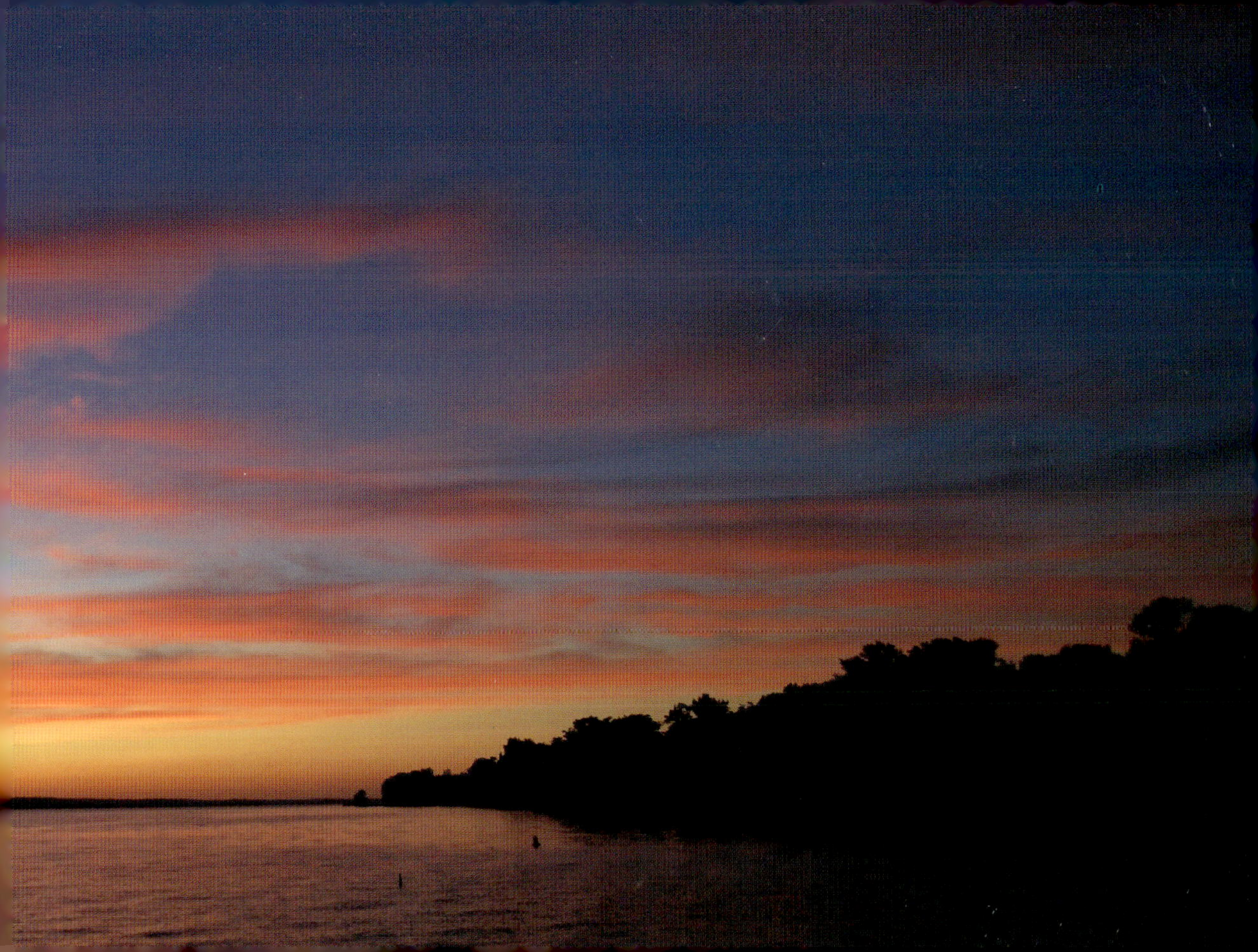

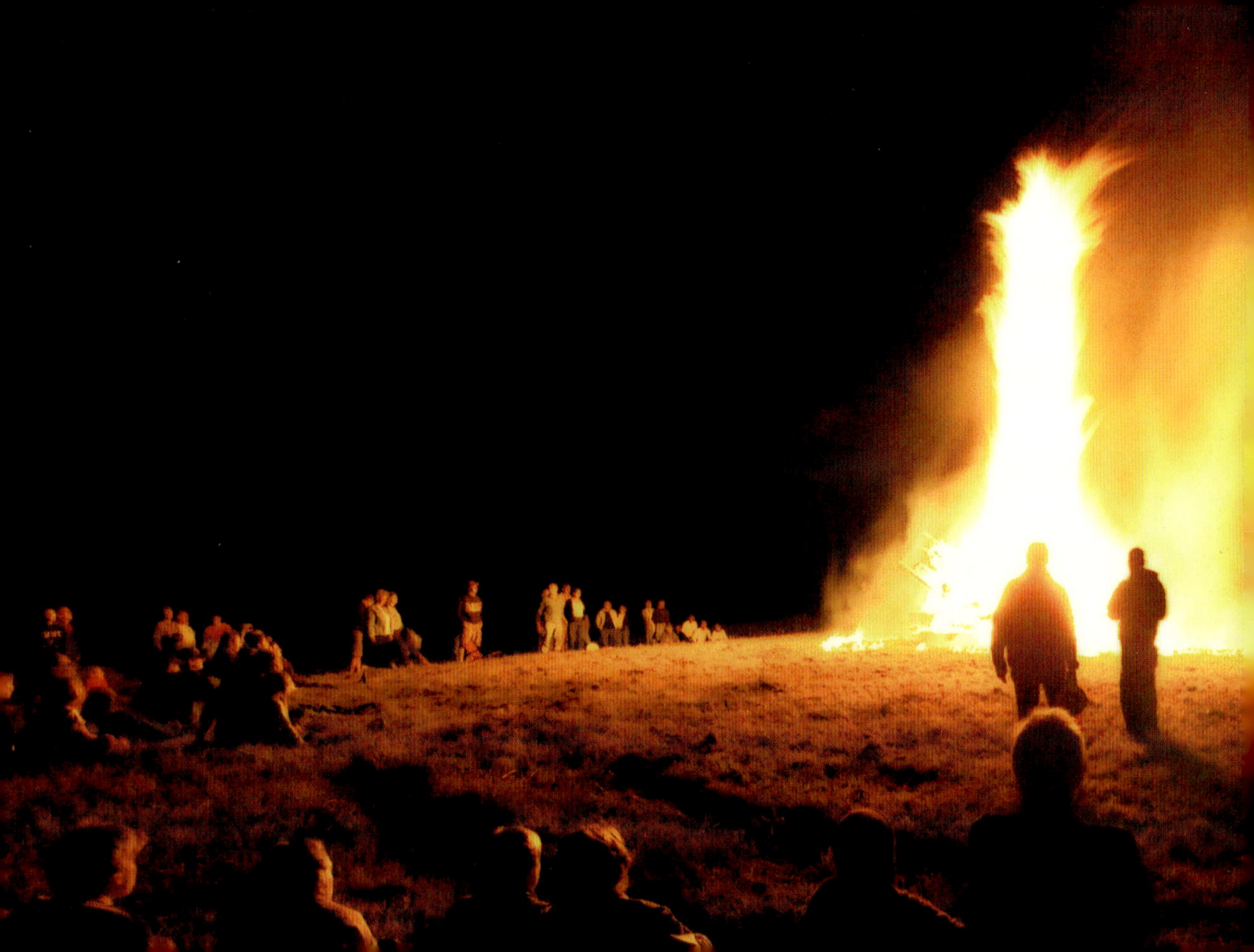

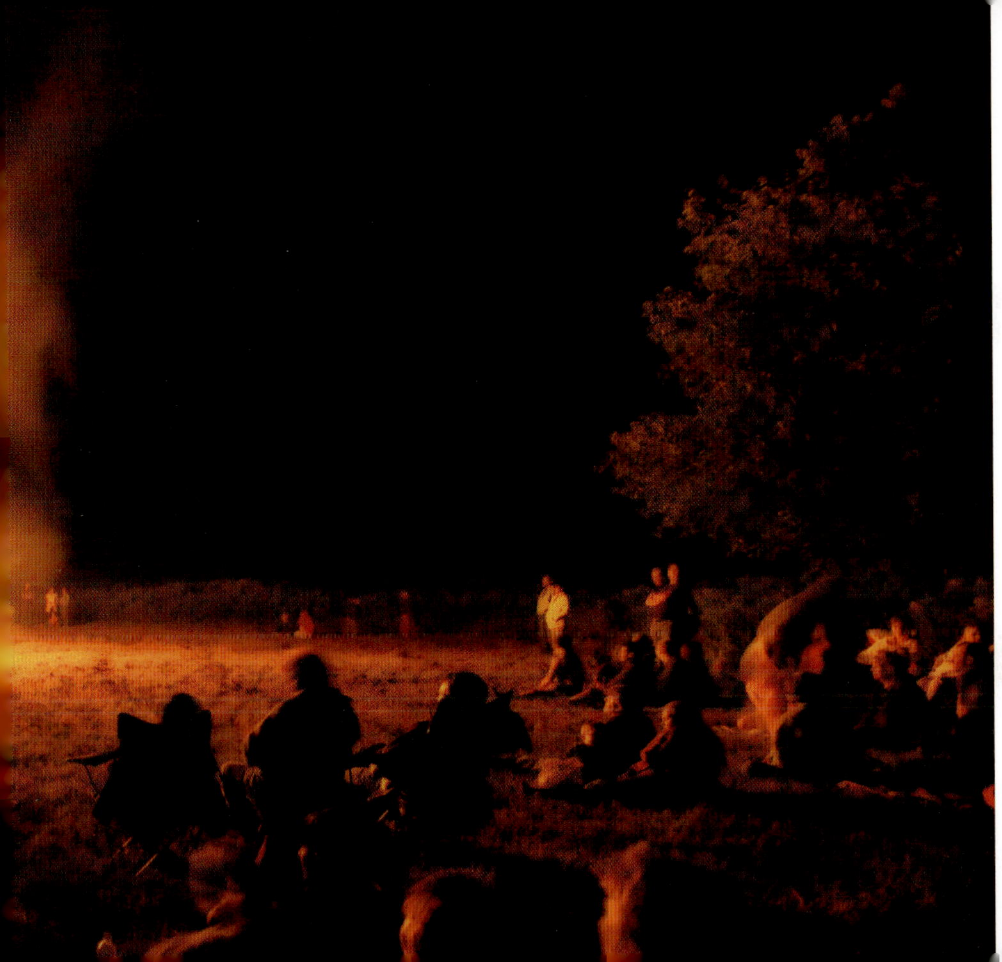

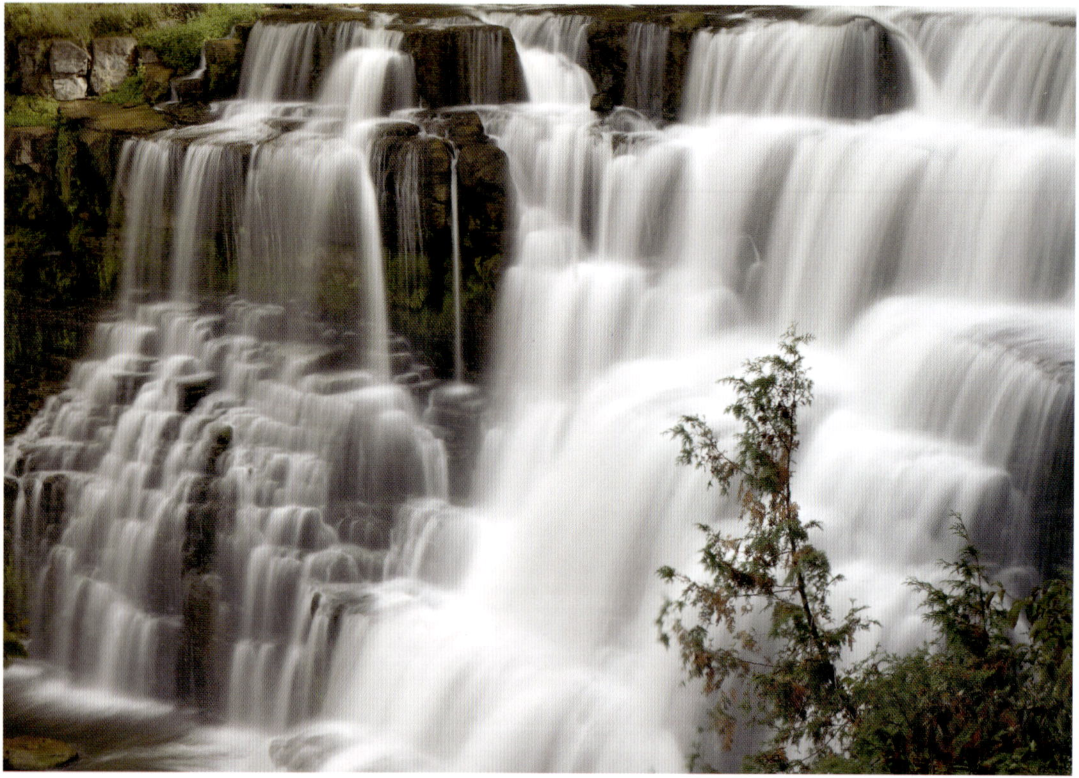

left The 167-foot-tall Chittenango Falls, east of Cazenovia Lake. right Countless hidden streams dot the Finger Lakes countryside.

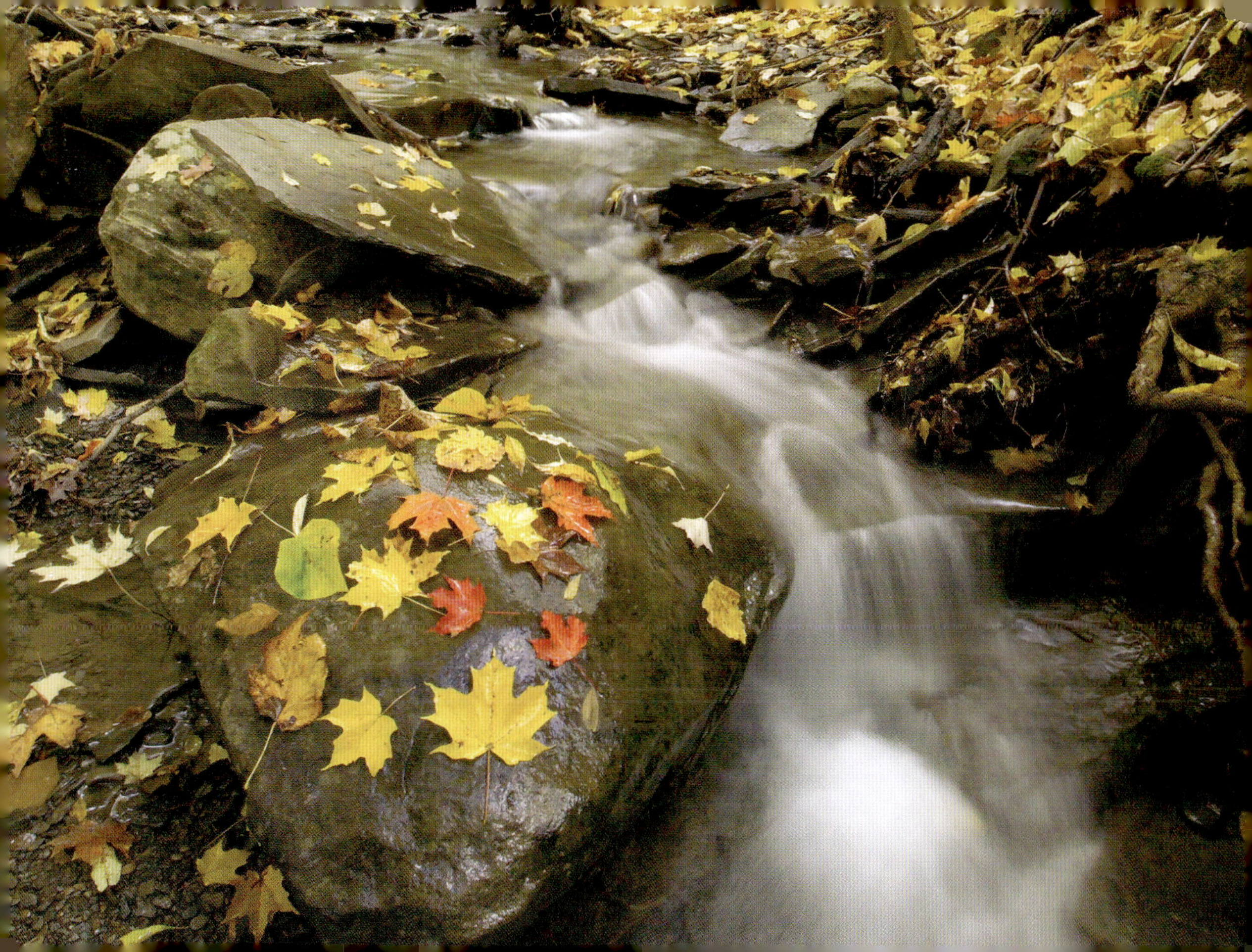

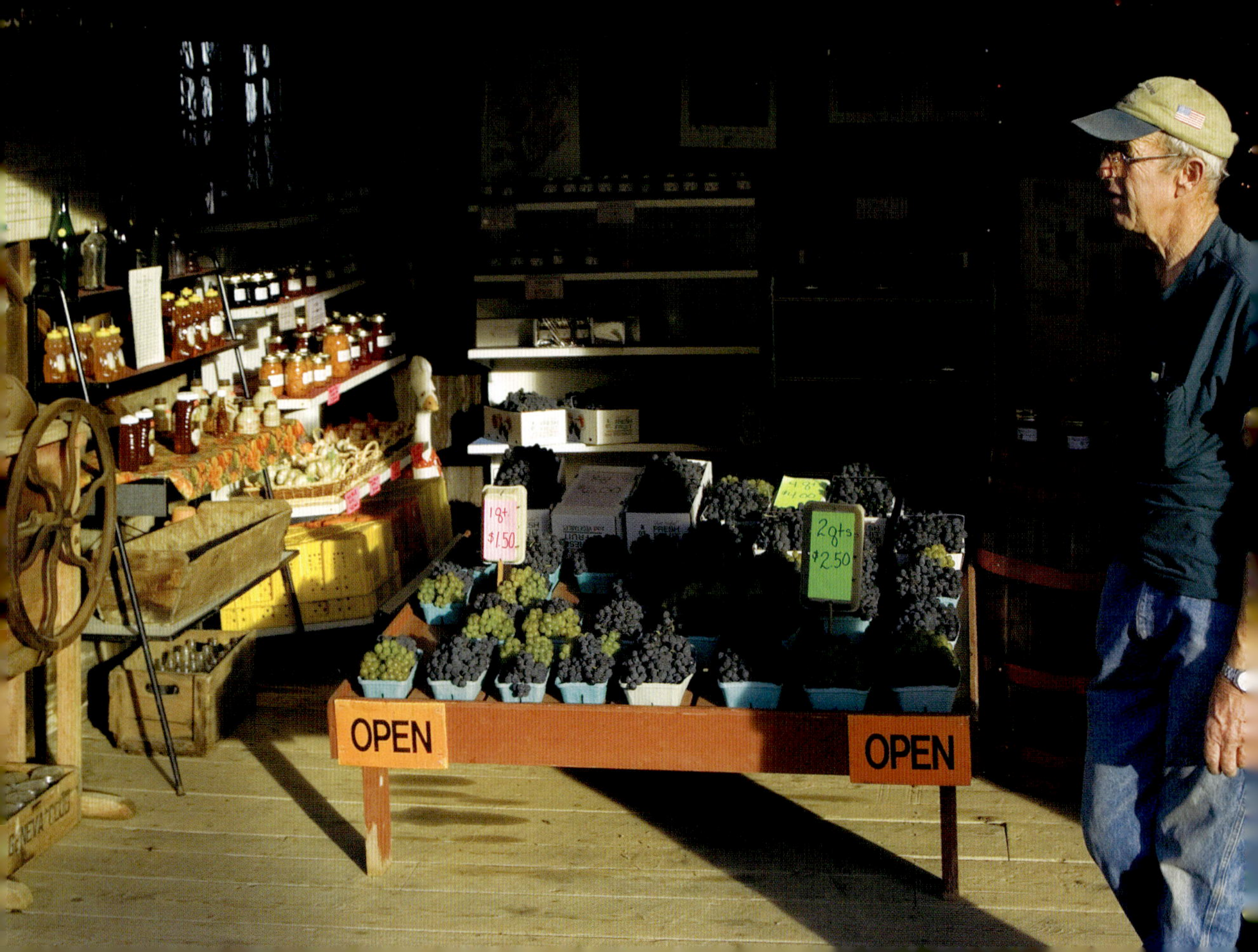
OPEN
OPEN
2qts
$2.50
$1.50

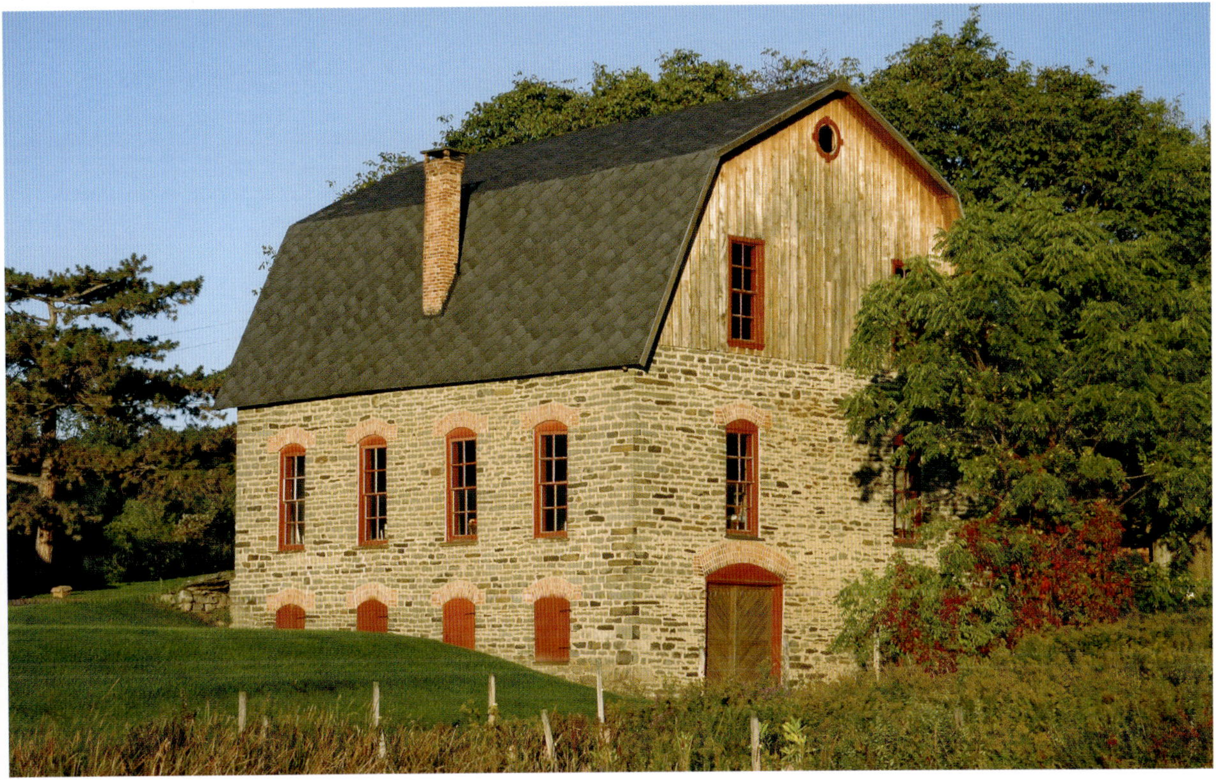

above A restored barn near Penn Yan once sheltered the apple crop from the hills above. left Gentner's Valley View farmstand, above the West River near Naples. next The Geneva Armory, on the right, site of the first indoor lacrosse game played in America.

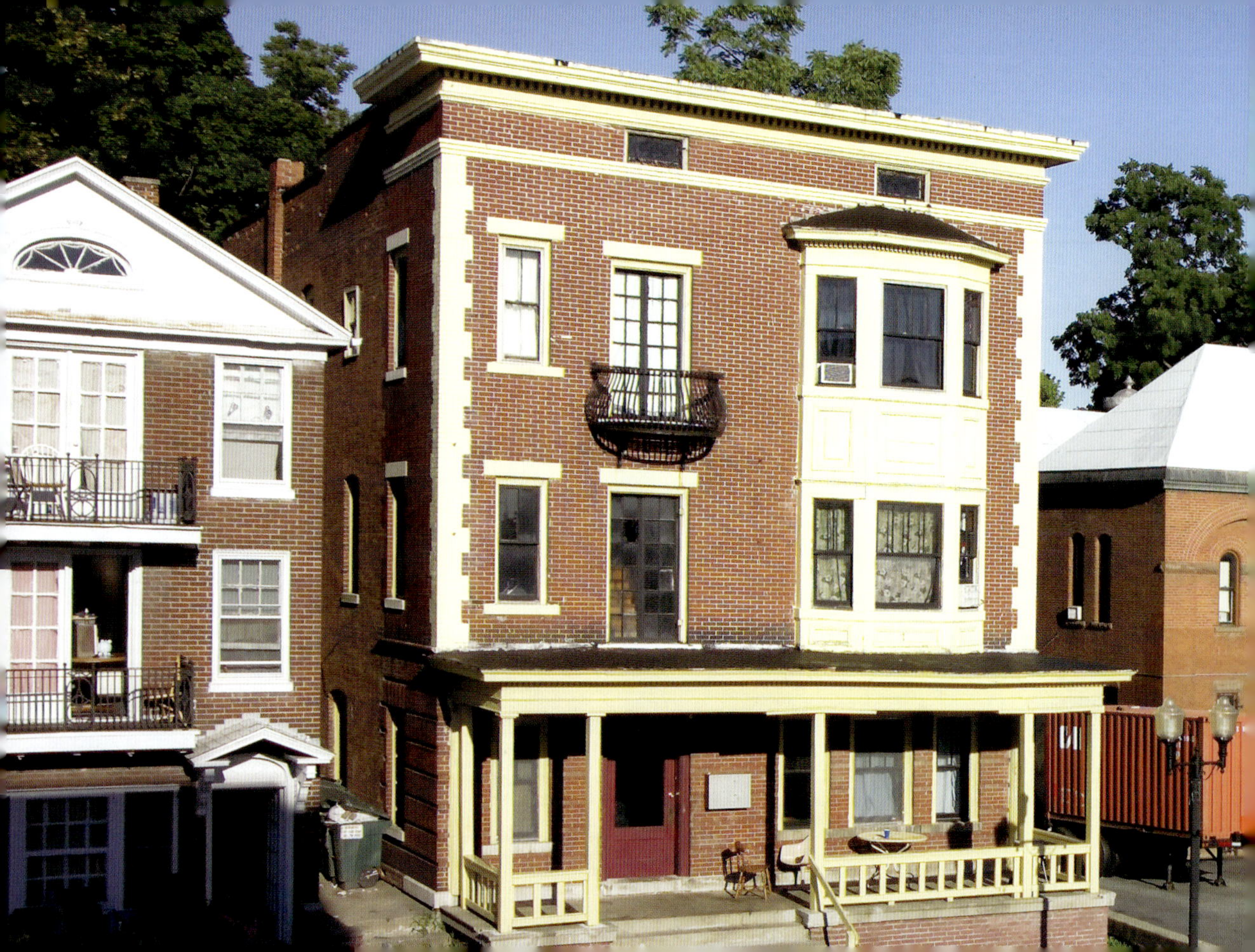

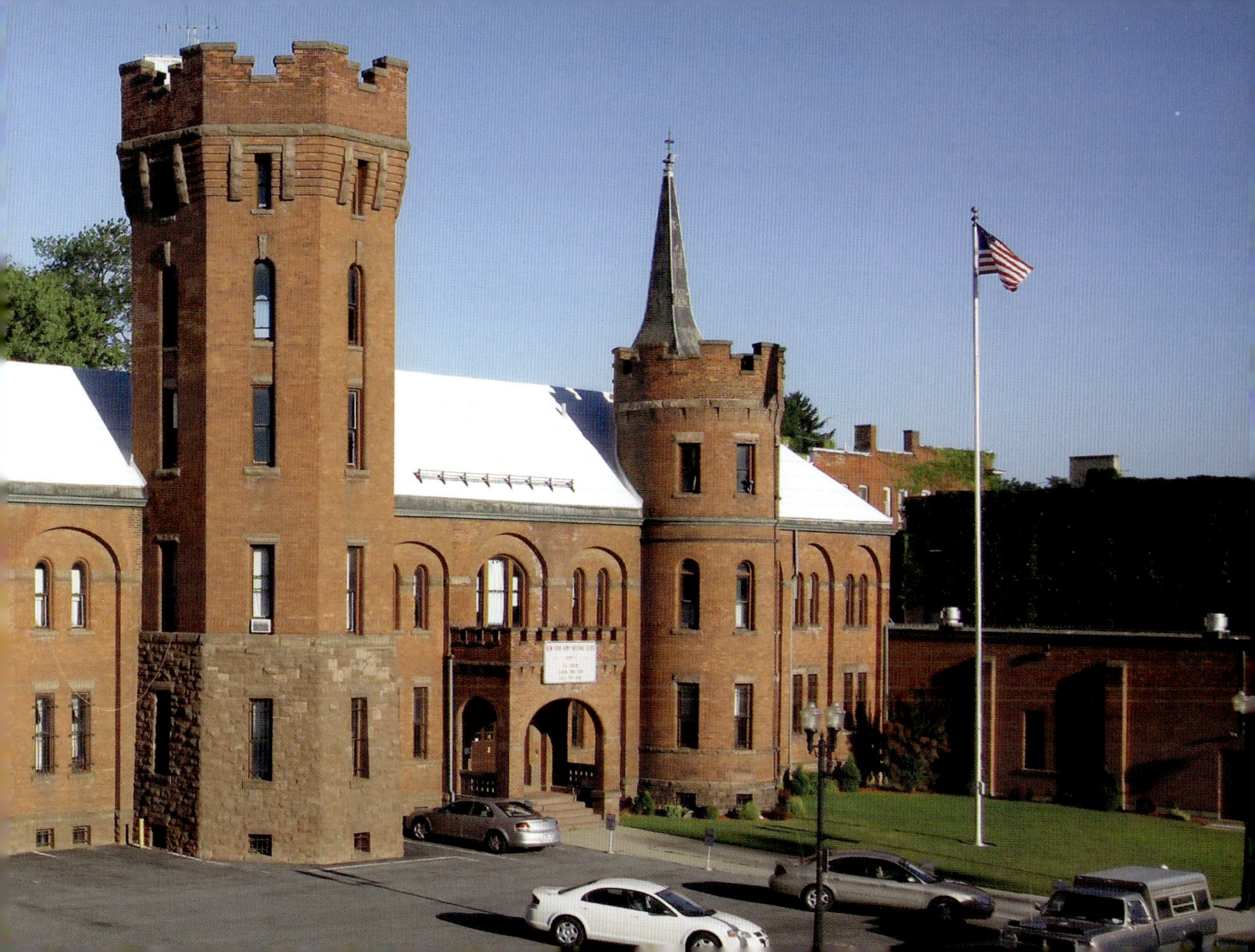

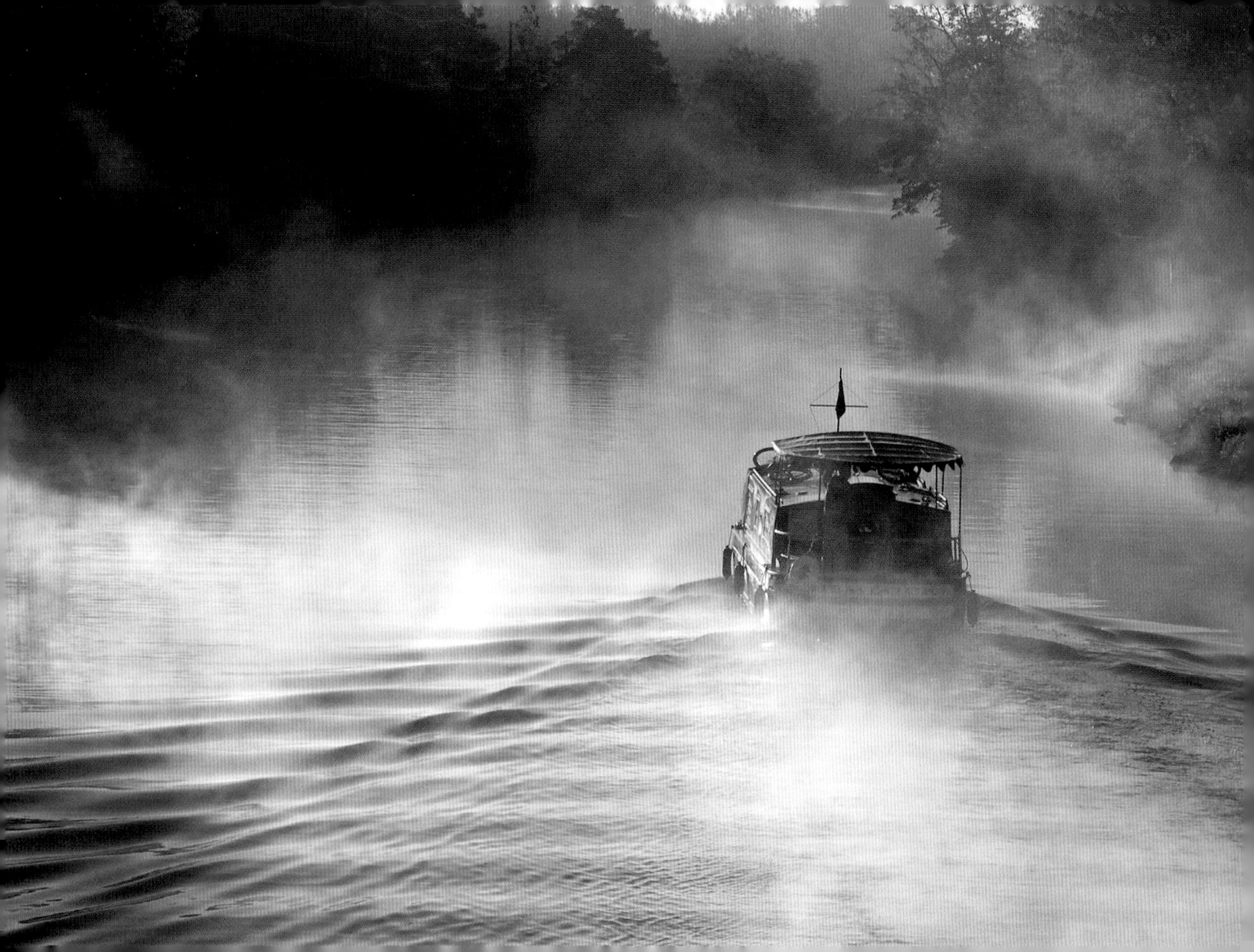

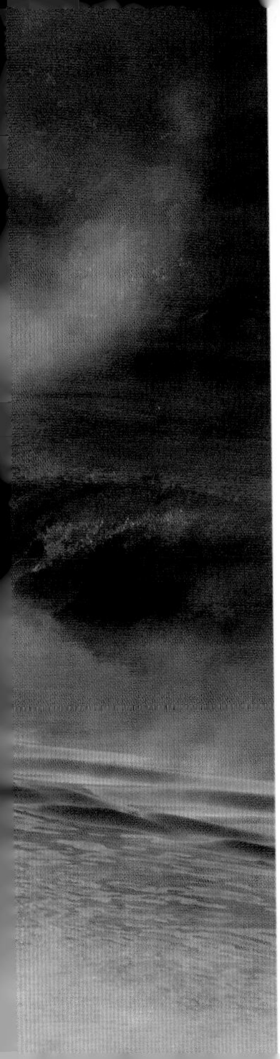

left Rental canal boats come equipped with bikes for exploring the towpath.

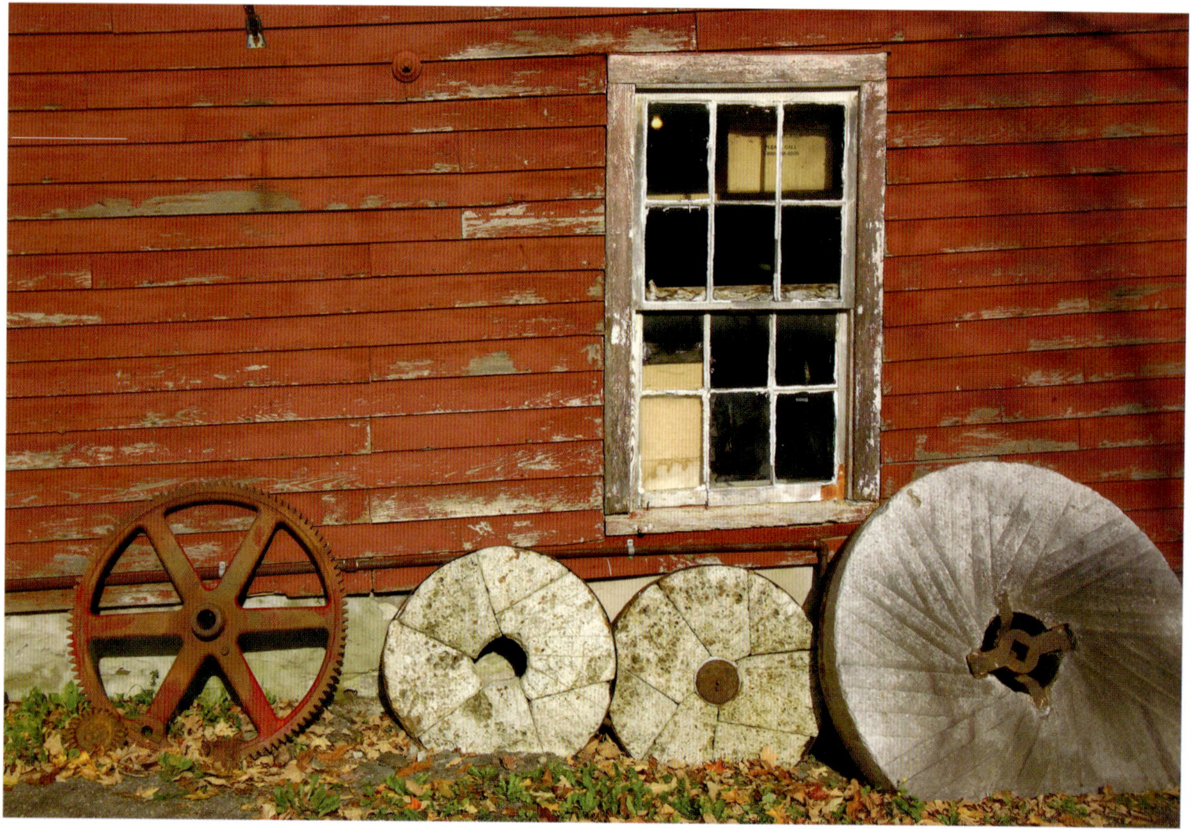

above and right Although now inoperative, New Hope Mills along Skaneateles Lake sells a variety of flours, mixes, and preserves.

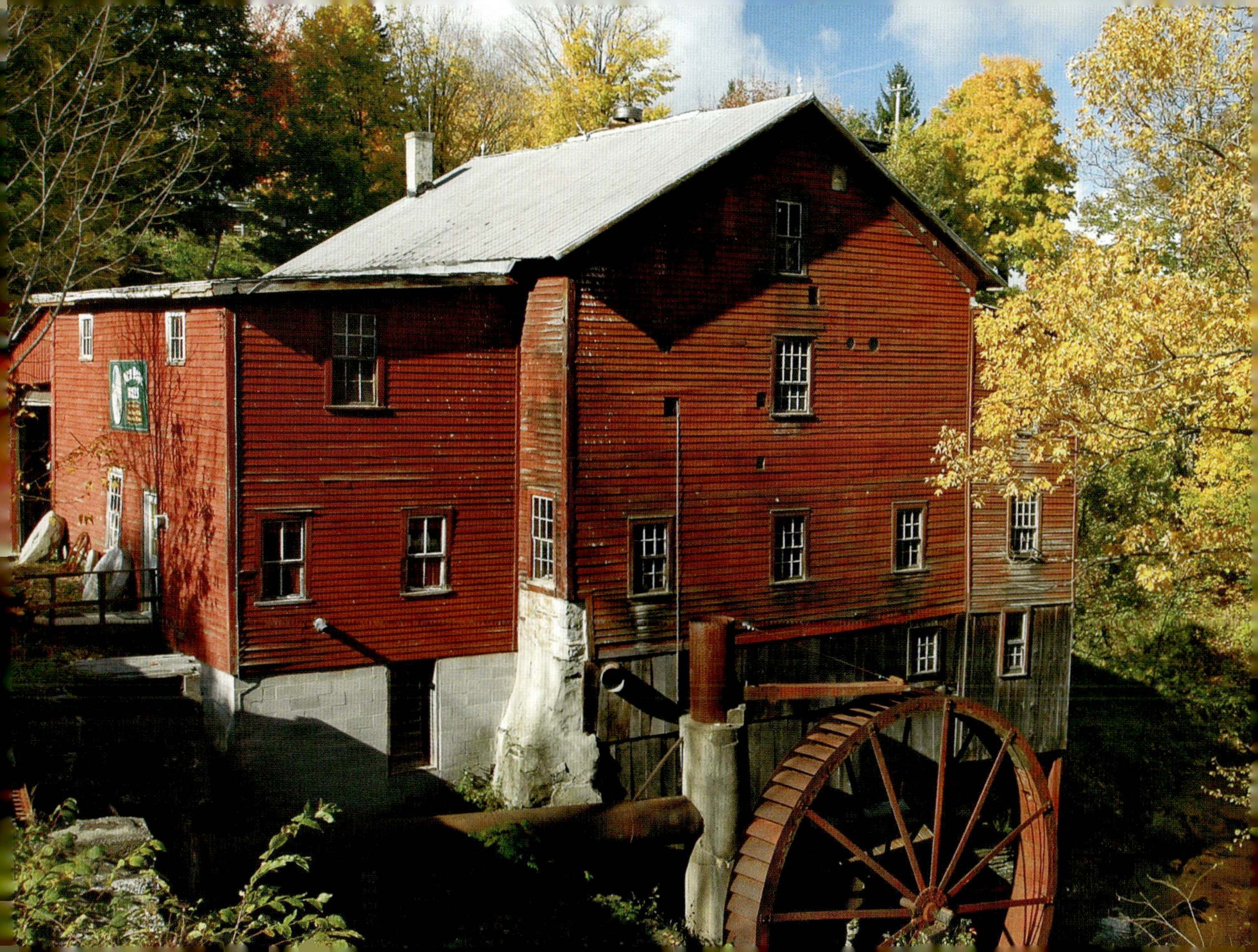

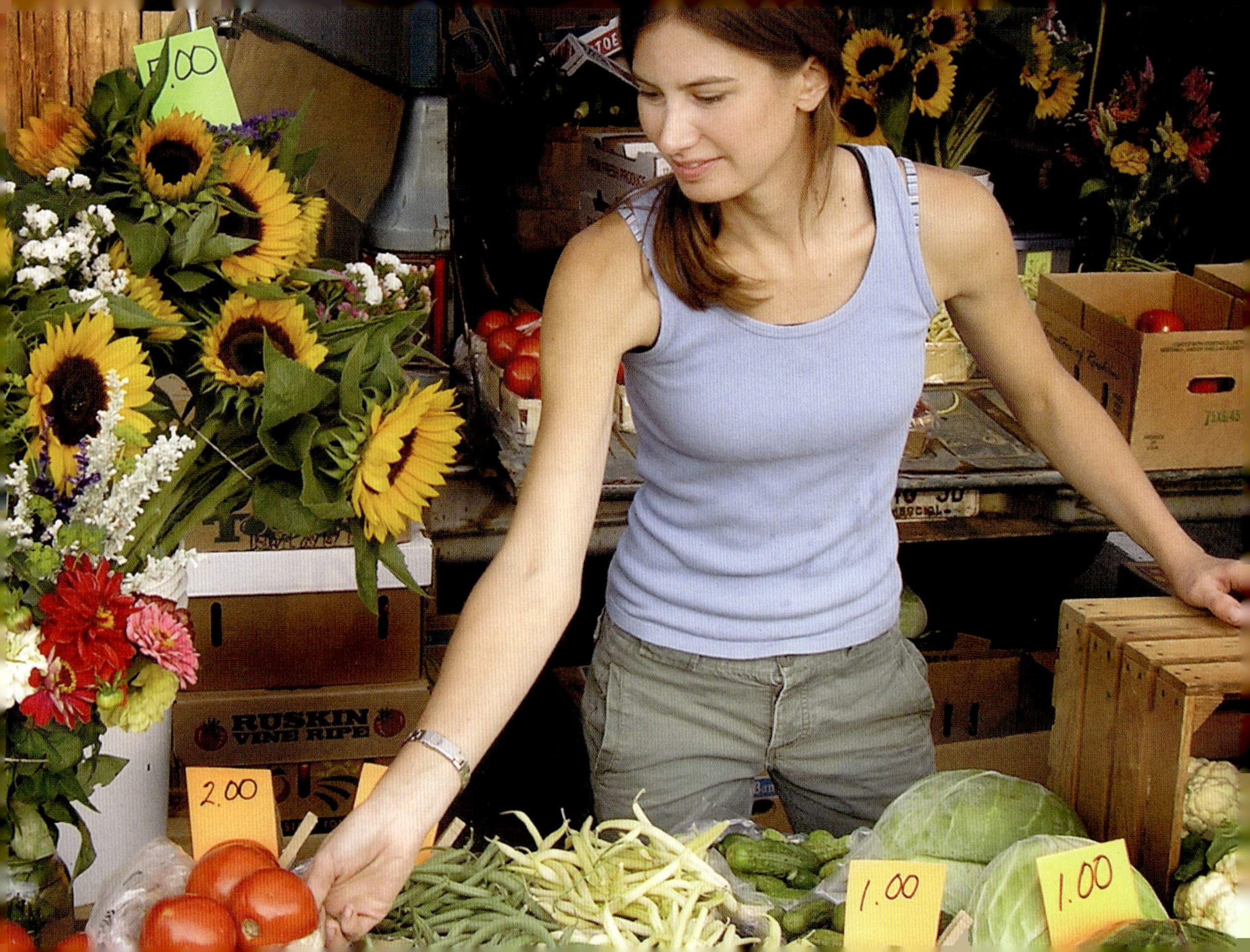

RUSKIN
VINE RIPE
2.00
1.00
1.00

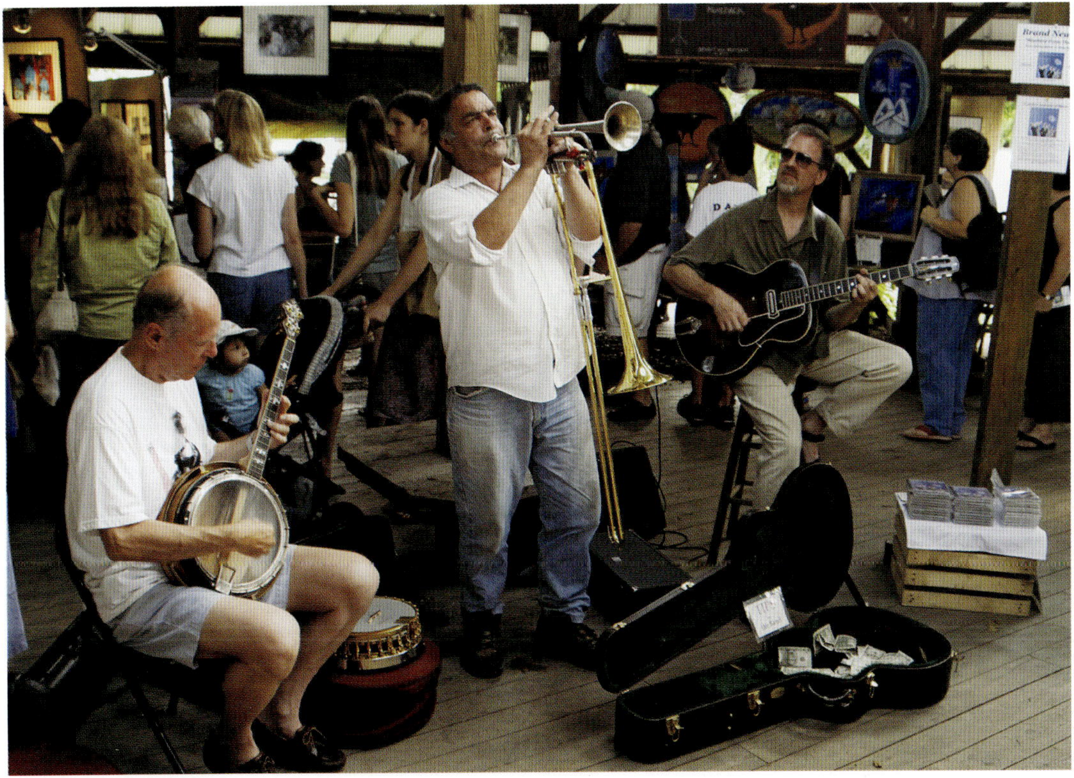

above, left, and next Farmers' markets abound throughout the region. The biggest, the Ithaca Farmers' Market, brims with musicians, artists, ethnic foods, and local produce.

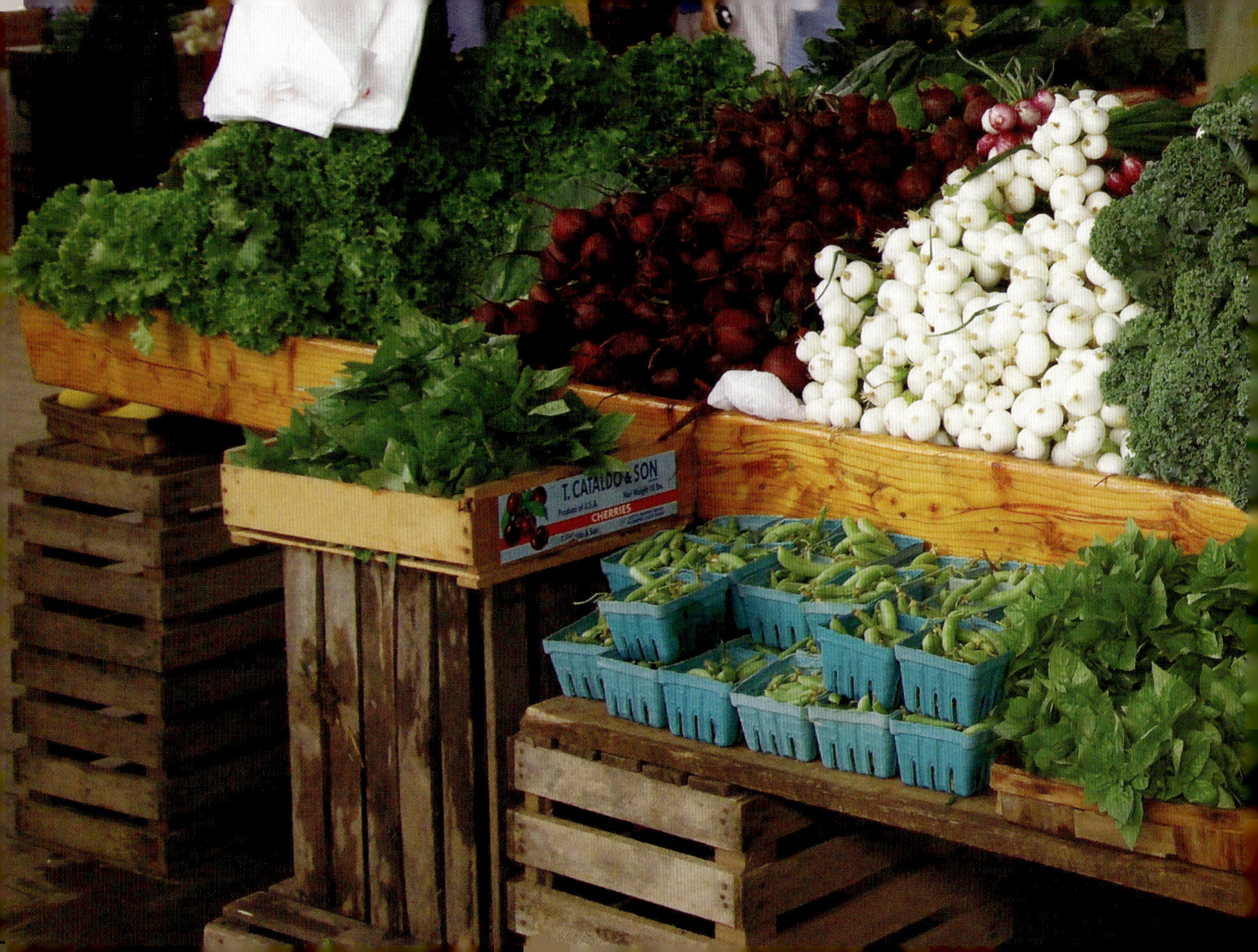
T. CATALDO & SON
CHERRIES

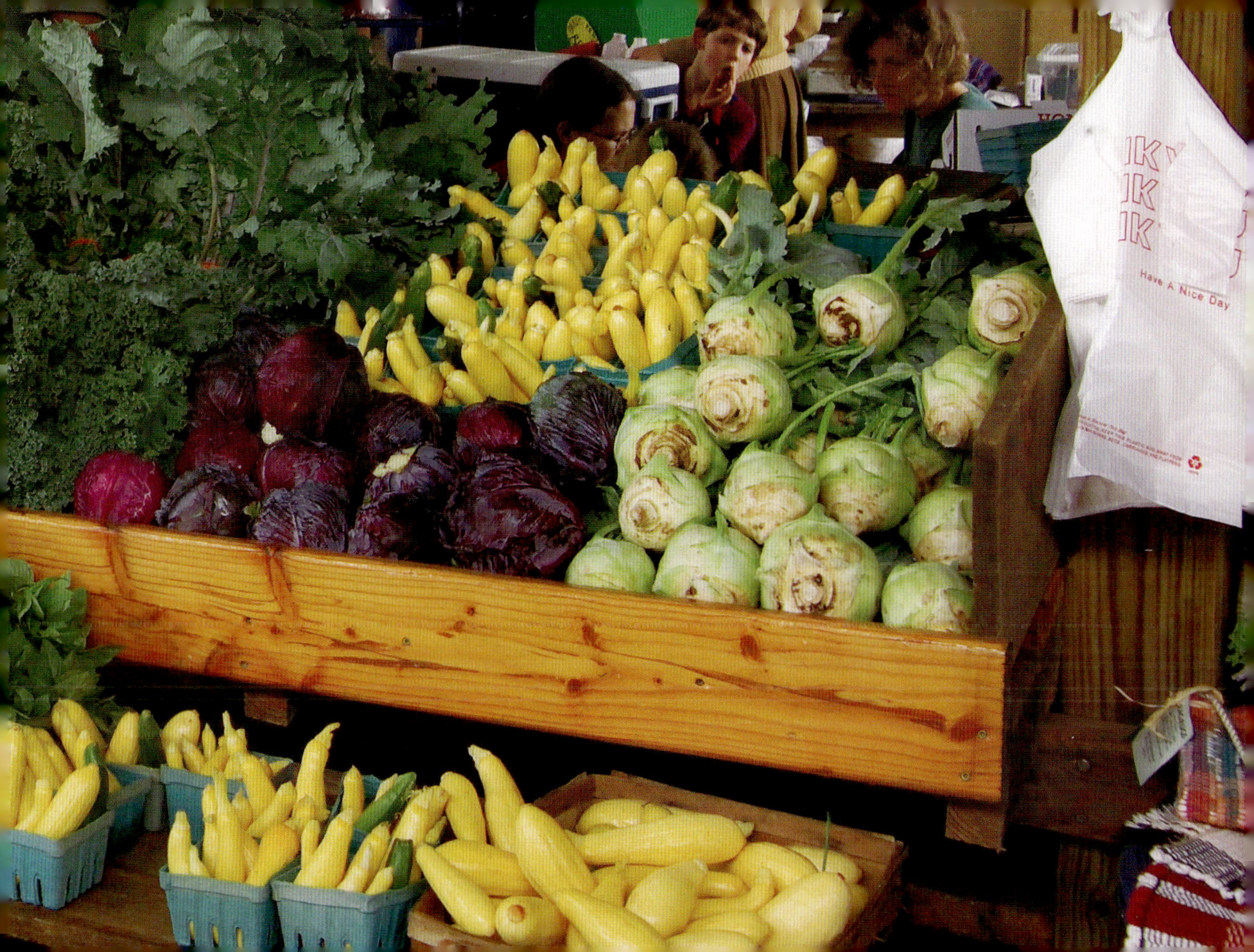
Have A Nice Day

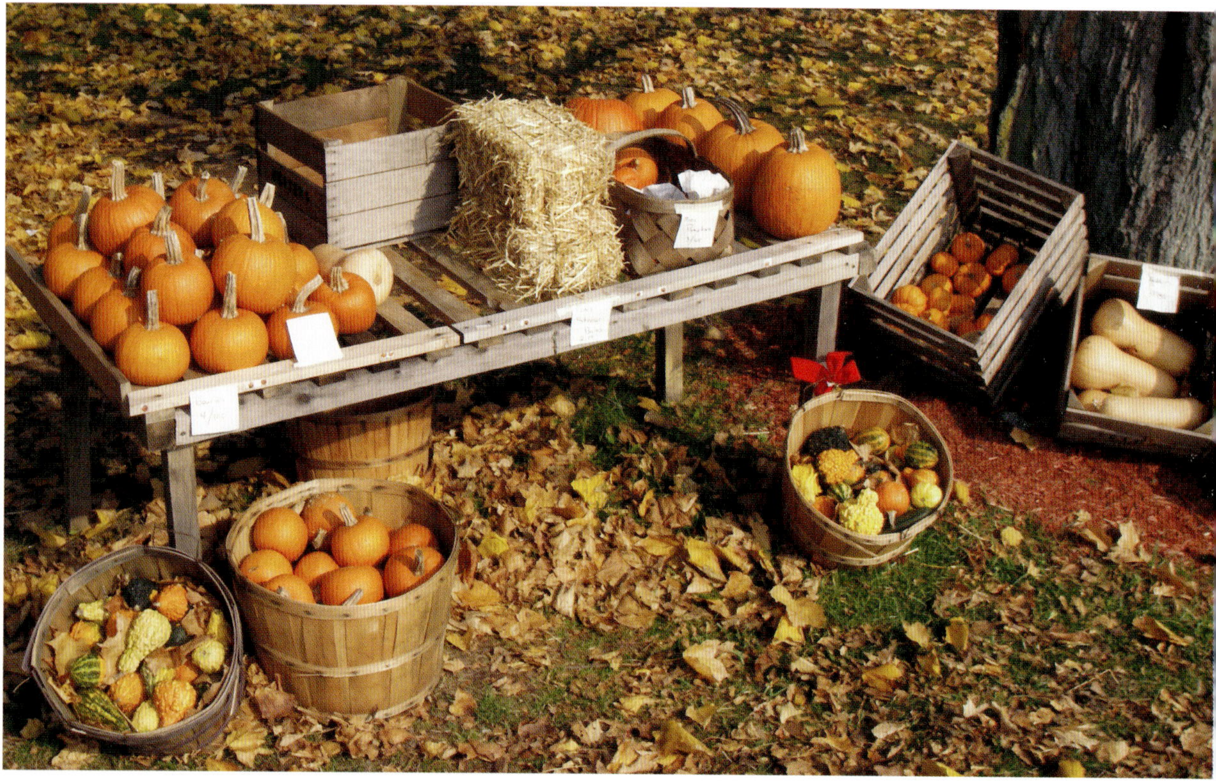

above and right Pumpkins, gourds, and corn are a plentiful autumn harvest in the Finger Lakes. next This field will yield almost half a million pounds of pumpkins. page after next Heidi and Jake in their pasture above Otisco Lake.

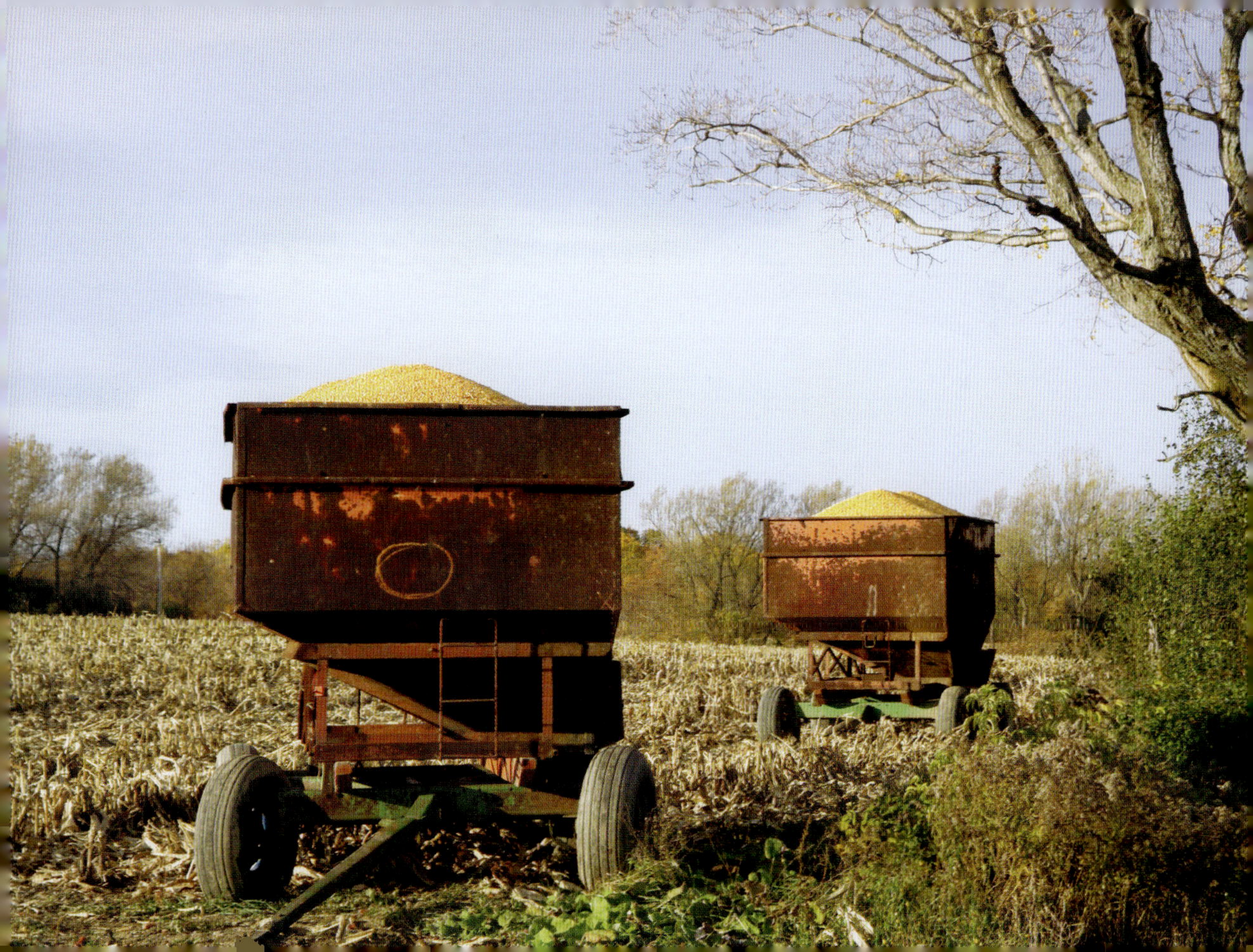

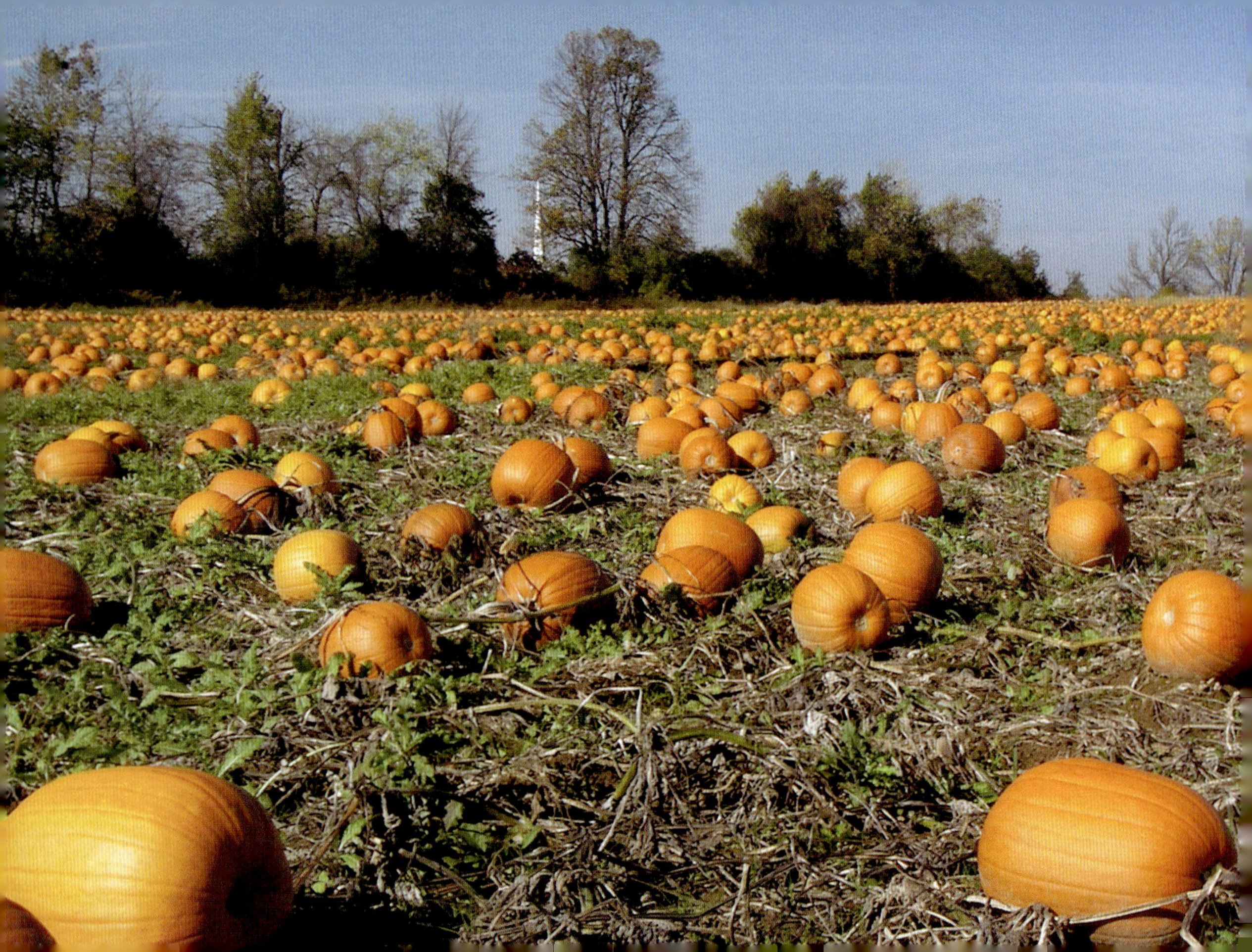

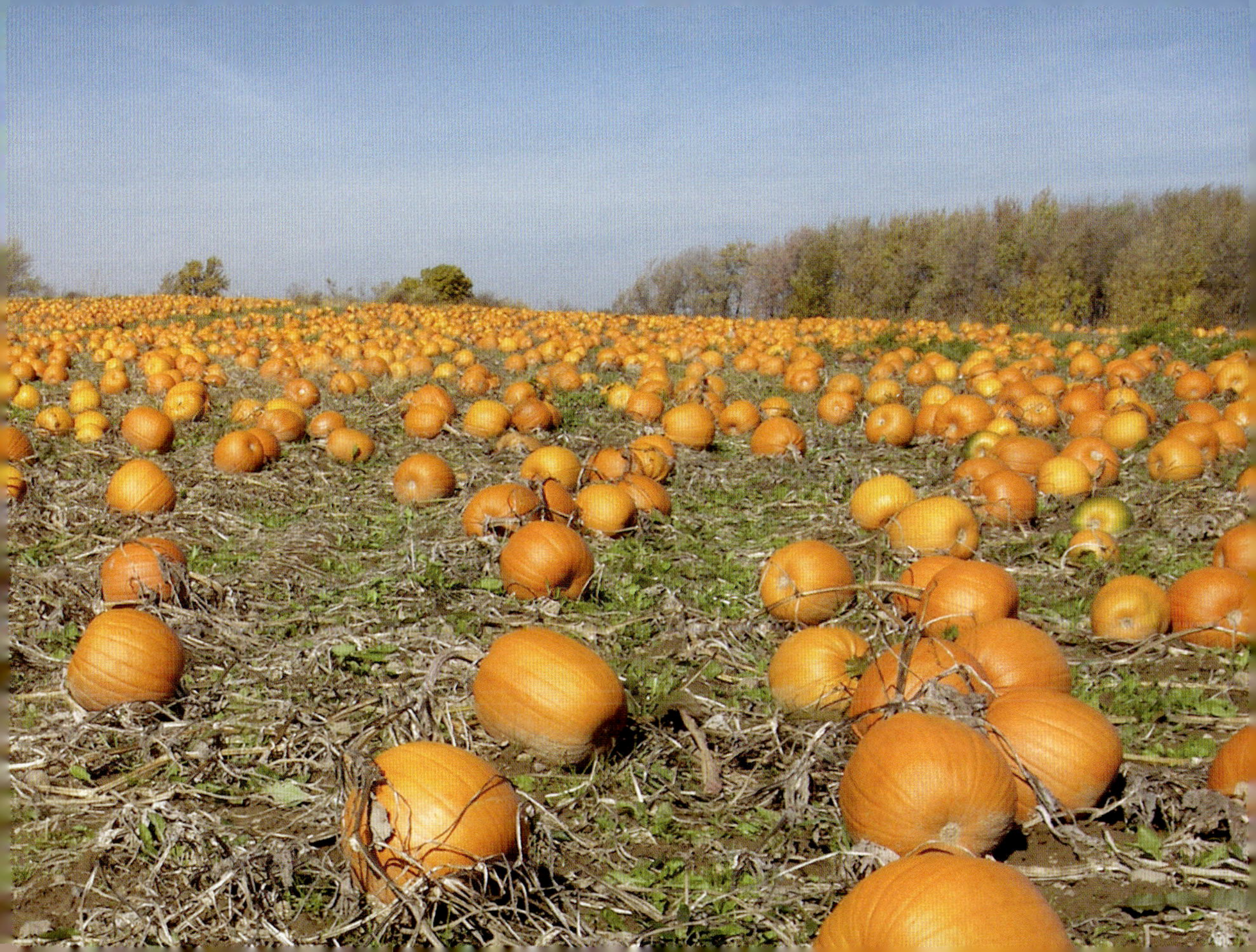

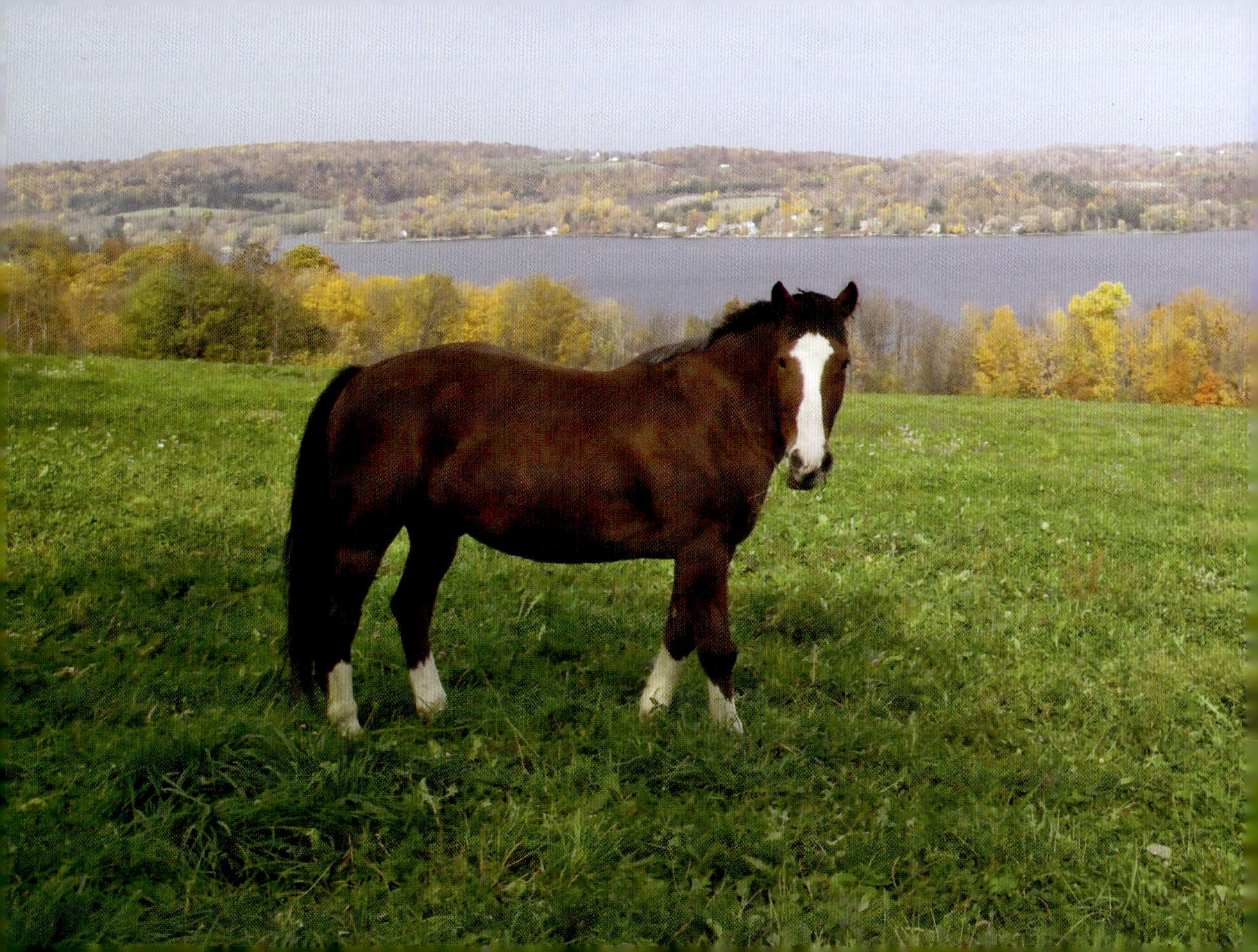

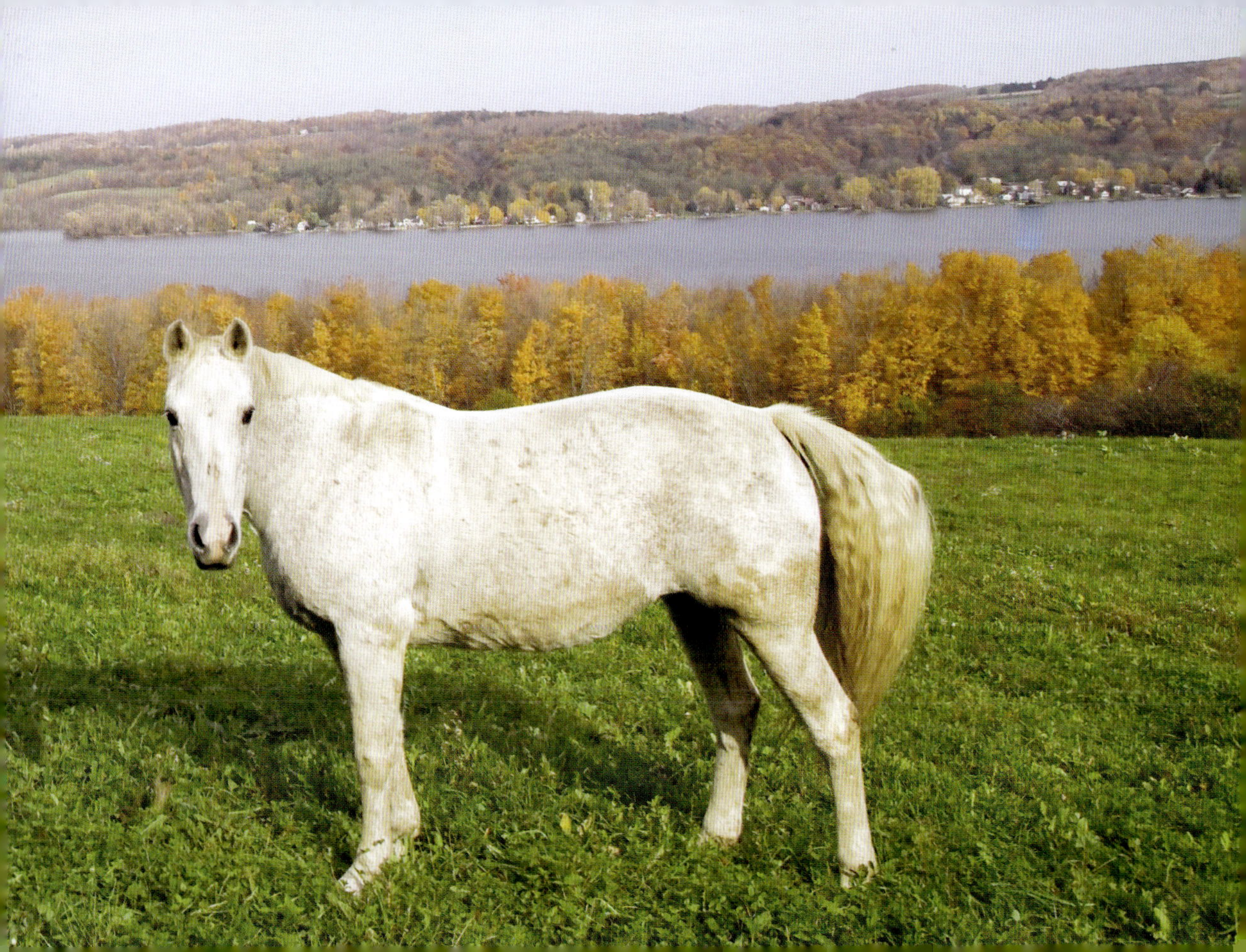

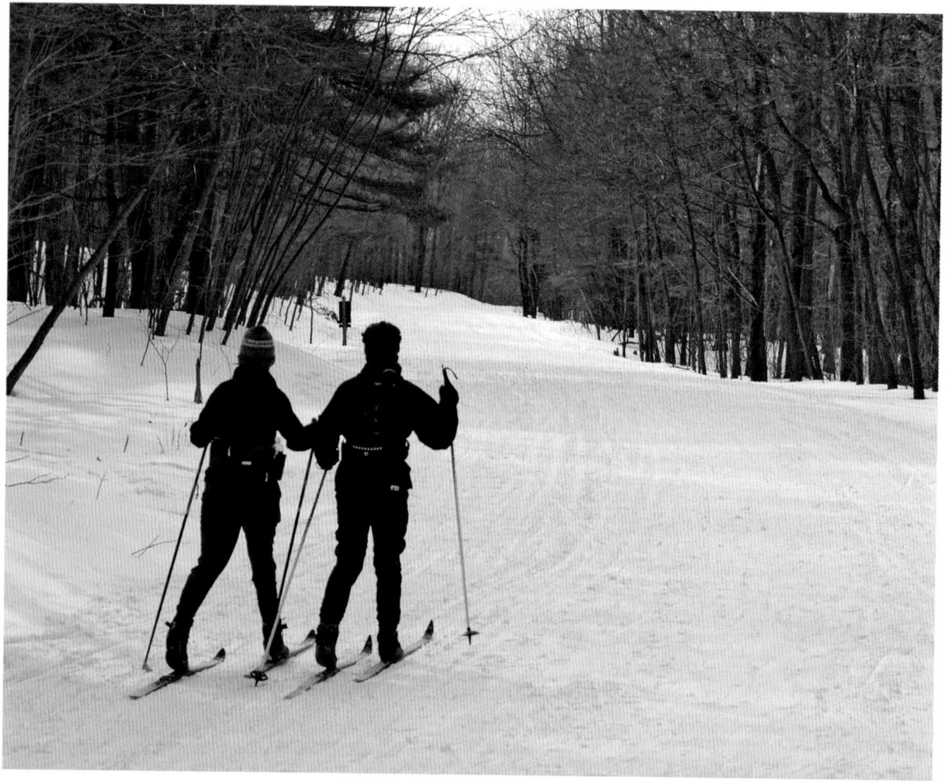

above Cross country skiers on the entrance road at Harriet Hollister State Park above Honeoye Lake.
right A roadside fence proclaims holiday cheer. next Mennonites head to church on a snowy Sunday.

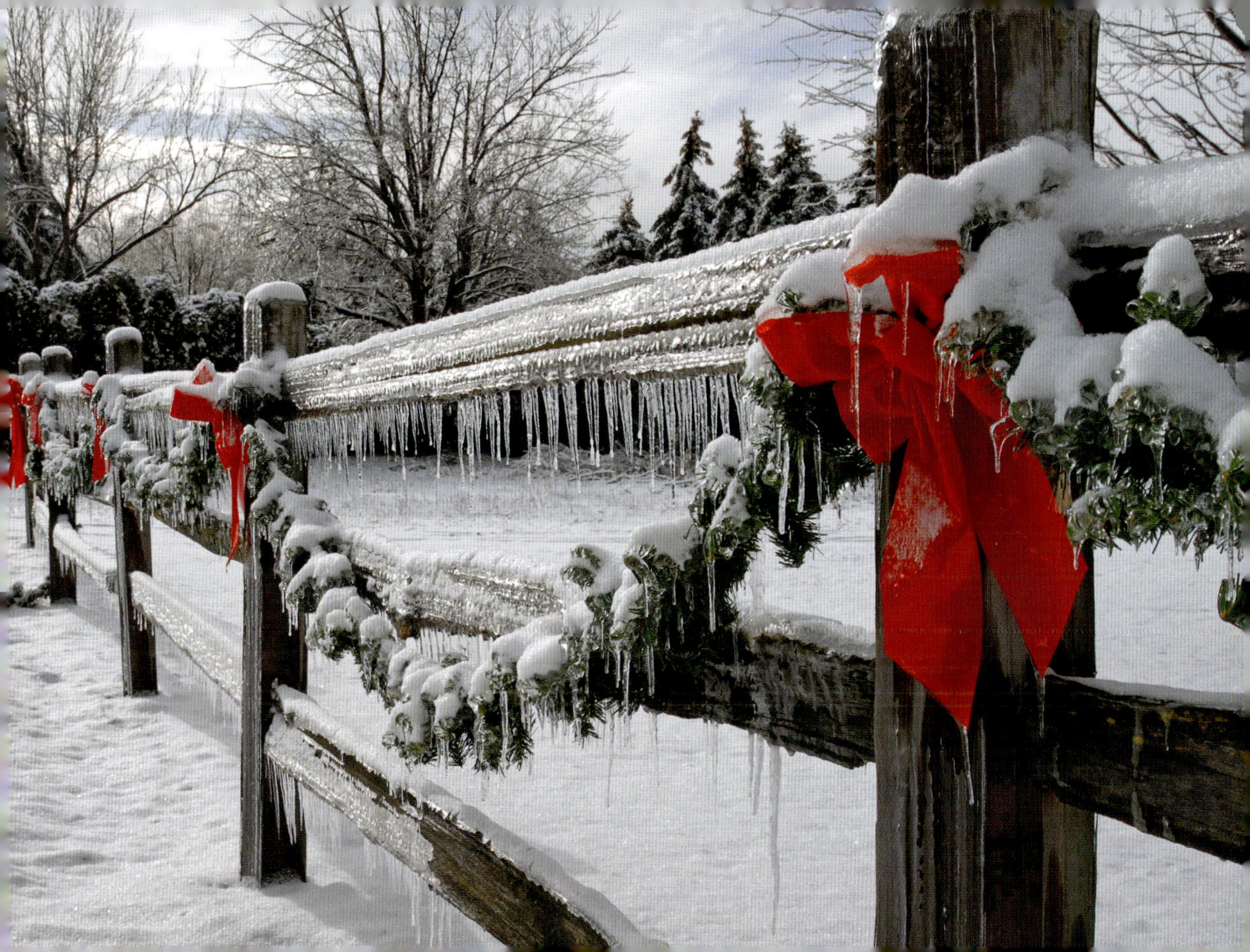

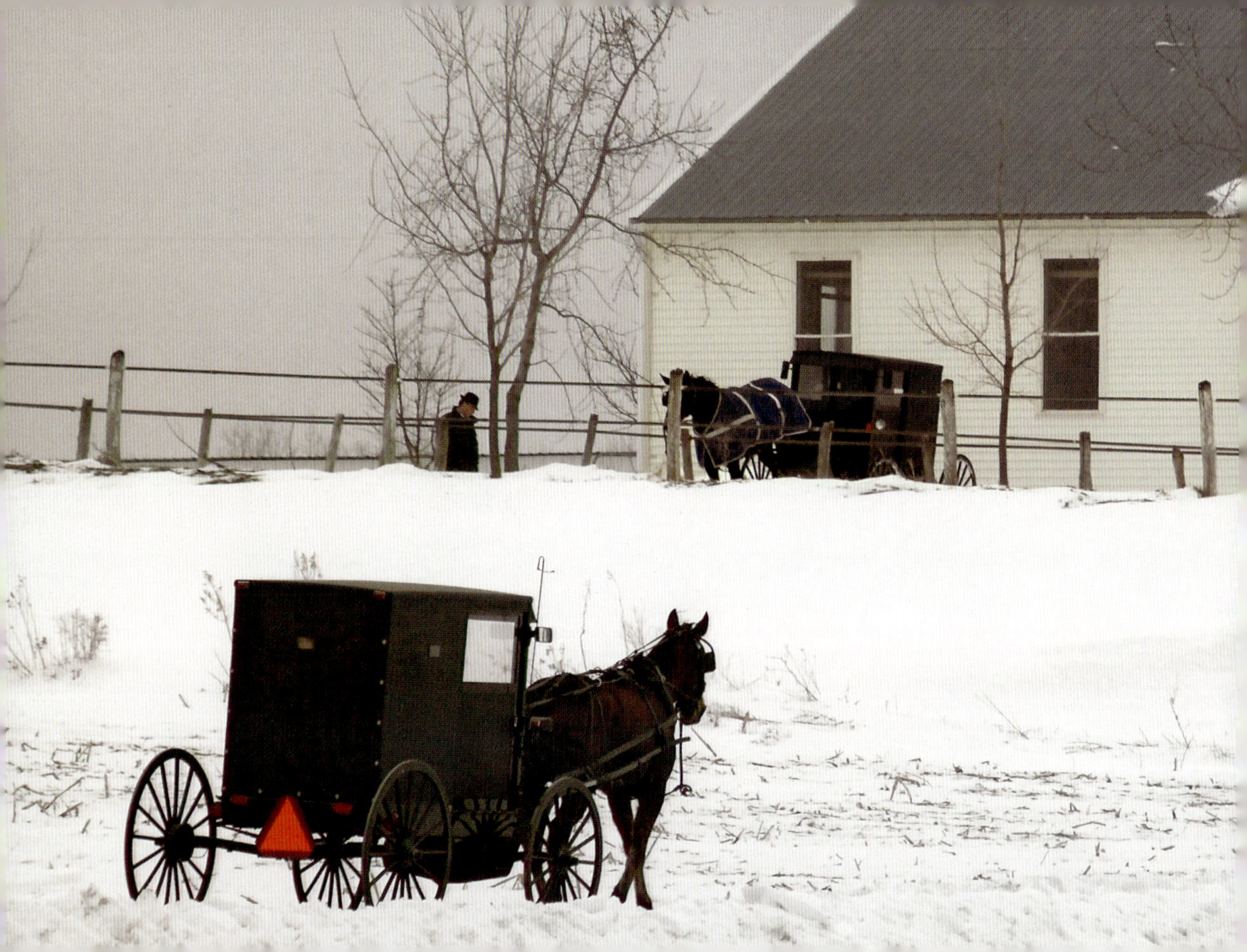

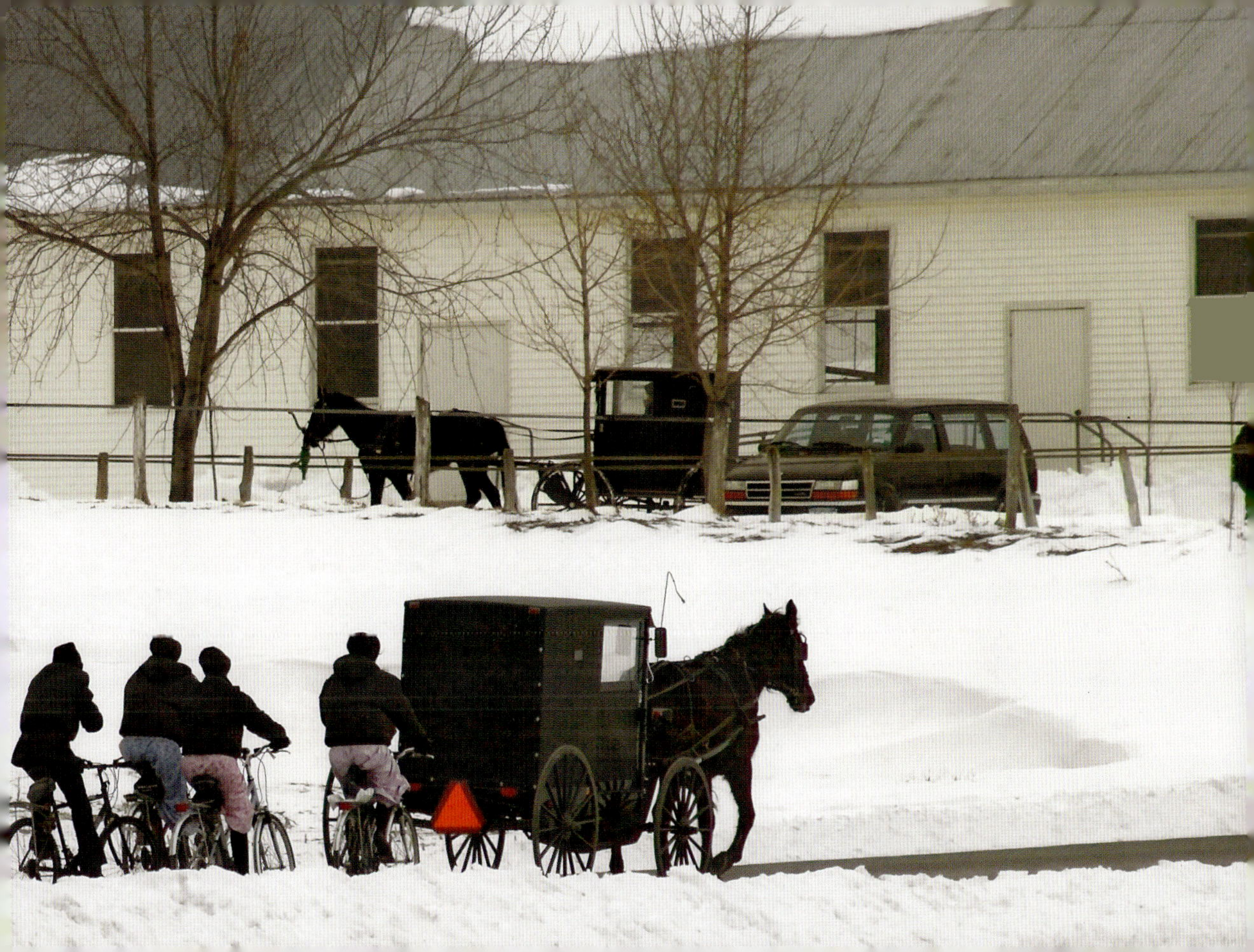

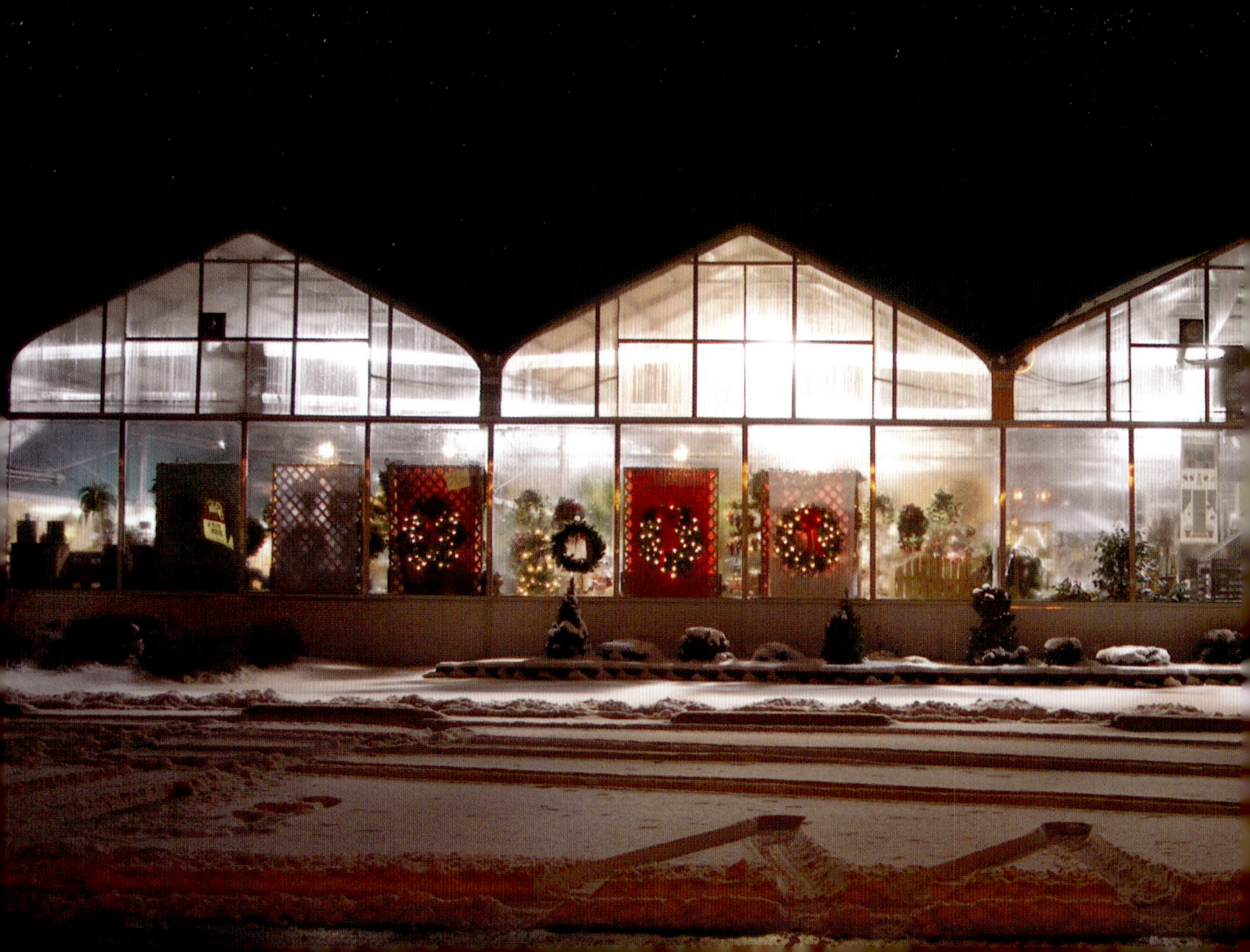

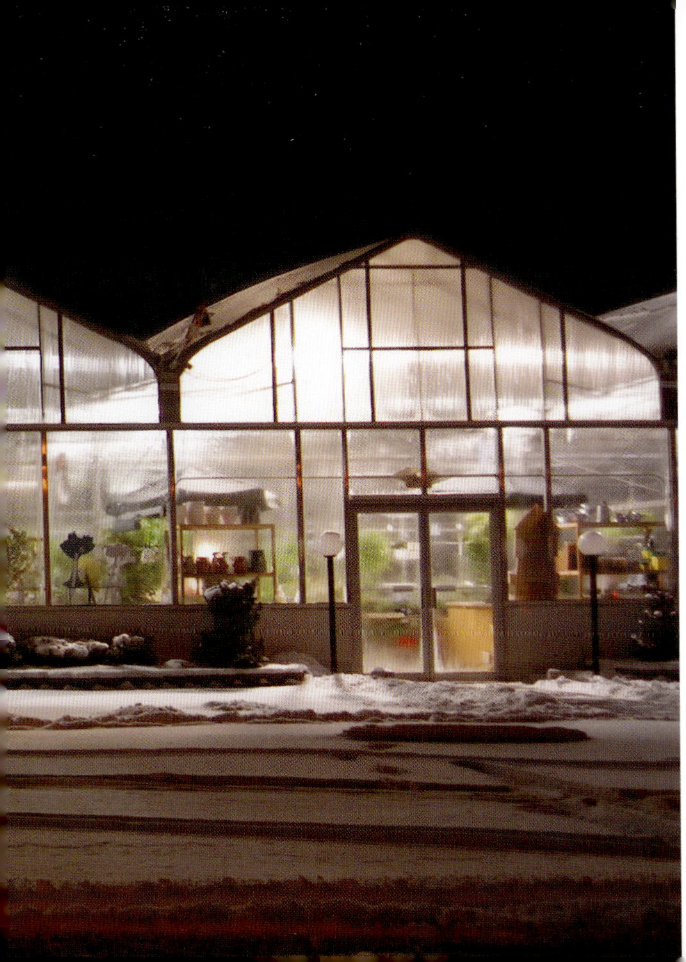

left Farmington greenhouses on an early December eve. next Near Farmington, an ice storm turns an ordinary field into a wonderland.

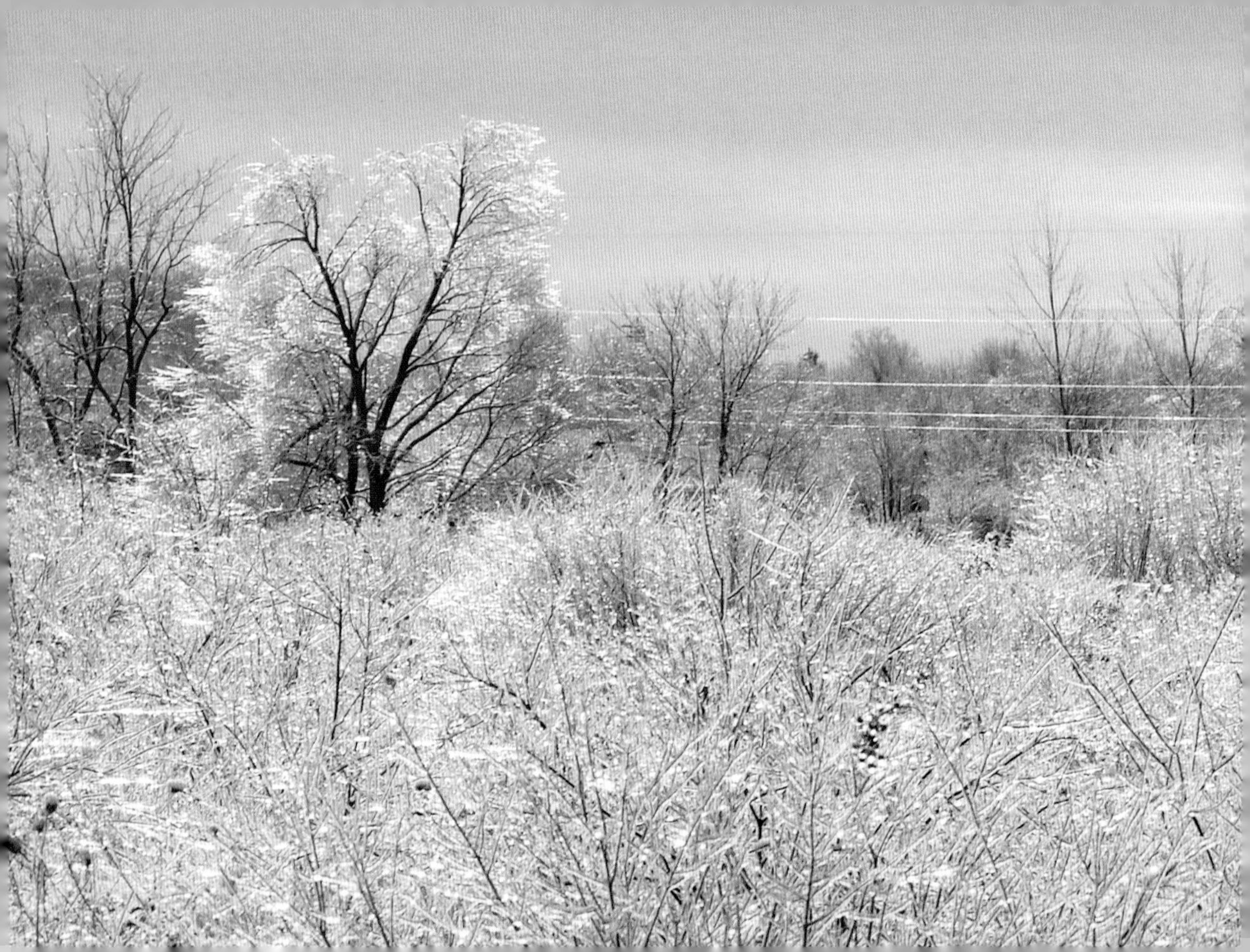

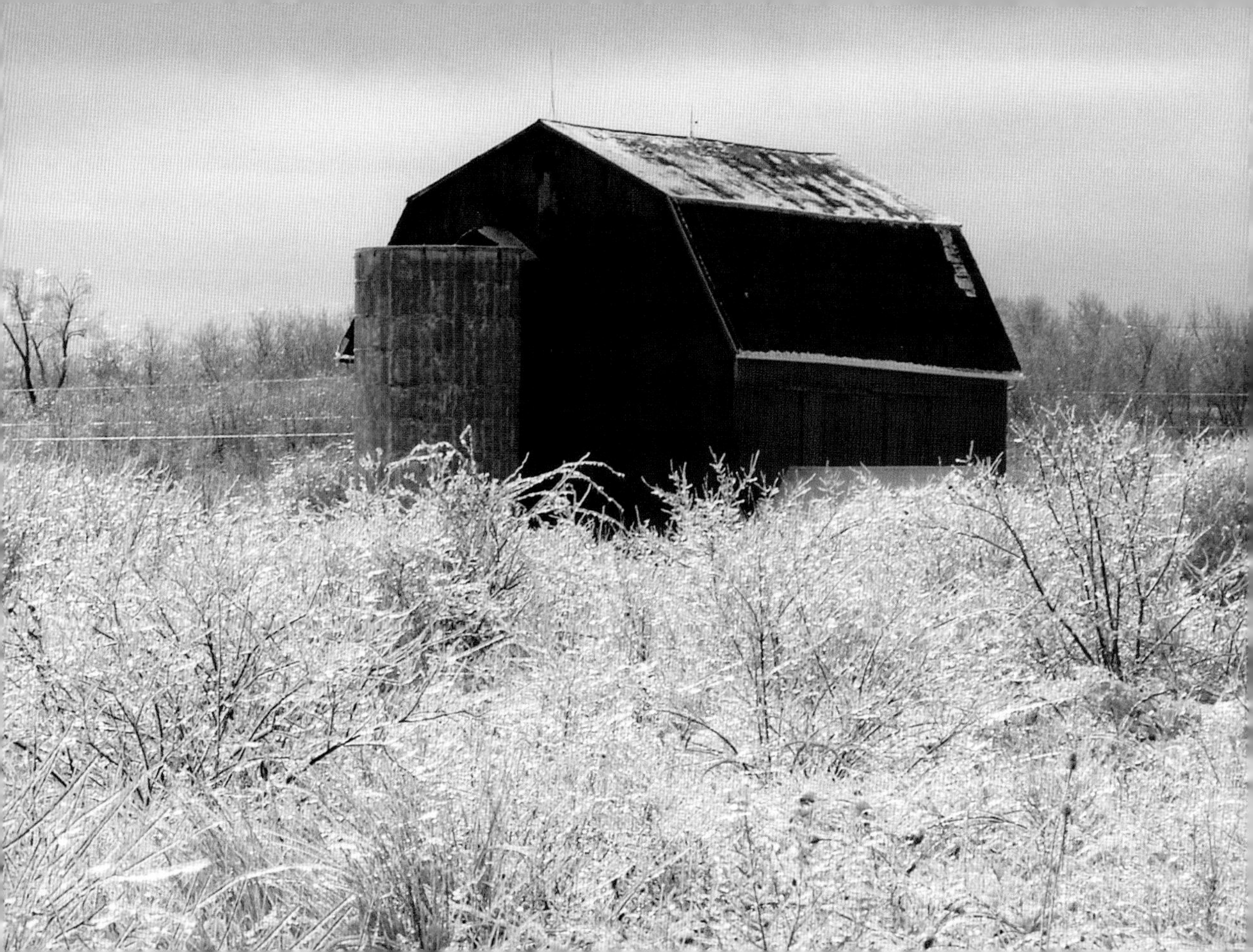

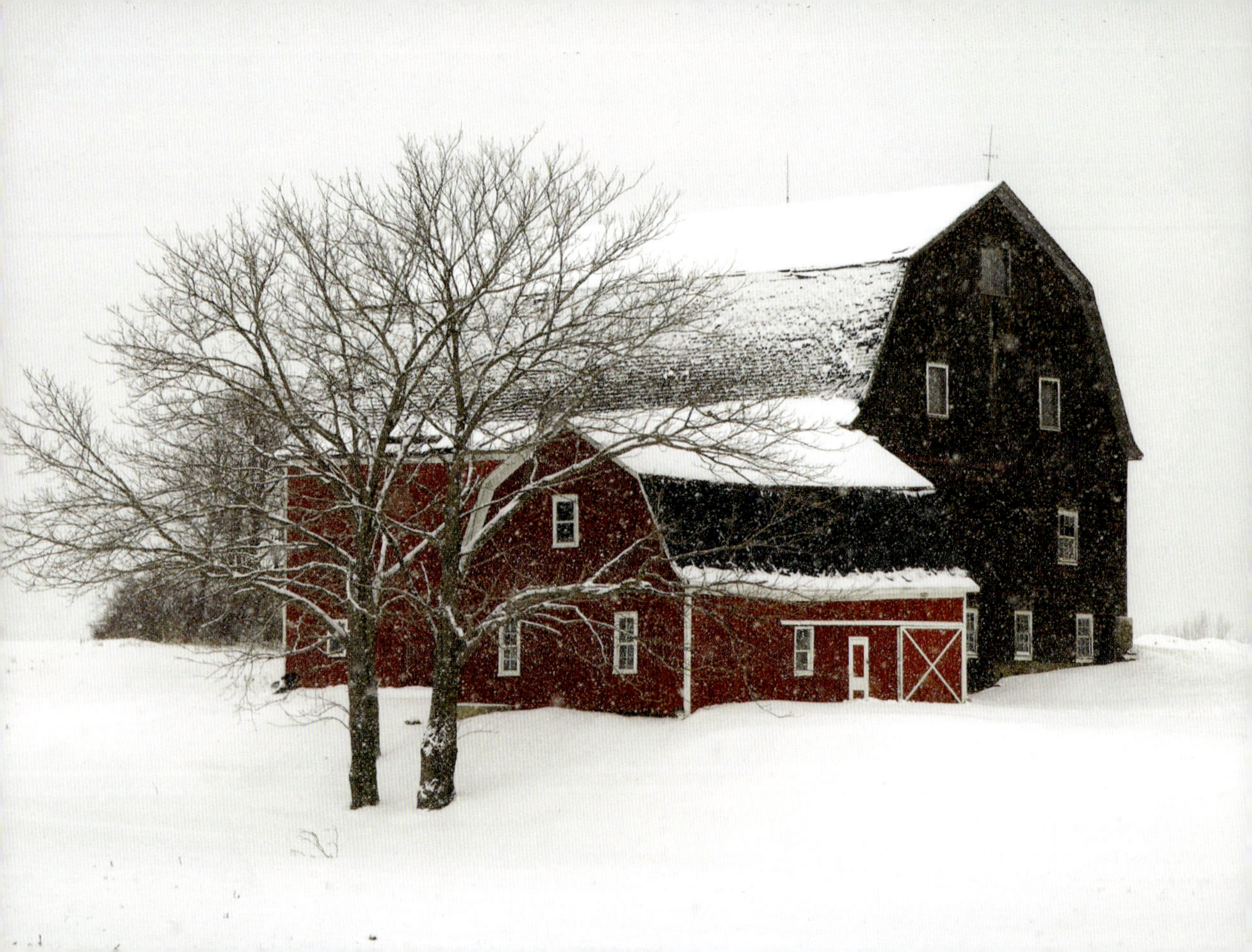

left A barn in Cohocton. right The 214-foot-high Taughannock Falls near Trumansburg. next Locked in by ice, the *Canandaigua Lady* waits for spring on Canandaigua Lake.

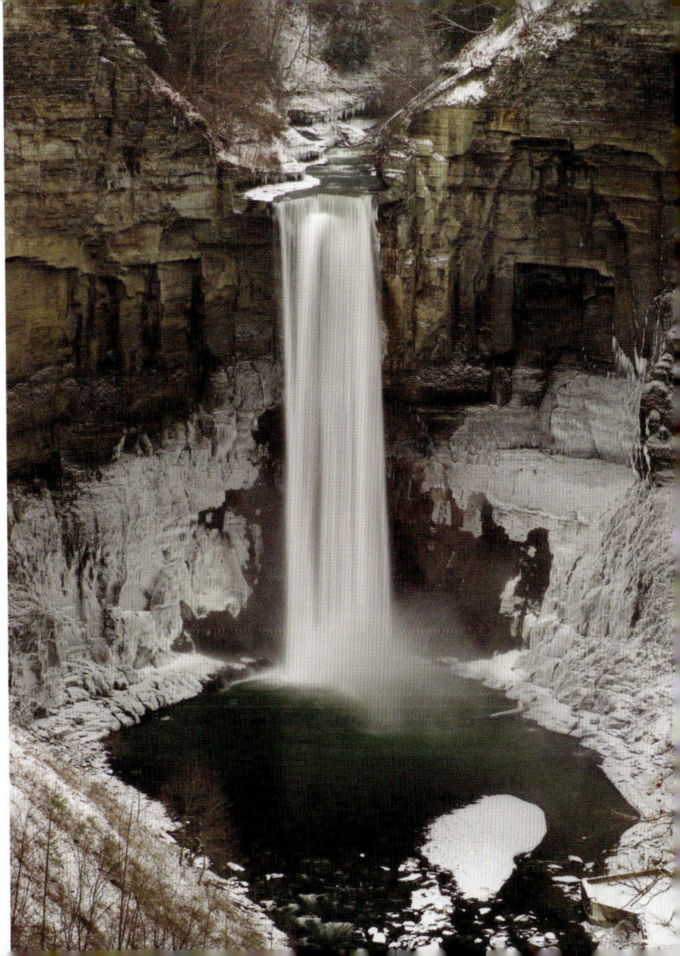

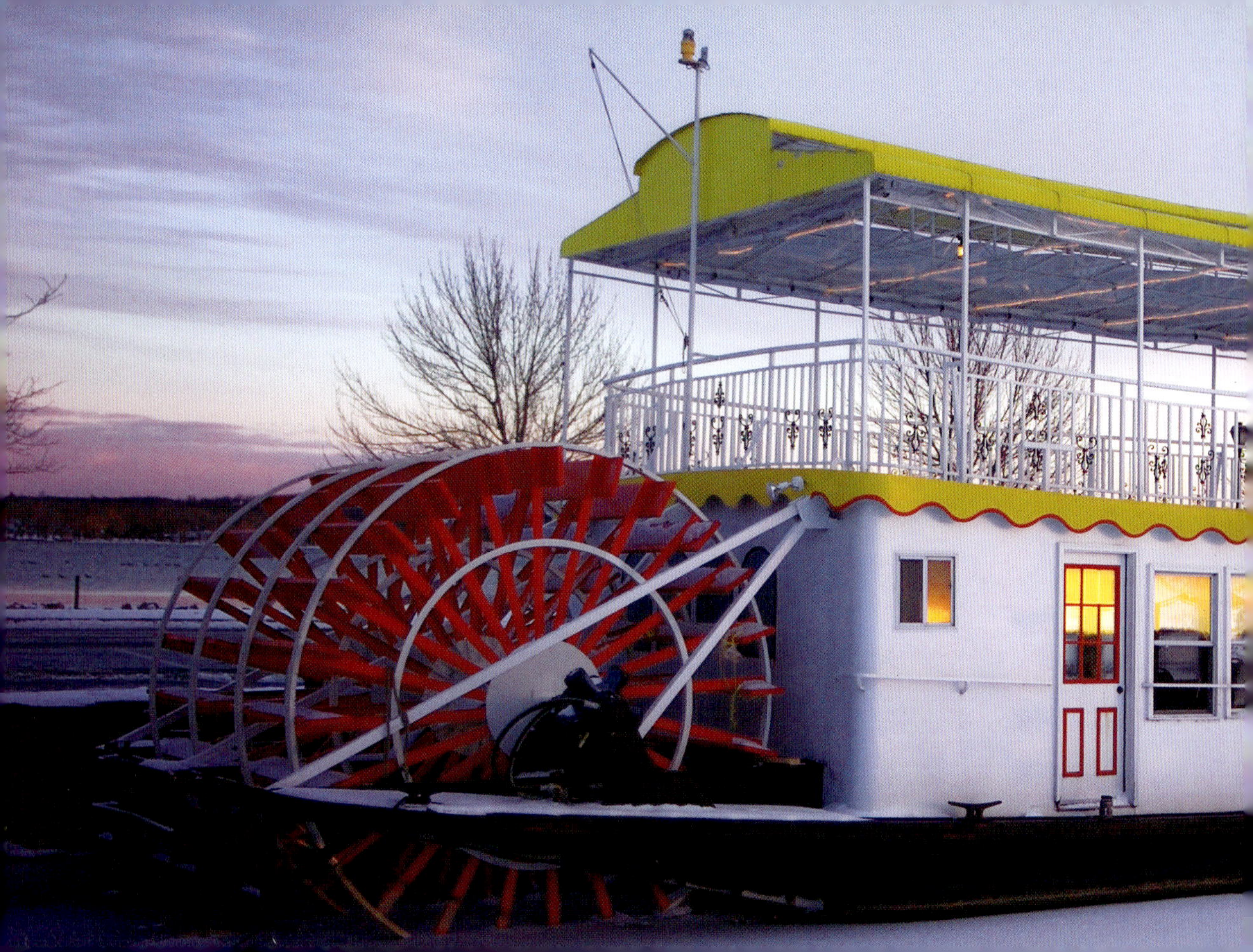

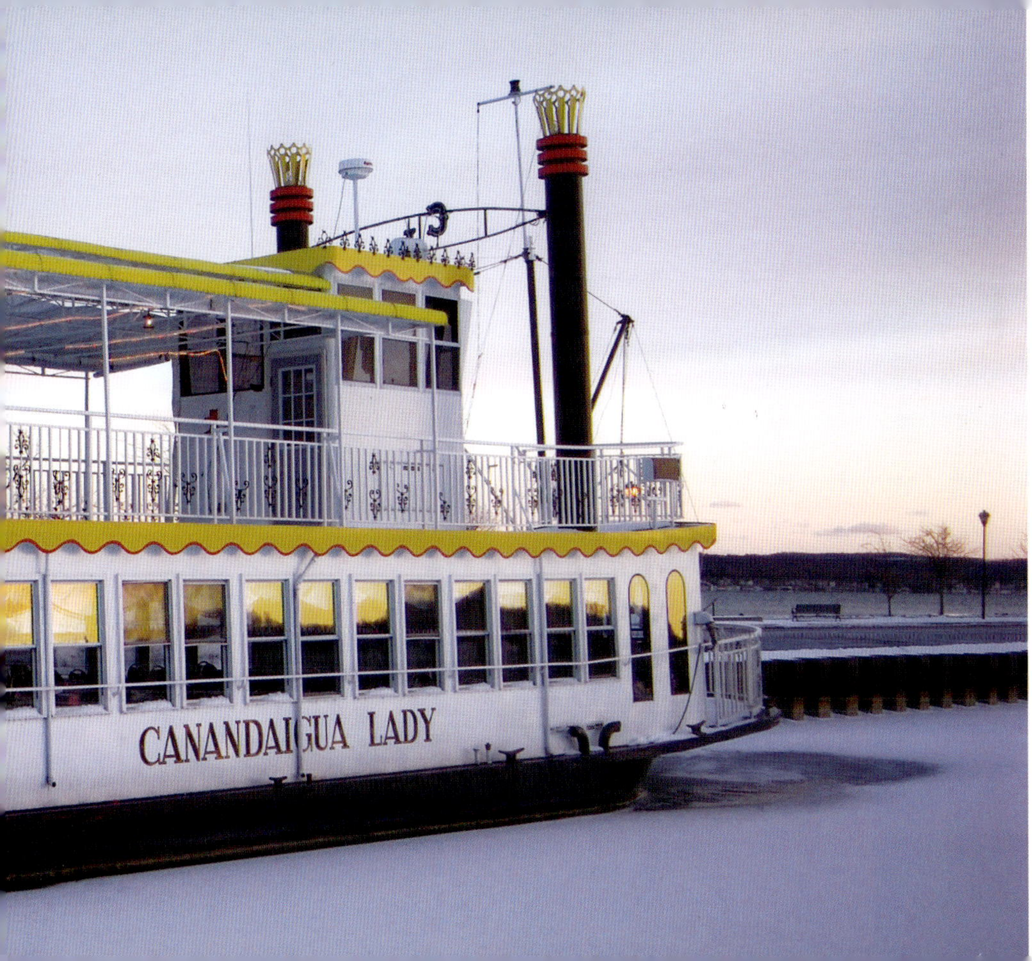
CANANDAIGUA LADY

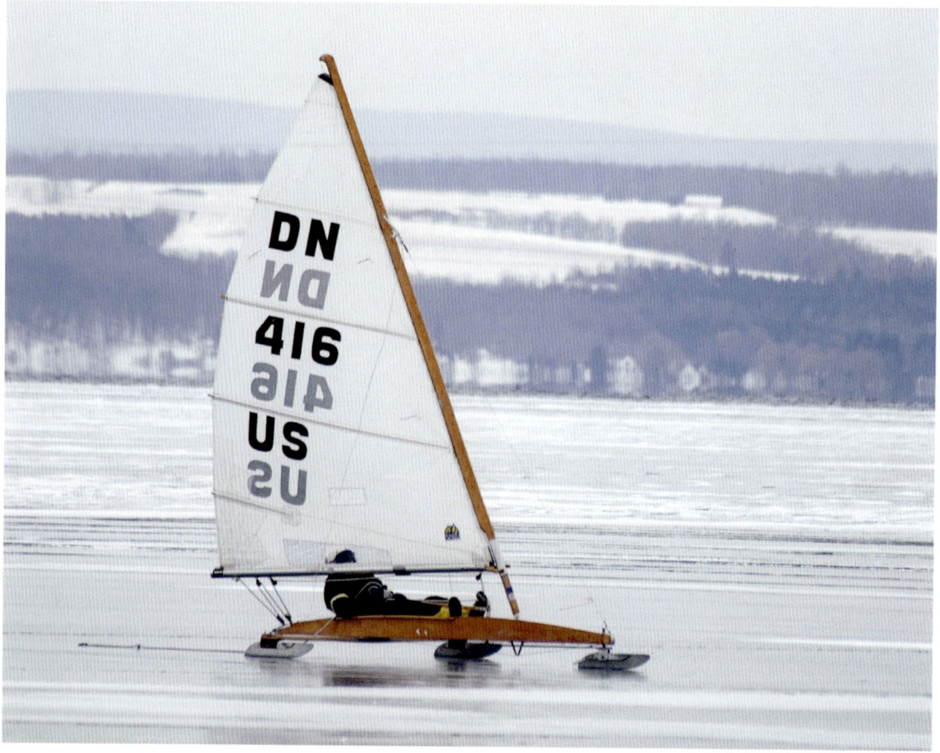

above On Canandaigua Lake, ice boats easily hit 35 mph. right A Toulouse goose on Keuka Lake. next An ice fisherman on Honeoye Lake.

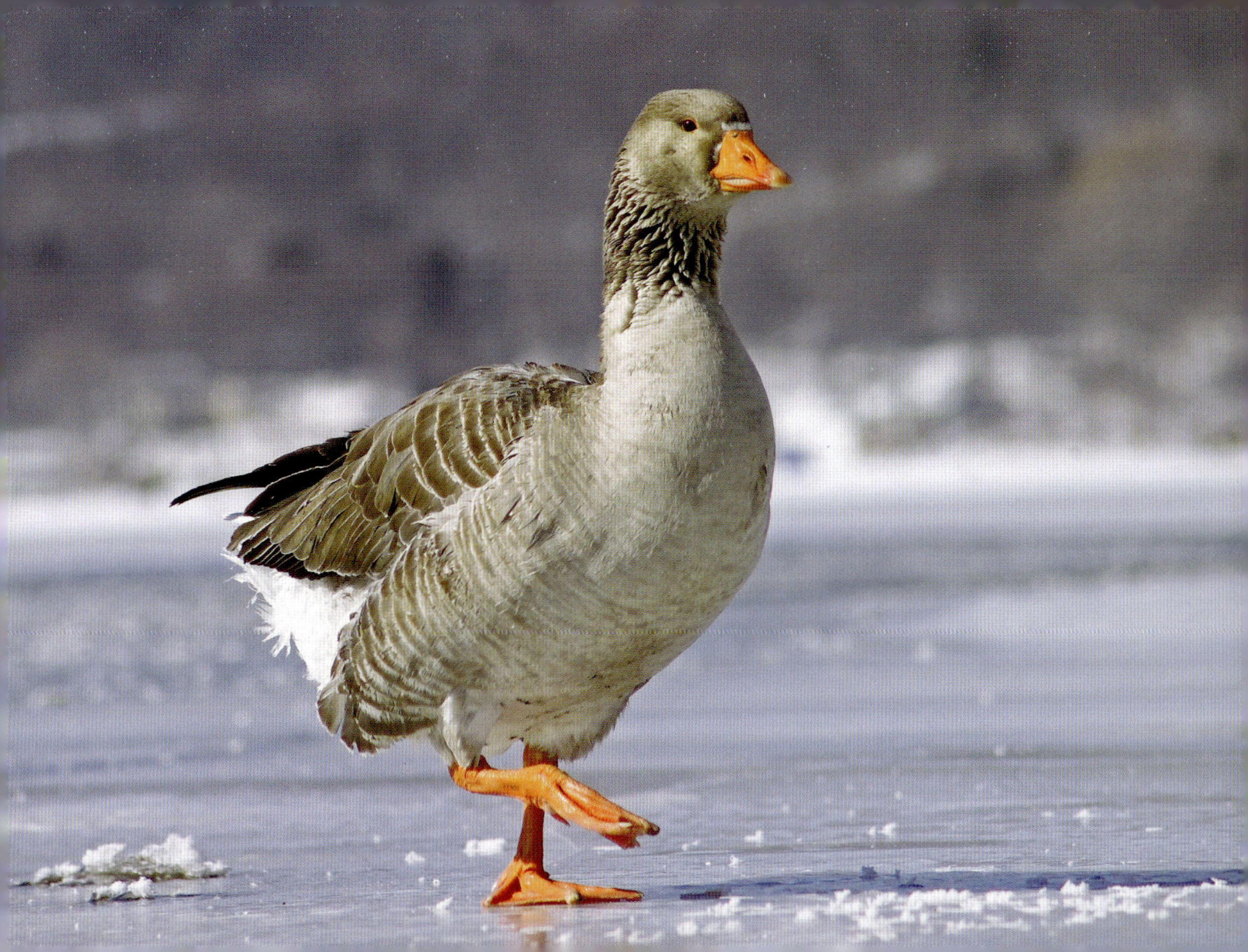

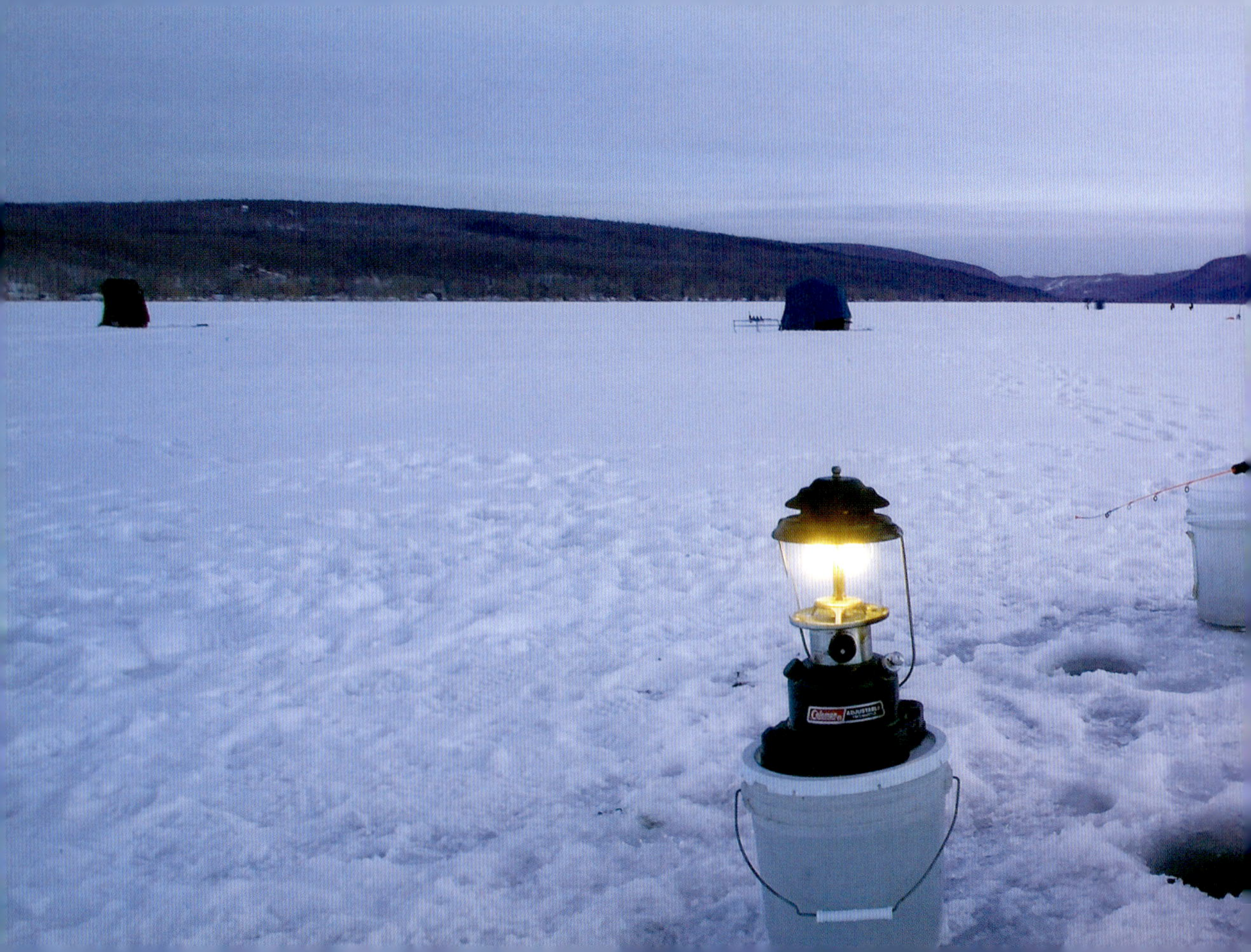
Coleman
ADJUSTABLE

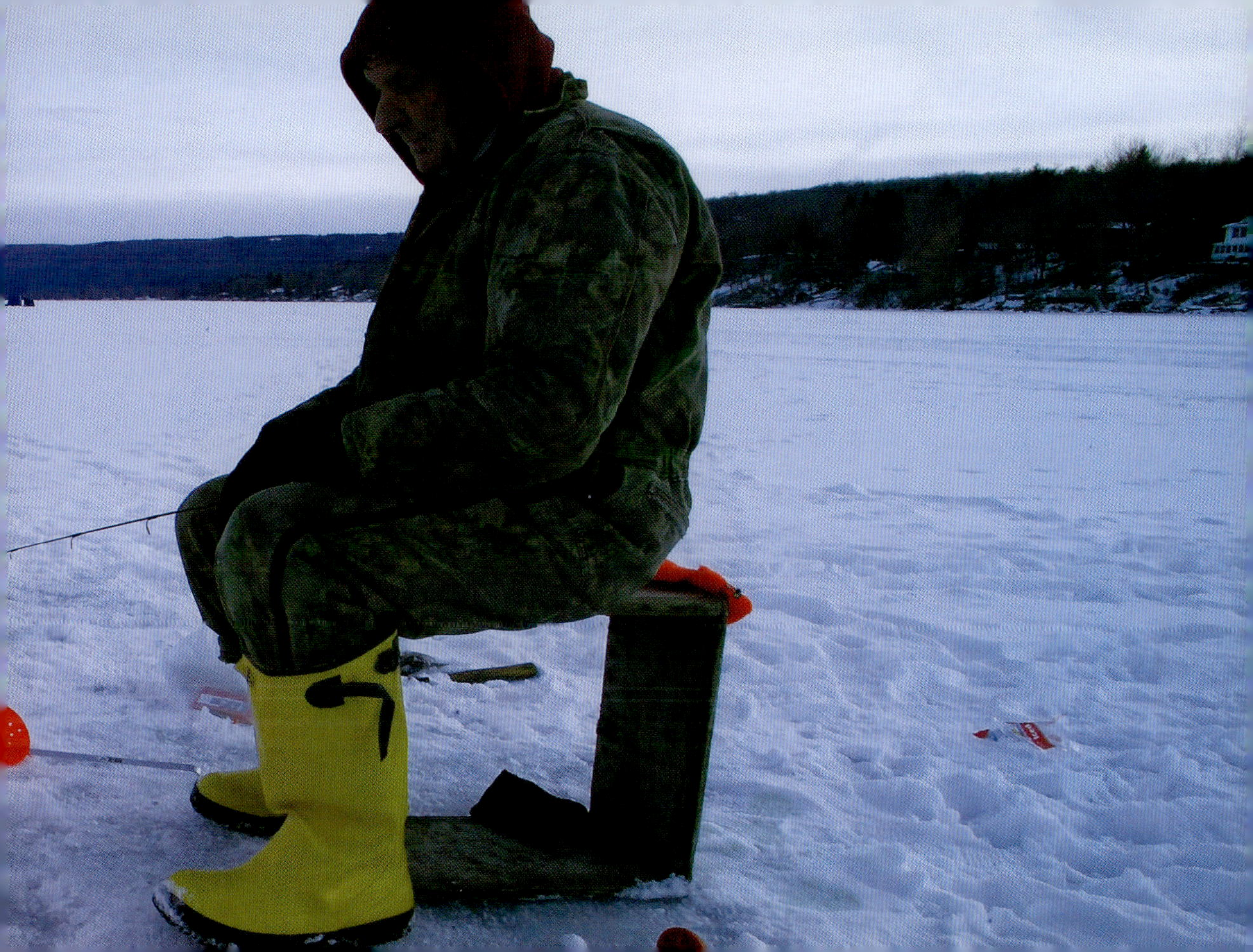

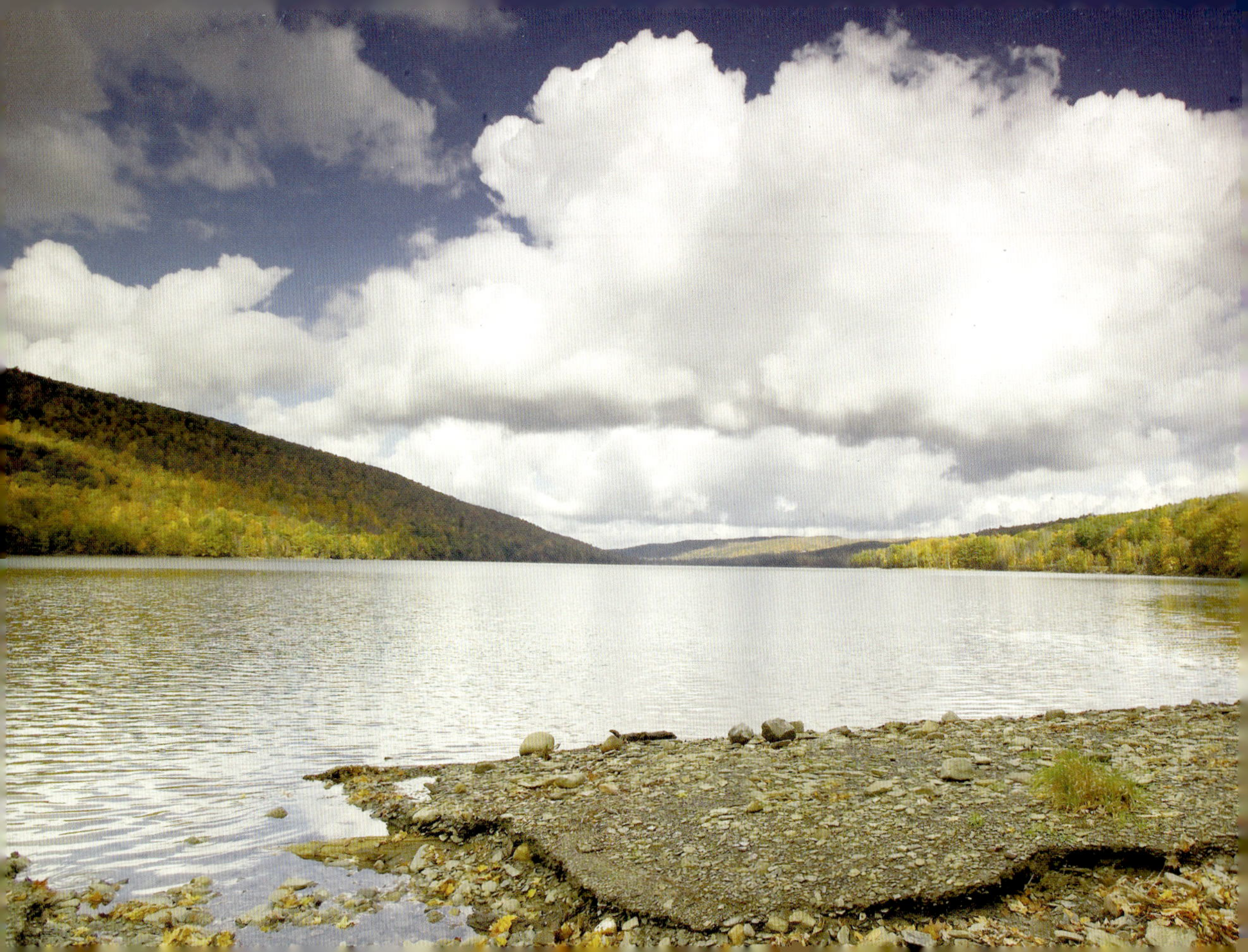

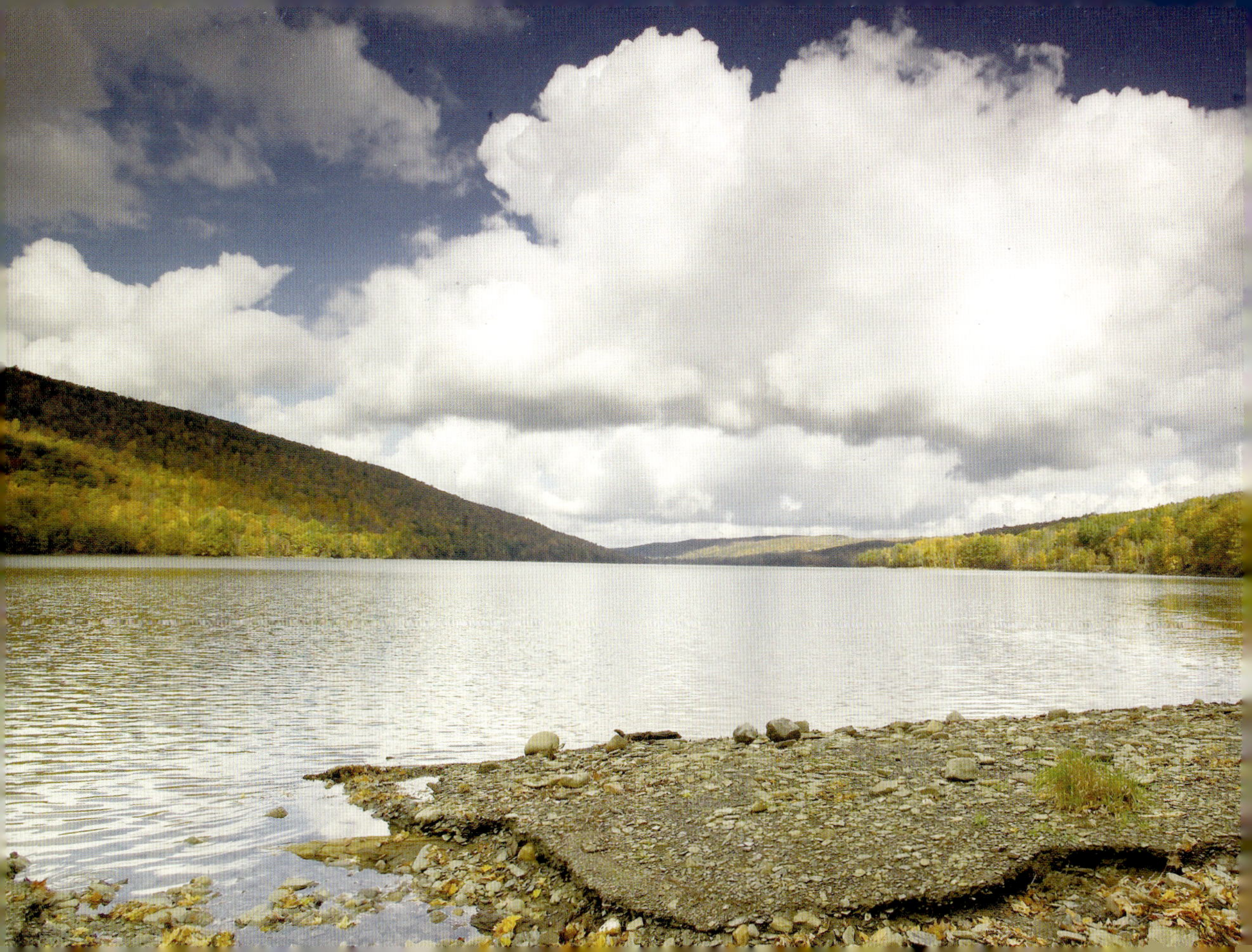

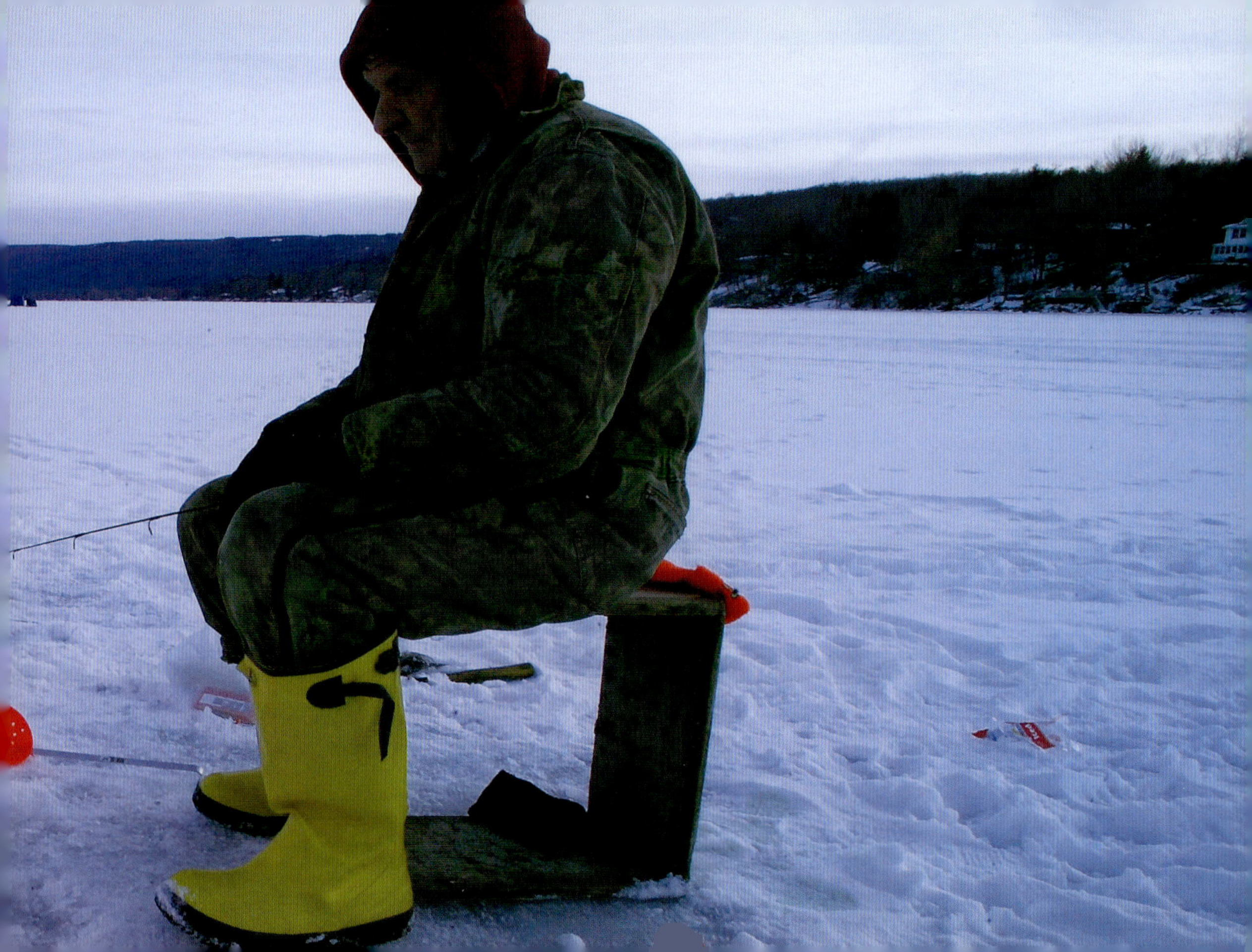

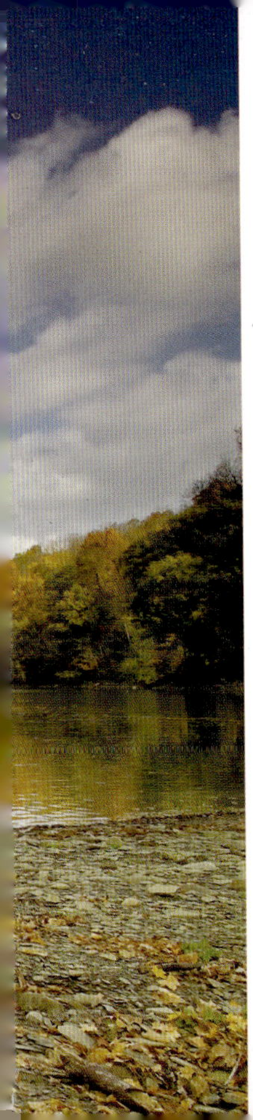

Acknowledgments

Thanks to

Marty Beckenbach of Finger Lakes Aerosports Park for scaring the heck out of me in his ultralight (assisted by Joel Spano and Rhett Radford),

Deanna Tiefenthal for her bonfire caption,

Terri Hoppenrath for riding her Harley for a photo shoot,

Carol Doeffinger for her research and help with the introduction,

Stephanie Albanese for the carriage photo and her encouragement,

Stephen Kimball for helping us get into wineries,

Ron Bennett for farming information,

John and Jan Fredericks for sunflowers,

Mid-Lakes Navigation for a mailboat trip,

and the Naples grape pie bakers for fattening us up for a long winter.

left Canadice Lake, three miles long, is the smallest of the Finger Lakes.

JAS,
CONGRATS ON BEING DONE! I'M SURE YOU'LL GO ON TO DO GREAT THINGS IN YOUR CAREER AND BECOME A BAD ASS PAIN PHYSICIAN. STAY GROUNDED AND DON'T LET IT GET TO YOUR HEAD.
BEST OF LUCK!
_GABY

BRO!
YOU KNOW I LOVE YOU AND THERE IS ALWAYS A PLACE FOR YOU AND YOURS WITH US!
_PHIL

Jas,

Good luck c fellowship
You will do great. Remember
to keep in touch

Grant

Jas!
My partner in crime!
I never would've made
it w/o you this year!
You made chief year
so much easier on me +
I wouldn't have wanted to
share it w/ anyone else!
Good luck next year. I
know you will be wonderful.
Keep in touch!

Love,
Casey